Germany and the Euro Crisis

A Failed Hegemony

Miguel I. Purroy

Germany and the Euro Crisis. A Failed Hegemony
© Miguel I. Purroy, 2019

First English paperback edition: March 2019
ISBN: 9781798759394

Translated into English by Patrick O'Callaghan

First Spanish edition: January 2019
ISBN: 978-1731493736
Original Title: *Alemania y la crisis del euro. Una hegemonía fallida*

Cover Design: Equis Creadores de Imagen

Interior Design and Formatting: Valentina Truneanu

All rights reserved. No part of this book may be reproduced, distributed, or transmitted in any form or by any means, including photocopying, recording, or other electronic or mechanical methods, without the prior written permission of the publisher.

TABLE OF CONTENTS

Preface. 11
Introduction 13

PART I
HISTORY OF A DIFFICULT RELATIONSHIP

I. THE CENTRAL PLACE OF GERMANY IN EUROPE: FOUR
   CENTURIES OF THE GERMAN PROBLEM 29
   Germany, from passive subject to leading role in European
      conflicts. 30
      From fragmentation to unification in the Congress of Vienna . 30
      The Prussian hegemony and the new unified Germany 33
      The anguish of being surrounded and besieged: a self-fulfilling
         prophecy. 35
   Two World Wars: Germany in the middle 38
II. CONTAINING GERMANY THROUGH EUROPEAN INTEGRATION 45
   The new European order: integrating to transcend war 46
   The British speciality: permanent ambivalence 52
   The Treaty of Rome and the European Economic
      Community. 58
   The Franco-German Axis: a marriage of convenience 62
   The Single European Act and the road to Maastricht: another
      power play between France and Germany 67
   The decade of great expansion and institutional reforms:
      1995-2005 75

III. THE EUROPEAN MONETARY UNION: A TROJAN HORSE FOR
THE DEUTSCHMARK?................................... 81
From the hegemony of the Bretton Woods dollar to that of
the EMS deutschmark.............................. 82
Milestones on the way to monetary union: the (supposed)
end of the deutschmark's dominance 87
Reasons of political economy: France and Germany united
in divergence...................................... 94
The central bankers: architects of the Monetary Union 97

PART II
AN ACCOUNT OF THE EURO CRISIS AND ITS CAUSES

IV. THE GLOBAL FINANCIAL CRISIS AND THE EURO CRISIS: A
FACTUAL ACCOUNT 103
The euro in Wonderland (1999-2007).................... 104
The 2008-2012 global financial crisis: this time was no different 109
The euro crisis: a tragedy in four acts 114
    Act I (2008-2009): Sub-prime banking crisis 114
    Act II (2009-11): Sovereign debt crisis..................... 115
    Act III (2011-2012): Widespread contagion 117
    Act IV (2012-2014): Lender of last resort................... 121
USA vs Europe: a comparative evaluation of how the crisis
was handled 125
The German prescription for overcoming the crisis: the austerity fallacy 134
APPENDIX IV-1. Self-fulfilling integration: Endogeneity Theory 140

V. CORE PROBLEMS OF AN IMPERFECT MONETARY UNION 143
The revenge of the theory of Optimal Currency Areas:
triggers of the crisis................................ 145
    The impact of the divergence of real interest rates on the economic boom at the periphery 147
    Diverging economic models, competitiveness differentials and
external imbalances................................ 149
    Excess private indebtedness and sudden stop 154
    Good and bad disequilibria: when capital stampedes......... 159

Incentives for fiscal indiscipline.................................. 160
Bundesbank über alles: the one-size-fits-all monetary policy 166
    A monetary policy based on averages 167
        Systemic fragility of financial markets in a monetary union:
            the original sin... 169
    A blinkered Central Bank: the absence of a lender of last
        resort... 172
        The vicious circle of banking and sovereign crises: the bond
            markets.. 174
    APPENDIX V-1. Was there no alternative? A comparison
        between the Gold Standard and the monetary union ... 177

VI. THE POLITICAL ORPHANHOOD OF THE EURO AND THE
    SOLIDARITY VACUUM 181
    The euro as an orphaned and stateless currency 182
    Is a monetary union possible without a political union?.... 185
    Political union or solidarity union?....................... 189
    Unequal sharing of the burden of adjustment.............. 191
    The (difficult) political economy of the adjustment 194
    APPENDIX VI-1. Two models of adjustment and burden sharing 196

VII. LOST INSTITUTIONALITY, HIERARCHICAL GOVERNANCE AND
    DEMOCRATIC DEFICIT....................................... 201
    Bad management, de-institutionalisation and discretion:
        from Brussels to Berlin..................................... 202
    Deficit of democratic legitimacy 208
        Some history to explain the concept....................... 209
        Citizen disenchantment and integration fatigue 214

PART III
GERMANY BETWEEN HESITANCY, HEGEMONY AND COERCION

VIII. GERMAN WAGE CONTAINMENT AND EXTERNAL IMBALANCES
    IN THE EUROZONE 219
    Europe's deep-pocketed moral arbiter 220
    The contribution of German wage restraint to the appearance
        of disequilibria in the eurozone........................ 223

Incomplete consensus narrative........................... 224
Wage containment, hero or villain?....................... 226
Economic and cultural structural dualism................. 229
The German trade surplus: the apple of discord 232
IX. ORDOLIBERALISM: THE GERMAN ECONOMIC CATECHISM .. 243
Ordoliberalism and the culture of stability 244
Ideological differences between Germany and Latin Europe 248
Principles, pragmatism or self-interest?................... 253
X. AN INCOMPLETE AND DISFUNCTIONAL HEGEMONY........ 259
Theory of hegemonic stability 260
Hegemons in monetary systems compared 267
Did Germany measure up to its hegemonic responsibility? . 270
The mark of history and German foreign policy........... 274
The watershed of the second unification.................. 279
Reasons for the reluctance: some more benevolent
    interpretations 284

PART IV
DESIRABLE, POSSIBLE, AND PROBABLE FUTURES

XI. THE DESIRABLE: PREPARE FOR THE NEW CRISIS........... 291
The calm before and after the storm: the state of the union.. 292
    Legacies of the crisis: sovereign debt and bank delinquency... 293
    More Europe or less?................................. 297
Risk sharing or submitting to discipline?................. 300
    A banking union to reduce vulnerability 302
    Shared fiscal stabilisation 305
    The moral hazard of solidarity 311
    Anything can happen, again 312
XII. BETWEEN DISINTEGRATION AND ORDERLY RECONFIGURATION 315
Can the Franco-German axis save the euro? The sacred and
    uneasy alliance..................................... 318
The refugee crisis and nationalist populism: a new existential
    threat 326
Brexit: the first step on the path to European disintegration? 332
    Why is the United Kingdom leaving? 333

  The second (dis)integration ring: Europeans outside the euro . 340
  Eurozone disintegration scenarios. 343
    Pedalling to stay upright 345
    Anomie / anarchy 345
    Orderly breakup 348
    Chaotic breakaway 351
  Dissent, consensus and new vision: the need to rewind and
    reshape. 351
    What do Europeans think and want? 352
    The battlefield of the proposals. 355
    A flexible, plural and democratic Europe 358
  The retreat of a hegemon and the new Europe. 361

Epilogue 367
Bibliography 373
List of Tables, Figures and Boxes. 383
Index 385
About the Author 393

PREFACE

After seeing the euro rocked in 2012, concern about its future and that of the European Union became a pressing question, especially for those of us whose research and teaching focus was international monetary systems and, more particularly, monetary integration between countries. The European Monetary Union (EMU) was the most important monetary union project in history and many hopes were tied up in it. I decided to write about what was happening, but there was always some good reason to keep putting it off. At first it seemed premature to do so before the euro crisis sorted itself out and one could assess the storm damage. Then along came the Alexis Tsipras Government in early 2015, which placed Greece on the brink of exiting the eurozone, and could have had unpredictable consequences for the entire monetary union. By 2016 the turbulence had receded and almost all the actors in the European drama became drowsy, complacent and exhausted. I became convinced that any hope of the union completing the task it had left pending at its conception had vanished. It was time to get to work.

I soon noticed that many pieces of the puzzle were missing, and that putting it all together would require more than the usual tools of macroeconomic analysis. The key insight was to understand that the problem was eminently political: political motives had created the EMU and there were political reasons for questioning its future. I went back to my academic origins and looked at the problem as a blend of economics and politics. I must admit it has been a stimulating exercise to jump between the realms of history, economics and political science and observe European integration from a 360° perspective.

I have tried to keep this book accessible for those who are not political scientists or economists. No special knowledge of economics is needed to follow the argument. Even Chapters IV and V, where the roots and evolution of the euro crisis are explained, keep the use of analytical tools to a minimum. The remainder relies on historical interpretations, descriptive economics and political analysis.

I am grateful to Herman Diekmann, Miguel Eduardo Purroy and Carlos Iván Bolívar for their valuable comments and statistical support. I thank my teacher and tutor in Political Science at the University of Hamburg, Franz Nuscheler, to whom I owe much of my special interest in crossing the frontiers between politics and economics. The reader will see that I assume critical positions regarding Germany's actions during and after the euro crisis, but always from a position of respect and equilibrium. I admire Germany, its thinkers, its social system, its attitude to life, its passion for work, its ingenuity, its generosity and its solidarity. I try to avoid value judgements, much less, moral judgements. My appraisal of Germany's conduct is based not on its subjective intentions, but on an analysis of the consistency and consequences of its actions, and above all of its omissions.

INTRODUCTION

Germany is the key to Europe's future, as it has been, one way or another, for at least a century.

(Timothy Garton Ash, 2012)

What is this book about? In recent years there has been a proliferation of accounts and analyses of what has come to be called the "euro crisis". Although the reader will find plenty of information on that episode here, our central theme has a different focus. What we want to explore is the role played by Germany in the crisis, and that country's contribution or lack thereof to the resolution of the euro problem. To understand the special role of Germany in Europe we will need to move between history, politics and economics. Here in the Introduction we will present a brief summary of the main ideas and conclusions. There is also a summary of the main points at the beginning of each chapter which should help the reader follow the central thread of the book.

From the second half of the 20th century up to the present day, Germany has preferred to stay out of the international limelight, while accepting shared leadership with other powers when multilateral cooperation was the best option. For seven decades, it has felt that European integration initiatives, from the European Steel and Coal Community to the European Monetary Union, were the natural stage upon which a new post-war Germany could grow economically and be seen as a pacifist, civic-minded and cooperative nation. The painful paradox of modern European history is that Germany, forced by the twin crises of the euro and of refugees, has found itself thrust into centre stage with no-one to share the spotlight. In an unintended and unwanted turn of events, it has become the dominant leader of the EMU and, by extension, of the EU itself.

Having not sought dominance, Germany didn't assume the responsibilities that a hegemon should have taken upon itself in an integrated monetary system. History shows that international monetary systems–and particularly monetary unions–have no chance of surviving in the long term unless their hegemon "benevolently" takes on the burdens of the role, or at least a disproportionate part of them. These burdens involve providing "public goods", necessary for the operation of the system, goods that no individual member country can provide or afford. In the case of a monetary union, the main collective good is the stability of the currency and of the financial system. This cannot be achieved by fiat but must be assembled by balancing multiple factors. When some of these equilibria are disturbed, a base level of solidarity among members must prevent countries in trouble from getting caught up in a vicious circle of growing instability. Germany did not think it was its job to take on this solidarity burden, which thus ended up falling onto the shoulders of those members most affected by the crisis. This was not out of selfishness or malice, but as a result of its ideological mindset. The fact remains that this "dereliction of duty" on the part of the hegemon was one of the drivers escalating the crisis and increasing the suffering of the debtor countries.

Germany's was a failed hegemony. During the euro crisis, the natural leader refused to act benevolently to stabilise the system and so the European Central Bank had to step in. During the refugee crisis, on the contrary, Germany decided to assume fully the role of benevolent hegemon and was willing to shoulder most of the burden. Its actions, however, were openly rejected by the principals in the drama. In the first crisis it turned down the role of stabilising the euro, and in the second it was not strong enough to get its partners in line for a Community response to the refugee problem. The reality is that the leader failed in both cases, albeit for different reasons.

Europe certainly had its Greek, Italian or Spanish Problems, but even more important was its German Problem. Connoisseurs of European history are well aware of the meaning of that expression. Germany was and remains a problem for Europe. It has always been too big not be feared, too big to avoid developing dominating tendencies but not big enough to exert hegemony efficiently. That was the case even when the pre-19th century German territory in the centre of Europe was composed of a mosaic of small principalities. Any of the four European Powers–France, Britain, Austria or Russia–that could dominate this territory would also dominate Europe. Until the second half of the 19th century Germany was at the centre of politics and war in Europe, more often than not passively. When all the principalities were amalgamated under the aegis of Prussia in the 1871 Pact of Versailles, the new unified German State became the Colossus of central Europe. The German Problem was now the presence of the new power in the centre. This generated a succession of fears and mutual distrust, action and reaction between Germany and the European Powers, which eventually led to the 20th century's two World Wars.

After 1945, the victorious Allies had one overriding goal in mind: that never again should there be a war within the confines of Europe. To guarantee this, the German Problem had to be solved once and for all. As a first step, they divided the country into four blocs, each under the command of one of the four allied Powers. However, this initial regime of submission had to evolve into something more permanent. Despite France's initial reluctance, the Allies conceived a project of European integration which would allow Germany to survive and develop, but always controlled–tamed–within European structures. It is interesting to note that the first and most fervent supporters of European integration were the United States and Britain. France ended up coming on board once she had been assured of holding political hegemony in Western Europe.

The United States unhesitatingly promoted the integration project. The support of the United Kingdom, however, was always ambivalent. For the first decade and a half after the war the British liked to say that, in the words of Churchill, they were *for* a United Europe without wanting to be *of* it. The final collapse of the British Empire and a domestic economic downturn forced them to apply to join the European Economic Community (EEC) at the beginning of the 60s. This was repeatedly blocked by France until General de Gaulle went into retirement. Even after being admitted at the beginning of the 70s, the British have always had one foot inside and one outside of the European Union, leaving the political leadership of the integration process in the hands of France. For its part, Germany regained its economic strength in surprisingly short order. Both countries established a marriage of convenience, to which Germany brought its economic weight while France took the political helm and enjoyed juicy agricultural subsidies. Having to pay the bills didn't matter to Germany as long as the framework of European institutions allowed it to reinsert itself into the international community.

The project of Monetary Union was primarily driven by France. The French found the hegemony of the US dollar around the world extremely irritating, and especially so in Europe. They were also upset at the predominant role that the deutschmark had taken in the European Monetary System (EMS). It had become the reserve currency of Europe and the Bundesbank the *de-facto* European central bank. The French franc, on the other hand, was subject to constant devaluationist pressures, with the consequent internal political unrest. France needed the stability of the deutschmark but replaced with a new common currency over which it would maintain political control, or so it thought … Germany dragged its feet all it could, but finally agreed to the common currency on condition that the design of the new monetary order resembled its own, with a European central bank based in Frankfurt and modelled on the German Bundesbank. Accidentally on purpose, Germany introduced a Trojan horse into Fortress Europe with which it would end up dominating the EMU.

There were no compelling economic reasons for implementing a common currency. The argument that a common currency was the corollary of a commercial union and would make it easier to move towards higher levels of economic integration had no theoretical support. Neither had the argument that a single currency would help convergence between countries that entered the union with diverging economic characteristics. The founding fathers of the euro ignored economists who warned that Europe was not yet prepared for a common currency. Tying together such divergent economies under the umbrella of a common currency ought to have meant equipping the union with fiscal institutions which could facilitate the transfer of resources to countries that, due to asymmetric shocks, might become unstable. The reality was that neither France nor Germany wanted any such element of fiscal solidarity in the design of the EMU.

Factors related to the political economy of economic adjustments also provided support for the creation of the EMU. The exchange rate crisis of 1992-1993 showed how speculative attacks and the devaluation of local currencies could give rise to political conflict, internally and externally. The common currency was supposed to do away with the need for exchange rate adjustments, when the external position of a country weakened against its peers. This did indeed hold until the euro crisis of 2010.

In the Global Financial Crisis of 2008, it seemed at first that Europe could dodge the blow that was hitting the United States. The unspoken reality was that in the 6 months after September 2008 European governments had to quietly spend 3 trillion dollars to bail out their troubled banks. In the case of the periphery countries, the main problem came from the abrupt departure of capital that up till then had been flowing in abundance to finance expansion plans. In the case of the strong countries' banks, the travails came from their excessive exposure to sub-prime investments. The ensuing recession, plus the effort to rescue the banks, put several countries in a vulnerable situation. This was more apparent after the financial markets became jittery on discovering the magnitude of the Greek problem.

Chapters IV and V give a detailed account of the development of the euro crisis, its origins and what actions were taken. Germany's diagnosis of the crisis missed the mark, as did its treatment of the problems. In the course of events, Germany became leader of the creditors and felt it had the moral right and duty to impose prescriptions of fiscal austerity that the debtors deserved for their profligate behaviour. This censorious approach, based on a misdiagnosis, served only to add fuel to the fire of the recession and exacerbate the distrust of investors. The contagion spread to the third and fourth eurozone economies (Italy and Spain) in the second half of 2011 and the first half of 2012. The euro ventured onto a terrain of imminent existential danger. The European Central Bank had to use its heavy artillery as lender of last resort to calm the markets in mid-2012, but the damage was done.

The emperor had no clothes. The crisis laid bare structural problems and failures of design that the EMU had been saddled with from the start. In the first place, structurally very divergent economies had to coexist under the umbrella of one currency, which was barely reconcilable with a monetary union with no risk-sharing cushions. To oversimplify, the debtor countries of the Mediterranean periphery (Ireland being a case apart), were characterized by economic models more focussed on their domestic markets, more prone to fiscal spending and less averse to inflation. The creditors, from North-Central Europe, had based their growth on export markets and had a clear focus on efficiency, productivity, fiscal discipline and the avoidance of inflation. It was evident that this latter model had emerged triumphant from the Global Financial Crisis. The creditors therefore felt that they had the moral authority to tell the debtors that the way out of the crisis was to embrace that winning model.

Secondly, it had become clear that the monetary union incentivised fiscal indiscipline of individual countries at the expense of their neighbours. Thirdly, the attempt to impose a one-size-fits-all monetary policy on a monetary zone as varied as the European one could not give good results. Before the crisis, for example, whenever the periphery needed monetary containment during a credit and demand boom, the ECB would orchestrate a lax policy of low interest rates. Fourthly, a Central Bank whose sole mandate was to preserve the stability of the currency at any cost was an oxymoron that was bound to fail. With financial globalisation, there is no way to protect the currency without at the same time preserving financial stability. This can only be done by allowing the central bank to act as the lender of last resort.

Aside from the economic inconsistencies, the edifice of the monetary union was not built on solid political foundations. The euro was and is an orphan currency without a homeland. It does not have the backing of a State as its ultimate source of strength. A very interesting discussion has arisen about how viable a monetary union can be without a framework of political union. In our opinion the existence of a conventional political union, which in any case would be unthinkable as things stand today, is not that important. What matters is the existence of mechanisms of fiscal solidarity that allow members of the union that are hit by some large-scale disturbance to cope with the problem and not get into a destructive spiral of recession and speculative attacks. The EMU not only did not provide such mechanisms during the crisis, but the leading member of the union imposed a philosophy dictating that the cost of resolving it should fall entirely upon the shoulders of the countries that had been "fiscally irresponsible".

While all this was happening, at the political level the institutional governance of the European Union began a process of accelerated deterioration. Firstly, Community institutions showed very little expertise in the management of financial and fiscal crises, which led them to much indecisiveness and frequent errors. Secondly, decision-making processes departed progressively from the institutional framework and rules of procedure enshrined in Union treaties. The European Commission was relegated to merely implementing decisions adopted by the Heads of State meeting in the European Council. Moreover, there came a time when not even the European Council was the highest decision-making body. That role fell to the German government. Berlin, not Brussels, became the capital of Europe in many aspects. It is not difficult to imagine the devastating impact that this situation had on the already deteriorated democratic legitimacy of the European institutions.

Germany was the country with the greatest economic weight and the deepest pockets in the EMU. Her policies had had a decisive impact on the accumulation of imbalances within the eurozone. Take for example the policy of wage restraint that Germany implemented once she embarked on the Schroeder Plan at the end of the 1990s. From being the "sick man of Europe", she became the star of export-led growth. While Germany applied wage restraint, fiscal austerity and saving, southern Europe embarked on an aggressive expansion, largely financed through the recycling of the German external current account surplus by German banks. When the tide turned in 2008 and German financing was abruptly withdrawn, the debtor countries of the periphery went into recession and fiscal difficulty. By this time, Germany had already consolidated its position in emerging markets as an exporter of high-tech goods, allowing her to ride the Global Financial Crisis with barely a scratch.

German domestic economic policy contributed to worsening the debtors' crisis. Wage restraint was largely responsible for the weakness of its internal market, which didn't absorb the potential exports her neighbours needed to balance their current accounts. Furthermore, the restraint resulted in low inflation within Germany, making it extremely difficult for its troubled neighbours to regain competitiveness through internal wage and price deflation. In this situation any basic economics textbook would have recommended that Germany relax its wage/fiscal restraint, allow some inflation and expand its domestic demand to help other Union members in difficulty. To the contrary, the German trade surplus continued its unstoppable rise and the burden of adjustment fell entirely on the shoulders of the debtors.

This non-cooperative behaviour had mainly to do with a basic body of beliefs very rooted in the German mentality and labelled the "ordoliberal" ideology. The fathers of the German economic miracle of the 50s and 60s and its particular brand of "social market economy" claimed that they were applying the principles of ordoliberalism. The same ideological stamp was applied to the second German economic miracle of the 2000s. Two basic pillars of this thought were the principle of responsibility (*Haftungsprinzip*) and the culture of stability (*Stabilitätskultur*). This was the prism through which the German authorities interpreted the euro crisis and according to which they created the recipes for solving it. Finance minister Wolfgang Schäuble liked to use the example of the "Swabian housewife" as a touchstone for what should have been–but wasn't–the behaviour of the eurozone's profligate members. When it came down to it, however, the yardstick applied to the neighbours was not that which was applied internally. In any case, an ordoliberal stance was a *sine qua non* for German politicians being able to connect with voters. The clear contrast between the German ordoliberal catechism and the economic philosophy of the more Graeco-Latin areas of Europe, including France, was not conducive to a common agenda.

Germany's economic superiority, combined with the desperation of debtors hounded by speculators, led to the emergence of a power dynamic in the eurozone in which the former clearly held a dominant position. Paradoxical though it may seem, this dominance wasn't necessarily undesirable. Historically, all international monetary regimes have required the most powerful of their members to take on the role of hegemon (*primus inter pares*) to lend stability to the system. Being the hegemon is associated with a set of privileges, for which the hegemon should compensate its partners/subordinates by absorbing more than its share of the costs of providing general stability. The problem arises when the hegemon evades this "benevolent" responsibility and the burdens associated with it. Germany did not want to accept them; it thought that each country should assume its own responsibility and pay the costs of its own rescue. It was all the same very proactive in enforcing austerity measures and imposing structural reforms on the debtors.

Anti-German name-calling was not long in coming, particularly in those countries most affected by the crisis, with some allusions to its warlike and totalitarian past. Even academic analysts pointed to the resurgence of the old German Problem from the second half of the 19th century and first half of the 20th. We believe that these unnuanced parallels are a distortion of history, but there is no doubt that after the second German unification in 1990 her foreign policy took a turn towards a more assertive defence of their own national interests, something that hitherto had been anathema. What did not change was the aversion to individually leading, much less dominating, international affairs. Germany has been marked by history, which explains her reluctance to dominate, and to some extent mitigates her unsatisfactory conduct. Be that as it may, her refusal to assume the responsibilities of a benevolent hegemon caused great damage to the EMU, prolonged the crisis unnecessarily, and imposed severe economic and social costs on the weaker EU countries.

Looking forward, are there any indications, or indeed likelihood, that Germany will decisively contribute to the future consolidation of the euro? It is not being alarmist to say that, as of today, the EMU would not survive a new existential threat against the euro. Nor is it too reckless to predict that such an existential crisis will inevitably arise at some point in the future. Since 2014, when the stress of the first euro crisis subsided, fundamental reform in the eurozone has come to a standstill. The two legacies of the crisis–sovereign debt and the banks' bad assets–are still there, dragging on the post-crisis recovery. Disagreement about the path to follow is very marked. The economic debate about what should be done to protect the euro swings back and forth. On the one side, there are those who advocate "more Europe", more economic government at Community level, more political and fiscal union. Others meanwhile propose "less Europe", the devolution of fiscal sovereignty to national levels, the freedom and right to move at different speeds of integration. In a second gamut of positions, there are those who think that the EMU edifice is already essentially built and that the existing rules merely need to be applied. Others in contrast think that fundamental parts of the edifice must be completely rebuilt or new ones added.

In general, the extremes of this second gamut move between two positions of principle on what it might take to buttress the euro. At one extreme are those who think that market discipline and compliance with the rules are enough to prevent a re-emergence of the crisis, or to manage it if it should occur. It is hardly surprising that this group includes Germany and the Northern Central European countries within her orbit of influence, including some in Eastern Europe. At the other extreme are those who consider it essential to create mechanisms of fiscal solidarity to help weaker Union members stabilize their economies should they be seriously disturbed, thus preventing a vicious cycle of recession. This solidarity is also more elegantly characterised as "risk sharing", the classic example being bank deposit guarantee funds that are triggered when a bank goes bankrupt. At this pole we find the Latin countries, led by France, as well as the leaders of Community bodies (the European Commission and its organs).

Given the apparently irreconcilable distance between these positions, much effort is being expended to design risk-sharing schemes that at the same time mitigate the "moral hazard" resulting from the exercise of fiscal solidarity. This moral hazard is the ordoliberals' main objection to solidarity. The sad fact is that, as of today, there is no consensus among European leaders about which path to follow. In France, Macron's attempts to agree a reform agenda have been met with a cold bucket of water from Germany. The latter won't accept any proposal that could mean unilateral fiscal transfers to other members of the Union. The engine of the Franco-German axis, which historically had promoted major initiatives of European integration, has lost power.

Just as the euro crisis seemed to be subsiding, a new and equally serious existential crisis erupted in Europe: the refugee crisis of 2015-2016. The wave of refugees engendered two serious threats to European integration. The first was the challenge to Germany's leadership in Europe. In an unexpected gesture, Chancellor Merkel opened the doors of Europe to more than two and a half million refugees in just two years. Germany's attempt to distribute the refugees according to quotas for each EU member met with frontal resistance from a number of countries, particularly those of Eastern Europe. Some of this was certainly retaliatory kickback for Germany's coercive style during the euro crisis. A second threat also emerged: in many countries the problem of immigrants and refugees had aroused the spectre of populist nationalism, which put at risk the stability of their respective governments.

Europe faces a serious risk of disintegration. Is Brexit the first step in this process? The United Kingdom's connection with Europe has always been very particular and ambivalent: even when it was insistently applying for admission to the European Economic Community, it was doing so for purely commercial reasons and to arrest the decline of its economy. It never accepted the idea of supra-national Community institutions with authority over its domestic affairs; whenever it decided to participate in Community initiatives, it always demanded special status and a right to opt out. Neither did it want to be part of the European Monetary Union. British society has always been deeply divided about its links to Europe, to the point that Prime Minister Cameron felt he had to promise a referendum on staying in Europe as part of the Conservative election manifesto in 2015. Historical circumstance meant that the June 2016 referendum took place in the midst of the refugee crisis, which tipped the balance in favour of leaving. Today the result might be different, but in point of fact half of British society has always been hostile towards Europe and always will be.

This British peculiarity, however, cannot disguise the fact that more than a few member countries of the EU share similar objections to the European project of an ever-closer union. There is integration fatigue among large parts of Europe: quite a few governments resent Community institutions invading their domestic spheres and there are serious doubts about the democratic legitimacy of the whole Community framework. There is a "rush to the rear" towards nationalism, nativism and autarchy. Populist parties, even when they are not in government, define and delimit the European political agenda.

It's time to face squarely the very real possibility of a process of disintegration. In the case of the eurozone, centrifugal tendencies could take several roads (or scenarios), some of them concurrently. A situation of anomie and anarchy could arise, like that which showed its head during the refugee crisis. Italy could revolt against the fiscal impositions of Community authorities. Some countries could organize a controlled breakup of the monetary union, creating new monetary areas or going back to more flexible exchange rate mechanisms. A new crisis could erupt that leads to a disorderly and chaotic breakup of the eurozone, with some members being forced to reintroduce their national currencies. Our view–and recommendation–is that it is preferable to rewind before it's too late, rather than plummeting into a chaotic breakdown. We should take advantage of the current relative calm on the European scene to prepare a framework that would allow one or more countries an orderly departure from the euro.

There is a growing intellectual consensus that long-term coexistence under a common currency of such divergent countries, with incompatible underlaying economic models and different fiscal and inflationary cultures, is not feasible unless the strongest members are willing to undertake solidarity schemes to compensate for that divergence. As this is not going happen in the EMU in the foreseeable future, the strongest members should take the initiative and pull out of the euro to create a new monetary area. Only Germany could lead this movement to leave, but so far has not given any sign that it is willing to do so. Its position remains that each country should assume the consequences of its actions, and that those who are unwilling or unable to comply with the requirements of the euro should pack their bags and leave. It just so happens that the conditions for staying are the ones imposed by the model that "won" in the crisis.

The euro, born to bring Europe closer together, has become an element of discord and tension. Over the years an inconvenient symbiosis has sprung up between the EU and the EMU. 19 of the 27 European members are part of the EMU, but the euro's travails have completely dominated the agenda of EU institutions. The eight members of the EU that do not belong to the EMU feel like second-class Europeans, as mere candidates for one day joining the monetary union. The greatest damage caused by this symbiosis has been in introducing a harmful element of totalitarianism–a monetary union is all or nothing–into the dynamics of integration. A common currency by definition does not permit divergence, speed differences, or the freedom to decide which elements of the monetary union a country wants to sign up for. When a member of the monetary union goes astray, and their actions cause negative spill-over effects on other members, the whole weight of the law comes down on the lost sheep, even going so far as forcing it to surrender its economic sovereignty to Community bodies. In other words, the government of a monetary union necessarily has a strong dose of authoritarianism.

There is nothing more alien to the founding spirit of the European Union than top-down authoritarian imposition, particularly when ordered by the most powerful member. Europe needs to rewind and reshape. The new Europe needs to recognise the plurality and diversity of its members, keeping its doors open to countries that only want to integrate in some respects, such as security and defence, or transport, education, environmental protection, customs union, tax regimes and a long *et cetera*. Each initiative should have a clear democratic mandate and corresponding political control. Rather than a uniform Europe, what is needed is a matrix of dynamic and flexible spheres of integration.

Can Germany be won over to this new vision? It is the direct heir to the grand visions of the founding fathers of Europe, so would need to go through a process of profound mental conversion. The German leadership is aware that Europe's current situation is not stable and that something has to be done. Internally, Eurosceptic forces have gained growing influence and the traditional pro-European political forces will have to reconcile themselves with this reality. On the other hand, the defenders of monetary union and the idea of an "ever more united Europe" know that this means someday having to ask German taxpayers to open their wallets to save the euro. This is utter anathema. In the light of this, the possibility cannot be dismissed that the German establishment might be willing to gradually abandon the original grand European ideology and explore new approaches to integration. A priority will be resolving the conundrum of the monetary union before it is too late.

The book is organised in four parts. The first part explains the birth and evolution of the European Union in terms of the German Problem. Every initiative in the process of European integration after the Second World War responded to the need to solve this problem. In the second part we give an analytical account of the origins and events of the euro crisis after 2008, using a multi-disciplinary focus which covers its macroeconomic, political and institutional aspects. The third part focusses on three facets of Germany's dominant influence in the eurozone: its economic policy of wage containment, its ordoliberal ideology, and its exercise of a hegemonic position. Finally, the fourth part looks at the prospects for solving Europe's existential crisis, and puts forward realistic proposals in the world of the possible. The beginning of each part and chapter includes a brief summary of their contents.

PART I

HISTORY OF A DIFFICULT RELATIONSHIP

In this first part we look at the birth of the European Monetary Union and the key role Germany played in it. The German Problem has always aroused passions and prejudices. The word conjures up visions of conflict, confrontation and enmities. Germany's defeats in two World Wars evoke strong overtones of violence, domination and destruction. However, despite these echoes, Germany has to be seen as more than just the protagonist of those 30 fateful years. Its contributions to the world since the Renaissance in the forum of ideas, political philosophy, industrial progress and social change have been immense, and since the mid-20th century its civic-minded attitude and integrationist international outlook have greatly contributed to world peace.

We have to look briefly at its history to understand the special place that Germany has always had in Europe. Its geographical location in the middle of the continent, and its size–too large for some tasks or roles and too small for others–has always put the country in an uncomfortable position as the focus of many paradoxes and contradictions. Before the 19th century, the fragmented German-speaking nations in the centre of Europe were a battleground for the European Powers of France, Britain, Austria and Russia. When in the second half of the 19th century Germany emerged as a unified nation under the aegis of Prussia, its relationship with Europe was marked by mutual distrust and fear which finally led to war. The project of European integration after World War II basically amounted to what the European leadership, with the decisive support of the United States, came up with to overcome the trauma of war and solve the German Problem.

The European Union was born in large part to assuage the anxiety of France and Britain (especially the former) at the vigorous recovery of the Federal Republic of Germany after World War II. Germany could not be denied its right to exist and prosper as a nation, so the victorious European allies found a way to neutralise German economic power by subsuming it into a larger entity. Subsequently, the transition to monetary union during the 90s was another attempt to control the dominance of the deutschmark, which had become the *de facto* European reserve currency.

The EMU was part of a political project rather than deriving from economic rationality. After having overcome the mutual resentment of the post-war years, France and Germany contracted a marriage of convenience which became the engine and axis of European integration. France kept its political standing, while Germany contributed its economic might. With the introduction of the monetary union however, Germany became the undisputed leader of Europe. The euro and the European Central Bank became a kind of German Trojan Horse inserted into the EMU's design, something that was far from the minds of the founding fathers of the European Union, and indeed from that of Germany itself, truly a historical paradox.

I

THE CENTRAL PLACE OF GERMANY IN EUROPE: FOUR CENTURIES OF THE GERMAN PROBLEM

Much of what has happened in Europe in recent decades, more specifically with the birth and development of the European Union, must be understood in the light of European history after the 17th century. Since that time, crises have been deep and transformational, military confrontations have been destructive and national borders have changed drastically. Still, certain persistent threads go to explain the behaviour of the diversity of peoples that make up Europe and the power relations between them.

Germany's geographical position in Europe, and its relative size, made it a key element in Europe's development, both when it was passive and fragmented, and when it became an active participant after the unification of 1871. Every major European confrontation has either occurred in Germany or has been about Germany. This refers not only to the 20th century's two World Wars, but to a much broader spectrum of conflicts encompassing several previous centuries. Germany was also the epicentre of major ideological clashes, such as those between Catholicism and Protestantism, capitalism and Marxism, or Western democracy and fascism. It was no accident that the major international organisations of the 20th century, the League of Nations after the First World War and the United Nations and NATO after the Second, were created because of Germany.

Germany, from passive subject to leading role in European conflicts

Irish historian Brendan Simms (2013) has developed an interpretative approach to European history according to which the centre of Europe, basically the region now occupied by Germany, was the field of play upon which and over which the Great Powers of the time, England, France, Austria and Russia, all faced each other. We will call this the "Germanic Region", because up until the second half of the 19th century there was no unified German nation but rather a multitude of small principalities with common elements of culture, language and physical proximity. The fact that they did not constitute a political unit with an army and common purpose did not mean that they were unaffected by the intense bellicose and diplomatic activity on the continent. Indeed, the greater part of this activity revolved around the Germanic Region, whether or not the Germans were actively involved.

From fragmentation to unification in the Congress of Vienna

The European Powers were constantly embroiled in an endless sequence of wars, skirmishes, alliances and betrayals, many of which had the Germanic Region as the object of dispute. In a world in which neither technology, nor population, nor other productive assets were increasing, fighting over territory was considered the best, indeed often the only growth strategy for the wealth of nations. Economic competition could only be expressed as a warlike struggle over material resources. Territorial conflict became the dominant States' driving force: the years of peace were no more than breathing spaces to allow recovery from the ravages of the previous war and to prepare for the next one. Preparing for and conducting wars to conquer land, take ports or create networks of trade was the *raison d'être* of the European monarchies and their bureaucracies, with the quasi-feudal nobility providing a warrior class and the commercial bourgeoisie supplying the material and financial means.

After the European Great Powers divvied-up their colonies on the Asian, African and American continents in the 16th century, their expansionist ambitions turned again to the European landmass, and the Germanic Region took on a pivotal importance. Whoever dominated central Europe, particularly the German territories, would control all of Europe. Thus, in the 17th and 18th centuries the plethora of German-speaking principalities and petty States that made up the Germanic Region were constantly being invaded and annexed by the four European Powers.

The Germanic Region shared borders with Russia, Austria and France and served as a buffer zone between the Powers. Any one of these felt existentially threatened if another of them occupied German territory and became a direct neighbour. Depending on how united the German principalities were, the territory of the Germanic peoples was either a power vacuum that awakened the ambitions of any of the surrounding powers, or a centre of power under the tutelage of one of them, and so would excite rivalries. The Region's central location in Europe meant that it could tip the scales of territorial European power.

The smaller German principalities could rarely do much but passively contemplate the destructive sweep of armies through their territories. At times they would try to exploit a conflict by providing military support for one of the larger contestants, possibly being forced to change sides according to how the winds blew. Nonetheless, beyond selling military services or entering into opportunistic alliances, the principalities were basically passive participants in European events, subject to constant impositions and abuses by the invading Powers. This period of history up to the beginning of the 19th century left a deep impression on the memory of the German peoples and explains some of the core fears that survived later in their collective consciousness, particularly the fear of being fenced in and territorially suffocated, or the threat of coalitions among their neighbours.

The successive defeats of the Napoleonic armies between 1813 and 1815 signalled a break in this pattern. At the Battle of Leipzig in 1813, Bonaparte lost control of central Europe. His defeat at the battle of Waterloo in 1815 at the hands of a British and Prussian coalition snatched from France any imperial claims inside or outside of Europe. Both battles marked a sea-change in European geopolitics, with the new rules of the game being reflected in the Congress of Vienna of 1814-1815. The Congress sowed the seeds of two gradual processes of unification, eventually leading to the birth of two new nations, Germany and Italy, with a significant impact on the future history of Europe.

The end of the Napoleonic Wars definitively crowned the United Kingdom as the world's undisputed dominant power. Napoleon defeated, the main concern of the British Empire, seconded by its allies Austria and Russia, was to contain once and for all France's ambitions to dominate Europe. In line with this British strategy, Russia and Austria had to boost their economic strength and military might to thwart France's inevitable revanchism.

Of great significance in all this was the emergence of Prussia as a medium-sized power on the European military scene, as witnessed by its success against Napoleon's forces. For the first time, one of the German States had taken part in the *ententes* and power politics of European affairs. In recognition of this, the Congress of Vienna allotted to Prussia the French territories of the Rhineland and Westphalia with the goal of reinforcing the military front against France.

Nevertheless, the most significant outcome of the Congress of Vienna was the germ of a federation of German principalities and States (the German Confederation), with Prussia playing the role of *primus inter pares* from the outset. The allies were very keen on filling in the void caused by the presence of a myriad of tiny German principalities in the historical centre of Europe, some of them mere cities or even parts of cities, unable to organize themselves militarily or economically. A goodly part of these mini-principalities was absorbed by larger ones after the Napoleonic War, while other medium-sized States such as Hanover, Baden, Württenberg and Bavaria came out of it strengthened and enjoying recognition by the allied countries. The *Deutscher Bund* (German Confederation) thus came to occupy a vital space at the centre of Europe, and for the first time in a relatively organic form. Although the German Confederation kept on being part of the Austro-Hungarian Empire, its position had gained in independence, importance and power. In the minds of the allied Powers, the Confederation was meant to keep the balance of power in Europe, with sufficient strength to serve as a buffer and containment zone against French and Russian adventures, but not powerful enough to develop its own hegemonic ambitions.

As for the process of Italian unification, nationalist impulses did not arise from the new model of Europe after Napoleon's defeat but were rather a rejection of the dismemberment and disposition of the Italian States by the Congress of Vienna, something which provoked strong popular reaction. Napoleon had occupied all the small Italian States, which the Congress subsequently handed over to the victorious Powers: Lombardy and Venice were given to Austria, the provinces of Parma, Modena and Tuscany remained under the control of the Austrian Prince Leopold, Naples and Sicily remained under the aegis of the Spanish Crown and Rome was given back to the Pope.

Vigorous and combative nationalist movements arose in answer to this stripping away of any trace of independence and "Italian-ness". Public employees and middle-ranking military officers formed a network of nationalist secret societies, known as the Carbonari, which were especially active from 1815 on. Later (in 1831) one of their members, Giuseppe Mazzini, created the Young Italy clandestine independence movement, that at its height had nearly 60,000 active members, before eventually joining Garibaldi's Red Shirts.

In the context of this nationalist effervescence, Tuscany and Florence rejected the authority of the Austrian Prince Leopold and won the backing of Carlo Alberto I, King of Piedmont and Sardinia, who declared war on Austria in 1849. The defeat of Carlo Alberto and his subsequent abdication led to the coronation of his son Vittorio Emanuele II, who together with his Prime Minister Cavour and Commander Garibaldi again declared war on Austria towards the end of the 1850s, this time in alliance with Napoleon III, King of France. The victory of Vittorio Emanuele II over Austria at the battles of Solferino and Magenta in 1859 represented a historic humiliation for the Austrian Empire and caused a resurgence of Italian nationalist feeling that culminated in the rapid unification of the Italian mini-States and the coronation of Vittorio Emanuele II in 1861 as first monarch of a unified Kingdom of Italy.

The Prussian hegemony and the new unified Germany

The Austrian defeat on Italian territory caused much disappointment in Prussia and the other German States, whose alliance with Vienna had guaranteed security for more than two centuries. On the one hand, German nationalist feeling was aroused by seeing what had happened in Italy, while on the other Austria's weakness increased anxiety about a possible isolation of German territory vis-a-vis the other European Powers. German States faced the crucial dilemma of whether to stay integrated with–indeed submissive to–the Austro-Hungarian Empire, or to set up shop separately and consolidate around Prussia. The decision tilted towards the latter option. In Prussia especially, but also in other areas throughout the German Confederation, there appeared nationalist movements advocating the definitive unification of Germany under one Parliament and the transfer of military and political power to Prussia, the *primus inter pares* of the German States. The key figure in this process was the Prussian Chancellor Otto von Bismarck, whose geopolitical vision brought him to the conclusion that the security of Prussia could only be achieved based on a unified Germany, which, if not realised peacefully, would have to be brought about through territorial annexations of the lesser German principalities. These annexations would clearly mean open confrontation with Austria, which still considered itself the titular head of the Holy Roman Empire of which the German principalities formed a part.

Prussian advances in its strategy of annexing the leading German States nudged the Austro-Hungarian Empire into declaring war in mid-1866. Many of the northern German States took Prussia's side, while the greater part of those in the south aligned with Austria. A newly unified Italy also sided with Prussia. After a short seven-week war, Prussia and its allies defeated Austria in the Battle of Sadowa in July 1866.

The subsequent Treaty of Prague sealed once and for all Austria's forced renunciation of any pretensions to possession of or tutelage over the German territories and gave the seal of approval to Prussia's annexation of several important German principalities and States (Hanover, Schleswig-Holstein, Hessen-Kassel and Frankfurt). A further 22 small principalities and States were absorbed into the new Confederation of Northern Germany, entirely supervised by and dependent upon Prussia. The three medium-sized States to the south (Baden, Württemberg and Bavaria) remained formally independent, but in fact linked to Prussia by a customs union and a secret mutual military defence pact. Curiously, Austria, despite being the loser, was treated with benevolence in the Treaty of Prague and its territorial integrity mostly respected, the exception being Venice, which was incorporated into the Kingdom of Italy. Bismarck knew that he needed the Habsburg dynasty as future allies against the potential threat of the other European Powers, especially Russia, and so could not leave Austria excessively weakened.

The most significant outcome of the Seven Week War and the Treaty of Prague was that for the first time the German Region was controlled and organized under one command, the Prussian State. The centuries-old conflict and instability that had characterised this enclave of German culture in the centre of Europe was at last resolved. However there remained one important task to attend to: the formal and definitive unification of Germany. And just as the defeat of Napoleon Bonaparte had opened the door to the appearance of Prussia on the European scene at the Congress of Vienna in 1814-15, it was once again France and another king of the same name, Napoleon III, who unwittingly both triggered and enabled this final process.

In effect, the triumphs of Prussia over Austria put France on maximum alert, given that the increasing military and economic power of Prussia and its North German Confederation were upsetting the precarious European balance of power. This had always depended upon the fact that Germany, while strong enough to offer a first line of defence against possible Austrian and Russian pretensions, was fragmented and unthreatening. Seeing this, in 1869 Napoleon III decided to launch a preventative attack against Prussia, using the support the country was giving to Prince Leopold of Hohenzollern as pretender to the Spanish throne as a pretext. This French aggression unleashed in the North German Confederation and the three southern German allies a wave of Pan-Germanic nationalism and solidarity in support of Prussia. The French army was defeated in 1870 at the Battle of Calm. It is an irony of history that a year later, in May of 1871, the emblematic Hall of Mirrors in the Palace of Versailles witnessed the signing of a peace treaty (the Pact of Versailles) between France and Prussia/Germany which proclaimed the birth of the German Empire. Once again, just as the Napoleonic wars of 1803-1815 had given a definitive boost to the gradual formation of Italy and Germany, the defeat of Napoleon III at Calm gave a final form to the powerful and unified German State with Berlin as capital.

The anguish of being surrounded and besieged: a self-fulfilling prophecy

The *de facto* unification of the North German Confederation and the southern States of Bavaria, Baden and Württemberg created a true European power with a population of 41 million, more than the 36 million French and 31 million British, endowed with a powerful army and undergoing an accelerated process of industrialisation. The result of this unification was not a mere aggregation of lands or peoples, but the birth of a new and qualitatively distinct nation. Its size, formidable military capacity, population, mineral resources, economic organisation and strategic geographical position made Germany a key player in European politics. But its location at the geographical centre (*Mittellage*), and its intermediate position in terms of relative power, constituted a permanent source of instability in Europe. Thus, the concept of the German Problem began to take shape: a country not strong enough to impose its will on Europe, nor big enough to exert hegemony, but certainly powerful enough to be perceived as a threat by the other powers.[1]

Germany ceased to be treated with the benevolent indifference of the past, when it didn't represent a threat to the great European Powers and was never more than a circumstantial ally in the permanent struggle over European hegemony. The attitude of the new Germany also played a part by arousing distrust and raising tensions with the rest of Europe. Unhappily, Germany's internal and external politics in the last third of the 19th century were marked by nationalism and the conviction that the country was on a "special path" to a "German destiny". This nationalism, accompanied by other factors of geopolitical and economic power, ensured that relations between post-unification Germany and the rest of Europe were characterised by fear and suspicion. The long-term dynamics of this relationship have marked European affairs up to the present day.

Two perceptions and two contrasting attitudes arose from the new geopolitical reality of the 1871 Pact of Versailles. On the one hand, the rest of the European Powers began to consider the German Empire–as Germany proclaimed itself to be in the Pact–an immediate threat to their own security. From then on, the German people and its leadership were thought to have expansionist pretensions and plans for European domination. As early as 1871, the Moscow Gazette ascribed to Germany *"an unstoppable and natural tendency to take the road of conquest"*; in

---

1 Brendan Simms (2013) defines the German Problem as the question of "how to organize the centre of Europe in such a way that it was sufficiently robust to dominate domestic and external challenges without at the same time developing hegemonic tendencies".

France, the Revue de Deux Mondes wrote in 1872 that *"like Napoleon, the House of Hohenzollern is committed to perpetual war because it refuses to accept limitations on its gains..."*; or the affirmation of Odo Russell, British Ambassador in Berlin in 1871, that *"Bismarck not only wanted to oppress France in perpetuity, but to achieve the supremacy of Germany in Europe and of the German race in the world."*[2] It is very striking that the German people were seen as having malicious plans for domination and conquest so early in the history of the new German Empire, a view that continued well into the second half of the 20th century.

On the German side, for its part, the new Empire continued to live under a permanent fear of being surrounded and besieged by foreign powers, the same fear that it had justifiably felt during the period of the principalities. This fear turned into the *leitmotiv* of German foreign policy, the driving factor that pervaded and drove its fundamental decisions for at least a good hundred years or more until the end of the first half of the 20th century. To counter the Germany-fearing views of the rest of Europe, Bismarck frequently repeated that Germany was a "satiated power", with no further territorial ambitions. Beyond the soothing words, the focus of Bismarck's foreign policy was the hurried formation of alliances to avoid isolation. He was accustomed to saying that the key to foreign policy was to be part of an alliance of two within a Europe of three Powers, or of an alliance of three in a Europe of five Powers (depending on whether this included Russia and Great Britain in the mix). During the years of his mandate from 1871 until 1890, Bismarck created and dismantled alliances with all the powers in every possible combination, either openly or in secret. Simultaneously, Bismarck worked discreetly at strengthening his military capacity. Military industries formed part of a greater strategy to create a wide, prosperous and disciplined economic base.

In Germany at the end of the 19th century the "doctrine of the global empire" (*Weltreicheslehre*) was very much in vogue. Its central belief was that the geo-economic power of the (other) European colonial empires would eventually crush the weak Central European block (i.e. Germany). Against this background, Germany embarked on a two-fold race to defend itself and to gain respect: on the one hand, it increased its activities on

---

2   Quoted by Simms (2013), p. 243.

the colonial front (South Africa, Asia, Oceania, Morocco...),[3] with consequent discomfort for the traditional colonial powers, and on the other hand it increased military spending, especially for the Navy, to be able to go one-to-one with Britain. Germany thus embarked on a perverse dynamic of action and reaction, of fear and shows of strength, of isolation and expansionism, which was interpreted by the other world powers as confirming their prejudices about the territorial voracity and warlike conduct of the new unified Germany.

As a consequence of its fear-driven policies, by the beginning of the 20th century Germany had become dangerously isolated. In a self-fulfilling prophecy, the dread of isolation and the measures taken to prevent it had led to actual isolation. In 1906, those two historical arch-rivals, France and Britain, signed a military alliance focussed on the German threat, an alliance which a year later was joined by Russia. All that remained to Germany was the alliance with Austria, whose military and political power was significantly diminished. Germany thus ended up as part of an alliance of two in a Europe of five Powers, something that Bismarck had fought so hard to avoid.

Two World Wars: Germany in the middle

In the years prior to the First World War, another of those paradoxes that characterized the ambivalent relationship between Germany and Europe came to the fore: in population and wealth, Germany was certainly a power within Europe, but its federalist political structure put it at a relative disadvantage in collecting enough taxes and organising under a single strong leadership that would lead to a military build-up. Germany had

---

[3] In the words of the then Chancellor Bernhard von Bülow, in a debate in the Reichstag on December 6, 1897, Germany claimed its right to *"ein Platz an der Sonne"*, a place in the sun, the same as its rival colonial powers. The expression became popular afterwards in reference to Germany's ambitions for territorial expansion. At the beginning of the 20th century, Germany's colonies included Togo, Cameroon, German Southwest Africa (now Namibia) and German East Africa (now Tanzania), three territories now part of Papua New Guinea (Kaiser-Wilhelmsland, the Bismarck Archipelago and the German Solomon Islands), and several territories in the Pacific: the Marshall Islands, Palau and the Carolines (now the Federated States of Micronesia), the German Marianas (now a US territory) and Samoa. In the north of China Germany leased a small concession on a strip of land called Kiautschou. Germany lost all of these territories in the First World War.

neither the resources nor the internal political structure to match Britain or France militarily in the time required.

Aware of this weakness, German strategists felt very inclined–indeed compelled on some occasions–to take preventative military action to avoid encirclement. This was a very dangerous strategy, because the opportunity (or the pretext) to undertake such preventative action could arise at any moment, igniting the spark of war. This explains the haste with which Germany aligned itself with Austria, when the latter declared war on Serbia and Russia following the assassination of Austrian Prince Franz Ferdinand in June 1914 at the hands of a young Serbo-Bosnian militant in Sarajevo. On Germany entering the conflict between Austria and Russia, France and Britain had no choice but to enter the war against Austria and Germany, if they wanted to avoid the precarious balance of power prevailing in Europe since the Congress of Vienna a century earlier being definitively shattered. Thus began the First World War (1914-1918), an extremely costly conflagration both in lives and in the destruction of wealth.

After Germany's defeat in 1918, the victorious Allies could not agree on how to deal with it. Their differences were evident in the Treaty of Versailles of 1919, which Germany knew very well how to exploit to recover its economic and geopolitical strength in a relatively short period of time. France wanted to teach Germany a lesson, prevent its economic recovery and eradicate any pretensions of future political or military domination at all costs. The United States and Britain, on the other hand, considered that Germany should retain sufficient, though modest, strength to continue acting as a buffer against the Russian, now Soviet, threat, at the same time preventing any future dictatorial, warlike or expansionist drift. Faithful to their democratic liberal traditions, those two countries considered that the best antidote against such radical tendencies was to support the implementation of liberal democracy in Germany and to re-educate the German people in the values of Western civilisation. This tension between these two views within the victorious Allied camp determined the agendas of their respective foreign ministries in the inter-war period. For its own part, Germany made every effort during the treaty negotiations to preserve the territorial integrity of the German Empire, with relative success. Even though Germany emerged weakened from the war, the treaty maintained the basic configuration of power relationships in Europe. Peace continued to depend on the balance of power between the Powers, meaning that the German Problem was anything but resolved; its ominous presence overshadowed European events of the inter-war period between 1918 and 1939.

Germany took advantage of post-war conditions to turn an internal weakness into a strength. It saw the opportunity to overthrow the old federal State structure, reduce its wide margins of autonomy, absorb the three strong southern States (Bavaria, Baden and Württemberg) and reorder the public finances. The new German Constitution of 1919 (the Weimar Constitution, which gave birth to the new Republic of Germany) created a more centralized, more unified, more cohesive and, in the end, much more powerful State.

Economically, the defeated nation showed a greater capacity for recovery than did its European conquerors. By 1921, Germany was already producing three times more steel than France, a country that was finding it difficult to rebuild its economy. Politically, the situation of each of the winning Powers greatly favoured the repositioning of Germany as a European Power. Russia was still mired in the convulsions of the early Soviet communist revolution. The British Empire had entered an irreversible economic decline, while France struggled with its own institutional hindrances and its inability to resume the path of economic growth. The United States had in truth become the greatest economic and military power in the world but had no interest in taking over the world's leadership from the hands of Great Britain.

History gives us examples of what happens when a global hegemonic power ceases to exercise its dominant role, either from isolationist self-interest or from simple weakness, while the emerging power does not have enough interest or strength to assume the leadership. Basically, the function of a hegemony is to provide what economists call "global public goods," such as world public order via military supremacy or international institutions that facilitate orderly world trade, international law or the preservation of the environment. If no single power has the strength or interest to provide these global public goods, the most likely consequence is permanent conflict, global recession, genocides and, in the end, war. Furthermore, when the ambivalence of the world's leader coincides with a medium-sized power harbouring pretension of domination in its region, as did Germany after 1925, the likelihood of a worldwide conflagration increases even more.

This vacuum in world leadership allowed Germany to recover its place in European and world affairs sooner than might have been expected after its defeat only a few years before. Indeed, in the 1925 Locarno Agreement, just 6 years after the end of the war, Berlin, Paris and Brussels, with Britain as a guarantor, signed a non-aggression pact and opened the door to the incorporation of Germany into the League of Nations.

However, neither victors nor vanquished had been satisfied with the territorial arrangements established in the 1919 Treaty of Versailles. The inter-war period was characterised by the continual emergence of revisionist and revanchist positions and groupings, making the establishment of cooperative relations and trade between European countries very difficult. The halcyon years of economic liberalism of the Gold Standard, which fostered so much international trade, investment flows and the coordination of economic policies, were forgotten. What took its place was a system of isolated economies, beggar-thy-neighbour exchange rate policies, tariff protections and internal controls of all kinds. This return to protectionism and non-cooperation had a strong inhibitory effect on the potential for growth of the European countries, which coupled with the widespread devastation caused by the war, led to the impoverishment of broad sections of the population and provided a breeding ground for the birth of extremist movements to the right and left of the political spectrum.

The revanchism of the elite and the hardship of the poorer classes provided the framework for the emergence of National Socialism and the rise to power of Adolf Hitler in 1933. The relevant point to highlight here is that the emergence of Hitler and his doctrine should not be understood as a fortuitous or isolated occurrence, but as an episode in a long chain of fear, prejudice and mistrust that strongly influenced Germany's foreign policy since the days of Bismarck.

Hitler's central thesis in Mein Kampf (1925-1926) was a vision of international politics as the backdrop in countries' struggle to defend or enlarge their "living space" (*Lebensraum*). The size of this space was what fundamentally determined a nation's power. To this central thesis was added the conviction that Germany had a territorial space smaller than its due, not only because of the loss of its eastern territories (Poland) at the end of the First World War, but because of a proper "natural right" to space in accord with the greatness of German destiny. Hitler stated in his manifesto that "*Germany ... should strive to eliminate the imbalance *between its population and its area ... Land in the East, in the territory of Russia and its vassal States, should be the goal of German foreign policy."* In November 1937, Hitler confessed that it was his *"unalterable determination to resolve the problem of German space by 1943-1945".*

The traumatic experience both before and during the First World War had sown deep roots of anxiety in the Germans at seeing themselves again fenced in, suffocated or crushed by a coalition of neighbours. Once again, Hitler and his foreign policy strategists felt that they needed to take "preventative" steps to deal with this existential threat. These went from investment programs aimed at increasing military capabilities, to launching pre-emptive strikes or occupying neighbouring territories to consolidate frontiers. This planned and systematic strategy of territorial expansion is what differentiates German foreign policy prior to the First World War from that leading up to the Second World War. Occupying neighbouring territories was not a core element of German policy before the Great War, but rather a consequence of preventative actions. For Hitler on the contrary, "expanding German living space" was the central plank and purpose of his foreign policy.

The "peaceful" annexation of Austria in March 1938 and the occupation of the Sudetenland, a predominantly German speaking region belonging to Czechoslovakia, in the autumn of that year, constituted the first tangible milestones in this project of territorial expansion. The tepid initial reaction of France and Britain, which calculated that Germany could be appeased through diplomatic efforts, boosted Hitler's confidence that this tolerance would continue when he invaded Poland in September 1939, and that any conflict would be limited to a war with Russia. Hitler was wrong. He should have realised that France and Britain would not allow aggressive German expansion to fracture the precarious balance of power in Central Europe. France and Britain declared war on Germany, which once again found itself in a conflict with the three great European Powers.

In summary, the World Wars of the first half of the 20th century are just two episodes in one long confrontation between Germany and the rest of Europe since the end of the 19th century.[4] The common thread was the problem of a Germany whose central position in Europe, industriousness

---

4   This line of interpretation is briefly noted in the work of Tony Judt (2005), Postwar: A History of Europe Since 1945, p. 4.

and size made her too strong and important to remain relegated to second place, but who was not powerful enough to dominate and subjugate her neighbours. The latter felt permanently threatened by what they perceived as the expansionist and militaristic nature of the Prussian State, while at the same time Germany lived in permanent anxiety because of a fear of being surrounded and crushed by its neighbours, as had happened so many times before German unification in the nineteenth century. This deep mutual distrust permeated the relationship between Germany and the European Powers. At the same time, this existential anxiety led Germany into a spiral of fear, arms races and acts of pre-emptive force, a spiral of self-fulfilling prophecies and self-induced isolation.

There was neither peace nor desire for peace after the First World War. Germany was neither destroyed nor neutralised. True, severe financial reparations were imposed and she was dispossessed of territories on the Eastern flank, but the aforementioned differences between the victorious Allies on how to handle the German Problem gave her an unusual freedom to rebuild in a relatively short time. The German Problem therefore lived on after 1918 and Europe returned to the old instability that had characterized several centuries of its history. European foreign and domestic policy during the inter-war years, as much on the winning side as on the losing, were dominated by populist revanchism, indelible offences, territorial pretensions, protectionism and isolationism. Virulent internal confrontations of all kinds sprang up: racial, social, class-based, ideological. All these elements lead us to affirm that German-European conflict did not cease between 1918 and 1939, but merely took on other non-military forms.

Against this backdrop, the outbreak of the Second World War should not have taken anyone by surprise. Once again Europe was ravaged, and once again Germany was defeated. Unlike in the aftermath of the First War, this time around the Allied Powers were determined to put an end to the German threat once and for all. In this task the victorious Powers were certainly successful but were less so in the task of solving the German Problem. In fact, the intense diplomatic activity in the post-war period, the arrangements for territorial dismemberment of Germany and the first steps towards European integration were dogged by the German Problem. Yet again the Allies could not agree on how to deal with it. Whereas Russia and France were radically against the reconstruction of Germany, the

United States and Britain favoured bringing it back into the world-wide community of nations once it embraced liberal and democratic values. In this dispute between the three Western Allies, the project of an integrated Europe acquired special relevance as the roadmap of consensus to handling the rehabilitation of Germany.

II

CONTAINING GERMANY THROUGH EUROPEAN INTEGRATION

An interesting discussion has developed on the question of whether it was primarily for economic or political reasons that the birth and major developments of the EU took place. Those who emphasize economics point to rationality and the advantages that economic cooperation, elimination of trade barriers, and the free movement of goods, services and people have for the well-being of populations and the growth of nations. Even though in many cases European economic integration has happened less through planned design and more as a response to crises and problems, this does not invalidate, say its advocates, the argument that economic reasons have prevailed. In contrast, those who emphasize politics find an explanation in the trauma of past wars, geo-political power relations and the respective political interests of European nations.

As so often happens in the interpretation of history, one-sided visions hardly do justice to reality. It could hardly be otherwise when the lives of human beings, institutions and nations are inextricably complex, multidimensional and systemic. This complexity naturally also applies to Europe and its process of integration. We do not, however, share the dull eclecticism of those who see everything as so complex, interconnected and nebulous that they are not able to discern the central threads that run through history.

The real engine, the real initial motivation behind the European integration project was the tragic state into which the continent was plunged after the Second World War. The deep conviction of both the leadership and the man in the street was that there could never again be another war on European soil. Everything done in the first decades after the war was imbued with this thought and drove the determination to solve the German Problem. The European endeavour was the solution.

The new European order: integrating to transcend war

The long history of mutual suspicion between Germany and the other European powers overshadowed European affairs after World War II and the path towards integration, especially in the first two decades. This time, however, unlike at the 1919 Treaty of Versailles, the defeated nation was treated much more severely. According to the agreements of the Yalta Conference of February 1945, Germany was split into four zones, each under the supervision of one of the four victorious Allied Powers: France, Britain, the United States and Russia. The capital Berlin, despite being within the territory under Russian control, was given special status and was also divided into four parts as a symbol of German dismemberment.

But once again the constellation of global geo-political power relations opened a window of opportunity for Germany's rapid economic recovery. During the Cold War confrontation between communism and democratic liberalism that began in the final phase of World War II, neither side wanted to allow a defeated Germany to fall under the influence of the other. Among the Allies there was a consensus that no form of German militarism could ever be allowed. Where consensus was not clear, however, was in how far to allow Germany to rebuild its economy and progressively implement forms of self-government.

It is not hard to draw parallels with the attitudes of the Allies in the 1919 Treaty of Versailles. France and Russia again took the radical line of not allowing any German economic recovery, nor letting it take the reins of its internal political life. The United States, in contrast, was more inclined to favour a gradual economic recovery, a gradual integration of Germany into the world's political system and the adoption of its own forms of democratic government. Apart from the genuine conviction that the USA might have had in favour of liberal democratic principles and values, a strong dose of realism was also present in this policy. In the context of the Cold War, the outlook of a power vacuum in the centre of Europe presented a serious danger that Soviet communism could fill it.

A subjugated, humiliated Germany living a regime of economic hardship could provide a breeding ground conducive to anti-Western feelings and facilitate the penetration of communism. For the United States, now undisputed leader in the Western Hemisphere, the Cold War Soviet threat decidedly tipped the balance in favour of allowing room for a German recovery. Britain, as a third player in the game, took a lukewarm position, oscillating between its traditional political liberalism and the anti-German resentment for the two wars fought against it.

The US Foreign Service did not ignore the potential danger of betting on the restoration of Germany as a nation, which is why in its medium- and long-term vision it enthusiastically favoured the European integration project. The renowned American diplomat George Kennan directly expressed the dilemma in 1948: *"If there is no real European federation and if Germany is restored as a strong and independent country, we must expect another attempt at German domination. If there is a true European Federation and Germany is not restored as a strong and independent country, we invite Russian domination…"*. A couple of years later, John McCloy (US High Commissioner for Germany) stated that *"no permanent solution to the German Problem seems possible without an effective European Union"*.[5]

These lapidary statements put a finger on the nub of what had been Europe's German Problem since the sixteenth century, and which we referred to in the last chapter. The power vacuum in the centre was ever an invitation for one of the European powers to occupy it, breaking the balance of power and unleashing war. But the powerful presence of a unified expansionist Germany after 1871 also posed a threat to the balance of power and ended up leading to war. After 1945, there was no wish for a vacuum caused by castrating the vanquished as a nation, nor for the threatening presence of an economic powerhouse with a bad record.

It became necessary to unite Europe, as much to prevent German domination as to stop Soviet penetration. This was key to what became the principal political motivation driving European economic integration, especially for France after it overcame a half-decade of visceral anti-German feeling. The message was simple: a true European federation–at the time understood in the style of the federation of the American

---

5   Simms, p. 381 and 403.

States–was the condition *sine qua non* for solving the German Problem, because if Germany's power were restored outside the containing framework of a European union, the result would be a resurgence of German domination. At the same time, if Germany was not allowed to raise its head and a united Europe did not exist, Soviet domination appeared inevitable.

This conviction also defined US policy priorities towards Europe after the war. In the context of the Cold War, a United Europe was vital to creating a counterweight to the Soviet Union. For this reason, American authorities always enthusiastically supported any initiative of European nations towards integration, a support that was often scantily rewarded and caused great disappointment in the US in the light of the internal disunity between European countries. In 1948, in the interest of revitalising Europe, the United States launched an ambitious plan for economic recovery, the Marshall Plan, with investments close to 200 billion dollars (at current values). France initially offered strong resistance to the inclusion of Germany in the Marshall Plan, but failed to deflect the US position. In the best French negotiating style, it managed to get a more substantial portion of the resources. This tactic later yielded much fruit in the negotiations for the European economic union, when it would sell dearly its lifting of vetoes to Community initiatives.

During the first decades of the post-war period, the victors worked towards letting Germany overcome hardship and make progress, but always under constraints, at first from the Allied armies, and later from the European Community institutions. The vanquished, for their part, wanted to show that they had learned the lesson of history and were capable of rehabilitating themselves in the eyes of the world by enthusiastically joining a Europe based on democratic values and peaceful coexistence. There was also a healthy dose of self-interest in the German attitude: only by being an exemplary European citizen were the vanquished going to be allowed to progress and, most importantly, gain future acquiescence in the main objective of German reunification.

It is fair to recognize that the European integration initiatives in the first decade of the post-war period mostly began in France, despite her deep dislike and distrust of Germany. At bottom, France understood and soon accepted the US thesis that the best way to neutralise Germany was to integrate it into a Europe where France would of course have some form of hegemony or political control. French integrationist efforts also drew on a long tradition of contributions to the construction of Europe. It was the French economist Charles Gide who prompted the International Committee for a European Customs Union in 1924. Two years on, the Steel Pact, a French-led cartel to regulate prices and production, was signed between France, Germany, Luxembourg, Belgium and the Saar Region, with Czechoslovakia, Austria and Hungary joining later. It was here that France and Germany began to recognize their mutual dependence in the field of coal, iron and steel. In 1940, Pierre Pucheu, a senior civil servant of the collaborationist Vichy Government, proposed a European economic union and a common currency, an idea that resonated among German officials because it would give supra-national validation to Germany's occupation of a large part of Europe. And in 1943 Jean Monnet, a member of de Gaulle's government in exile and later one of the founding fathers of the European Union, forcefully expressed his conviction that the only way to achieve peace, prosperity and social progress in Europe was for its States to join in a unitary European organisation, a Federation of Nations: *"There will be no peace in Europe if the States are reconstituted on the basis of national sovereignty... The nations of Europe are too small to guarantee to their peoples the necessary prosperity and social development. The European States must constitute themselves into a Federation..."*.[6]

France was very reluctant to allow Germany to participate in Europeanist discussions and initiatives during the early post-war period, but opposition began to crumble under the impact of a series of events in 1948-49. Those two years witnessed the Prague Coup, the Soviet blockade of Berlin, the creation of NATO and the agreement of the Allies, under US pressure, to allow the establishment of West Germany as a State. This momentous step allowed the unification of the three Occupied Zones in a Federal Republic of Germany.

These geopolitical realities were compounded by French concern about the rapid recovery of the German iron and steel industries across the Rhine. The main reserves of coal and iron ore were on the German side and France needed to maintain some sort of control or access to them. Thus was born Jean Monnet's 1949 proposal to put mineral reserves and steel production under the control of a joint supra-national authority. This proposal came to fruition in 1950 with the Schuman Plan, named

---

6 Mentioned in Judt, p.153

after the French Minister of Foreign Affairs at the time. In true French pro-European tradition, Robert Schuman looked far beyond the joint management of iron and coal. For him, the integration of coal and iron production *"should lead immediately to the construction of common foundations for economic development as a first step towards a Federated Europe ..."* (statement given on May 9, 1950).

The founding treaty of the European Coal and Steel Community was signed in Paris in April 1951 by the six participating countries that would later promote the European Economic Community (France, Germany, Belgium, The Netherlands, Italy and Luxembourg). This was a European solution to a French problem, since France was thus able indirectly to assume control over German basic industries. Germany gained little or nothing from the treaty but signed up wholeheartedly as denoting the first act of recognition and formal acceptance of the German State as an equal member in the European partnership. The priority of German Chancellor Konrad Adenauer had been *rapprochement* with France, which became the backbone of European integration for several decades.

The decade after the war also saw multiple efforts to move towards greater levels of military cooperation. The Cold War was taking an increasingly confrontational direction, with a Soviet Union very sure of itself and ready to dispute hegemony with the United States, mainly in Europe. European countries of the Western Alliance felt an imminent threat and although they knew they could count on the military might of the United States to defend them, especially after the North Atlantic Treaty Organisation (NATO) was established in 1949, they would still need to build up their own lines of defence for lower-intensity conflicts.

France and Britain decided to get into the nuclear arms race and did not sign up to continual US proposals for a United Europe to create its own nuclear deterrence capability. Like the Americans, many Europeans saw military integration as a gateway to further political integration, but the resistance and individualism of Britain and France, especially the latter, made progress slow and tortuous. At the centre of the conflict was, yet again, the German Problem. The main, one could almost say obsessive, objective of France was to keep Germany from rearming. Britain, while not in favour of German rearmament as such, saw the German Problem in the same light as the United States, i.e. in the wider context of the Soviet threat and the Cold War. It therefore tended to be pragmatic about some degree of West German participation in European-American defence, albeit with typical British ambiguity and reluctance.

France looked with suspicion on US enthusiasm for NATO because it considered that organisation to be the Trojan horse inside of which the remilitarisation of Germany could take shape. West Germany astutely showed itself reticent about any involvement or military rearmament in the framework of NATO, at first because it needed to overcome the trauma of the two wars, and later because it was the most interested party in its European neighbours perceiving it not as a threat, but rather as a reliable partner to be enlisted in Europe's recovery. In this context, with the dual aim of having control over European military affairs and heading off independent German rearmament, France decided to take the initiative by introducing a proposal for military cooperation. Thus, in October 1950, René Pleven, the French Prime Minister, put forward the establishment of a European Defence Community, which would organize European military matters through an Assembly of Heads of State, a Council of Ministers and a Court of Justice. The treaty creating the European Defence Community was signed in May 1952 by the same six signatory countries of the Steel and Coal Community. Each could maintain its military units under the direct command of the respective Government, except for Germany, which would be under the unified command of the European Defence Community.

Paradoxically, although consistent with other episodes of self-sabotage, the French National Assembly refused to ratify the European Defence Community Treaty in August 1954, supposedly because it did not offer enough guarantees to prevent the resurgence of German militarism. This rejection created a dangerous vacuum that prompted a boomerang reaction against France. The United States and Britain took up the initiative and pushed for an update of the Treaty of Brussels. This treaty, originally signed by Britain, France, Belgium, The Netherlands and Luxembourg in 1948, had been a conventional post-war mutual defence pact, aimed especially at responding to a possible future German military threat. Six years later, with the Cold War, both the threat and the enemy had changed. In conferences held in London and Paris towards the end of 1954, the foundations were laid for what would be the policy and institutions of common European defence for the remainder of the century. The Treaty of Brussels was later transformed into the Western European

Union, incorporating Italy and Germany as well as the five founding countries. It allowed Germany to raise an army of no more than half a million troops and paved the way to its full incorporation into NATO as a sovereign State. Another main objective of post-war German foreign policy had been achieved. Allied military forces remained stationed in the three zones of the divided Germany, no longer as occupying armies but as a joint European-American force to deter the Soviet threat.

The British speciality: permanent ambivalence

From its beginnings up to the present day, the British attitude towards European integration deserves special mention. Britain decided not to be a part of the Coal and Steel Community, thus revealing another constant in the dynamics of European integration: British ambivalence. Winston Churchill was decisive in shaping the British position. The British always liked to sit at the European table and design the menu, but without ultimately taking part in the meal. As Churchill would say in a speech before the House of Commons in 1953 on the occasion of the discussion of a French proposal to establish the European Defence Community: "*We are with Europe, but not of it. We are linked, but not combined. We are interested and associated, but not absorbed.*"[7] British ambiguity about Europe could hardly have been better expressed. From the very beginning of the European post-war initiatives, British rhetoric supporting the union was muted when some degree of decision-making power had to be transferred to supra-national bodies. That is as far as their Community enthusiasm would go. They were only willing to join collegiate bodies where all the power resided in the respective government delegations, be they officials, ministers or heads of State. They avoided those institutions that could impose decisions on national governments and could mean some degree of loss of sovereignty. And if Britain was going to join a Community institution, the negotiations around involvement always came with an opt-out clause. Europe has always had its British Problem as well as its German Problem and its French Problem,

---

7 Simms (2017) gives a historical overview of the 1000-year long complex relationship between Great Britain and Europe, which has constantly oscillated between conflict and cooperation.

all of them radically different but each one distorting and hindering the whole process of integration.

In addition to not feeling fully part of Europe, in reality Great Britain didn't think that it needed to be part of it, or didn't think so until its own economic decline became apparent. This perception of being able to dispense with Europe was especially strong during the first fifteen years after the war, when the special British relationship with its former colonies gave it some real competitive advantage. Despite the huge material sacrifice which it had had to undergo during the war, what remained standing of the British Empire–which was still appreciable–conferred on Britain reserves of resources and trade relations that the other European powers did not have. Being part of the British Commonwealth gave it important access to raw materials and export markets. Suffice it to say that in 1947 British exports to the rest of the countries of the Commonwealth were equivalent to the total of exports from the six countries of the Coal and Steel Community. In fact, the main argument that the British initially gave for not taking part in the various European trade or customs treaties was their incompatibility with existing commitments to the countries of the Commonwealth, something which would later prove to be only partly true.

However, the relatively stronger initial position of Britain's economy should not hide the fact that she too emerged very impoverished from the war. British citizens had to endure a continuation in practice of the war economy until well into the 1950s, characterized by restrictions on consumption, acute shortages, price controls, rationing, queues for everything, austerity and exchange rate crises. The difference with Europe, especially France and Germany, was that these countries resumed the path of growth and prosperity much more quickly. It took the British almost two decades to realise that they had been left behind and that they needed Europe more than they thought.

Nor did the special relationship she wished to maintain with the United States help with Britain's incorporation into European affairs, at least in Britain's view. The priorities and focus of the British Foreign Office were concentrated on the other side of the Atlantic, especially when Winston Churchill returned to lead the government from 1951 to 1955. By then the centre of political, economic and military power had moved across the Atlantic, while Britain was mired in an accelerated process of decline, due not only to the final collapse of the Empire, but also to its mistaken economic thinking. The truth was that the United States, rather than valuing and cultivating the "special relationship" with Britain, was often irritated by the country's refusal to integrate with Europe, or at least facilitate the processes of European collaboration in military and economic matters. There is no doubt that US foreign policy always favoured a Europe as united as possible. In the end, Britain was in an uncomfortable position: on the one hand, the special relationship with the United States ceased to be so special, and on the other it left the field open to France to dominate the European scene at will.

To better understand this uniquely ambivalent relationship of Britain to Europe, it is worth looking briefly at the "Europeanist" thought of Winston Churchill, the man who marked British political life both during and after the war. Churchill was a passionate defender of the idea of Europe in the post-war years, at least until the beginning of his second government (1951-1955). However, his actions in this government would later call into question the honesty of his European vocation. Roy Jenkins (2001), in our opinion the best biographer of Churchill the politician, provides interesting insights that clarify and correct the more extreme interpretations of both defenders and detractors of Churchillian Europeanism. Winston Churchill was a sincere and enthusiastic advocate for the European Union once the war ended, but he always swam in that ambiguity that British politicians and diplomats so elegantly continued to manifest. In Churchill's case this was perhaps less noticeable in the first five years after the war, but it became more visible on his return to government responsibilities. It was one thing to evoke grand Europeanist visions while out of power, but quite another to commit as a government to being part of a united Europe.

Winston Churchill was a passionate man. When he embraced a cause, he did so with enthusiasm and had an enormous ability to infect many people with that passion. He loved grandstanding in his speeches; nothing he said could have the slightest tinge of banality. His sentences were fashioned with the majesty which grand visions of the world and of history required, and with which he liked to delight audiences. He prepared his speeches carefully and reworked them as often as necessary, but once on the speaker's podium, the words flowed with fluidity, elegance and solemnity.

One of these memorable speeches was the address he gave in September 1946 at the University of Zurich.[8] On that occasion he condensed his thinking about the reconstruction of Europe and the pillars on which the process of unification should rest. Churchill was at that moment fully convinced that only a united Europe could leave behind the tragedy of two world wars that had happened only 20 years apart. Beyond this conviction, shared by the vast majority, the core idea of his approach was that unity should build on the partnership between France and Germany. The central message of the speech was the need to *"... recreate the European family, or as much of it as we can, and to provide it with a structure under which it can dwell in peace, safety and freedom ... We must build a kind of United States of Europe based primarily on French-German reconciliation... There can be no revival of Europe without a spiritually great France and a spiritually great Germany."* These lapidary and visionary words, pronounced barely a year after the end of the war, clashed head-on with the enmity that still burned between the French and Germans and with France's determination not to allow Germany to raise its head for the foreseeable future. Only with the passage of time did it become clear that the Franco-German axis was to become the backbone for creating the European Union.

The problem was that neither of the two countries concerned, especially France, was yet ready to reach an understanding unless Great Britain took on the role of honest broker. Charles de Gaulle made this clear to Duncan Sandys, Churchill's son-in-law, whom he had sent to France to explore the reaction of the French political establishment to his proposals. The foundational core, replied de Gaulle, should be the alliance between France and Britain, and this only once both countries had agreed on how to deal with the German Problem, or in other words how to definitively neutralise Germany.

Churchill's contribution was not only in the realm of ideas. It was of equal importance in the construction of the initial institutional scaffolding for Europe. In 1947 he promoted the formation of a "Movement of European Unity" and used it to contribute to multiple initiatives in concert with other European leaders. These initiatives culminated in the

---

8   Churchill, W. (1946), Speech, University of Zürich, 19/IX/1946. http://www.churchill-society-london.org.uk/astonish.html

Hague Conference of May 1948 with the creation of the European Council, followed by the first Assembly of the European Council in Strasbourg in the summer of that year, with the participation of around 200 delegates from Great Britain, as well as delegations from Ireland, France, Italy, the Benelux countries, Sweden, Denmark and Norway. Even though this European Council had no institutional authority, other than as a forum for the discussion of proposals, it contributed greatly to creating the momentum for other more concrete European initiatives. On the occasion of the second Assembly of the European Council, Churchill gave a speech in Strasbourg's Place Kléber before 20,000 people enthused about the idea of Europe.

In one of his speeches before the British Parliament in the framework of discussions on common defence policy, Churchill even went so far as to suggest the need to cede parcels of sovereignty in order to move towards political union in Europe: "*Mutual aid in the economic field and joint military defence must inevitably be accompanied step by step with a parallel policy of closer political unity.*" During the parliamentary debates in 1950 about the Schuman Plan for the formation of the European Coal and Steel Community, he lambasted the "insular" attitude of Atlee's Labour Government, which had chosen to participate as a mere observer with third-level delegates.

But in October 1951 Churchill again assumed the post of Prime Minister and did nothing to reverse the Labour Government's decision to stay out of the European Coal and Steel Community. More telling still, Churchill did not want Great Britain to be a member of the European Defence Community, the initiative launched by René Pleven in 1951. This position is particularly striking given that just a year earlier, in August 1950, at the Second Assembly of the European Council, Churchill had put forward a resolution in favour of the principle of a "Unified European Army". Nor did the government of Churchill nor that of his successor Anthony Eden take an active and enthusiastic part in the Messina Conference of June 1955 and in the successive rounds of negotiations that culminated in the Treaty of Rome, the constitutional text of the European Economic Community.

This strikingly ambivalent attitude of Churchill towards Europe was consistently echoed by successive British governments to this day. It was not that Churchill did not sincerely wish European unity to succeed, but that he preferred to see Great Britain as a benevolent observer. No great perceptiveness is required to imagine that behind the ambivalence was something more than mere caprice. A first line of interpretation that seeks to exonerate Churchill from the accusation of inconsistency is that his second Government's foreign policy was managed by Anthony Eden, who clearly never communed with the cause of European unity nor indeed with Britain's participation in it. The political survival of Churchill in the Government depended in good measure on support from Eden, the party-anointed successor, with whom Churchill tried to avoid conflict. However, Churchill was not one to shy away from a fight for ideas that he considered important. Europe was simply not a high enough priority for him in his second Government.

More well-founded is a second interpretation, which points to Churchill's view–shared by the British establishment–of Great Britain's special place in the world. According to this view, this British distinctiveness arose from belonging simultaneously to three interlinked circles: Europe, the United States of America and the British Commonwealth. Europe, the first circle, could not impede or restrict Britain in terms of meeting the special "Atlantic" and "Imperial" missions of the other two circles. This is why in fact, beyond the dreams and speeches of Europhiles like Churchill, Britain never truly felt entirely European, and felt less so when it might involve more costs than benefits. The other two circles more directly touched material interests and were seen as incompatible with full membership of Europe. As regards the "Atlantic mission", i.e. the special relationship with the United States, it turned out that Churchill's reading of this relationship and its hypothetical incompatibility with Europe was plainly wrong. The Americans were from the first day of the post-war period ardent supporters of European union, especially military union and were in fact somewhat disappointed and baffled by the British refusal to take concrete steps towards integration with Europe.

Only the third circle, the Imperial Commonwealth, which involved ties and commitments with former colonies, especially Australia and New Zealand, could actually conflict with membership in the European Community. Churchill was emphatic in saying that Britain would never take steps that could damage or weaken the Commonwealth, because "*Britain cannot be thought of as a single State in isolation. She is the founder and centre of a world-wide Empire and Commonwealth. ... For Britain to enter a European Union from which the Empire and the Commonwealth would be excluded would not only be impossible but would, in the eyes of Europe, enormously reduce the value of our participation."* The economic and military contribution that the former colonies made during the war was certainly very important, and no less important was the flow of goods and financial resources for the reconstruction of the country after the war. Britain already had a customs union and a common market much earlier than Europe, which would explain its scant initial interest in an economic community or customs union to trade its products. Against such a complex and weighty background as the British Commonwealth, attempting to enter an incipient and fragile European Economic Community was genuinely difficult and without clear benefits. With the passage of time the cohesion of the British Commonwealth gradually slackened and the benefits for the Mother Country lessened, but it was not till the early 1960s that Britain realised that the balance was definitively tilting in favour of joining the European Community.

The ambivalent attitude of the United Kingdom towards Europe continued even after its application for admission to the European Community was accepted in 1969. The British would repeatedly push for greater integration, then jump off the bus and slow down the process. Curiously, British analysts liked to allude to the process of formation of the United States of America after independence as a case of exemplary integration. Perhaps they were unaware that by doing so they were setting out on a course where one day they would face existential decisions that collided with the sacred legacy of British uniqueness and independence. The decision of the United Kingdom in 2016 to withdraw from the European Union, so-called Brexit, must be seen as a natural culmination of the ambivalence and ambiguity that have always characterized the relationship between Great Britain and Europe.[9]

The Treaty of Rome and the European Economic Community

The failed efforts at European military integration had a decisive effect on the emergence of the European Economic Community. The lack of

---

9 See Brunnermeier, James and Landau (2016)

progress on political and military integration following the French referendum convinced Konrad Adenauer that the path of economic integration was the easiest way to advance European union, even though that way had not been Germany's priority. Economic union seemed to be the path of least resistance in moving towards political union. Negotiations in the military and political fields had been very laborious and tortuous, with the shadows of ancient mistrust, revanchism and nationalist sensibility always hovering over them. The refusal of Britain and France to give up one iota of their sovereignty, their initial reluctance to accept Germany into the European club as an equal member, and in the end the lack of will for political integration had all become evident. In view of this difficulty of moving towards political union, the founding fathers of the European Union (Monnet, Spaak, Adenauer, de Gasperi, Schuman, Mansholt, *et al*) concluded that a preliminary step and indirect route to union was to encourage greater levels of economic integration. The experience of the Coal and Steel Community had been frankly positive, so the time had come to take a step forward and extend integration to the sphere of trade and the economy at large.

At the beginning of 1955, Jean Monnet founded the Action Committee for the United States of Europe. The Belgian interior minister, Paul-Henri Spaak, also played a very active role in promoting this initiative to move towards an economic community. In the Conference of Messina in June 1955, the six founding countries (Germany, France, The Netherlands, Luxembourg, Belgium and Italy) began to discuss proposals for a customs union, trade agreements and sectoral policies. Great Britain, which took part in the initial talks, withdrew in November of that year.

The Suez Crisis finally convinced France that it should turn towards European integration and accept Germany as a full member of the same. In 1956, following the forced nationalisation of the Suez Canal by the government of Egyptian President Nasser, Great Britain and France embarked on a joint military intervention that ended in total failure. This compelled the embarrassing admission that the power of the old European empires had vanished and that without the support of the United States, which had not been previously consulted, Europe could no longer stand firmly on its own two feet. For France, ever irritated by the growing US dominance over Europe, this humiliation led to several conclusions that would colour its later attitude towards Europe: first, that it needed to build up its own nuclear and military power, second, that it needed to foster a strategic relationship with Germany, and third, that negotiations for the creation of the European Economic Community had to be accelerated. Great Britain, on the other hand, came to the opposite conclusion: that it needed to remake the special relationship with the United States, which in practice subsequently resulted in a relationship of subordination. Germany, for its part, took advantage of the situation, was receptive to French concerns and won a preferential seat at the European table.

A year later, in March 1957, the six countries of the Messina Conference signed the Treaty of Rome that proclaimed the birth of the European Economic Community. In the Treaty, besides solemn declarations of support for European unity, the foundations were laid for trade agreements between member countries, reductions in tariffs and the free movement of goods and people. An important milestone was the creation of the European Court of Justice.

Unsurprisingly, the economic negotiations were no easy matter. Once again, France played hardball and got the most benefits. The main French interest was in gaining access to European markets for their agricultural products, especially meat, dairy products and grain. France had a larger cultivated area and more advanced levels of agricultural production than its European partners, which generated significant production surpluses. The French State had to absorb this surplus production at a high cost. The lobby and the votes of agricultural producers were determining factors in French politics, which explains why the government had created an expensive and complex scheme of agricultural subsidies, guaranteed minimum prices, purchase of surpluses and production ceilings to satisfy that key electorate. Skilfully, French negotiators shifted the brunt of the agricultural subsidies scheme onto the shoulders of the EEC, which would now be shared by less agricultural European nations. The inefficiencies, protectionism and aberrations of French agricultural policy were extended to the remaining five members, some of them, such as Italy, less agriculturally advanced. In 1958 the EEC adopted the Common Agricultural Policy (CAP), which validated all of these distortions. Thus agricultural Europe entered a vicious circle in which subsidies and guaranteed minimum prices encouraged expansion in exploited acreage and generation of greater surpluses, with the consequent snowball effect on the mass of subsidies.

The EEC was thus born with a heavy burden. At the beginning of the 60s, the CAP absorbed 70% of the budget of the EEC and 80% of its administrative personnel. Germany was willing to accept this arrangement because that was the price it had to pay to be a full member of the Community. France dictated the policies and Germany paid the bills. France didn't have to give up any aspect of its sovereignty, because most of the decision-making bodies had been designed by the Treaty of Rome to be run by intergovernmental consensus and not by supra-governmental authorities. When France didn't get its way, it used the policy of the "empty chair" until its goal was achieved, a favourite tactic of General de Gaulle. On balance, France and Italy obtained important economic benefits from the Treaty of Rome, but Germany won the political recognition for which it had worked so patiently since the end of the war.

Great Britain did not participate in the Treaty of Rome because it considered that elements in it implied a loss of sovereignty. A very convenient argument to justify its refusal to participate, though one without much substance as we said before, was that it did not wish to disturb its relationship with the countries of the British Commonwealth. Furthermore, the British political establishment was convinced that any economic union would eventually lead to German primacy. Four years were enough for Britain to see the error of having stayed on the side-lines. In 1961, the Conservative Prime Minister, Harold Macmillan (1957-63), formally requested the incorporation of his country in the EEC. In his opinion, "... *only by entering the European Economic Community could the nation hope to regain the weight she has lost on the international stage.*" Curiously, this precise argument was later applied in reverse by Brexit defenders in the campaign leading to the 2016 referendum. France, however, frustrated Britain's attempt to join and the British application was rejected. In view of the continued deterioration of the British economy, episodes of currency crises and the need to alleviate the burden of defence spending, the Labour government of Prime Minister Harold Wilson (1964-70) made a new attempt in 1967, only to be rejected again by the France of General de Gaulle. De Gaulle's obsessive and visceral animosity against US pretensions of world supremacy always made him see European affairs in that light. To him, allowing Britain, traditional ally of the United States, to join the EEC was tantamount to giving free entry to a Trojan horse in whose belly was concealed a project for American domination in Europe.

After de Gaulle's departure from power, Britain returned with a third request for membership at the end of 1969, in the closing months of the Labour Government of Harold Wilson. On this occasion, the request was admitted and the parties entered into the long and detailed negotiations that usually precede such accession. The task of negotiating the terms of accession fell to the Conservative Government of Edward Heath (1970-74), a convinced pro-European. On January 1, 1973, Great Britain became a full member of the Community, at the same time as Ireland and Denmark. Norway, which had also applied to join at the same time as its British ally, didn't follow through because its voters rejected joining in a referendum in June 1972. In the British general election of 1974, Heath was replaced by the Labour leader Harold Wilson (1974-76), which had included in his election manifesto a promise to renegotiate the terms of the EEC membership agreement and to hold a referendum. It was not that Wilson disagreed with European membership–he had after all been the initiator of the two earlier applications–but in his opinion his Conservative predecessor had not negotiated accession in sufficiently favourable terms. After a few brief months of negotiations and without substantial changes in the accession terms, the Labour Government held a referendum in June 1975 on Britain's remaining in the EEC, resulting in a clear mandate from two-thirds of the electorate in favour of staying in Europe.

The Franco-German Axis: a marriage of convenience

The gradual establishment of a European economic union can only be understood in the context of the political power relationships between European countries, particularly between France and Germany.[10] Each country had its own reasons for promoting integration. Germany's actions were always aimed at achieving its two main foreign policy objectives in the post-war period: being accepted back into the international community as a civil and civilised power and reuniting the two Germanys. Its political establishment was convinced that both goals were achievable only within the framework of an integrated Europe, with Germany as

---

10 Dutch central banker André Szasz (1999) says emphatically that to discuss European monetary integration is to discuss relations between France and Germany.

an enthusiastic driving force. The only way to recoup its strength was within Europe and at the service of Europe, not as a lone power that might reawaken the ghosts of the past. It would be a long-term process, moving step-by-step, which should start from a basis of economic integration and move towards higher levels of political and military union. The alliance with France was essential if this was to work.

France had other concerns and other motivations. The French would not accept any weakening of their political and economic sovereignty due to actions of the economic and military superpower, the United States. It would not countenance Europe becoming America's back yard. Containing US influence was a permanent obsession of French governments, particularly that of General Charles De Gaulle. To the discomfort of the French, the Marshall Plan was a constant reminder of American superiority. The clearest and most irritating sign of this subservient position was the weakness of European currencies, the French franc included, against the almighty dollar. Conscious of its limited power as a single country, France pushed for an integrated Europe as a greater counterweight to the US, and a stronger voice on the world stage. The inclusion of Germany was essential, due to its population and economic might. France thus went from vetoing Germany's attempts to raise its head, to becoming its strategic partner. Nonetheless, in the view of the French establishment the European project was to be at the service of France regaining power and prestige on the international scene, not the other way around. Political leadership of all integrationist efforts, and at a later stage of all European institutions, should therefore fall to France, all the more so since Britain had walked away from it.

Progress in the early years of the EEC did not live up to the founding fathers' expectations that economic integration would lead to greater political unity. Seeing the slow rate of progression, in 1961-62 France put back on the table plans for a European Political Union, stressing the need to overcome the lack of military integration among European countries, but as always looking for independence from the United States. Other than West Germany's automatic solidarity with anything France proposed around that time, the other European countries showed no enthusiasm for these proposals. Some considered them too "inter-governmentalist", i.e. devoid of real European or supra-national decision-making authority. Others didn't share de Gaulle's phobia concerning the United States and Britain.

France did not let up in its efforts at creating distance between Europe and the United States-Great Britain duo. One such effort was the Franco-German Friendship Treaty, signed by de Gaulle and Adenauer at the Elysee Palace in January 1963, and designed to put an end to the long history of tension and conflict between the two countries. Among other points, there was a commitment to meetings at ministerial and Heads of State level with established frequencies, agreements on cooperation in the areas of education and youth, and other usual niceties. So far all very normal and commendable, but there was no reference to existing agreements on military cooperation in the Western Hemisphere, such as NATO, or to trade agreements such as the General Agreement on Tariffs and Trade (GATT). This was seen as a rebuff to the United States. De Gaulle's veiled intention was to put Germany in the uncomfortable position of having to choose between the alliance with France and the alliance with the US. Faced with this existential quandary, Adenauer, convinced that only a French alliance would allow him to attain the great long-term objective of German reunification, signed the agreement with France, a gesture that ended with his fall from power.

As might have been expected, the confrontational aspect that de Gaulle wanted to give to the treaty had little appeal for the German establishment, especially to the Atlanticist faction which advocated closer relations between Germany and the United States and Britain. Before ratification by the German Parliament, pressure from this faction forced the inclusion, in the preamble to the Treaty, of references to all the existing agreements in the framework of the Western Alliance. Strong criticism from this quarter finally led to the resignation of Chancellor Adenauer in October 1963. This was more than just another mundane incident in European history, as Adenauer was the man who had played a decisive role in the reconstruction of Germany and the creation of the European dream. All the same, German establishment criticism of Adenauer, and his subsequent resignation, did not mean an abandonment of the central pillar of Germany's pro-European policy, i.e. the *rapprochement* with France. They also knew that, without the cooperation of France, it was not possible to move decisively towards the European integration which Germany badly needed.

The rest of Europe also wanted to avoid confrontation with the United States, despite France's insistence on the estrangement. In 1964, de Gaulle rejected the combined efforts of Monnet and the US Government to revive the process of European integration via a common defence platform centred on a Multi-Lateral Force (MLF). Not only was de Gaulle opposed to this initiative, but he once again threatened to apply the "empty chair" policy in the EEC, flirted with the Soviet Union, and finally in 1966 pulled France out of the NATO command structure, though remaining a member. Luckily for Europe, in 1969 the contentious de Gaulle departed from the scene. The arrival of Pompidou greatly facilitated continuity of the Franco-German alliance, which continued to be the backbone of Europe until into the 21st century.

Second only to the military imbalance, the French establishment's biggest headache was the French franc's weakness against the all-powerful dollar. For the French, their currency was not just a unit of account or a means of exchange, but a veritable national symbol, an expression of sovereignty, all very much in tune with their statist/chartalist vision of monetary matters. Hence the defence of the *franc fort* as an integral part of State policy. The franc suffered frequent speculative attacks throughout the 60s and 70s, forcing the Banque de France to come strongly to its defence. The vulnerability of the franc contrasted with the strength and stability of the deutschmark, which was no more to French liking than the supremacy of the dollar.

The hurricane unleashed by the extinction of the Bretton Woods agreement in 1970-71 threw European financial and foreign exchange markets into turbulence mode. To deal with this, the EEC member countries implemented a coordination mechanism for their exchange and monetary policies. They committed to intervening in foreign exchange markets to keep European currencies within certain margins or zones, in what was called "the Snake in the Tunnel". For the first time, European countries tried schemes of macroeconomic and monetary coordination at institutional level, leading governments to a greater level of political and economic integration. At last France saw fulfilment of its dream of essaying Europe-centred alternatives to the dollar, this being the reason why it had taken the lead and exerted enough pressure for Germany to join in. In a *quid pro quo* characteristic of the history of Franco-German cooperation, France validated Germany's citizenship in Europe and Germany endowed France with the power, prestige and stability of the deutschmark.

The Snake was not particularly successful: countries fluctuated in and out of the Tunnel, and the exchange rate coordination mechanisms were so lax that they did not really work. Learning the lessons of the Snake, at the end of the 70s France actively promoted a more institutional and binding exchange rate arrangement. The details were entrusted to the technical experts of the Bundesbank, which by that time had acquired a solid and prestigious reputation. France's support during the design and implementation of the European Monetary System (1978) was enthusiastic, not only because of its European character but because it allowed her to indirectly enjoy the stability of the deutschmark after the franc's very turbulent 70s.

A constant of the process of European union was that these jumps towards higher levels of integration, large or small, were always the outcome of special understandings, the mutual empathy of pro-European leaders amongst themselves, especially the leaders of France and Germany: examples include that between Konrad Adenauer and René Pleven for the creation of the Coal and Steel Community; between Konrad Adenauer and Pierre Mendès-France in laying the foundations of the Western European Union and the European Economic Community; between Konrad Adenauer and Charles de Gaulle for the powerful Franco-German pro-Europe axis; between Willy Brandt and Georges Pompidou for the implementation of the Snake; between Helmut Schmidt and Giscard d'Estaing for the creation of the European Monetary System; and between Helmut Kohl and François Mitterrand for the Single European Act and the Treaty of Maastricht, which together created the framework of the future monetary union. The impetus of great leaders, among whom flourished relationships of friendship and mutual trust, managed to overcome the quagmire of EU bureaucracy and to neutralise internal opposition to some essential projects.

An important point to note is that this friendly Franco-German alliance did not eliminate all rivalry between them. Rather, it was a means of handling clashes, explicit or otherwise, between the two main powers and their circumstantial allies in the struggle for power in Europe. As we have already mentioned, the French were always guided by a dual objective: first, to eradicate American hegemony from European soil, and second to neutralise growing German power by tying that country to a united Europe. This would contain any aspirations to domination it might have, while leaving political primacy to France. Germany had no qualms about playing that game, as long as the prize was attaining its two major post-war foreign policy objectives: full membership and recognition of the Federal Republic in the European and international community, and the consent of the Allied countries for an eventual reunification of the two Germanys. The German leadership was well aware that its impressive economic success would inevitably provoke anxieties and echoes of the past, against which an enthusiastic integration into Europe was the only antidote to hand. Thus, France and Germany both needed Europe for their respective national projects, though for very different reasons. The important point to stress is that, independently of their individual motives, the France-Germany duo was the key to explaining the advance–or sometimes the stagnation–of the European integration process.

The Single European Act and the road to Maastricht: another power play between France and Germany

In the 1980s, several countries joined the EEC: Greece in 1981, Spain and Portugal in 1986. Internal negotiations in the EEC were not easy. The three Mediterranean countries, being predominantly agricultural, supposedly represented a competitive threat to the powerful French agricultural establishment. Only after difficult negotiations and generous concessions did France agree to the incorporation of the three new members.

The expansion to twelve nations highlighted some institutional failures of a community designed for only six founders thirty years earlier. The system of decision-making by unanimity became increasingly cumbersome. Negotiations on important issues turned into the horse-trading of support and alliances in exchange for privileges and concessions. The rule of intergovernmentalism–that everything should be approved by the respective governments at ministerial level–and unanimity in decision-making slowed down the integration process and generally resulted in sub-optimal decisions. Progress was achieved basically by "negative economic integration", i.e. giving concessions, lowering tariffs or rates, or increasing subsidies or aid. Very rarely did Community bodies make courageous "positive" decisions where only the common good prevailed. Only when the great leaders decided to promote some project did it manage to make positive progress.

One such positive moment of relaunching the communitarian process occurred in 1983, when in a Solemn Declaration the Heads of State proclaimed their willingness to accelerate progress towards a European Union. The moment was auspicious for two reasons, one negative and the other positive. The negative reason, as mentioned above, was the disappointing slowness of Community processes, trapped in the quagmire of Brussels bureaucracy and intergovernmental skullduggery. At the time, the term used to label the stagnation of the European integration process was "euro-sclerosis". Positive momentum came from the optimism generated by the relative success of macroeconomic and monetary coordination, which was functioning reasonably well after the implementation of the EMS in 1979. This time the expectations of the founding fathers, that economic progress would open the door to political advances, became reality. Another very important facilitating factor was the recent appearance on the scene of two new European leaders, to wit, French President François Mitterrand (1981-95) and German Chancellor Helmut Kohl (1982-98), who played an instrumental role in the birth of the EMU.

In that spirit, in February 1984 the European Parliament adopted the Draft Treaty of the European Union, to reform European institutions and move towards greater degrees of unity. This political will prompted several rounds of negotiations, whose agreements were finally set forth at the end of 1985 in a key document, the Single European Act, which formally came into effect in July 1987. After the 1957 founding Treaty of Rome, this was the next most important milestone in the history of European integration. The decision to create a single market and to establish the four fundamental freedoms of movement (of people, goods, services and capital) meant a quantum leap forward, a decision to set Europe on the path to a qualitatively superior union. The subsequent decision to create the Monetary Union with the Treaty of Maastricht was for many a natural consequence of the Single European Act and its necessary complement. For others, it was a step too far; it was not essential for deepening the economic union that the Single European Act was meant to promote.

The Act was the first proposal for fundamental reform of Community statutes since the Treaty of Rome in 1957. It established the calendar for creating the single market for goods, services, labour and capital, with the deadline being the end of 1992. It also conferred on the European

Parliament greater powers to make legislative proposals, which would then be carried out by the European Commission. Of great symbolic importance was the proposal to rename the European Economic Community as the European Union, which came into force with the Treaty of Maastricht in 1992. Decisions by unanimous vote were replaced by the mechanism of qualified majority voting. This certainly represented an advance, although in practice the largest countries, especially Britain, Germany and France, kept a sort of right of veto. The largest could no longer impose their will but could still block decisions they did not like. The Act laid the foundations and gave the necessary impetus to the efforts and agreements that concluded in the Treaty of Maastricht, the founding document of the European Monetary Union.

Another milestone in the path of European political integration was the Schengen Agreement reached by five of the ten members of the EEC in June 1985 (France, Germany, Luxembourg, The Netherlands and Belgium) and which responded to the Treaty of Rome mandate to allow free movement of people within the Community. Its objective was the gradual elimination of internal border controls and the adoption of a common visa policy. By its very nature, negotiations on this issue were complex, and it was not until 1997 when countries belonging to the European Union finally acceded to the Schengen Convention, even though Britain and Ireland reserved a right to opt-out.

An important role in this rebirth of the integrationist spirit was played by the former French Minister of Finance, Jacques Delors, who was appointed President of the European Commission in January 1985, a position he held for three terms until the end of 1994. From this position, Delors pushed forward key initiatives for the creation of the European Monetary Union. In June 1988, the European Council of Heads of State agreed to request the European Commission to form a working commission with the specific purpose of advancing ideas and proposals on a common monetary area in Europe, as well as a European Central Bank. A year later, the Delors Commission, so-called because it was presided over by the President of the European Commission himself, presented its proposals to the European Council, which accepted them as a basis for discussion. Very intense technical and political discussions on how to give shape to the idea of a monetary union took place in the second half of 1989 and throughout 1990 and 1991.

Many academic economists were sceptical or even openly opposed to the proposal, because they felt that the necessary conditions for adopting a common currency were not present in Europe. The political leadership of the time, however, was fully determined to move towards monetary union, believing that only through the progressive creation of integrated economic blocs could the edifice of the European Union be constructed at the political level. In retrospect, Mario Draghi, President of the European Central Bank from 2011, recognises that the EMU initiative *"... was driven primarily by the political will to give de Common Market a stable monetary anchor and to set Europe on course toward an ever closer integration..."*. The politicians were undoubtedly the key players in the process leading to monetary union and they took the key decisions on where to go to and when.

Meanwhile, Eurocrats and most officials thought, naively, that the momentum of economic-monetary integration itself would encourage–or force–higher levels of integration in other areas. This way of thinking was a constant from the beginning of the construction of Europe. Another constant of the process was that, having received the political mandate of the European Council, the Community institutions in Brussels and the Eurocrats took total control of the process without any political checks. In the specific case of the monetary union, it was the Committee of Governors of the European Central Banks who received the design mandate, and they handled it with that secrecy and aversion to political control for which central bankers are well-known.

It is incorrect to say that the European political leadership simply ignored the shortcomings attendant on the birth of the monetary union, especially in terms of the lack of fiscal and political integration considered by economists to be indispensable for the sustainability of a common currency. The leadership did not ignore them, but they also firmly believed in the stimulating power of crisis and trusted that the feedback dynamics (positive or negative) would later force putting in place the pieces needed to complete the jigsaw puzzle. Romano Prodi, twice Italian Premier and President of the European Commission between 1999 and 2004, stated that *"I am sure the euro will oblige us to introduce a new set of economic policy instruments. It is politically impossible to propose that now. But some day there will be a crisis and new instruments will be created."*[11]

---

11   Interview Financial Times

If so many independent experts were opposed to a European monetary union or were sceptical regarding its desirability and feasibility, why did the idea prevail and take shape in such record time between the Delors report in mid-1989 and the Draft Maastricht Treaty at the end of 1991? Clearly, the key driving forces behind the monetary union project were not economic interests or rationales, but the political necessities of the main participants. It should be no surprise that States respond to their national interests when it comes to integration processes involving some kind of cession of sovereignty. In the case of France, her interest was twofold. In the first place, French national pride was closely tied to the currency; to the French way of thinking, a strong nation should have a strong currency. The policy of the *franc fort*, driven primarily by François Mitterrand (president from 1981 until 1995), was a reflection of this grandiose and nationalistic view of the currency. This explains how this policy was maintained against all odds, often with painful consequences, even when economic reality required a devaluation of the franc.

This became apparent in the currency crisis after the collapse of the Bretton Woods system between 1969 and 1971, or more dramatically in the EMS crisis of 1992-93. The failures and consequent political costs of devaluing the franc brought the French leadership to the conviction that subsuming their national currency within the project of a common European currency was the way to elude those devaluation costs in the future. Knowing that the battle between the franc and the deutschmark had been lost, France saw in the euro the opportunity to regain control of its monetary affairs. She believed, naively, that she was going to have political control over the new common currency while taking advantage of the strength conferred by an ECB conceived as a carbon copy of the reputable German Central Bank.

This nationalistic vision of the currency is the frame of reference for understanding the almost obsessive determination of France, from the time of General de Gaulle onward, to neutralise the monetary hegemony of the US dollar. As early as 1965 Giscard d'Estaing coined the term "exorbitant privilege" in referring to the dollar's position as a global reserve currency.[12] But awareness of the vulnerability of national currencies, including their beloved franc, brought the French political establishment

---

12 See the reference in Eichengreen (2011)

to the conclusion that only a common European currency could provide a sufficient counterweight against the hegemony of the dollar. At the geopolitical level, Europe could only be a player in the international power game if it had a currency of its own as strong as the dollar or the yen.

The second concern of France had to do with the German Problem. 45 years after the war, this had re-emerged with full force with the fall of the Berlin Wall in October 1989 and the reunification of the two Germanys a year later. This was the decisive factor that eliminated once and for all the barriers to the creation of the EMU that might hitherto have existed in French thinking. German reunification revived the enduring concern and anxiety about the economic and political power of the country which, in France's opinion, had threatened peace and equilibrium in Europe since the beginning of the 19th century. The only way to neutralise and control German power was to tie Germany into deeper and irreversible European integration, in which of course France would retain political leadership. This could be accomplished through monetary union. In her nationalistic view of the currency, France thought that wresting the deutschmark away from Germany was like depriving her of the source of her economic power, like Delilah depriving Samson of his strength by cutting his hair. So, the second political motivation for France promoting the EMU was her desire to control and neutralise the new power that German reunification had granted to her eternal rival. This was nothing new, because this distrust and the desire to contain Germany had been the constant theme permeating the actions of France throughout the process of building European integration, from the very creation of the Coal and Steel Community in the early 50s.

Paradoxically, Germany also had political motivations to deepen European union through a common currency. Helmut Kohl, German Chancellor from 1982 to 1998, was convinced–as were his predecessors–that only by being wrapped up within and subject to the European Union could Germany obtain approval for its reunification project from the Allied Powers (United States, Britain, France and Russia). Germany understood that its reunification would only be accepted if it was part of a broader process of the integration of Europe. So it was that, by wrapping itself in the cloak of Europe, Germany could once again re-emerge as a united nation on the stage of world and European powers. Kohl's political capital let him brush aside internal resistance to giving up the deutschmark, especially from the powerful and independent Bundesbank. Kohl thought that there was too much at stake politically to risk everything by listening to economic or monetary objections, which might have had much technical validity but would have to be sacrificed on the altar of German reunification.

It is curious to note how the French and German governments sold the idea of monetary union to their respective national audiences. It seemed almost as if they were talking about two different things. Germany framed the euro as the direct successor to the strong deutschmark, and the European Central Bank as a mirror of the Bundesbank. For France, the common currency would be the way to partially recover her monetary leadership, lost in the currency debacle of 1992-93. Germany assured its public that both the new common currency and the public finances of the members would be subject to strict rules and procedures of supervision and sanction. France was satisfied with an arrangement in which she shared with Germany control over the currency and monetary policy, and at the same time fully preserved her sovereignty over fiscal decisions. Quite different versions of union went through the minds of the French and the Germans.

Some historians, such as Oxford's Timothy Garton Ash (2013), have claimed that European monetary union cannot be seen as a German project to dominate Europe, but on the contrary as a project for Europe, especially France, to control a reunified Germany. The reality is that Germany had, from an economics standpoint, little to gain from monetary union and much to lose, specifically her revered and beloved deutschmark. But at the time the German political position was not strong enough and she needed the acquiescence of France and Britain. Timidly, and rightly, Chancellor Helmut Kohl said in 1991 that a monetary union required some form of fiscal, and therefore political, union. That was not in fact part of France's thinking. Her main goal was to draw on the strength of the deutschmark and control the new common currency, but not to surrender control over its national budget to any Community body.

In the end, however, Germany managed to sell dearly her renunciation of the deutschmark. Her reward was the imposition on the EMU of a monetary architecture in the image and likeness of the Bundesbank. Paradoxically, this monetary architecture was what later allowed her to turn the tables and assume her position of dominance.

The United Kingdom, as the third European power, also viewed with great concern the events that led to the fall of the Berlin Wall and the *de facto* German reunification that came from it. Margaret Thatcher once said emphatically to the Soviet leader Gorbachev: "*We don't want a united Germany*".[13] She thought that a reunified Germany would end up, once again, dominating the rest of Europe. But there wasn't much she could do to prevent it, inasmuch as the United States always wanted a strong Germany within a strong Europe, and because the Soviet Union was facing its own collapse, while France had negotiated the reunification in exchange for a Europe designed to suit it. In any case, showing little or no interest in monetary union, the British continued step by step in their progressive process of alienation from the European integrationist spirit.

The rest of the member countries of the EEC had no opportunity to exert much influence in this critical phase of European integration. Countries in Germany's area of influence (the Benelux countries and Norway), were in no doubt that their destiny was inevitably linked to the deutschmark. And the Mediterranean countries could not afford to miss out. They also shared the arguments of the French position, although with some nuances. In consequence, political conditions were definitely ripe for monetary union.

After presenting the Delors Report in mid-1989, the European Commission opened the internal discussions and prepared its own report with the title "*One Market, One Money*", whose fundamental thesis was that a common market needed a common currency in order to be further improved. The proposals of the Delors Committee to advance in stages towards monetary union were the object of intense implementation debates at the level of the various European Community technical and political bodies during 1990 and 1991. In December 1991, the European Council meeting in Maastricht agreed to draft a treaty on the European Union, based on the conceptual framework and recommendations of the Delors Report. Thus, the seminal agreement of the current European Monetary Union was born: the treaty was signed by the Heads of Government in the Dutch city of Maastricht in February 1992, and became effective in November 1993.

---

13   Quoted in B. Simms, p. 483

At the same time, and fulfilling the mandate of the Single European Act of 1987, the European Single Market came into force on the 1st of January 1993, its central tenet being the freedom of movement of goods, services, capital and people (the four core freedoms). Freedom of movement meant the abolition from that moment on of any borders or obstacles in these four fundamental categories.

The decade of great expansion and institutional reforms: 1995-2005

The incorporation of three major countries (Austria, Sweden and Finland) as full members in 1995 came to enrich the best spell of Community spirit that Europe had had since the mid-80s. At the same time, during the first half of the 90s, a pivotal debate took place on the incorporation of new members. This was triggered by the collapse of the Soviet Union and the insistent request of the countries of Eastern Europe for admittance to the European Union. For these countries, being part of Europe was the key to definitively freeing themselves from communism and dictatorship and protecting themselves against possible future attempts by Russia to re-establish her tutelage over them.

Incorporating 12 new countries almost simultaneously was a controversial decision that would subsequently have serious implications for the viability of the Union. It was also a Herculean task that demanded an excessive degree of attention by Community institutions–attention that might have been better directed towards anticipating and mitigating the disastrous financial crisis coming at the end of the 2000s–and altered the equilibrium that the founding countries had painstakingly carved out over five decades. In spite of all the risks, the doors of the Union were in the end thrown open to the countries of Eastern Europe, albeit after long waiting periods and very demanding preconditions had been established. Thus in 2004 the EU took in the Czech Republic, Slovakia, Slovenia, Estonia, Lithuania, Latvia, Hungary, Poland, Cyprus and Malta. In 2007 Romania and Bulgaria also joined.

Why, then, did the European Union take such a risky step? The three principal European Powers were engaged in a power-game guided by their own special interests that, as usually happens, led to a poor collective outcome. Beyond the integrationist and pro-European rhetoric that they all officially declaimed, three divergent positions became clear in the discussions. France was not in favour of enlargement because she felt that this would weaken her political power base in the Union. Her political reluctance came clothed in the discourse of the need first of all to "deepen" the European Union: before expanding, it was necessary for the existing group to become more integrated. At the other extreme, Britain was in favour of enlargement towards the East, but, although this was not openly stated, the intention was not to strengthen or deepen the Union, but to turn it into a loose federation of sovereign nations. At bottom, the veiled intention of this approach was to throw sand into the wheels of European integration which, in the opinion of the British, was moving too fast and was too invasive of national sovereignty. Incorporating such a large number of countries, of diverse cultural backgrounds and with different levels of economic development, would certainly not facilitate deeper vertical integration.

With her well-known style of "both the one and the other" (*sowohl als auch*), Germany wanted both to broaden and to deepen at the same time. It tried to become the hinge on which the divergent interests of France and Britain would pivot. At the end of this long discussion, Britain aligned itself strongly with Germany in a Faustian pact to enlarge Europe eastward. We say Faustian, because the consequences were subsequently harmful for both the United Kingdom and Europe, as the Brexit decision subsequently proved. A major factor in the British man in the street's progressive disillusionment with the EU was precisely the mass migration of citizens from Eastern Europe towards the UK, having acquired the Community right to free movement of people. Nearly a million new European citizens from the East settled in Britain after 2004, initially putting stress on public services and jobs. This fact was undoubtedly decisive in tilting the balance of the 2016 referendum towards the Leave option, no matter how misguided was public perception about the effects of immigration on public services, wages or jobs.[14]

---

14 Hill (2018) refers to the incomprehensible decision of the British government not to invoke the moratorium on the flow of East-European immigrants for a transition period, something that both France and Germany did do. This led to a wave of immigrants from Eastern Europe, which diluted the climate of tolerance for immigration. On the erroneous perception of the impact on jobs, wages and public services, see the Report of the London School of Economics (http://cep.lse.ac.uk/pubs/download/brexit05.pdf)

If we had to answer the classic question of *"cui bono?"*, clearly Germany benefited. Indeed, the enlargement of the European Community to 28 members represented a remarkable strengthening of Germany's political position in Europe. In addition to the countries incorporated in 1995 (Austria, Sweden and Finland), all belonging to Germany's natural sphere of influence, the 10 countries of Eastern Europe belonged to a second German sphere of influence. This web of special bonds was the result of the German government's consistent *Ostpolitik* (also known as *Realpolitik*) approach to the countries of the Warsaw Pact, especially during the long regime of Helmut Kohl. In its delicate balance between West and East, between the United States and Russia, German foreign policy had cultivated trade and cultural relations with the whole of Eastern Europe during the 80s and 90s. By 2004, the level of integration and trade between Germany and the Eastern Europe countries was far greater than that of any other country in the European Union. After the expansion, this allowed Germany to establish financial, industrial and commercial relations with these countries to a depth that the other European Union partners could not match. The two waves of EU enlargement thus reaffirmed the status of Germany as the "central space" (*Mittellage*) in the new geography of the European Union. In other words, she became the uncontested central European power, as much as or more than she might have been at some point in the past.

Paradoxically, the macro expansion did not politically strengthen the European Union as such, in fact quite the contrary. The decisions on new memberships were taken several years before countries actually joined, at a time when Europe still enjoyed the integrationist impulse carried over from the mid-80s. But the enthusiastic and positive momentum that the European Community had lived through in the decade between 1985 and 1995 cooled when the expansion got to the phase of detailed execution, where things were much less glamorous and were replete with episodes of tension and skulduggery. In other words, a return to realism. With the enlargements of 1995, and especially of 2003-05, the political power of the founding members was diluted at the institutional level, and as a result the old natural leaderships were also diluted. The European collegiate bodies turned into Towers of Babel, where each of the 28 countries wanted to be represented on each of the Commissions and internal bodies. The game of alliances became complicated and decision-making processes inefficient, or even crippling in some cases. All this clouded the atmosphere of the original EU, and Germany inevitably clinched its position as Europe's centre of gravity.

Also relevant to explaining the return of "realism" was the resounding failure of Europe in its efforts to face such an eminently European event as the Balkan War in the second half of the 90s. Its demonstrable inability to come up with a military, diplomatic or political solution to the conflict was humiliating. The United States and NATO had to intervene to tackle the ongoing humanitarian disaster. A decade later, with the war in Libya and the West's military intervention, Europe's military and diplomatic incapacity was once again in evidence. Both events poured buckets of cold water on European self-esteem, which had been *in crescendo* since 1985 with the monetary union decision, the single market and the membership expansions. These events, however, made evident the gap between ambitions of acting as a United Europe in the field of foreign policy and defence, and the real capacity to do so.

These facts, coupled with the mismatches arising from the accelerated membership expansion, forced a rethink and relaunching of much of the institutional and legal framework of the European Union. The entire apparatus of Community technical and political bodies went into an intense process of revision. Several proposals were elaborated to adapt the European constitutional framework to the new challenges. First in line was the Treaty of Amsterdam, approved in October 1997 and coming into force in May 1999, which transferred areas such as immigration, police coordination, security and defence to Community level. The new figure of a European High Representative for Foreign Policy was established. The treaty also defined the bases and criteria for the entry of the new batch of countries from Eastern Europe. The Treaty of Nice, approved in 2001 and ratified in February 2003, carried on with the task of adapting structures and Community procedures to the new reality of enlargement to the East. A central point of this treaty was the reform of majority voting. Large countries such as Germany demanded a voting system weighted by population. As a compromise, a double majority system was approved: certain matters would be decided by a majority of population and also by a majority of member countries. The principle of unanimity remained only in areas such as taxation and defence. The treaty extended the number of members of the European Parliament to 732 (!).

More ambitious were the objectives of the Treaty of Lisbon, which ended up being ratified in December 2009 after a long and bumpy approval process. This treaty was aimed at equipping Europe with a new constitution and a fundamental charter of human rights. The initial impulse came from the Declaration of Laeken in December 2001, in which the Europeans Heads of State expressed their willingness to write a new Constitution to improve the democracy, transparency and working efficiency of the Union. This task was entrusted to a European Convention chaired by former French President Giscard d'Estaing. A first proposal was adopted in the European Council of June 2004 by the 25 Union Heads of State. However, the French and then the Dutch electorates rejected the proposal. This forced a new phase of revision of the text, which ended up being simplified and diluted significantly. The new text was approved in Lisbon in late 2007, but again experienced setbacks owing to the Irish electorate's rejection in a 2008 referendum. A new Irish referendum the following year removed the last obstacle, so the Treaty of Lisbon finally came into force at the end of 2009, together with the European Union Charter of Fundamental Rights. The intention of the Treaty of Lisbon was to improve the efficiency and democratic legitimacy of the Union. It gave additional powers to the European Parliament and extended the scope of decisions that could be made by qualified voting in the various Councils of Ministers.

III

THE EUROPEAN MONETARY UNION:
A TROJAN HORSE FOR THE DEUTSCHMARK?

The European project was predominantly a political one. The European Economic Community, born out of the Treaty of Rome 1957, had been a political project, as had been the European Monetary Union born of the Maastricht Treaty of 1992. In due course, however, political interests aligned with economic circumstances favourable to integration. Additionally, the economic interests of the countries involved also converged. This type of large international project only advances when the Member States consider that progress in economic interdependence favours their own national interests. Of such conjunctions is history made.

Certainly, after the initial political impetus, economic integration usually gains a life of its own and responds to arguments about the need to amalgamate for further growth, or to the economic dynamics of steps that are a logical consequence of previous ones. In the case of Europe, when and why economic integration processes were triggered had mainly to do with challenges from the international economic environment, manifested both in exchange rate crises or as imperatives of external competition, which forced the creation of higher levels of coordination and integration. For example, the Werner Plan of 1969 and the Snake in the Tunnel were the European response to the dollar crisis at the end of the 60s and to the collapse of the Bretton Woods system. The EMS of 1978 was a response to the decline of the dollar in 1977-78. The revaluation of the dollar in the first half of the 80s and then its rapid decline finally made apparent to Europeans the need to disassociate themselves from the dollar, which had become a source of monetary and exchange rate instability.

In this chapter we will focus on the economic dynamics of the European integration. We will analyse the international circumstances that gave rise to the first schemes of monetary and exchange integration, such as the Snake and the EMS. We will give an account of the gestation of the monetary union with emphasis on the monetary and exchange rate events that prompted it, from the collapse of Bretton Woods to the exchange rate crisis of 1992-93. These traumatic economic events brought out the difficult political economy of the adjustment processes, which ended up convincing the traditionally weaker countries that they should take shelter under the umbrella of a strong common currency.

From the hegemony of the Bretton Woods dollar to that of the EMS deutschmark

It is usual to organise accounts of the economic history of the European Union according to a conventional sequence of phases of economic integration. A process of integration should proceed sequentially through commercial, financial, monetary, and finally political levels. At first glance, these conventional steps seem applicable to the European experience, but a more careful look at how it developed reveals a crucial fact: the process of trade integration was preceded by, and then accompanied by, monetary schemes aimed at financial and exchange rate stability.

Already by 1962 the EEC Commission submitted for discussion a report entitled "*Program of Action for the Second Phase of the European Economic Community*", a first proposal for a monetary union, which was to be completed in nine years. However, as long as the Bretton Woods monetary system ensured a stable framework of exchange rates with all currencies anchored to the U.S. dollar, the European monetary integration agenda couldn't become relevant, nor did it need to do so, as Bretton Woods met the European need for monetary stability well enough during the first two decades of the post-war period. Liquidity needs, for their part, were provided by the Marshall Plan (1948), which was also decisive in getting Europe, especially France and Germany, out of the terrible post-war depression. However, the Marshall Plan had the side-effect of establishing a skewed pattern of international commercial relationships almost exclusively centred on the United States, for the simple reason that it provided international liquidity in dollars. To boost intra-European trade, countries needed to break the straitjacket of currency scarcity, which is why the European Payments Union (EPU) was created in 1950. This was the first truly European integration effort. The Payments Union made regional trade possible by arranging compensation (settlement) of net bilateral trade balances in the respective national currencies. When there were trade imbalances, the EPU granted temporary lines of liquidity from surplus countries on terms longer than the natural payment periods.

What did Bretton Woods mean for Europe and why did it fail? The Bretton Woods Conference, held in 1944 at the Bretton Woods Resort Hotel in the White Mountains region of the State of New Hampshire in the United States, laid the foundations of the new post-war world monetary order, with full operation starting five years later. The goal was to establish a system of institutions focussed on the management and regulation of the international financial system.[15] Once the war ended, countries began to gradually release current account transactions, a process which was completed towards the end of the 50s in Europe and allowed the provisions of the agreement to enter into full operation.

In the Bretton Woods system the US dollar became the base currency or monetary standard for the rest of the world and its value was established at a fixed parity with gold. The other currencies were valued against the dollar. That was not the original intention, since gold was supposed to play the role of base currency and the others, including the US dollar, would have the same peer status (i.e. a system of N+1 currencies). The geopolitical and geo-economic reality after World War II, however, had been the emergence of a fully-fledged US hegemony. All non-US currencies had to establish a fixed parity to the dollar, which could only be adjusted according to certain parameters and mechanisms. Each currency could fluctuate 1 percent up or down with respect to the dollar. The signatory countries to the agreement, except the United States, pledged to defend the fixed parity, which could only be adjusted in the event of fundamental imbalances and with prior approval of the International Monetary Fund.

---

15   The two core institutions of the new order were the International Monetary Fund and the World Bank.

The monetary policy and the level of world inflation were determined by the US Federal Reserve. The other countries had to subordinate themselves to this policy and intervene in the exchange market to defend the parity of their respective currencies with the dollar. Despite this subordination, the existence of controls on capital flows–convertibility only existed for current-account transactions–left national policies with some room for manoeuvre in monetary matters.

From the second half of the 1960s onwards, the massive involvement of the United States in the Vietnam War led to a relaxation of the fiscal and monetary discipline of the one country that, as the guardian of the reserve currency, was responsible for global financial stability. This indiscipline resulted in domestic inflationary pressures which, via the fixed exchange rate, spread to the rest of the world and engendered distrust concerning the strength of the dollar. Capital flight and the need to contain inflation would later oblige the US monetary authority to raise interest rates, further upsetting the international financial markets. Some European central banks, especially the French, began to demand that their dollar reserves be swapped for gold, until in September 1971 the Nixon Administration decided to close the cashier's window for gold and stop the exchange. Additionally, the United States imposed a general 10 percent duty on imports, in what amounted to a unilateral *de facto* devaluation of the dollar.

That was the end of a system that had lasted for two and a half decades with very positive effects for the world economy. The system came to an end because the hegemonic country, the United States, failed to meet its responsibilities and obligations as world monetary anchor. All currencies were forced to modify their parities against the dollar. The formalisation of this realignment of currencies and the suspension of dollar convertibility took place in December 1971, at a meeting of the Group of Ten at the Smithsonian Institution in Washington.

During this progressive breakdown of the stability of the Bretton Woods system, European interest in isolating themselves from the disturbances caused by the American monetary instability meant that in December 1969 the Heads of State Summit of the European Economic Community in The Hague confirmed its intention to implement a monetary union by stages. A committee headed by Pierre Werner, Prime Minister and Minister of Finance of Luxembourg, was charged with the design of an alternative European exchange and monetary system.[16] The implicit conviction in the committee's mandate was that exchange rate stability was a prerequisite for making headway in the process of economic integration. In October of 1970, the Werner Report put on the table a new plan to achieve monetary union in 10 years (1971-80) via a progressive process of monetary and currency integration. The plan was approved by the European Council of Ministers in February of 1971.

The 1971-73 period witnessed several attempts at restoring fixed exchange rates. These were short-lived and gave way to increasingly frequent exchange rate realignments. From 1972, the Japanese yen and most European currencies began officially to float against the dollar. Three large blocks and their respective anchor currencies dominated the world monetary scene since then: the US and the Americas around the dollar, Europe around the deutschmark and Asia around the Japanese yen (China practically did not exist on the financial world scene at that time). The death of Bretton Woods officially occurred in January 1976 with the amendment of Article IV of the Statutes of the International Monetary Fund, which formally recognized that countries had the right to choose between a fixed or a floating exchange rate system, whatever suited them most.

Of the three blocks, only Europe managed to implement plans for internal exchange rate stability. In April of 1972 a cooperative system of exchange rate stability known as The Snake in the Tunnel was implemented. The idea was that European currencies would fluctuate within a band as a block vis-à-vis the rest of the world's currencies. Basically, the system consisted of an agreement on central bank intervention to keep exchange rates within a band of +/-2.25% (6% in the case of the peseta, lira and Portuguese escudo). European countries outside the EEC Six could also participate in the scheme.

However, the absence of mechanisms and rules for monetary and fiscal convergence soon made the Snake break down under the ravages of the inflationary shocks of the 70s. Due to divergent monetary policies and widening spreads of inflation, Britain, Denmark and The Netherlands left

---

16 See Eichengreen (2011) for a detailed account of the interactions between the Bretton Woods crisis and the process of exchange rate discussions and proposals in Europe. The monetary initiatives of the EEC were reactions to the breakdown of the Bretton Woods system.

the Snake two months after its inception, Italy did so in February 1973, and France followed in January 1974. Some of these countries entered and left the Snake system more than once. By 1978 the participants had been reduced to the deutschmark's natural sphere of influence (Germany, Belgium, Luxembourg, The Netherlands, Denmark, Sweden and Norway). The relatively short and tumultuous life of the scheme left two things clear: first, that stabilising exchange rates in a region required a minimum level of coordination of fiscal and monetary policy; and second, that the deutschmark had advanced by leaps and bounds to its position of the reserve currency of Europe.

In May 1978, France, Germany and Great Britain began to work on a proposal for a "zone of monetary stability" to replace the Snake. In December of the same year, after intensive discussions, the European Council agreed to establish a EMS, which came into force in March 1979. For the first time, with the creation of the EMS, parameters and workable mechanisms were established to help countries to stabilize their currencies. This made all the difference with respect to the earlier experiment of the Snake. The EMS contemplated three central elements, namely: 1) the creation of the ECU (a basket of currencies to be used as a reference for central parities and as a clearing currency between central banks), 2) an agreement on the Exchange Rate Mechanism (a system of bands, interventions, and rules of parity adjustments), and 3) credit support mechanisms between central banks to manage temporary exchange rate misalignments.

Even though the EMS was supposedly meant as a cooperative arrangement *inter pares*, in practice the deutschmark soon assumed the same hegemonic role that the dollar had had in the Bretton Woods system. The ECU was relegated to a mere unit of account and the deutschmark became the reserve currency of Europe, the currency of central bank intervention and the reference currency for the system. In this way, European countries submitted voluntarily to the monetary policy discipline of the German Bundesbank. It was up to the rest of the EMS members to adjust their monetary and fiscal policies to keep their currencies within the exchange rate band. In other words, Germany was autonomous in its fiscal and monetary policy (it did not have an exchange rate target), while the other countries had to adjust their internal policies to preserve parity with the deutschmark.

The reason behind this fundamental asymmetry being accepted by the European partners can be found in the traumatic experience of a decade of speculative attacks on their currencies, devaluation and high inflation during the life of the Snake. Motivated by widespread interest in taking monetary policy outside the reach of political influence, they all wished to seize the anchor of stability that the Bundesbank and its deutschmark represented. Luckily, and this element was crucial for the relative success of the EMS, restrictions to capital movement granted members some freedom to implement internally autonomous counter-cyclical policies. Additionally, the EMS contained provisions to deal with temporary or permanent misalignments of an exchange rate in an ordered and consensual way. In fact, realignments of European exchange rates were frequent at the beginning, the first of them coming as soon as September 1979 with a revaluation of the DM (*deutsche mark*) and devaluation of the Danish krone. The process of such realignments was however fairly orderly, and their frequency diminished as time went on.

Milestones on the way to monetary union: the (supposed) end of the deutschmark's dominance

The Werner Report proposals to advance towards EMU in three stages, approved by the European Council in early 1971, had been temporarily frozen due to the exchange rate turbulence of the 70s. The first stage of the Werner Plan consisted in a comprehensive coordination of economic policies, with a view to achieving stability of exchange rates in a second stage. However, the breakdown of the Bretton Woods system, the oil-price shocks and the accommodative monetary policies of some European countries blew the coordination and harmonisation of EEC members' economic policies to smithereens. The frustrating experience of the Snake and the laborious implementation of the EMS were necessary for Europe to learn what it really meant to coordinate its policies and stabilise its currencies. But the reasonable success of the EMS exchange rate mechanism, especially from 1983 on, rekindled enthusiasm to put the great topic of monetary unification back on the agenda.

In this context, the countries of the EEC signed the Single European Act in 1986, undertaking to remove all obstacles and restrictions on the free movement of goods, services, people and capital before the end of 1992. Two years later, the European Council formed a committee, chaired by Jacques Delors, to carry out a new study on the feasibility of complementing the common market with a common currency. The Delors Committee proposals to advance in stages towards monetary union were accepted by the European Council in mid-1989 and their implementation was intensively debated by the technical and political bodies of the European Community during 1990 and 1991. An important document in the context of these discussions was the report prepared in 1990 by the European Commission itself and entitled *"One Market, One Money"*, the central thesis of which was that a common market needed a common currency in order to prosper. In December 1991, the European Council, meeting in Maastricht, The Netherlands, agreed to draft a treaty on the European Union, based on the conceptual framework and recommendations of the Delors Report. Thus was born the seminal agreement of the current European Monetary Union: the treaty was finally signed by the Heads of Government in the Dutch city of Maastricht in February 1992, becoming effective in November 1993.

Unlike the Werner Report, Delors proposed the liberalisation of financial markets and the removal of capital controls at the beginning of the convergence process. Werner left that to a final stage. Rather than the cooperative federalism between central banks advocated in the Werner report, Delors proposed a single independent European Central Bank with a clear mandate for price stability. This robust monetary unification proposal explains why the Delors Report is laxer than Werner's in terms of provisions and mechanisms for fiscal coordination. Governments were willing to submit to the monetary discipline of a single central bank in exchange for preserving their freedom to collect taxes and spend. For Werner, on the contrary, fiscal harmonisation was a fundamental prerequisite of monetary union. Time proved Werner right, because fiscal harmonisation later turned out to be of the greatest importance. Successive attempts were made to correct this design flaw in the monetary union, but the right of the member States to fiscal sovereignty, consecrated in the Maastricht Agreement, imposed severe restrictions on any scheme of fiscal integration.

The central core of the Maastricht Treaty was the commitment of governments to the schedule of monetary unification, which consisted of three phases:

- Phase I: from July 1990
  - Removal of capital controls
  - Reduction in exchange rate variations
  - Reduction of interest and inflation rates spreads
  - Strengthening the independence of national central banks
- Phase II: from January 1, 1994
  - Convergence of economic policies (inflation, fiscal deficit and public debt)
  - Creation of the European Monetary Institute (EMI), predecessor of the European Central Bank (ECB)
  - Mandate to the Heads of State in the European Council to decide on the initial members of the Union before the end of 1997
- Phase II: from January 1, 1999
  - Formal beginning of the Monetary Union
  - Conversion of the EMI into the ECB
  - Final setting of fixed exchange rates
  - Circulation of the euro as the only legal currency from January 1st, 2002

Why did this third project of creating a European Monetary Union end up becoming reality? The Delors Report proposal could well have been derailed, as with other proposals in the past, but the virulent exchange rate crisis of the second half of 1992 ended up pushing aside all political reticence about a common currency. The crisis brought to light two facts. First of all, the dominance of the deutschmark imposed a monetary policy on Germany's neighbours that was inconsistent with their national economic cycles. A common currency was supposed to hand back to all countries power that should never have been lost. Secondly, the crisis demonstrated the long-term non-viability of a system of fixed parities in a context of national monetary autonomy and free movement of capital. This last factor, the liberalisation of capital flows after July 1990, constituted an entirely new situation. Europe suffered at first hand the consequences of what in the literature has been called the "inconsistency triangle".[17] The

---

17 The inconsistency triangle (also called the "unholy trinity") refers to the incompatibility of three elements existing simultaneously: fixed exchange rates, mobility of capital and autonomous monetary policies. For a more detailed description, see Purroy (2014), p. 71

combination of fixed exchange rates and free movement of capital with no shared monetary policy was the perfect breeding ground for the crisis.

A brief account of events is instructive. The seeds of the 1992-93 crisis were planted by Germany, when it put its national interests above those of its partners in the EMS. Specifically, the fall of the Berlin Wall in October 1989 and the process of German unification at the end of 1990 represented a formidable fiscal and monetary shock for West Germany and the deutschmark (DM), which initially affected only that country, but went on to destabilise the rest of Europe. The decision to lock the Eastern German mark to the deutschmark (DM) at 1:1 parity quadrupled overnight the purchasing power of East Germans, unleashed a voracious demand for Western goods, rendering non-competitive and sweeping aside virtually the entire industrial base (and jobs) of the former German Democratic Republic. In 1991 alone, transfers and fiscal subsidies from the West to the East side represented 5 percent of GDP and placed German fiscal accounts in deficit. Intense inflationary pressures emerged following the explosion of demand and fiscal expansion, which the Bundesbank, faithful to its militant anti-inflationary philosophy, countered with contractionary monetary policies and interest rate hikes.

The impact of these German policies on the rest of Europe was devastating. Her European neighbours suffered the effects of the inflation imported from Germany and subsequently the recessive impact of German contractionary monetary policy and high interest rates. They were caught in the classic trap of exchange rate rigidity in a context of capital mobility, which allowed no leeway to deal with the economic downturn by devaluing their currencies or through autonomous monetary policies. They had no room for manoeuvre because in the EMS their currencies were tied to the DM and their monetary policies subordinated to the Bundesbank.

Europe's growing commitment to monetary union made a return to exchange rate flexibility unthinkable, despite the currencies of weak European partners experiencing a real appreciation that was highly inconvenient for overcoming domestic recession. On the contrary, the recession was aggravated by the pro-cyclical policies imposed by the national interests of the hegemonic country. While it is true that some imbalances in the real exchange rates of some European countries had been building up for years via persistent inflation differentials, the monetary shock of

German unification and the consequent recession quickly made these mismatches unsustainable.

In this context of real appreciation and implicit commitment for exchange rate stability there arose in the financial and foreign exchange markets a curious "convergence business", which encouraged the accumulation of massive speculative positions and ended up triggering the crisis of September 1992. Indeed, the combination of real exchange rate appreciation and recession in several European countries elevated the risk premium (and interest rates) of their currencies, which encouraged the inflow of capital to these high yield countries. And the belief that those countries were going to continue their process of convergence towards the DM kept down the cost of hedging future exchange rates, generating a lucrative arbitrage between the high yields in weak financial markets and the low cost of FX hedging.

In practical terms the convergence business worked like this: an American investor, for example, would trade dollars for Italian lire and invest in the high yield Italian financial market. Simultaneously, the investor would ensure the recovery of his dollars by purchasing dollar futures against the delivery of DM. Due to the credibility of the European commitment to exchange rate stability, the risk of exchanging lire for DM was left open or covered at relatively low cost. Arbitrage between high yields in Italy and the low rate of exchange risk coverage generated the incentive for capital movements.

This convergence business continued until confidence in European exchange rate stability began to erode, especially when Denmark rejected the Maastricht Treaty in mid-1992 and France announced a referendum for the fourth quarter of the year. At that point violent speculation took off against countries that had earlier received massive capital inflows. The action of Hungarian-American investor George Soros, who gained celebrity by betting aggressively against the pound sterling, was particularly noteworthy. Once the speculative attack had been unleashed, capital abruptly abandoned markets such as Italy or Britain and fled massively to Germany. Those currencies perceived as weak were depreciated even more, until their permanence within the EMS exchange rate band system became untenable.

Due to Germany's fear that its foreign exchange interventions in supporting the parities of weak currencies would undermine its restrictive internal monetary policy, it pressured the Italian government to devalue by 7 per cent on September 14, 1992. The markets considered this devaluation to be insufficient. Two days later came the massive speculative attack of Black Wednesday, forcing the Monetary Committee of the European Commission to suspend EMS membership for the lira and pound sterling. From September 1992 onwards, several other currencies were gradually forced to withdraw from the EMS Exchange Rate Mechanism, as was the case with the Finnish mark, the Swedish krona and the Spanish peseta.

There followed several months of turbulence and successive devaluations of several European currencies, until in July 1993 France, Belgium and Denmark also decided to abandon the EMS Exchange Rate Mechanism. In recognition of this collapse of the system, but with the intention of signalling a desire not to abandon efforts towards exchange rate convergence agreed in the Maastricht Treaty, the Council of ECOFIN (European Finance Ministers) and the governors of the central banks decided on August 1, 1993, to expand the fluctuation bands to ±15 percent, maintaining the other attributes and mechanisms of the previous system. This exceptionally large margin was established mainly to allow some *soi-disant* "strong" currencies, such as the French franc, to be devalued against the deutschmark in an orderly manner. The new rule of the Exchange Rate Mechanism validated the devaluations that took place and allowed a very large flotation. Little by little, the excluded countries returned to the EMS Exchange Rate Mechanism, helped by the credibility they all gained from the prospect of the approaching Monetary Union. This devaluation round of European currencies, simultaneously with the strengthening of the dollar during the first Clinton administration, allowed Europe to emerge from recession, and to handle the years of convergence towards Monetary Union membership standards with relative economic tranquillity.

Apart from these speculative episodes, underneath the 1992-93 crisis there lay the structural problems that often appear in fixed exchange rate arrangements, and which should have sounded an early alarm for what the future of the EMU would be like. In the first place, such rigid arrangements are prone to the aforementioned misalignment of nominal exchange rates with respect to their level of real equilibrium. Secondly, a contradiction sooner or later appears between the national interests of the hegemonic country and the rest: Germany pursued a tight monetary policy after the monetary and fiscal overspill associated with unification, but what suited other countries was monetary expansion and a reduction of interest rates, which would have been advisable in a situation of recession. These contradictions always arise when there is an asynchrony in economic cycles but monetary policy is dictated by another country or by a supra-national central bank.

There are obvious parallels with the collapse of Bretton Woods, when the United States–the hegemonic country and currency–experienced a series of disturbances in the second half of the 60s that led to fiscal and monetary disarrays, in turn forcing European countries to realign their exchange rates and import American inflation. In the 90s Germany–the hegemonic country of the EMS–also prioritised her own national interests, adversely affecting the economic cycles of her neighbours. German actions created the conditions for a speculative tsunami, putting paid to the EMS exchange rate system which had functioned relatively well until then. Both hegemons buried their respective exchange rate systems, with the difference that the EMS revived temporarily in 1993 with the promise of monetary union agreed in the Maastricht Treaty.

The clash of national interests and policies, where the hegemon ends up imposing its will, created the conviction in the rest of Europe that the asymmetry of the EMS had to be replaced by a symmetrical mechanism around a new common currency and a single impartial central bank. France especially resented the German monetary hegemony. Another lesson learned from the 1992-93 exchange rate crisis was the impossibility of maintaining exchange rate stability simultaneously with freedom of movement of capital and monetary policy autonomy, the aforementioned inconsistency triangle. Fixed parities, with currencies being issued by independent governments, are inexorably abandoned when the inconsistencies explode. From this lesson was born the conviction of the need to move towards higher degrees of monetary integration, which gave the final decisive impulse to the project of Monetary Union. After the Single European Act, which liberated capital flows in 1990, the only alternative to monetary union was to return to exchange rate flexibility. But was this flexibility compatible with an increasingly integrated common market? The promoters of the monetary union project certainly felt that it wasn't, contrary to the opinion of many academics.

Reasons of political economy: France and Germany united in divergence

The contentious argument that a common market requires a single currency was often ventilated in Europe, and it became the central theme of the document of the European Economic Commission in 1990, "*One Market, One Money*". The argument was that the presence of multiple currencies and the associated transaction costs constituted a brake on the processes of commercial integration. And if currencies were experiencing strong and frequent parity variations, this instability would inhibit investments in export markets and disincentivise international trade activity. However, these arguments were supported neither by economic theory nor by empirical evidence. There is no strictly economic reason why markets cannot be integrated in a context of floating exchange rates. The floating of currencies certainly imposes some costs and frictions on trade, but these are not large enough to impede the advance of commercial integration. In addition, with the accelerated development of financial markets, there are sufficient risk coverage mechanisms to mitigate the negative impact of exchange rate variability on trade.[18]

As theory did not clearly support the need for a common currency for economic integration, reasons of political economy did definitely carry weight in the decision. The traumatic experience of the currency crises of the 70s, 80s and early 90s taught politicians several lessons. The dynamics of the competitive devaluations that broke out as the crisis developed, together with protectionist retaliation from the affected countries, not only imposed barriers to trade but also put at risk their political will for integration. To give just one example, in the five months following the outbreak of the crisis of September 1992, the pound sterling depreciated 25 percent with respect to the main European currencies. This resulted not only in a sudden improvement in Britain's balance of trade at the expense of her neighbours, but also began to spark transfers of factories, and the associated jobs, from the European continent to the British Isles. Aside from the political tensions that these beggar-thy-neighbour attitudes generated, such an approach was not compatible with a community

---

[18] See Purroy (2015) for a detailed account of the discussion about the pros and cons of exchange rate flexibility and its effects on trade.

project. Hence, moving towards monetary union was also seen as a way of preventing or dissuading its members from using exchange rate policies to the detriment of others.

An additional driver to promote monetary union came from the political dynamics of the adjustments needed to resolve balance of payments imbalances. Countries customarily in deficit, such as France, Italy or Spain, regularly faced episodes of recessive adjustments, austerity measures, unemployment, deflation and/or devaluation. And those customarily in surplus, like Germany and the Benelux countries, faced the prospect of expansive and inflationary adjustment if they were forced to share symmetrically the inter-European adjustment burden. The reality was that this burden ended up predominantly on the deficit countries. It is therefore not surprising that these countries were sympathetic to the idea of a monetary union wherein not only would imbalances be theoretically reduced, but any adjustment burdens would be evenly distributed if they should become necessary. If exchange rate variations were causing so many problems, thought the politicians, why not subsume all currencies within a common currency, abandon exchange rate flexibility once and for all, and allow a common monetary authority fiercely committed to price stability to impose the necessary discipline?

By means of a common currency and a common central bank, politicians wanted to remove from the political arena those cyclical episodes of contraction and expansion often produced by mistaken policy decisions. The weaker countries of the southern periphery also needed to bask in the anti-inflationary credibility of their stronger neighbours and stabilise their foreign exchange markets once and for all. Even some stronger countries such as France, whose currencies were exposed to the ravages of speculative markets, needed to depoliticise their economic adjustment processes and hide behind an automatic mechanism imposed by a common currency. These common rules would restrict autonomous (national) monetary policy choices and thus dampen internal political brawling.

As a result, the reasoning and motivations that prevailed in the minds of the political decision-makers during the integration process were more in the field of political economy than in the realm of pure economic theory. Politically, it was irritating to have to deal with frequent adjustments to keep the national currency within the band of the EMS, because those adjustments inexorably went through recessive phases. The irritation was increased by the fact that the countries with stronger currencies did nothing to relieve the burden of the weaker ones. Another source of irritation, especially for France, was having to bow to the dictates of the Bundesbank, whose monetary policy was not always aligned with the interests and concerns of the French economy. That is why, among the other reasons already cited, it was France especially which promoted the idea of a common currency.

Germany, on the other hand, dragged her feet. German economists and the Bundesbank were against monetary union, because they thought that abandoning the deutschmark would open the door to instability created by the inflationary tendencies of her European partners.[19] Nothing was more precious to the Germans than their *Stabilitätskultur*, their culture of stability. So as not to risk this stability, the German leadership thought that some form of political and fiscal union should precede monetary union. Their European partners, however, saw the common currency as a means of regaining sovereignty, by not having to submit to the designs of the deutschmark and by being able to keep their fiscal autonomy.

The interests and economic approaches of the two main European partners could not be more divergent, but curiously the monetary union constituted a meeting-point. Each of them thought they could accomplish their respective political goals: France wanted to put an end to the "exorbitant privilege," of the dollar and the deutschmark, while Germany knew that she had to sacrifice her own currency for the sake of the reunification of the two Germanys and of the European project. The French felt that they were the winners because they managed to preserve their fiscal sovereignty. They also believed naively that they would continue to exercise the same political control over the monetary union which, with Germany's acquiescence, they had had over the rest of the affairs of the European Union. Germany, for her part, managed to bring the single central bank into her sphere of influence and replicate the structure and statutes of the Bundesbank. In terms of fiscal and political union, the Germans thought naively that monetary union would eventually lead to a more federal Europe, in which the profligate and inflationary inclinations

---

19 See, for examples, the manifestos of German academics in the 90s in Ohr, R., Schäfe, W. (1992) or Kösters, W. et al. (1998).

of her European partners would be repressed by Community institutions. It did not occur to them that a federal fiscal Europe would sooner or later require some form of free transfer of resources, something which Germany would thereafter radically oppose.

The central bankers: architects of the Monetary Union

The truth is that it was Germany that ended up getting her own way, by managing to have the central bank's technical bodies be those commissioned to design the edifice of the European Monetary Union. The preponderance of the Bundesbank in the process of defining and shaping the European Monetary Union was aided in the sphere of economic thought by the growing conviction in the 80s and 90s that it was necessary to "tie one's hands" to achieve inflationary stability. By the nineties it was universally accepted thinking, almost amounting to dogma, that an independent central bank with an unequivocal mandate to ensure price stability was a necessary condition to achieve low inflation. So it was that European countries were willing to delegate their monetary autonomy to a sole Community authority, the European Central Bank, and that that central bank should be heir to the credibility won by the German Bundesbank with its relentless anti-inflationary zeal. A single central bank based in Frankfurt, and a single currency, became the central dogma of the European project. It was believed with almost religious fervour that, if the central bank pursued price stability as its only objective, the financial stability of the EMU would also be guaranteed. There was no particular concern for fiscal discipline, because it was believed that monetary discipline would force governments into maintaining it as well.

In the book "*Making the European Monetary Union*", commissioned by the European Central Bank and the Bank for International Settlements, British economic historian Harold James (2012) takes on the task of showing in detail the decisive role that the Committee of Governors of the European Central Banks played in assembling the scaffolding of the monetary union. Even when politicians took key decisions at the macro level, such as on whether and how to proceed, on where the European Central Bank would have its headquarters or on who would appoint its board, the definition of the type of monetary and exchange rate regime, its rules of operation, its institutional architecture and its detailed planning was in the hands of the technical teams of the Committee of Governors. This fact acquired fundamental importance in the EMU's (defective) design.

The central concern of the politicians was to prevent the instability generated by the episodes of exchange rate and monetary turbulence from ruining the common market and European integration. The central bankers were immediately won over to the idea of removing monetary policy from the sphere of government politics. By abolishing national currencies and adopting a common currency, exchange rate instability would be eliminated at its roots. With this purpose in mind they designed a powerful, fully-independent, central bank, answerable to no community or political body and with the sole and exclusive mandate of price stability. That is, a carbon copy of the Bundesbank.

The EMU was born with this indelible seal of the Committee of Governors. The Committee had the usual inability and/or reluctance of central bankers to give thought to political or fiscal structures that should accompany a common currency. It was probably too much to ask of the Governors and their technical bodies to maintain such a breadth of vision and themselves consider the political, financial and fiscal aspects. Those concerns weren't central to their mental outlook, and the belief that price stability was sufficient for financial and fiscal stability acted as ideological blinkers that made other dimensions invisible. The blame for this abdication really lies with the politicians and other Community agencies that should have assumed the responsibility to think broadly and failed to do so.

Formally, after 1994, EMU candidate countries were subjected to a process of 'convergence' based on five nominal criteria, as a central element in the preparatory strategy for the beginning of the Union, with a view to proceeding to the third phase beginning on January 1st, 1999. These criteria were as follows:

1. Price stability: a country's inflation rate could not exceed by more than 1.5% the average rate of inflation of the three member States with the lowest recorded inflation.
2. Interest rates: a country's long-term interest rates could not vary by more than 2% relative to the average interest rate of the three member States with the lowest interest rates.

3. Fiscal deficits: national budget deficits had to be below 3% of gross domestic product (GDP).
4. Public debt: the country's debt could not exceed 60% of its GDP.
5. Exchange rate stability: exchange rates should remain stable within the authorised fluctuation margins during the two years prior to the effective date of unification.

Already by 1997, it was clear that several candidate countries would not meet the required levels of convergence, especially Italy and Greece. It thus became necessary to relax the measurement criteria and use a fair amount of manipulation and concessions to get these countries past the final exam. From January 1999, 11 countries went in to form part of the EMU: Belgium, Germany, Spain, France, Ireland, Italy, Luxembourg, The Netherlands, Austria, Portugal and Finland, representing more than two thirds of Europe. Greece joined the group on January 1st, 2001, also after getting considerable exemptions and no small degree of turning a blind eye.

TABLE III-1
EMU - Representative Convergence Variables, 1998

	Inflation %	Unemployment %	Current Acct Balance % GDB
Austria	0,8	4,3	-2,5
Belgium	0,9	9,3	-1,0
Finland	1,3	11,4	1,6
France	0,7	10,3	-2,6
Germany	0,6	8,9	-2,2
Greece	4,5	11,2	-3,8
Irland	2,1	7,6	2,3
Italy	2,0	11,5	-3,1
Luxembourg	1,0	3,1	3,4
Netherlands	1,8	3,9	-0,9
Portugal	2,2	4,4	-3,4
Spain	1,8	14,6	-3,2

Source: OECD, Economic Outlook

Table III-1 shows that in the year prior to the launch of the euro (1998) there was a high degree of nominal convergence (represented by the rate of inflation). However there remained latent imbalances in the real economies (represented by levels of unemployment and current account deficits). On the eve of the EU, unemployment rates varied from 3.1 percent in Luxembourg to 14.6 percent in Spain. Slightly less serious, though by no means negligible, were the differences in current account balances. More on this later.

It is striking that the convergence criteria focused exclusively on nominal variables, ignoring the importance of substantial convergence of the real economy. Divergences in unemployment levels, productivity rates, current account deficits, effective real exchange rates or other indicators that were equally representative of possible underlying imbalances in the real economies, were systematically set aside. Even though these divergences would later produce asymmetries in economic cycles that were frankly inconsistent with a monetary union, the political haste to celebrate the union prevailed.

The irrevocable fixing of the parities of the 11 founding countries to the euro took place on January 1st, 1999, the date on which the European Central Bank fully took over the reins of monetary policy from the European Monetary Institute. This should be considered the real date of birth of the EMU, since the circulation of the euro in the form of coins and banknotes from January 1st, 2002 was of secondary importance compared to the irrevocable fixing of exchange rates and the handing over of monetary policy by national central banks to the European Central Bank. The European Monetary Union had been born, showing the distinctive features of Germany. Accidentally on purpose, this central bank was the Trojan Horse smuggled within the walls of the EMU, which was going to have such a decisive effect on the emergence of German hegemony on the European scene.

PART II

AN ACCOUNT OF THE EURO CRISIS AND ITS CAUSES

We are all the product of our history and the EMU is no exception. The EMU was basically a political project, cooked up in haste and contrary to the recommendations of many qualified experts. This haste left a series of weaknesses that would cost it dearly later on. Some of the fathers of the EU, such as Monnet, wanted to move forward at all costs, assuming that moments of crisis would provide the stimulus necessary to supply the missing bricks for the Union's edifice. This somewhat perverse theory proved fatal when the first great crisis of the euro occurred. Part II is devoted to an account of the crisis, an analysis of its causes and an understanding of the core problems behind it.

The German narrative of the crisis as a result of the profligacy and fiscal disorder of a number of countries is simply inaccurate. This interpretation would not have mattered, had it not given rise to the austerity recipe prescribed to the debtor countries, and had the government that proposed it not had its hand on the helm of Europe. As a consequence of these mistakes the euro was on the point of perishing in 2012, were it not for the intervention of the ECB as lender of last resort.

The global financial crisis of 2008 was "the mother of all crises". Europe, and particularly the eurozone, was affected more destructively than the rest of the Western world. The causes for the increased damage were of two kinds. The first had to do with the problems associated with the existence of an imperfect and incomplete monetary union. The second relates to the inability shown by the Community's institutional apparatus to cope with a crisis of this magnitude.

The question once again arises of whether a monetary union is possible in the long run without a corresponding political union. A full union along the lines of a United States of Europe is probably not necessary–and certainly not viable today–, but theory and history say that there has to be some degree of solidarity among members in difficult times. To handle this, there must be democratically legitimate organs for managing resources and settling distributive conflicts.

IV

THE GLOBAL FINANCIAL CRISIS AND THE EURO CRISIS: A FACTUAL ACCOUNT

We have seen in previous chapters how the EMU baby was born. Its gestation was long and complicated, but there was a European leadership willing to carry the pregnancy to term at all costs. We will now look at how the baby handled itself in the wide world, to what extent its genome helped or hindered it in facing the turbulent years of the financial crisis that erupted in 2008, and how its performance fared in comparison with the rest of the world.

The EMU's first nine years of life gave cause for optimism. Never before in history had so many major countries achieved such a degree of monetary integration. All eyes were on the historic experiment. The doubts that many may have had prior to the launch gradually dissipated in the face of the sustained growth of every country in the Union, the closing gaps between rich and poor members, and a more assertive presence of Europe on the world stage. It looked as if the founders were right in their optimistic vision that the endogenous dynamics of the Union would correct any deficiencies or shortcomings that may have existed at the outset.

The post-2008 Global Financial Crisis was not just another in the long list of booms and busts in world economic history, not just another episode in the economic cycles that have characterized the capitalist dynamic. What made it unique and extremely destructive is that it was a crisis of excess private debt, which simultaneously affected a large part of the universe of major developed countries. With the global financial meltdown that happened in 2008, the structural flaws of the EMU edifice soon became apparent. Optimism gave way to pessimism, to accusatory finger-pointing, to the discontent of the citizenry and to a very severe recession in countries that a moment earlier had been examples of the miracle that a monetary union could produce.

It wasn't just that the theoretical focus on austerity as a way to handle the crisis was mistaken, but that the crisis management itself also failed. Policy responses to handle the crisis at the level of the Community institutions were both slow and late. By virtue of the complex intergovernmental decision-making process, most of the time the agreed measures were also incomplete and insufficient, more a product of political compromise than of economic rationality. In the following pages we will discern what happened worldwide, what happened at the European level and what were the fundamental milestones and phases of the eurozone crisis.

The euro in Wonderland (1999-2007)

An evaluation of the performance of the EMU must be divided into two clear stages: before and after the Global Financial Crisis of 2008. Until 2007 the achievements of the monetary union seemed quite remarkable. As shown in Table IV-1, the convergence of inflation rates was accomplished, even in the countries of the Mediterranean periphery.

Table IV-1

Inflation in the eurozone and selected countries, 1990-2007

	Greece	Italy	Portugal	EMU	non-EMU Europe	OECD-5
1990	19,9	6,3	13,3		6,6	5,3
1995	8,9	5,4	4,0	2,4	2,5	2,7
2000	2,9	2,6	2,8	2,1	1,6	2,5
2005	3,5	2,2	2,1	2,2	1,5	2,1
2006	3,3	2,2	3,0	2,3	1,9	2,5
2007	3,0	2,0	2,4	2,1	1,9	2,0

Note: non-EMU Europe covers the United Kingdom, Sweden and Denmark
OECD-5 covers the United States, Japan, Canada, Australia and New Zealand
Source: European Central Bank and OECD

Nevertheless, these numbers also reveal two very important facts. In the first place, by the year 2000, practically at the beginning of the monetary union, convergence had already been reached, not as an effect of the monetary union itself, but as result of the self-discipline of the candidate countries during the convergence efforts prior to joining. Secondly, the European countries that did not enter the monetary union also managed to bring down inflation substantially, with averages even lower than those of the eurozone. A similar achievement was shown by major non-European OECD countries. It is hard to defend the thesis that the striking price stability shown by the EMU members in the 2000s was the result of any monetary union. The favourable global economic environment of low inflation and high growth rates that prevailed in the first 7 years of the 2000s blanketed members and non-members of the eurozone equally.

The world economy, and the European economy was no exception, enjoyed a prolonged bonanza since the beginning of the 2000s, which led to the belief that this time it was different and that the policy makers had found the magic formula of "the great moderation" required to break the violent cycles of boom and bust that had characterized the world economy in the two previous decades. The fact is that in Europe this bonanza was mixed with the successes of the nominal convergence and was subconsciously linked to the existence of monetary union, with the consequent monetary-unionist euphoria. At the same time, the degree of financial globalisation in the world, especially on the European continent, climbed geometrically. This accelerated the spread of the Asian and American bonanza, but at the same time meant that the European continent was more vulnerable to contagion coming from other regions.

A positive effect of this confluence of euphoria due to the bonanza and financial globalisation was the striking worldwide and European convergence of interest rates (see Table IV-2). The countries of the eurozone periphery managed to converge and finance themselves at the same interest rates as the rest of the partners. Greece and Portugal, for example, which in 1990 had double the interest rates of the rest of Europe, went on to enjoy the confidence of the financial markets from the very beginning of the monetary union, enabling them to be financed at the same low cost as the best of the world's economies.

Table IV-2
Interest rates in the eurozone and selected countries, 1990-2007

	Greece	Italy	Portugal	EMU	non-EMU Europe	OECD-5
1990	23,0	13,5	20,8	10,8	11,9	10,4
1995	15,5	12,2	11,5	8,4	7,0	8,9
2000	6,1	5,6	5,6	5,4	5,5	5,4
2005	3,6	3,6	3,4	3,4	4,2	3,7
2006	4,1	4,1	3,9	3,8	4,4	4,0
2007	4,5	4,5	4,4	4,3	4,6	4,5

Note: non-EMU Europe covers the United Kingdom, Sweden and Denmark

OECD-5 covers the United States, Japan, Canada, Australia and New Zealand

Source: European Central Bank and OECD

This convergence of interest rates was mirrored in the evolution of risk premiums applied to European countries by the markets. Premiums for the group of countries on the Mediterranean periphery are shown in Figure IV-1. At no time between 1999 and 2007 did differentials against German bond rates exceed 40 basis points (0.4 percent). Greece, which joined the union in 2001, immediately enjoyed the same risk premiums as Italy (between 20 and 30 basis points). Spain's risk premium from 2003 to 2007 was positioned below 5 basis points, i.e. virtually without a premium. Judging by this convergence of interest rate differentials, up until 2007 the financial markets perceived the situation in Europe and each of its members to be extremely positive, that the union faced no systemic risks, there was no likelihood of dismemberment and consequently no exchange risk. Applying differentiated risk premiums was not justified. This was the perception of the markets only a year before the outbreak of the crisis of 2008...

The combined presence of low-cost financing, structural lags in investment and the perceived absence of exchange rate risk unleashed massive capital flows in the first half of the 2000s towards the countries of the eurozone periphery (the Mediterranean coast and the new members from Eastern Europe). The closing of the gaps in physical infrastructure and public services helped these countries grow at more accelerated rates under the umbrella of the Union's anti-inflationary credibility and without the impact initially being reflected in their fiscal accounts. The fiscal figures looked healthy due to economic expansion and growth-induced increase of tax revenue.

Figure IV-1
Evolution of risk premiums, 1999-2007

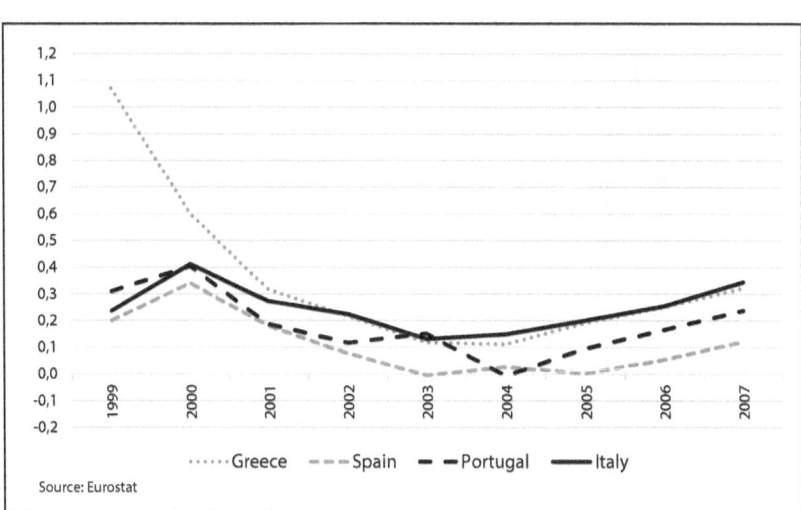

Source: Eurostat

Additionally, an average annual growth rate of 5.2% in the Mediterranean periphery (Greece, Italy, Spain and Portugal) between 1998 and 2007, compared to 3% in France and Germany, allowed the periphery to reduce the gap in GDP per capita (see Figure IV-2). Taking the average of the 6 European countries as an index of 100, the relative GDP index per capita of Germany and France decreased from 125 to 116 in the period 1998-2007, while the index of the four countries in the periphery went up from 75 to 84, meaning they were catching up. As a preview of what would come later, the figure shows how after 2008 the periphery lost ground with respect to the leading European countries. This is due to the total loss of dynamism in those countries, since while Germany and France grew at an annual average rate of 1.73% between 2008 and 2016, the Mediterranean periphery decreased at an average annual rate of 0.37%.

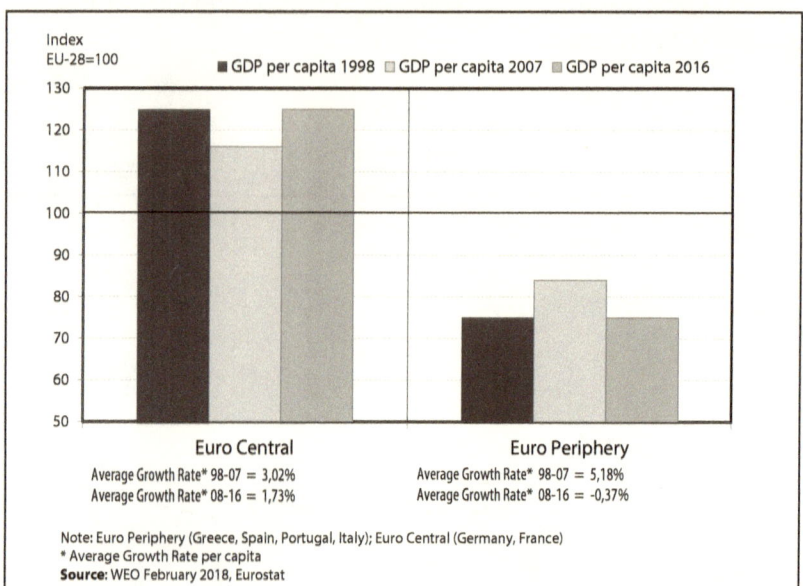

FIGURE IV-2
Convergence of per capita GDP and growth differences, 1998-2016

Note: Euro Periphery (Greece, Spain, Portugal, Italy); Euro Central (Germany, France)
* Average Growth Rate per capita
Source: WEO February 2018, Eurostat

At the time, most academics and politicians thought that this vigorous initial rate of catching up justified some imbalances, which they considered temporary and beneficial. Any deficits in the periphery countries' current accounts were considered natural, as they were supposedly a reflection of the "good disequilibria" often associated with processes of real convergence. The massive inflow of capital to periphery countries comfortably financed the current accounts deficits. The fact that investment far exceeded national savings, with the consequent accumulation of foreign debt, was considered a positive development. It was assumed that all this would lead to an accumulation of capital which would substantially increase future levels of productivity and the capacity to generate surplus resources to meet the debts that might be piling up. So why worry?

In the early years of the EMU there were no major asymmetric shocks. Furthermore, trade integration was flowing properly and holding to its moderate and steady increase. The financial markets underwent significant advances in integration. Was the success of the first years of the EMU the proof that Europe was indeed an optimal currency area? Some economists, who before the implementation of the EMU harboured some doubts about the macro-economic advisability of creating the eurozone, began to temper their initial scepticism and recognised that the European experience was proving to be a "great success".[20]

The theory of endogeneity became a fashionable way to reconcile past scepticisms with present successes. Basically, the theory said that monetary integration, once begun, generated a virtuous circle of greater integration as time went on (see Appendix IV-1). This, though less analytically elaborated, had also been the belief of the European Union's founders. The eruption of the financial crisis in 2008, however, showed that endogeneity had feet of clay.

THE 2008-2012 GLOBAL FINANCIAL CRISIS: THIS TIME WAS NO DIFFERENT

What has been termed the Global Financial Crisis (GFC) matched in its magnitude and effects the Great Depression of the late 1920s and early 1930s. What happened, in essence, was that in the United States, as in much of the rest of the Western industrialized world, serious imbalances accumulated during the decade of the 2000s under the cover of abundant liquidity, low interest rates, abundant bank credit, low inflation and high growth. Households, corporations and financial institutions strongly increased their levels of debt, and directed their demand to certain speculative markets, the main one being the housing market. The housing bubble was irresponsibly funded by mortgages granted in breach of the standard practices of good lending, because banks would then package and sell them off to third parties as "collateralised debt obligations" (CDOs), offloading the risk (see Box IV-1). When the housing bubble burst, a large number of financial and insurance companies found themselves in situations of illiquidity and insolvency, leading to the rowdy collapse of Bearn Stearns in March 2008, and of Lehman Brothers and AIG in September of the same year. The markets realized that the financial companies' balance

---

[20] Wyplosz (2006) was of this opinion, not without simultaneously warning about certain "dark sides" of this success. De Grauwe (2005), another recognised expert on issues of monetary union, did not hesitate to call the EMU a great success six years after its inception.

sheets were loaded with junk bonds. The banks then began a desperate race to reduce their indebtedness and clean up their balance sheets. Credit dried up and the economy plummeted into recession.

Box IV-1
THE SUB-PRIME BUBBLE

In the first half of 2000 there was a boom in residential and non-residential construction, especially in the United States, but also in much of Europe. The expansion was fuelled by a very lax financial environment and hyperactive capital markets which knew how to take advantage of this environment. Financial institutions and any agent authorized to originate mortgages relaxed credit standards irresponsibly and approved mortgage financing to people without the capacity to pay. The belief that housing or commercial property prices would continue to rise indefinitely kept the mortgage machine turning over. This irresponsible behaviour proliferated because the mortgage machinery was also responsible for "bundling" mortgages in financial instruments, which then ended up in mutual funds or bank portfolios in the far corners of the world. Governments turned a benevolent blind eye because they thought that democratising people's access to home ownership was "politically correct"–and won votes. The mortgage originators, on the other hand, were not particularly worried because they dumped the risk–the mortgages were sold off–and so the risk was diluted in a highly complex and opaque web of bonds and derivatives collateralised by junk mortgages.

But United States real estate prices stopped rising in 2006, unsold property inventories grew exponentially and real estate delinquencies jumped from just 6 percent by the end of 2005 to more than 30 percent three years later. A large part of the funds available for construction and mortgages were short-term and came from wholesale funds institutions (banks, pension funds, insurance companies, etc.). These began to pull out of the credit market on the first signs of construction cooling down, and past dues on mortgages going up. When funding pulled out, construction stopped cold, properties began to be auctioned off and the value of bonds underwritten by sub-prime mortgages collapsed. Mortgage financing institutions and anyone who had these bonds in their investment portfolio had to get rid of them at fire-sale prices to address the shortage of liquid funds.

Several alarm bells had already been causing panic in 2007. In June of that year, Bearn Stearns suspended redemptions of two of its funds. In August, BNP, the largest French bank, also shuttered the redemptions window for three of its investment funds that had American sub-prime mortgage-backed instruments on their balance sheets. Rhineland, a German investment company specialising in the same type of instruments, had to be rescued by its owner, IKB bank. The mania[21] that had inflated real estate property prices turned into a panic selling of any mortgage-related financial instrument, which seriously hit the balance sheets of all the financial institutions. As no-one could be sure of anyone else's degree of involvement, funds providers completely withdrew from the market, liquidity problems became acute and the whole financial system, including the good banks, became contaminated with widespread distrust. Box IV-2 presents a brief description of the perverse dynamics of financial crisis, which were also present in the GFC.

The result was a virulent financial crisis that had been hatching progressively from the second half of 2007. The second semester 2007 results of the big American banks, such as Merrill Lynch and Citigroup, already reflected the losses suffered by the fall in value of real-estate mortgage investments, causing the collapse of their own share price and that of other financial institutions. In March 2008 the Federal Reserve was forced to rescue Bearn Stearns, an investment bank, with an injection of 30 billion dollars.

September 2008 was the month of total financial Armageddon: Washington Mutual, a bank very active in mortgage loans, was subjected to an intervention by the Office of the Treasury and then forcibly acquired by JP Morgan Chase. The same fate befell Merrill Lynch, a second investment bank, which was acquired by Bank of America. Lehman Brothers ran out of liquidity in the middle of the month and, given the systemic risk implied by its size, the Federal Reserve had to step in and close it. The insurance giant AIG had to be rescued and its shares seized by the U.S. Government. On the other side of the Atlantic and in the same month, the British bank Northern Rock, the French-Belgian bank Dexia, as well as the German mortgage bank Hypo Real Estate were nationalized by their

---

21 A term coined by Charles Kindleberger in his classic description of the pattern of financial crises, to describe the upward phase of the crisis. "Mania" is an immoderate appetite for some real or financial asset accompanied by a credit boom. See Kindleberger and Aliber (2011)

respective governments with taxpayers' money; the Belgian bank Fortis was placed under administration and later acquired by BNP Paribas.

Box IV-2
MANIAS AND BUBBLES: THE DYNAMICS OF FINANCIAL CRISES

In his classic analysis of financial crises, Charles Kindleberger gives a stylized description of common patterns that have underlain almost all the episodes of financial crisis of the past four hundred years, including the GFC of 2008.[22] Kindleberger's account says that at some point, for whatever reason, the availability of credit increases, economic activity accelerates, and there is a growing optimism among investors, who then borrow and begin to buy real or financial assets, whose prices then rise and spur new purchases of those assets. Households and individuals see their equity increased through the greater value of their assets and incur more debt to ride the wave of price increases of the assets that are attracting investors; companies meet the growth in demand and the Treasury fills its coffers. It is this credit spiral that fuels the formation of speculative bubbles in the prices of certain assets: this is the mania phase. At some point, unfailingly, lenders perceive that the bubble is not sustainable and reduce their willingness to lend. Debtors need to sell assets to meet their debts, bringing down the prices of those assets, upon which the bubble explodes and the markets panic. When the debtors fall into insolvency and the assets given as collateral lose their value, the institutions that financed the bubble collapse and the financial crisis explodes.

During the formation of the bubble there are always voices of calm who claim that "this time it's different". Only this short-sightedness can explain Alan Greenspan's lax monetary policy between 2002 and 2007, while the immense sub-prime bubble was building up, or the bubble of capital flows to the European periphery was forming. The crisis of 2008 was no different from the classic pattern, neither in the United States nor in Europe.

The only thing different in the four waves of financial crises that have hit the world since the 1970s is the frequency with which one crisis has followed another,

---

22 Kindleberger and Aliber (2011): "Manias, Panics, and Crashes: A History of Financial Crises", 6th edition. Reinhart and Rogoff (2010) empirically corroborate the presence of the same pattern in more recent times.

and the large number of countries affected simultaneously by similar bubbles. The new and aggravating factor has been the disappearance of a global system of exchange rate stability (Bretton Woods) and the progressive liberalisation of international financial markets. These two factors mean that credit bubbles are potentiated, because they are now fed by international capital flows, which, as part of the balance of payments adjustment process, lead to currency appreciation in the countries which are recipients of capital. Once international lenders perceive the unsustainability of recipient countries' debt, capital flows are reversed, currencies are attacked and depreciation feeds back and accelerates the classic pattern of panics and financial crisis explosions. In this way, banking crises and currency crises now go hand in hand. And the number of infected countries grows to the rhythm of financial globalisation.

After the category 5 hurricane of September 2008, the heads of State of the G-7 met in Washington in October and decided to deploy a set of actions to prevent new failures of systemically important institutions, provide the markets with liquidity, recapitalise the banks and extend the insurance of deposits. The US government and its Federal Reserve adopted an aggressive policy of providing liquidity or bailing out financial institutions–by means of buying shares–to cut the spiral of distrust that had already left so many victims in its wake. European actions were less determined but were enough at first to stop the avalanche that had begun.

Following the typical sequence of these crises, 2009 was the year when the financial crisis turned into economic crisis: banks stopped lending, companies were left without working capital, consumers reduced their debt and bought less, investment stopped, governments collected less tax and unemployment rose. By 2010 unemployment in the United States had risen to 10 percent of the workforce. The resolute stance of the American government and the Federal Reserve, however, succeeded in lowering the unemployment rate by one percentage point per year so that by 2014 it was already below 6 percent, close to the level of full employment. The well-timed actions of the Federal Reserve as lender of last resort, the speed and size of monetary and fiscal stimulus and the consistency of the "macro-prudential" approach of the American authorities to supervision and regulation, were decisive in overcoming the GFC in a relatively short time.

The euro crisis: a tragedy in four acts

For Europe, 2008 also marked a before and an after. The GFC's impact was somewhat delayed with respect to the United States, but was longer lasting and more virulent, to the point of threatening the very survival of the monetary union. We can identify four phases in the euro crisis: the first (the sub-prime banking crisis) covers 2008 to the end of 2009, the second (the sovereign crisis in Greece, Ireland and Portugal) from late 2009 to mid-2011, the third (contagion and the euro crisis) from mid-2011 to mid-2012 and the fourth (recessive austerity crisis) from July 2012. Some countries such as Ireland and Spain began to climb out of the cellar in 2014, but others, such as Portugal or Greece, struggled for longer.

Act 1 (2008-2009): Sub-prime banking crisis

At first, until well into 2009, Europe seemed to look on events on the other side of the Atlantic with some complacency and *Schadenfreude*. More than one accusatory finger pointed to the United States as a case of capitalism run wild, unregulated and with a bloated and reckless financial system. However, even in 2008 European governments had had to start discreetly implementing significant bank bailouts with resources from the public treasury. By March 2009 European governments had disbursed or pledged 3 trillion dollars for this purpose. Bank bailouts occurred in Germany, where the government committed resources equivalent to 8% of GDP, in France to 5% of GDP, and in The Netherlands to 12% of GDP.

One exception was Spain, where the authorities initially adopted an attitude of denial and went about bragging that they had a solid banking system which did not require corrections, something that was far from the truth. This inaction from Spain–and to a lesser extent from other countries–during the phase in which the financial markets were still willing to assist States in the processes of restructuring, would later prove to be extremely costly. Italy experienced a similar fate, as it too was unwilling to expose its own banking problems. In Ireland, the European country with the most serious banking problem, the magnitude of the financial hole was such that the government could only apply band-aids.

Even back in 2008, more or less underground capital reversals and spontaneous adjustment processes had been taking place within the eurozone, gradually accumulating tensions in the financial markets. It would soon become clear that much of the periphery countries of the EMU, the so-called PIIGS (Portugal, Ireland, Italy, Greece and Spain), had committed the same or worse credit excesses as the US and had their own speculative bubbles: a housing bubble in Spain and Portugal, a banking and real estate bubble in Ireland, fiscal excess in Greece and Italy. On the eruption of the crisis, consumer confidence collapsed, and over-indebted households began to implement their own deleveraging (debt reduction), with the consequent effect of depressing aggregate demand.

Economies that had been buoyant until 2007 went into recession in 2008, with a rise in unemployment, fiscal deficits and accelerated public debt. It was an abrupt change in the landscape, much of it to do with the problems of the banks. Financial institutions saw their sources of liquidity dry up due to the deterioration of their balance sheets and the general distrust coming from ignorance of how much each bank was affected by investments in sub-prime bonds or real estate loans. Public finances were also hit by the cost of bank rescues and the fall in tax revenue caused by the recession. Bank credit evaporated, companies were left without working capital and consumers had no way to finance their purchases. Economies were stopped in their tracks.

Act II (2009-11): Sovereign debt crisis (Greece, Ireland, Portugal)

It was not however until the end of 2009 that all these components began to crystallise in what became the "mother of all crises": the European sovereign debt crisis. Up until then, the crisis had many similarities with the GFC in the United States. The first alarm bells of the European home-grown sovereign crisis sounded in Greece, when in October 2009 the new Greek president Papandreou acknowledged that the previous government had blatantly lied about their public accounts and that the fiscal deficit for 2008 was triple what had been officially reported. A large part of this excess public spending had gone into funding bureaucracy and lavish pension plans. Serious doubts then arose about Greece's ability to honour a debt which already amounted to 130% of GDP (compared to a eurozone average of 79%). These doubts raised the Greek debt risk premium to the 25 percent and turned the Greek case into a self-fulfilling prophecy of collapse.

Community organs reacted timidly and late. The financial markets and their agents, better informed as usual, confronted the authorities with the evidence of the severity of the crisis, arguing that the first 110 billion euros Greek rescue package presented in May 2010 was utterly insufficient. The ensuing relentless speculative attack forced Community authorities to create a European Financial Stability Fund and a program to support the stock market (the Securities Markets Program). These initiatives were correct in principle, but once again the markets considered that their dimensions and activation mechanisms were inadequate and not enough to deal with the Greek insolvency. All this indecision and inconsistency significantly raised the ultimate cost of the rescue. Barely a year later, therefore, in July 2011, the "Troika" in charge of the negotiations (IMF, European Central Bank and European Commission) had to put on the table a new bailout package of 130 billion euros, additional to the unreleased funds of the first bailout of 2010.

The handling of the "Greek tragedy" was unfortunate. In hindsight, the main criticism is that it was neither understood nor accepted that the Greek debt burden was unmanageable. The country should have declared default, Greek debt should have been restructured realistically and creditors should have assumed the necessary debt cuts. Once this orderly default had been declared, the European Central Bank should have assisted Greece with Open Market Operations (OMO), as they belatedly did in 2012. If this had happened, it is highly likely that the sovereign debt crisis would have been contained to an exclusively Greek and not a European problem. By not recognising Greece's insolvency, the distrust of the financial markets towards Greece spread to other members of the eurozone, which also had evident, though manageable, problems.

The other two countries bailed out by the European Community and the IMF in this first phase were Ireland and Portugal. Ireland's sovereign crisis originated in the State's commitment to guarantee all deposits in the banking system. And the Irish was no normal banking system but a seriously oversized one, representing more than 700 percent of GDP (!). This government's guarantee was the way to save the country's major banks, six in total, which had financed the Irish housing bubble. The cost to the Irish Treasury of honouring that obligation was to go from being in fiscal balance up to 2007, to incurring a deficit of 14 per cent by 2009 and 31 per cent by 2010. Unemployment rose from 4.6 to 13.6 percent from

2007 to 2010. Given the magnitude of this bust, Ireland became the second European country which had to sign a rescue package in November 2010.

In the case of the sovereign crisis of Portugal there was no cheating and abuse in the style of Greece, nor a real estate bubble as in Spain or Ireland, but a profligate public administration, disorganised, inefficient and committed to infrastructure projects and investments exceeding its capacity for management and repayment. The fiscal deficit, which had already averaged an unsustainable 4% of GDP since 1999, went to 10 per cent in 2009-2010. Portugal's rescue package was implemented in May 2011.

Act III (2011-2012): Widespread contagion

In mid-2011 the European financial crisis entered a qualitatively new phase of widespread contagion, which put the very existence of the euro at risk. Up to that time the vicissitudes of Greece, Portugal or Ireland had not seriously affected the economic situation of the rest of the eurozone, but that changed when the European political leadership gave signs of not being willing to support distressed sovereign debt. Investors were increasingly impatient with the dithering efforts of Community institutions to confront and overcome the crisis. Additionally, the austerity measures imposed by the IMF-ECB-European Commission Troika on the debtor countries in crisis were only producing more recession and increased insolvency. The alleged positive effects of austerity in generating market confidence and creating an environment to promote growth were nowhere to be seen.

Unfortunately, the Europe that was still relatively unharmed, especially Germany, was unwilling to help countries in crisis via a more expansive fiscal policy and some encouragement of financial flows. Neither was the European Central Bank, under the direction of Jean-Claude Trichet, helping to stimulate economic activity, already deeply depressed at that time. Rather the opposite: in April and July of 2011 interest rates were raised twice, something that could well be described as madness, ignorance, ideological subservience, or a mixture of all three, on the part of those who were then in charge of the ECB.

The crucial trigger of contagion was the political decision to let the financial markets take charge of disciplining and punishing investors. The need for a second Greek bailout was announced in July 2011. Once again, the size of the rescue package was seen by the financial markets as insufficient and even hypocritical, owing to the persistent denial of a reality that everybody was aware of: that the Greek debt burden was unmanageable. The lack of confidence of the financial markets turned to panic when at a meeting in the French city of Deauville on the 18th of July, 2011, Merkel and Sarkozy decided that this time bondholders had to assume a significant cut (i.e. loss) in the value of the restructured debt. This new scheme was called Private Sector Involvement (PSI). To put it bluntly, everyone would have to swallow their losses. There was nothing wrong with letting the markets do their job and penalising investors; the problem was that this new policy wasn't complemented by mechanisms to allow an ordered restructuring of debt, or measures to ensure the future viability of the remaining Greek debt.

The Deauville decision was a very serious mistake, based on ignorance of how financial markets work at the height of a crisis, particularly when the markets know that there are no concomitant mechanisms in place to stop the bleeding. Making investors assume sovereign losses in this way caused panic in the European bond markets, who read into it a clear message: the European sovereign debt would no longer be guaranteed by national governments, nor the European Union, nor the European Central Bank. It was the financial markets, particularly the bond markets, which would have to resolve the debt crisis alone using "market mechanisms". But the market had disappeared: no-one would buy anything at any price. It was ironic indeed to expect private investors to maintain a confidence that governments themselves were not showing. And if sovereign debt had no Community guarantee or backstop, there was also no guarantee that countries would stay within the eurozone. The ghost of exchange risk, which had disappeared from the eurozone scene since 1993, reappeared. The very foundations of the euro were shaken.

Some analysts have pointedly highlighted the coincidence of this radical policy shift represented by PSI with the fact that after the first Greek rescue German and French banks had got out of the danger zone represented by their high initial exposure to Greek debt.[23] Two years gave them

---

23   Between 2008 and 2012 the German banks were able to reduce significantly their exposure to the other European countries. Measured as a percentage of GDP in the respective countries, German bank assets were reduced by 5.2 percent of Italy's GDP, 10.3 percent of Spain's, 8.2 percent of Portugal's, 10.6 percent of Greece's and 43.2 percent of Ireland's (data in Steinberg and Vermeiren, 2016).

time to dilute the impact of the exposure. Whatever the Franco-German motivations, the truth is that the Deauville decision was foolhardy and inconvenient at that precise moment of the financial markets.

After arduous negotiations with the private holders of Greek bonds, the resources available for this second rescue package were increased to 246 billion euros in March 2012.

The rapid increase of risk premiums is an indicator of how serious the crisis became in this third phase; they are the thermometer of the stress on a country's financial system and its public finances, because they reflect the premium demanded by investors according to the perceived risk. Figure IV-3 shows that 2011 broke the record in three of the four Mediterranean countries. From a relatively low and, above all, uniform level of around 200 basis points up until 2008, risk premiums for Greece began to climb in 2009 and those for Portugal and Spain in 2010. Greece and Ireland were then beginning to look like the first dominoes to fall in the European sovereign debt crisis. The interest rate spreads for Greek debt reached levels of 10 percent by the end of 2010 and 32 percent by the end of 2011. Portugal sailed into troubled financial and fiscal waters in 2011, when her risk premium reached levels of 12 percent before the rescue.

Figure IV-3
Evolution of risk premiums, 2008-2015

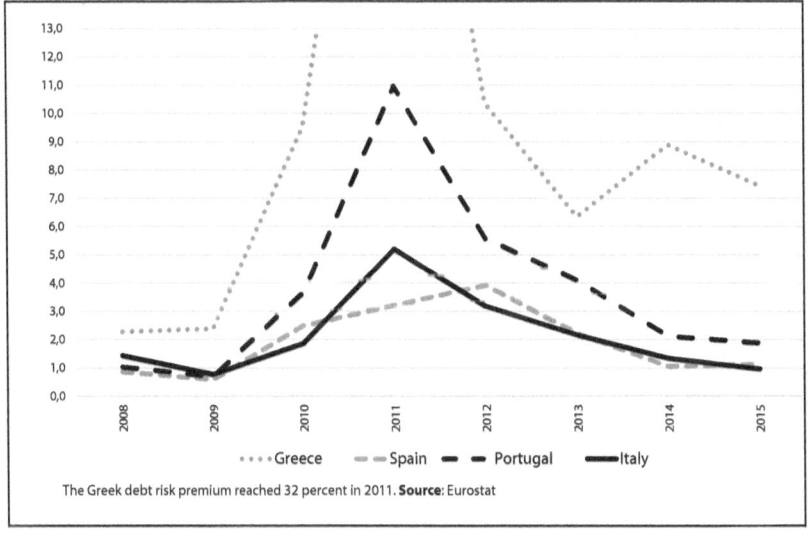

The Greek debt risk premium reached 32 percent in 2011. **Source:** Eurostat

Even though the three rescued countries (Greece, Ireland and Portugal) did not account for more than 7 percent of European sovereign debt (see Figure IV-4), their contagious potential in terms of generating market distrust in several of the largest European countries was huge. The problem, in the markets' view, was that Europe and the EMU had shown that there were no flood defences in the event of a downturn. Thus from mid-2011 the risk premiums demanded by investors to acquire Italian and Spanish debt also started to rise, more markedly in Italy because of its high level of public debt. At the end of 2011, the Italian risk premium stood at 519 basis points and the Spanish at 326. If the Greek and Irish crisis had unfolded in 2010 and the Portuguese in 2011, 2012 was when the third and fourth largest eurozone economies were attacked by the financial markets. Until the end of July 2012 the Italian risk premium stayed at levels of around 500 basis points, while the Spanish premium reached 547. There came a moment when both brushed against the ceiling of 7 percent that some analysts consider the point of no return for a destructive spiral of worsening sovereign debt burden.

FIGURE IV-4
EMU Public Debt 2011: size (billions) and weight (% of GDP)

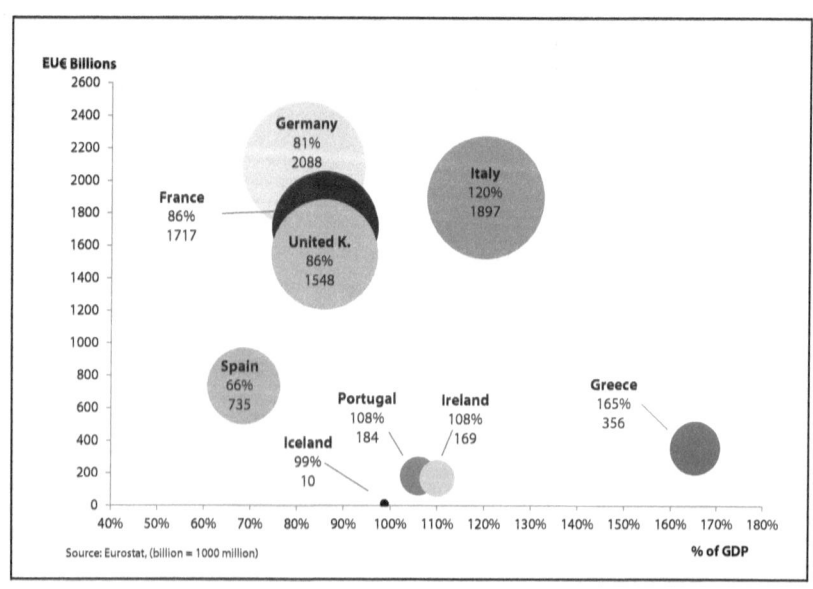

By then the public debt of Italy, the third largest European economy, had reached almost 1,897 billion euros in 2011, with an excessively high debt to GDP ratio of 120 percent (see Figure IV-4). This situation was the cumulative result of several decades of fiscal deficits.

For its part, although Spain showed in 2011 a much lower volume of sovereign debt in terms of size and relation to GDP (735 billion of euros or 66 percent of GDP), the trend towards deterioration was already very marked. Two things were taking place: firstly, the huge economic recession generated by the explosion of an unprecedented housing bubble, and secondly, the process of dismantling an extremely high level of private debt. Financial institutions had accumulated part of that private debt, which had to be absorbed by the State in the form of bank bailouts. Additionally, the inevitable deleveraging by households fed back into the recession day by day.

Unemployment rates of close to 25 percent and associated high welfare payments became a heavy burden on the Spanish fiscal coffers. In addition, the announcement of the European Commission in June 2012 that several stressed Spanish banks would be rescued with public resources (up to 100 billion euros) was not well received by the markets, because it would add a further burden of 10 percent of GDP on the sovereign debt. This would incrementally affect the Spanish economy's ability to bring down its global (public and private) debt to sustainable levels. The pro-cyclical austerity measures imposed by the Troika, which fed the vicious circle of recession and insolvency of banks and government, were not helping.

Act IV (2012-2014): Lender of last resort

When the cost of public debt in countries as important as Italy or Spain brushed against the point of no return, the European Central Bank had no choice but to take serious steps to support the sovereign debt markets. No intergovernmental fund could face an Italian or Spanish debt debacle, since these countries exceeded the Community's capacity to supply resources. The ECB's main channel of intervention was to provide liquidity on preferential terms to banks (one trillion euros for 3 years at 1 percent interest between December and February 2012). However, the European Central Bank was very worried because the connection between monetary policy and the real economy had been broken. Put simply, the

ECB's low rates were not being passed on by the banks to their customers to stimulate economic activity.

Fortunately, the misguided mandate of Jean Claude Trichet as ECB President had come to an end in late 2011. He was replaced by Mario Draghi, an Italian economist with more political experience, more open to Keynesian demand support measures in times of crisis. His decisive and historic statement of the 26th of July 2012 that the ECB would do "... *whatever it takes to preserve the euro...*" marked a before and after, an inflexion point in the euro crisis. Debt markets breathed a sigh of relief and risk premiums began to fall rapidly. The subsequent mere announcement in September 2012 that the ECB would buy unlimited sovereign debt of countries that formally requested rescue in accordance with the rules set by the EMU, called the Outright Monetary Transactions (OMT) programme, brought immediate relief to new debt issues and roll-overs of countries that were in trouble. The Spanish risk premium declined 130 basis points in just two months after July. The same happened with Italian debt. Figure IV-3 shows this relative levelling off of risk premiums for Spain and Italy between 2012 and 2014. It took Portugal longer to recover the confidence of the markets, while Greece would need five years and two more bailouts to gain access to the financial markets in manageable conditions.

After the decisive intervention by the European Central Bank, Community institutions adopted a more energetic and interventionist attitude towards the countries with debt problems. They had finally understood the gravity of the crisis, but their diagnosis was still mistaken. And not only was the diagnosis wrong, but they also didn't recognise that much of the problem arose from the lack of institutions and mechanisms to handle the rigidities and imperfections of the European Monetary Union's architecture (we will discuss this in the next chapter). It would probably have been too much to expect self-criticism from the Community authorities towards the edifice that they themselves had built and were struggling to shore up. That is why the measures imposed revolved exclusively around the reduction of fiscal deficits through policies of tax increases and lower spending in the short term. In the longer term, a conventional set of structural reforms were imposed on the rescued countries.

The range of fiscal measures went from laws and regulations that had to be modified, to which State enterprises should be privatised, which

State institutions should be re-dimensioned or disappear, which welfare benefits should be reduced or eliminated, which salary cuts should be implemented, etc. In addition to the measures imposed on the individual countries receiving bailout packages, in December 2011 the European Commission adopted a first package of regulations and fiscal guidelines for all the eurozone countries. This so-called "Six-Pack" basically consisted of an update and broadening of the Stability and Growth Pact reformed in 2005. The name came from the fact that the Commission sanctioned 5 Regulations and one Directive, all of them aimed at improving systems for monitoring and sanctioning the compliance of the eurozone countries with their fiscal deficit limits. The most relevant was the regulation on prevention and correction of "macroeconomic imbalances", called the Excessive Imbalance Procedure, which extended the discretionary powers of the Commission to a broad spectrum of areas of the economy beyond those of taxation and public expenditure.

A second package of regulations, called the "Two-Pack", was proposed concurrently in draft form at the end of 2011. Due to the legal extent of its impositions this required approval by the European Parliament, the individual governments and the European Council, which finally sanctioned it in May 2013. The first regulation established measures to monitor and evaluate the eurozone countries' budgets, while the second referred more specifically to deepening the surveillance system in euro member countries that faced threats to their financial stability.

In the area of structural reforms, attention focused on flexibility of labour markets, liberalisation of financial markets and cleaning up of the banking system. With these regulations the European governance system was sailing into uncharted waters. From a Community governance that basically issued non-invasive and consensus-based recommendations, it became a regime of hard requirements, practically eliminating the autonomy of national governments to manage their own economic policies if they were going to receive rescue funds.

A quintessential example of poor Community crisis management was the succession of Greek rescue packages. After the second package in 2012, Greece entered a perverse process of decline and inability to generate the resources to carve its way out of the crisis. Between 2010 and 2016 the Greek Parliament had to approve thirteen austerity packages to meet the bailout conditions. At the political level, the country staggered from crisis to crisis, swaying between governments of the Right and the Left. In 2015 the leftist Tsipras government and its controversial Finance Minister Varoufakis failed in its attempt to lift the "financial siege". What they got instead, in July 2015, was a third rescue package that was even tougher than the previous ones and even more invasive of the country's sovereignty, in exchange for 86 billion euros and ECB liquidity support to avoid Greece's imminent exit from the EMU. Despite the hardships, the Greeks had to accept the harsh bailout conditions because they could sense what awaited them on the other side of the door: disorder, confiscation of deposits, a financial *corralito*[24] and, eventually, departure from the eurozone.

Once again, the Community institutions rejected the IMF's strong recommendation to accept that the Greek debt was unpayable in a reasonable timespan and that creditors should accept a significant write-down of the debt stock. The European Commission, under the aegis of Germany, was utterly opposed to taking this route, alleging that the European Union's legal framework did not allow a State's debts to be condoned. Economic reality, however, was stubborn. Proof of this had been the repeated–and ongoing–Greek bailouts, all of them exercises in wishful thinking and hypocrisy. Right after the first bailout, Greece was caught in the fatal trap of fiscal austerity, which caused recession, which in turn did not allow the generation of resources to serve the debt.

This third act of the Greek tragedy, however, did not have much contagious impact on the rest of the European debt markets. The lender of last resort was still committed to the stability of the eurozone and the Community institutions had also built some (low) walls of containment. But what was truly relevant is that in the midst of negotiations of this third bailout package an option was put on the menu that so far no official body had dared mention outside whisperings in European corridors: the possibility of the exclusion of a member from the eurozone. In 2015 the Community leadership, especially Germany, seriously considered Greece's exiting the EMU if that country did not accept the rescue terms. This altered fundamentally the future rules of the game, regardless of whether Greece moved towards exit or not. After that, financial markets incorporated into their calculations the possibility that a country could

---

24 Diminutive of corral (stockade), a term originating in Argentina's financial crisis after the collapse of the Currency Board.

at some point leave the common currency. Once the taboo was broken, exchange rate risk broke out again on the eurozone scene. The monetary union was no longer irreversible and irrevocable. The acceptance of the bailout by a humiliated Greece thus really meant a Pyrrhic victory for European leadership: obstinate German orthodoxy prevailed, but the monetary union had lost its virginity.

USA vs Europe: a comparative evaluation of how the crisis was handled

It was no minor sacrifice that the debtor countries were being asked to accept, both in terms of governance and political cost in the eyes of their electorates. There was also no little sacrifice in terms of recession. Was it worth it? Did this loss of economic sovereignty help to turn the crisis around and return to growth? A comparison between the responses to the crisis from the United States and the EMU sheds some light on the matter. Whereas the United States reacted vigorously and, judging by the results, correctly in confronting the Global Financial Crisis, Europe did so timidly and, also judging by the results, misguidedly.[25]

The Government of the United States and the Federal Reserve lost no time looking for those guilty of the crisis and for ways to punish them. They understood that the contagion from the sub-prime crisis threatened to shake the foundations of the whole financial system, not just in the US but globally. They understood that the stampede of sources of financing had to be confronted with a vigorous response of liquidity endowment and massive fiscal stimulus. They knew that a financial meltdown would have immediate and devastating consequences for the real economy and for employment, comparable to those of the Great Recession of 1930. The presence of Ben Bernanke as Chair of the Federal Reserve was decisive. Bernanke had devoted much of his prior academic career to studying the Great Recession and the policy mistakes committed at the time.

To halt and reverse the recession, the US authorities used a combination of support and expansive measures, ranging from fiscal stimulus

---

25 See Matthijs (2014). After an initial phase of synchronisation, European policy completely separated from North America's at the point of the Greek sovereign debt crisis in 2010.

to the critical intervention of the Federal Reserve to lower interest rates, inject liquidity into the economy and put together credit support programmes for banks and businesses. It was the Fed that assumed leadership to contain the crisis because it was the institution with the greatest arsenal of instruments, with more financial resources and not subject to the cumbersome political processes of approving fiscal packages. The Fed was in no doubt that it should assume its role as "lender of last resort" at times of systemic crisis. The investment bank Bearn Stearns was rescued in March 2008. The decision to let collapse Lehman Brothers, also an investment bank, in September was an unfortunate hiccup, product of a confluence of events,[26] but a few days later the Fed and the government decided to rescue the insurer AIG with a package of about $100 billion.

In October 2008, the American authorities orchestrated a financial rescue package of $700 billion, followed in early 2009 by a nearly $800 billion fiscal stimulus package. As a result of these massive stimuli, the US economy began to grow again by the third quarter of 2009 and showed a significant growth of 2.5 percent in 2010 and 1.6 percent in 2011. This speedy recovery of the leading world economy allowed global growth to resume its upward path with annual growth rates of 5.2 and 3.9 in 2010 and 2011 respectively.

Contrast this account with Europe's response to the GFC. There was an initial phase (2008-2009) of reasonable assertiveness by most European governments. The financial Armageddon of September 2008 also hit several major European banks: Northern Rock in the United Kingdom, Hypo Real Estate and its subsidiary Depfa in Germany, Dexia in France-Belgium, Fortis in Belgium-Holland. These episodes of crisis and bank rescues were adequately addressed by the respective governments. Also proper were some fiscal stimulus packages arranged by individual European countries in 2009 to mitigate the recession, to the point that the eurozone went from decreasing by 4.5 per cent in 2009 to growing by 2.1 percent in 2010 and 1.6 percent in 2011.

The road began to diverge from the United States when the Greek crisis in 2010 prompted moralistic finger-pointing by some European countries, led by Germany, which divided eurozone members into a

---

26   Ben Bernanke (2015), Federal Reserve Chairman at the time, takes a special interest in explaining why they had to let Lehman Brothers fall. This decision was widely criticised.

dichotomy of good and evil, the fiscally virtuous and the sinners. The sinners of the Mediterranean periphery and Ireland had to swallow the bitter pill of austerity to balance their accounts and compel them to undertake painful structural reforms. German ordoliberal ideology prevailed over the pragmatism shown by other world economies in handling recessions, and reduced the understanding of the complex eurozone crisis down to a mere phenomenon of fiscal indiscipline, profligate governments and lazy citizens. It was that same ideology that led to the European Central Bank raising interest rates twice in 2009, something completely inappropriate at the time and the contrary of a much needed stimulus. This lack of coordination between monetary/financial strategy and fiscal stance was a key difference compared to the American handling of the crisis.

Although it is true that from 2011 the ECB orchestrated an expansion of its balance sheet[27] similar to that of the Federal Reserve through operations to provide liquidity, the orthodox wing, represented by the Bundesbank, demanded the incorporation of automatic exit mechanisms, that is, the automatic winding-up of operations. This is how the ECB's balance sheet shrank by 35 percent between March 2011 and January 2014. In simple terms, this meant a contractionary monetary policy at a time when the whole of Europe was still immersed in the recession and in need of fiscal and monetary stimulus. The concern of the German authorities was that these unconventional liquidity operations represented an indirect support to debtor countries, whose governments were going to feel themselves under less pressure to undertake structural reforms and that ultimately it was the virtuous German taxpayer who was footing the bill.

It was no surprise then, that the eurozone relapsed into another serious recession after 2010, while the rest of the world was heading towards recovery. The disappointing economic performance of the eurozone is evidenced by the average growth rates in the eurozone in comparison with the United States and the OECD (see Figure IV-5). The figures show that the 2008-10 period was tough for the entire developed Western Hemisphere. The United States decreased by 0.2 percent, the OECD countries by 0.1 percent and the eurozone by 0.7 percent.

---

27 The expansion or contraction of a central bank's balance sheet is an indicator of how expansionary or contractionary the monetary policy has been.

FIGURE IV-5
Average Growth: Eurozone (EMU-19), USA and OECD

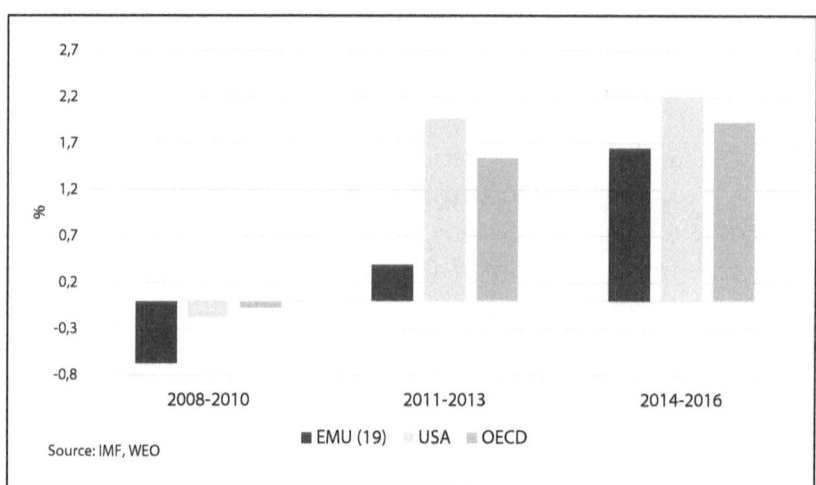

Source: IMF, WEO

The gap opened in the period 2011-13, when the United States grew by an average 2 percent annually, the OECD by 1.5 percent and Europe virtually stagnated. The United States managed to reduce the unemployment from 10% in 2010 to 6% in 2014. In the same period, Europe actually increased the rate of unemployment from 10% to 11.25%. Viewed comparatively with the rest of the developed world, the speed of the post-crisis recovery was highly unsatisfactory in the EMU. It wasn't until 2014 on that the eurozone began to grow moderately and continuously, though still below the US and the OECD countries.

As is often the case with averages, the numbers in Figure IV-5 hide an even less satisfactory reality within the eurozone. The Mediterranean countries decreased strongly in the four years between 2010 and 2013. The insistence on recessive fiscal adjustments, coupled with the forced process of deleveraging, plunged these countries into a second serious recession between 2011 and 2013. (See Box IV-3 for how and why deleveraging aggravates and lengthens recessions.) It was only in 2014, four years after the US and the other Western developed economies, when the Mediterranean periphery began to grow at the same pace as central Europe. For their part, the countries of central Europe, unaffected by sovereign debt problems, grew by more than 2 percent in 2010 and 2011. From 2012 onwards, these countries at the centre grew at sluggish rates that were inferior to the rest of the developed world, although higher than the Mediterranean periphery.

Figure IV-6
Growth: Centre vs Periphery, 2010-2017

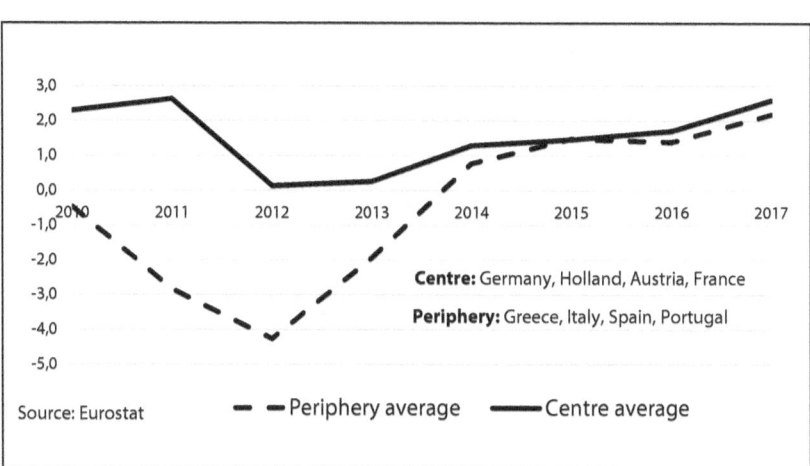

Source: Eurostat

Only from 2014 do all the eurozone countries begin to grow and rates of growth at the periphery and the centre begin to converge. These were not, however, rates as are usually seen in recoveries after severe crises, confirming that a set of structural burdens was still affecting the European economies. The decline in living standards during the crisis was very severe. For example, the nominal *per capita* income of Greece in 2017 was still equivalent to that of 2003, and that of Spain, Italy and Portugal was equivalent to that of 2008.

Looking at the individual economic performance of the periphery countries in the aftermath of the crisis, Figure IV-7 shows that all the countries left negative terrain in 2014, two years after Mario Draghi's "whatever it takes" statement. Only Spain, however, began to grow consistently above the European average starting from 2014. Despite a severe banking crisis, the country was able to get its homework done on time and avoided being stigmatised by having to sign a formal bailout agreement. The 2012 commitment of the European Stabilisation Fund to provide up to 100 billion euros to capitalize and salvage the bankrupt Spanish banks was enough to fend off the worst scenarios. Rajoy's centre-right government launched the country on a consistent programme of structural reforms. Italy also made its way out of the recession but continued in the same lethargic situation of quasi-stagnation from before the crisis. Of the two countries that had been bailed out by the Troika, Portugal had a difficult time initially due to the drag of an unresolved banking crisis, but its efforts at reform allowed moderate growth from 2015 on. Even the Greek submarine surfaced in 2014, although it continued in a zero-growth zone until 2016.

FIGURE IV-7
Periphery Growth, 2010-2017

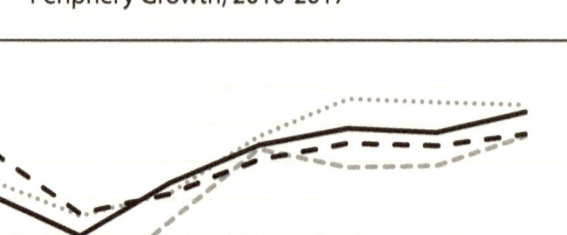

The unemployment rate is a better indicator than the growth rate for gauging the seriousness of the eurozone crisis and the slowness of the recovery. Figure IV-8 shows the evolution of this indicator from 2010 to 2017. In all the countries of the Mediterranean periphery, the number of unemployed as a percentage of the economically active population reached alarming levels during the peak of the crisis and descended very gradually once GDP growth recovered. The levels remained high, however, so we cannot speak of a true recovery. The leaders in the unemployment stakes were Spain and Greece, which at the peak of the crisis had one out of every four potential workers unemployed. Spain and Portugal then saw the greatest post-crisis reductions in relative terms, but their absolute levels remained unacceptably high four years after the crisis. In Greece, the unemployment rate in 2017 was still 6 points above its level at the start of the crisis. Somewhat different, though no less worrisome, was the evolution in Italy, where the decline during the crisis was relatively less, but where exiting the recession was not accompanied by job creation.

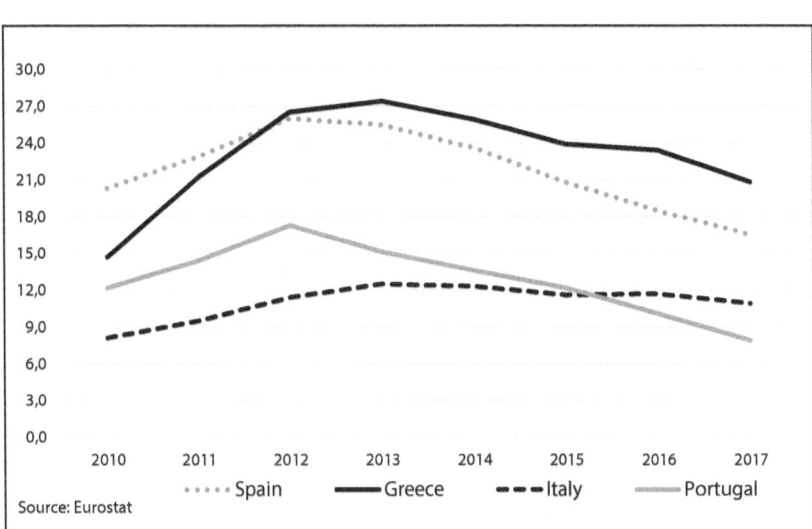

FIGURE IV-8
Periphery: Unemployment Rates, 2010-2017

Source: Eurostat

If we turn our attention to the countries of central Europe, the lukewarm growth of these economies is also striking (Figure IV-9). The euro crisis affected them only moderately, because the markets did not perceive risks of fiscal or financial sustainability and the adjustments were small. Except for The Netherlands, none of the other three countries representative of the European centre, in which we include France, ventured onto negative terrain during 2012 and 2013. The important issue to highlight is rather that from 2014 growth was modest, with France and Germany between one and two percent. This performance cannot be considered satisfactory for two reasons. First, the strong countries did not "do the right thing" to lessen the burden of a recessive adjustment of the weak members of the union. They should have become the engine pulling the train of growth. Secondly, because it points up how the EMU, compared to other regions, still has serious growth problems. In short, the eurozone did not pass the test in the areas of crisis management and providing employment and welfare to its citizens during the crucial first half of the 2010s.

FIGURE IV-9
Centre: Growth Rates, 2010-2017

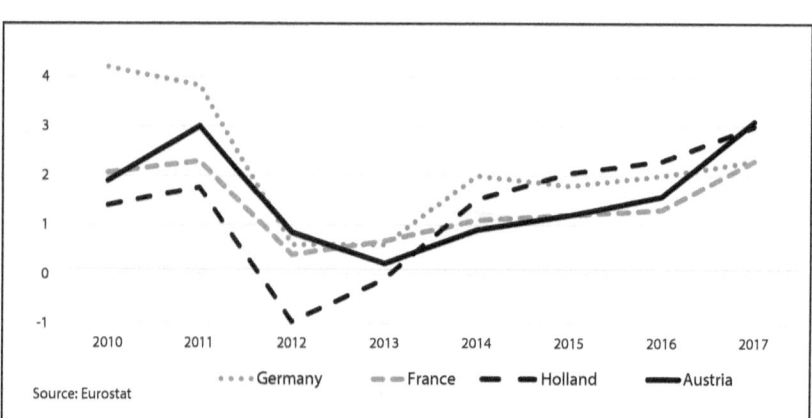

Source: Eurostat

One of the main reasons for the unsatisfactory growth of employment and production in the eurozone was the hefty legacy of sovereign debt with which countries were burdened. This severely limited the use of fiscal policy or new debt to inject life into their economies. In terms of proportion of GDP, Greece increased its debt burden by 75 percent between 2007 and 2016, Italy by 32 percent, Portugal by 90 percent, Spain by 178 percent and France by 50 percent (see Table IV-3). The sovereign debt burden of these countries in 2016 was markedly above the 60 percent threshold established by European regulations. The situation of Greece, Italy and Portugal was particularly serious.

TABLE IV-3
Evolution of sovereign debt burden (% of GDP), 2007 vs 2016

	2007	2016	% Increm.
Greece	103	181	75%
Italy	100	132	32%
Portugal	68	130	90%
Spain	36	99	178%
France	64	97	50%
EMU	65	89	37%

Source: Eurostat

Box IV-3
THE PERVERSE DYNAMICS OF DELEVERAGING

The gravity of the European recession was due among other things to the proven fact that economic contractions that come after the collapse of credit bubbles, and of their debt bubble counterparts, usually last longer than those derived from causes more tied to the real economy. This is because the deleveraging process takes time and has a delayed and cumulative effect on economic activity.

The evolution of the European crisis is a good illustration of this deleveraging dynamic. In a <u>first round</u> of effects, European financial institutions proceeded to clean up their balance sheets and to radically curtail lending among themselves and to non-financial parties. As the crisis unfolded, banks stopped financing households and businesses, which in turn fuelled the vicious cycle of recession, as no growth can be expected without credit. Due to widespread mistrust, some banks found themselves in situations of illiquidity or insolvency as the vicious cycle of recession and degradation of the quality of their assets became evident. This was especially the case for the assets related to activities inflated by manias (real estate mortgages in particular). To avoid a sharp fall into recession, governments had to support their banks using taxpayers' money or by issuing new public debt, whose increase accelerated accordingly.

In a <u>second round</u> of effects, households also boarded the deleveraging train, saved money to pay off debts and postponed buying decisions, causing an additional fall in aggregate demand.

Finally, in a <u>third round</u>, the markets were unwilling to keep financing additional volumes of sovereign debt, because it was perceived to have increased to dangerous levels during the effort to save the crisis banks. As a product of this forcible debt reduction, the economies of crisis countries entered a dangerous downward spiral, in which spending cuts and recession fed on each other, lowering tax revenues by decreasing activity and increasing fiscal expense on unemployment benefits.

Each of the three rounds of deleveraging triggered its own recessive wave, with cumulative effects: contraction of bank credit, contraction of household consumption and, finally, fiscal contraction.

The German prescription for overcoming the crisis: the austerity fallacy

The figures show that the eurozone crisis lasted longer and was more severe in terms of depression than was the Global Financial Crisis in the United States or other Western economies. Several elements can be put forward to explain this specificity of the eurozone:

- Given the impossibility of making adjustments via the exchange rate changes or individually-targeted monetary policy, the common currency exacerbated economic imbalances.
- Right from its original design, the EMU lacked the institutions and safeguards necessary for the management of severe financial crises.
- Germany, as the eurozone leader, erred in its diagnosis and applied undesirable remedies.

We will leave the first element to the next chapter. The second element became clear after 2011, when the Community institutions had to rush to reform the fiscal framework of the EMU and create rescue funds. Regrettably, neither of these reforms were ready in time, nor were sufficient resources made available, so they did not avoid the European Central Bank appearing on the scene as the lender of last resort to calm the markets. Incidentally, this intervention teetered on the edge of illegality, because the Treaty of Maastricht did not contemplate such a role for the Central Bank.

As Mario Draghi, President of the ECB, said in 2017, *"the incompleteness of the EMU has made the crisis more severe"*.[28] A paper from the CID at Harvard University, coordinated by Alessio Terzi (2018), confirms that the poor institutional framework of the EMU and its improper handling of the crisis were responsible for its unusual severity. Quantitative research shows that between 2010 and 2015 the *per capita* product in the European periphery shrank by 11 percent over what would have been expected in a "standard counterfactual scenario".[29] Similarly, the average

---

28   Mario Draghi, President of the ECB - 7 September 2017

29   A term used in the methodology of impact assessment, meaning a scenario with which one could compare the eurozone, if it had not had the institutional treatment given to the crisis by the EMU.

unemployment rate was 5 percent higher than what pre-2010 economic imbalances could explain. The crisis also lasted longer than it would have if the deficient institutional structure of the EMU had not limited its ability to handle it.

As for the third element–the mistaken diagnosis and prescription–there is broad agreement among analysts that this was a decisive contributor in worsening the crisis at the periphery. Countries at the centre of Europe, led by Germany, watched the recessive post-2010 downward spiral on the periphery with no little glee. They considered the hardship these countries were going through to be not only a well-deserved retribution for past excesses, but as something absolutely necessary. The thesis imposed by Germany on the periphery was that austerity was the only way to overcome the imbalances and restore the confidence of the markets, not unlike a penance to atone for sins and be accepted back into the community of the faithful. In this way, to the harmful dynamics of deleveraging was added a fiscal austerity policy. It was the perfect storm for a recession shipwreck.

Austerity, as a macroeconomic adjustment mechanism, is a set of measures aimed at putting the economy on a deflationary path (i.e. internal devaluation) by cutting public expenditure, reducing real wages and lowering prices, all with the primary purpose of restoring balance and the subsequent one of recovering the country's competitive position. This recipe had its ideological basis in the theory that austerity was conducive to economic growth, because it would restore investor confidence and thus reopen the access to capital markets to finance a renewed growth. This explains why austerity ideologues call this policy "expansionary fiscal contraction", a term as euphemistic as it is contradictory.[30]

Given the results, it is clear that austerity as a recipe for emerging from the crisis in a reasonable time did not work. Rather than restoring the confidence of the markets and stimulating growth, it prolonged the recession and sank countries further into crisis. The reason for the failure was very simple: the macroeconomic policy response of European institutions and governments was based on a mistaken diagnosis of the crisis and, as a result, in a mistaken recipe for solving it. Very much in line with their ordoliberal and moralistic thinking, Germany considered that

---

30   See Blyth (2014).

the crisis countries were victims of their own excesses and should tighten their belts to restore fiscal and external equilibrium.[31] It was believed that fiscal deficits were caused by an excess in demand that had to be eliminated via austerity measures. The reality was that excess demand had already disappeared by then, and that what were really needed were measures to prop up demand.

Indeed, public finance theory recommends that fiscal management have a buffering (counter-cyclical) effect in short-term economic cycles: recessive phases should bring an increase and expansive phases a decrease in fiscal deficit. To this end support comes from what are called the fiscal "built-in stabilisers". Unemployment benefits are a good example: in times of recession the burden of unemployment benefits increases and with it the public deficit; the opposite occurs in phases of expansion. The European austerity recipe, however, cancelled the dampening effect of stabilising mechanisms by forcing debtor countries to reduce deficits. The result was that the eurozone as a whole, reduced its primary deficit from 350 billion euros in 2010 to only 10 billion in 2014.[32] Even "healthy" countries of central Europe adopted contractionary fiscal policies, i.e. they did the opposite of what counter-cyclical theory recommended.

The error was in not understanding that the triggers of the crisis had not been the fiscal excesses of governments, but overgrown demand and private spending, basically fed by a boom in bank credit. Proof of this is that the countries most impacted by the crisis had previously had their fiscal accounts in balance, except in the case of Greece. Despite being an exceptional situation, the Greek case was used as a platform–or rather an excuse–to generalise the ordoliberal narrative, in which everything was blamed on the profligacy of the peripheral countries. It was very simple: if the diagnosis was that the crisis had been caused by fiscal excesses of the affected countries, the prescription could not be other than austerity.

It was not understood that the lack of institutions and mechanisms to resolve the banking crisis was what turned the financial crisis into a fiscal one. Indeed, the abrupt constriction of bank credit generated by the reverse of capital had forced companies and individuals to deleverage

---

31   A more malicious view of the purpose of austerity was that it served to ensure that debtor countries freed up enough resources to honour their obligations to creditors.

32   See Richard Baldwin and Francesco Giavazzi, (2015)

and reduce spending, thus contracting economic activity. The banks were affected in two ways: on the one hand, the recession had propelled delinquency (past dues), especially in mortgage loans. And on the other, the reversal of capital flows had dried up the banks' liquidity. As no one knew how much each bank was affected by past dues and bad investments, the national interbank markets also dried up. In the absence of a lender of last resort to stop the panic in its tracks, national governments had to come to the rescue of their troubled banks, to which end they had to use taxpayers' money and/or borrow on the bond market. Thus began the fateful vicious circle of governments increasing public debt to bail out the banks and the banks buying sovereign bonds to bail out their governments. Additionally, fiscal accounts were very affected by the recession-induced fall in revenue and the increased welfare burden related to the rise in unemployment. Fiscal deficits were therefore really caused by the original crisis of credit crunch and collapse in aggregate demand, not the other way around.

Was austerity at least an efficient remedy for restoring external imbalances? Certainly, current-account deficits diminished considerably. This improvement, however, was not so much due to a sustainable recovery of the countries' competitive drivers, but to the brutal contraction of internal aggregate demand, in particular the demand for imports. Unfortunately, this domestic deflation was not properly rewarded with an improvement in exports and higher growth. When all countries, including those in surplus, simultaneously adopted programmes of retrenchment in public expenditure, consumption and imports, none of them saw its efforts to improve its competitiveness rewarded, because there was no external demand to absorb their exports. This is what is called the "fallacy of composition": what can make sense for individual countries can be disastrous for all of them as a group. In the same way, austerity does not work when all the surrounding countries apply it simultaneously, including those that don't theoretically need it–for example, Germany. This fallacy meant that the austerity programs were ineffective and very expensive: ineffective, because they required a huge dose of sacrifice to achieve a small improvement, and socially costly, because on the road to austerity many jobs were lost and economies were much damaged.[33]

---

33   Details on the impact in de Grauwe and Yuemei (2013)

In terms of fiscal imbalance, it may sound paradoxical, but the reality is that austerity had little or no impact on closing fiscal gaps. On the contrary, economies went into a downward spiral of recession that strongly reduced tax revenues, increased unemployment benefit costs, and led to bankruptcies of companies and banks, some of which had to be rescued by the State, which was then forced to borrow even more. In other words, a genuine boomerang effect. The financial markets, far from gaining confidence, distrusted the sustainability of the austerity efforts. Governments were faced with the drift to populism that came hand in hand with the hardships imposed on large masses of the population.

Empirical research by the IMF has shown that an increase in public spending has a greater multiplier effect in the recessive phases of the economic cycle than in the expansive. At times of falling real income, consumers tend to spend a larger share of any additional income they get. This means that it can make sense to increase spending to get out of the recession and balance the fiscal accounts in the medium term. A suitable combination of fiscal stimulus and structural reforms is therefore often a better recipe that just contracting spending, no matter how much reform is undertaken. Much more than a policy of fiscal containment, what post-crisis Europe needed was a policy of proactive management of aggregate demand that avoided extreme swings. After the 2008-2009 financial tsunami, Europe needed a coordinated policy of fiscal and monetary expansion, especially in the surplus countries of the European centre. Unfortunately, what it got was the opposite. The austerity policy that was implemented loaded countries in crisis with a burden of unemployment and public debt, which then made recovery extremely slow and painful.

Aside from the basic mistakes of diagnosis and prescription, in what else did the Community's handling of the euro crisis fail, and what could it have done? There are two sides to the story: the sovereign debt of the debtor countries and the exposure of the lending banks in creditor countries. On the debt side, it should have been recognised that the Greek sovereign debt was unsustainable. The successive rescue packages consisted basically of granting more loans so the country could continue to fulfil its obligations. Lending more money meant swamping the country with still more unsustainable debt. The solution would have been to call in the IMF, which knows a lot about these things, right from the beginning, ask creditors for a significant write-off, agree on a programme of structural reforms and give Greece the long-term funds to undertake this programme. The European Commission and the ECB, however, preferred the path of successive bailouts, infringing the express prohibition of the Treaty of Maastricht.

The facts support the suspicion that the reforms and actions taken during the sovereign debt crisis in 2010 and 2011 responded more to the interests of the creditor countries that to the needs of the debtors. New funds provided to the debtors were meant in the first instance to rescue the German, French and Dutch banks that had lent generously to the Mediterranean periphery during the boom years. This was also the reason behind the creation in 2010 of the European Financial Stability Facility (EFSF) and the European Financial Stability Mechanism (EFSM), which were replaced in 2012 by the European Stability Mechanism (ESM).

This observation ties into the other side of the coin of the failure of crisis management, that which relates to the lending banks. The Community authorities and national governments lacked the courage to face up to the problem of the banks. Instead of implementing mechanisms for restructuring–and, where necessary, for liquidation–of banks with large exposures to debtor countries, they preferred to give money to the debtors, so they could pay. Nor was there the courage to face starkly and realistically the banking calamity that from the outset had underlain the heart of the crisis in the peripheral countries, especially in Italy and Spain. Too little, too late and too slow.

What would have been appropriate was to define an EMU framework to resolve cases of insolvency, which would liquidate non-viable banks, ensuring that the unavoidable spread of distrust would not lead to a systemic collapse. Depositor guarantee protection was needed up to a reasonable amount. The shareholders, creditors of subordinated debt and major depositors, should nevertheless have taken on their proportion of the bust from the beginning, but always within an ordered frame of restructuring banks and sovereign debt, not in the improvised fix agreed by Merkel and Sarkozy in Deauville. In cases of liquidity problems, the ECB should have carried out its function of lender of last resort more expeditiously and, when it began to do so, without the ambiguity signalled by Germany's continually challenging Mario Draghi's "whatever it takes".

Finally, the timing of decisive interventions in crisis episodes was out of sync. The main responsibility for this was Germany's constant putting-off of decisions. As Wade Jacoby points out in his contribution to the book by Matthijs and Blith (2016), Germany was caught in the dilemma between "the timing of politics" and "the politics of timing": it was not deaf to the urgency of adopting policies on time, but usually postponed rescues until the last minute to ensure that there was no moral hazard of the rescued debtor having an incentive to behave badly in the future and expecting to be rescued.

Appendix IV-1
SELF-FULFILLING INTEGRATION: ENDOGENEITY THEORY

Since the beginning of the 2000s, in seeking to reconcile past critical positions with present realities, a theoretical framework and empirical line of research took shape on the benefits of monetary union "endogeneity". The main thrust came from the economist Andrew Rose who, in the context of studying the impacts of different monetary unions, affirmed that monetary integration led to a significant deepening of trade flows.[34] The result was that, although a group of countries could not or would not fulfil *ex ante* the optimality criteria for a currency area, the decision to adopt a common currency could be justified on the expectation that *ex post* the union would increase the degree of integration and symmetry. In fact, prior to the launch of the union, this was the argument given by the technical and political experts of the European Commission against the scepticism of the academics.

The endogeneities of a currency area would cover the four major criteria always mentioned by theory:

- endogeneity of commercial integration
- endogeneity of financial integration
- endogeneity of symmetries of shocks and economic cycles, and
- endogeneity of labour flexibility and mobility

---

34   See Rose (2000) and Frankel and Rose (2002), who come to the conclusion that countries in a monetary union trade three times more with each other than could have been expected without a union. They also estimate that for each one percent of GDP of increased trade, *per capita* income grows by one third of one percent. Subsequent studies have found these figures to be greatly exaggerated (see Baldwin 2006), but no one disputes that the so-called "Rose effect" exists.

The economic logic of the phenomenon of endogeneity would reside in monetary integration being accompanied by a radical elimination of frontiers and barriers. This substantially modifies the structure of incentives for economic agents to reorient their transactions to the integrated region. Trade is increased because the existence of monetary union sends a strong signal to investors that the countries' commitment to integration is irrevocable, that there will be no competitive devaluations in the future, and that governments will create the institutions and arrangements to facilitate more integration.

Now, what can be concluded from later empirical studies on the effects of endogeneity? What does the theory get right? With specific reference to the EMU, research on the effect of monetary union on trade integration shows a positive effect, but its size varies widely across studies.[35] The difficulty of estimation comes from the fact that the European Community had already reached very advanced levels of commercial integration by the beginning of the monetary union in 1999, after a 40-year long period of custom and trade union. Furthermore, trade-generating effects take much longer than 5 years to make themselves felt.

Equally ambiguous and long-term are conclusions about the endogenous effect of the monetary union on the flexibility and mobility of the workforce; these studies do not show significant advances in labour flexibility in the first years of the EMU. In contrast, the endogenous effect of integration on the financial markets seems to have been more clear-cut and of a short-term nature. The existence of a single currency accelerated the process of financial globalisation, especially in giving the money markets depth and liquidity. In the bond and equity markets the process was slower, though still intense, as the voracity of the post-2008 contagion phenomenon showed *a posteriori*.

As to the expectation that monetary integration would increase the symmetry of shocks and economic cycles, empirical observations prior to the crisis of 2008 seemed to justify moderate optimism on the beneficial effects of the union.[36] However, this initial optimism came from the fact that the first seven years of the EMU coincided with the period of the "great moderation" in the global economy, in which there simply were no shocks, symmetrical or otherwise. There were no events that could validate or invalidate the assumption that monetary

---

35 A good review of the specialized literature on this subject can be found in Beetsma and Giulodori (2010). De Grauwe and Mongelli (2005) present the state of the art on the subject up to the mid-2000s. Lane (2006) focuses on the effects of monetary union on the real economy.

36 See Wyplosz (2006).

union would reduce the asymmetries of economic cycles. Endogeneity effects related to the symmetry of economic cycles were severely challenged, however, after the outbreak of the financial crisis of 2008.

V

CORE PROBLEMS OF AN IMPERFECT MONETARY UNION

In the previous chapter we gave some clues to how a phenomenon of contagion coming from another continent could have unleashed a crisis of such magnitude and, above all, how it could have impacted so asymmetrically on the member countries of the EMU. The question we now ask is to what extent the structural elements of the crisis were in some cases caused, and in other cases exacerbated, by the very existence of an imperfect and incomplete monetary union. What were the design faults that compounded the difficulties already present in any fixed exchange rate regime?

There is a consensus that the eurozone crisis was primarily a crisis of excessive debt, private debt first of all and sovereign debt later on. It is also agreed that the effects of the crisis were aggravated by the straitjacket of a monetary union with no lender of last resort and with no banking integration. Nor was the European Union institutionally prepared to offer efficient and effective policy responses for halting and unravelling the crisis. Lastly, Germany, the country that should have assumed the duties proper to her role as *de facto* European hegemon, did nothing of the kind. On the contrary, she insisted on a mistaken ideological diagnosis and imposed solutions skewed in favour of the creditors, further aggravating the hardship of the countries in crisis.

The quasi-dogmatic article of faith of the architects of the monetary union, under the decisive influence of Germany, was that low and stable inflation was a sufficient safeguard of financial stability. They also believed that by establishing certain rules and exhorting individual countries to avoid fiscal excesses, their work was done. They believed that economic and monetary integration was going to cause economies with radically different cultures and economic models to converge. They thought that the straitjacket of the common monetary policy would discipline governments fiscally. They also thought that imposing fines and high interest rates on rescue funds would sufficiently deter fiscal follies. There was a lot of naiveté and wishful thinking in these beliefs. There was also a good deal of ignorance about the destructive financial and fiscal dynamics which an imperfect monetary union would sooner or later unleash. Insufficient consideration was given to the various "trilemmas" affecting open and globalised economies, in particular the impossibility of trying to have integrated financial markets, fiscal independence, and financial stability simultaneously.[37]

In this chapter we will deal with four core problems that defined the European crisis, all of them sown in the original design of the eurozone itself. In the first place, there was ignorance of the basic postulate of the Theory of Optimal Currency Areas, i.e. that countries that are monetarily integrated and suffer asymmetric disturbances, especially those related to the real economy, need to substitute exchange rate adjustments with other mechanisms in order to help restore the balance of their external and internal accounts. In the absence of these mechanisms, real imbalances or asymmetries created financial vulnerabilities for which the eurozone was not prepared: credit bubbles, over-indebtedness, excess demand, current account deficits, sudden stop of financial flows, banking crises, etc. Secondly, the European experiment underestimated the need for a minimum level of fiscal integration or risk-sharing schemes, just as it ignored the incentives for fiscal indiscipline that the members of a monetary union are prey to. Thirdly, the monetary dominance of a single central bank–and its unique mandate–did not allow the complexity of the crisis to be tackled using a varied arsenal of tools, nor did it allow the divergent economic cycles to be adequately dealt with, before and after the crisis erupted. Finally, the absence of banking integration, and above all the absence of a lender of last resort, allowed the emergence of a perverse doom loop of

---

37   See Obstfeld (2013) and Obstfeld (2014) for a detailed description of the trilemmas that confront modern economies. Other economists use terms like "impossible trinity" or "inconsistency triangle" to describe the same phenomenon of incompatibilities.

banking and sovereign crises that exponentially aggravated the effects of the crisis. The conclusion is that incomplete currency unions place their members in a situation of greater systemic financial fragility than would happen without the common currency.

THE REVENGE OF THE THEORY OF OPTIMAL CURRENCY AREAS: TRIGGERS OF THE CRISIS

The first problem of the EMU is that the 11 countries that created it on January 1, 1999 (Greece would be added two years later) did not meet the requirements to be classified as a feasible and desirable monetary area, especially for the persistence of divergences in the real (productive) sphere of their economies. The euro united two groups of economies with very different production models and cultures: those oriented towards export and those oriented towards the internal market. This led to multiple problems that became evident on the outbreak of the financial crisis. Europe's decision to form a monetary union did not have a solid basis in economic rationality.

The body of theory that analyses the convenience, costs, benefits and viability of monetary unions is the theory of Optimum Currency Areas.[38] In its initial version, developed by Mundell (1961) and McKinnon (1963), the theory said that adopting a common currency could suit a group of countries or regions only if perturbations affected them symmetrically; in the absence of this symmetry, countries or regions that were to integrate monetarily should have sufficient mobility of the labour force or of other production factors to deal with the effects of asymmetric shocks. Later, Kenen (1969) introduced the element of fiscal integration or fiscal federalism that would allow for compensatory transfers to countries or regions that were negatively affected. In the light of the European experience, this recommendation by Kenen turned out to be even more important, if possible, than the original Mundell focus on the mobility of production factors.

---

[38] A detailed development of the postulates of the theory of Optimum Currency Areas can be found in Purroy (2014). We have borrowed the title of this section from an article by Paul Krugman (2012). See also Eichengreen (2014).

When the idea of monetary union was taking shape in Europe in the 80s, many economists warned that the European countries did not meet the criteria to form an optimum currency area.[39] Truth be told, however, it must be said that the reasons given by these and other economists were quite different from each other and, what is more important, did not give enough importance to what later turned out to be the real problems that were to place the common currency under existential threat.

Economists on the other side of the Atlantic particularly, when comparing the degree of symmetries/asymmetries between the various regions of the United States or Canada with respect to those existing between European countries, showed that the mobility of production factors was significantly higher among geographically very remote regions on the American continent than existed between close European neighbours such as France and Germany. Due to cultural, social and linguistic barriers, labour mobility between European countries was also much lower. They further noted something of vital importance: when the asymmetric effects of shocks negatively affected a region in the United States or Canada, fiscal transfers from one region/state to another went into action to ease adjustment to the disturbance and contribute to a prompt recovery of the affected region/state. Additionally, banking and financial markets integration, were in general another mechanism to soften asymmetric shocks, since financial institutions with widespread presence could continue to lend money in the affected regions or states.

These warnings were disregarded, partly due to ignorance of the theoretical postulates, and partly from the belief that the union would set off a subsequent "endogenous" dynamic of integration. This would *ex post* create the necessary conditions of symmetry and mobility of production factors, particularly the labour force, for the success of the union. This argument was music to the ears of politicians who were determined to promote a united Europe at all costs. To be fair, however, we have to say that at that time the theory of Optimum Currency Areas was not yet sufficiently developed to constitute a solid guide to enable politicians and Community institutions to take more informed decisions. With the benefit of hindsight, we now understand that the theory could not have known about the effect of globalisation on the dynamics of debt, or about

---

[39] See Feldstein (1977), Eichengreen (1991), Wyplosz (1997), to name but a few.

the need for resolution mechanisms for banking crises, the need for a central bank with responsibility for stabilising the financial system, the need for fiscal integration in a framework of political solidarity, etc., etc. Moreover, Mundell and McKinnon were focussed on the asymmetries and disturbances of the real economy. In the 60s they could not know that financial globalisation was going to transform the world the way it did and transfer the principal risks and challenges to the financial sphere. This explains why they could not be aware that a monetary union needed to be accompanied by a banking union and a deep integration of the financial markets.[40]

The truth is that after integration the economies of the EMU did not converge as the theory supposed they should have.[41] Inflation differentials and consequent productivity differentials led eventually to greater divergence in real economies. Labour mobility and trade integration were lower than expected. Financial integration progressed as expected, but with the absence of other components of the scaffolding of the union, it became a boomerang of contagion during the crisis years.

The impact of the divergence of real interest rates on the economic boom at the periphery

In the previous chapter we described the speculative bubbles that appeared in Europe. Why did they do so especially in the countries of the eurozone periphery? The explanation lies in the very essence of an imperfect monetary union. In a theoretically ideal world, members of a monetary union should converge towards a single rate of inflation. However, and despite the advances achieved during the period of convergence prior to 1999, some European countries, especially those located in the Mediterranean periphery, kept inflation levels higher than the countries with traditionally better performance in terms of price stability. Efforts to converge could not eliminate certain cultural traits that made those

---

40 This awareness of the importance of financial integration for the feasibility of monetary unions is a relatively recent development in the literature on Optimal Currency Areas (see Mongelli, 2008).

41 Franks et al. (2018) of the IMF present a detailed study of the process of convergence or divergence in the EMU, coming to the conclusion that levels of divergence in the real economy remain incompatible with a monetary union. See also Wortman (2018), Botta et al. (2018)

countries more prone to spending and distributive policies than to austerity and hard work. Once the monetary union launched under a single central bank, what did converge was the nominal interest rate, which in the absence of exchange risk, was uniform throughout the length and breadth of the EMU. This incongruity between a single nominal interest rate and diverging inflation rates was not an unfortunate and avoidable development, but something inherent in currency unions between countries with cultural differences.

Diverging inflation rates and a convergent nominal interest rate are a sure recipe for imbalances in the medium and long term. Why is this? The impact of the interest rate on consumption and investment demand is well-known, which is why interest rates are the monetary policy instrument *par excellence* of the central banks. The lower the interest rate, the greater the stimulus for economic activity. To be precise, what affects the decisions of investors and consumers is the "real" interest rate, defined as the difference between the nominal interest rate and the inflation rate. For a given common nominal interest rate, the higher a country's inflation rate, the lower the real interest rate and the greater the incentive for investors to invest and consumers to consume.

The British economist Alan Walters warned in 1990 that not all countries would be joining the monetary union with the same inflation rate, but that the nominal interest rate would indeed converge quickly. This meant that countries with higher initial inflation, and thus lower real interest rate, would experience a higher growth of aggregate demand, which would produce greater inflationary pressure. Furthermore, companies and consumers in countries with lower real interest rates would also have greater incentive to borrow, because of the lower cost of bank credit, which would lead to excess demand. Due to the greater stimulus of demand in countries with lower real interest rates, initial inflation differentials would not only fail to disappear, but would increase in an unstable spiral of divergence.[42]

The union's architects underestimated the asymmetry of the inflationary cultures of countries that decided to join the monetary union.

---

42 Walters' Theorem (1990), also known as the Walters Critique, has received renewed attention after the financial crisis. Walters was worried about the implications of a possible entry of Great Britain into the European Monetary Union and so warned about the risk of inflation divergence.

Certainly, European countries converged a lot prior to 1999 (see Tables III-1 and IV-1), but much of the progress resembled a student's all-night study session before a final exam. The student gets a pass, but without the knowledge getting a chance to embed solidly in his brain. There was also a good deal of statistical fudging and turning a blind eye before the inaugural group photo in 1999. Be that as it may, the differences in inflationary cultures remained. The seriousness of the non-convergence of real interest rates was in the impact it had on feeding the unsustainable growth of aggregate demand in some countries. This was one of the main causes of the appearance of current account deficits in the periphery countries. Obviously, these current account deficits could not have reached the levels they did, nor could they have been maintained for so many years, had there not been a group of wealthy European countries willing to lend huge sums of money to banks in those countries that had a greater tolerance of inflation. The abundant credit therefore validated and encouraged the exuberance of consumption and investment in the peripheral European economies, with the consequent increase in the indebtedness of households and corporations.

Diverging economic models, competitiveness differentials and external imbalances

A second crucial aspect in explaining the origins of the crisis is that when the European Monetary Union was born in 1999 it already had important imbalances in its members' real economies, especially in their productive strengths. The convergence efforts during the previous decade had focussed exclusively on nominal magnitudes of a fiscal or monetary nature, but the reality was that at the beginning of the Union there were important asymmetries between countries in terms of their level of productive development and underlying economic models.

In Europe, long before 1999, there were two groups of countries with very different economic models. It is no coincidence that these models were aligned with entrenched cultural differences regarding consumption and inflation. Cultures, social preferences and economic models tend to be aligned. The Centre-North countries, wedded to the Protestant ethic that extolled frugality and hard work, tended to be more efficient and to have more competitive export sectors. The Mediterranean countries, for their part, tended to give priority to consumption, redistributive public expenditure and real wages, meaning that their main engine of growth was the domestic market.[43] The result was two clearly differentiated models of economic growth: that based on the export sector and that based on domestic demand. During the exchange rate vicissitudes of Bretton Woods, the Snake or the European Exchange rate Mechanism, the first model gave rise to "hard" or strong currencies (especially the deutschmark) and the second to "soft" or weak currencies (including the French franc, despite all the political efforts to defend a *"franc fort".*)

As long as the monetary arrangement allowed exchange rate adjustments to compensate for differences in productivity, the two models coexisted within the framework of the European Economic Community. From time to time devaluations compensated for the higher propensity for inflation and monetary expansion. There was an internal coherence within each model, facilitated by the exchange rate flexibility: monetary and exchange rate policy counterbalanced greater or lesser fiscal discipline, as well as greater or lesser wage containment. The problem appeared after the introduction of the common currency, which excluded the use of exchange rate adjustments to compensate for differences. From that moment on, wage and fiscal policy had to be consistent with a fixed exchange rate and a monetary policy fully committed to price stability. Germany and its peers had no problem, because the new economic model embraced by the EMU was clearly cut to the template of its frugal export model. The Mediterranean countries did not want to–nor, to be fair, could they–change their growth model, and therefore began to diverge more and more from their partners in the Centre-North. The consequences were disastrous.

There are also doubts that the exchange rate parities at which national currencies converted to euros on January 1st, 1999 truly reflected the real productivity levels in each country. Most of the periphery currencies were overvalued, which dragged down their competitiveness from the outset. These initial misalignments of the nominal exchange rates further burdened the start of a union full of asymmetries.

---

43   Scharpf (2018) characterises both economic models in detail and insists that their coexistence has become impossible after the common currency was set up. Previously, the possibility of adjusting exchange rates would offset imbalances as they appeared.

The divergent levels of competitiveness ended up being reflected in external account imbalances. Per-unit labour costs are the standard indicator of productivity. As this component of competitiveness is easily measurable, unit labour costs (ULC) are used as a proxy of a country's competitiveness. As evidenced by Figure v-1, the evolution of this indicator during the first decade of existence of the EMU was markedly divergent.

FIGURE V-1
Unit Labour Cost, 1999-2016

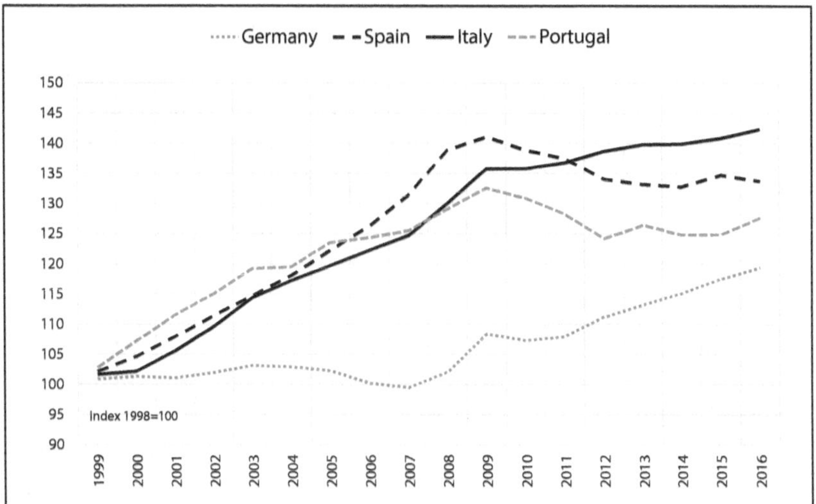

Source: European Commission. AMECO, Eurostat

The sample of four countries includes Germany as a reference point for labour cost containment, and Spain, Italy and Portugal as peripheral countries heading for crisis (excluding Greece, as it is a particular case). The ULC of the periphery, rather than converging towards Germany as would have been necessary in a monetary union, began diverging from the very start. Germany, in contrast, was able to maintain a strict control of labour costs, because the social, economic and political actors had forged a social pact (the *Agenda 2010*, promoted by Chancellor Schröder) to work cohesively towards recovery of the competitiveness lost in the 90s after German reunification. As proof of the effort, in 2007, eight years after the start of the EMU, the German ULC index was below its 1998 level.

The post-2009 evolution shows the significant efforts of countries such as Spain and Portugal to reduce their labour costs through austerity policies. Behind this reduction was hidden a tough process of falling real incomes and rising unemployment. Italy's evolution was different. ULCs continued their uninterrupted rise as the country undertook no adjustment of real income or structural reform process. Germany, for its part, returned after 2008 to the "normal" increase of ULC after attaining the competitiveness objectives of Agenda 2010.

There is a known link between productivity differentials and external imbalances, because in the long term these differentials end up being reflected in competitiveness of exports and imports. By the purchasing power parity theorem[44] we also know that inflation differentials are reflected in real long-term currency appreciations or depreciations, which, in turn, lead to imbalances in current account balances of payments. When there exists the option of adjusting the nominal exchange rate, these imbalances are of short duration, since devaluing the currency makes it possible to compensate, at least temporarily, for the loss of competitiveness. But when a country is part of a monetary union, this exchange rate adjustment option is not available and one must resort to the automatic mechanism of internal adjustment of prices and wages. As this deflationary mechanism is slow and painful, the imbalance in external accounts tends to persist for longer than is desirable.

If we look at the evolution of current account deficits on the balance of payments (see Figure v-2), we see that the evolution in the ULC indicator (a proxy for productivity) from Figure v-1 mirrors the deterioration or improvement trends in the current account. Particularly marked were the situations of Spain, Greece and Portugal, where current account deficits reached unsustainable levels, especially from 2003. With the disappearance of sources of external financing from 2009, the three countries were forced to drastically reduce their current account deficit. Spain and Portugal managed to reach solid ground in 2013, while Greece was still in a negative

---

44 This theory, which goes back to the beginnings of economics as a science, was first developed at the beginning of the last century in the work of Gustav Cassel (1918), a Swedish economist, who considered the impact of inflation differentials on the exchange rate during the years of World War I and said that *"the widespread inflation that took place during the war has decreased purchasing power parity in all countries, although to varying degrees, and exchange rates should deviate from their old parities in proportion to the inflation of each country".*

zone in 2017. The cases of France and Italy were of a different nature. Their current balance-of-payments situation deteriorated, but to a much more moderate degree. These were two economies with a historically firmer industrial and technological base, giving some stability to their competitive advantages. Germany, meanwhile, recovered from its late 90s deficit situation as of 2002 and continually improved its trade surplus, reaching an average of between 6 and 8.5 percent of GDP from 2007.

Figure V-2
Current Account Balance (% of GDP) 1999-2017

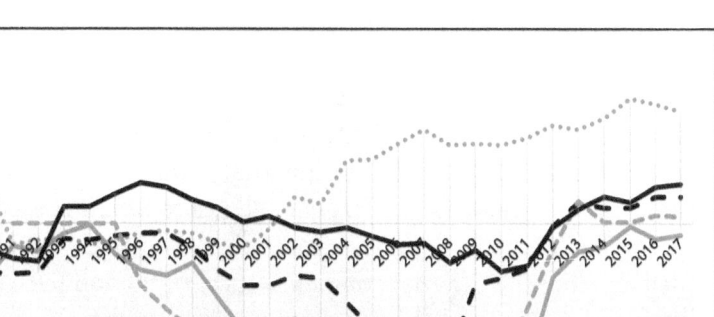

The orthodox German diagnosis of this situation was simple: wage increases and the lack of control over fiscal spending were responsible for the loss of competitiveness in the periphery countries and for their current account deficits. A logical consequence of this simple view was that wage restraint and labour market reform would be both necessary and sufficient to restore external balance. This approach was put into practice when it came to designing the structural reform programs that the eurozone core imposed on the periphery countries. However, the reality in Europe in the years prior to the crisis was different, and more complex than what the orthodox diagnosis indicated. The principal causes of the external account imbalance were the boom in bank credit and the concomitant boom in demand, both through the direct route of a demand excess that could only be met by imports, and by the indirect route of inflationary pressures that affected the competitiveness of domestic producers. The excessive focus on wage restraint therefore did not attack the full problem of external imbalances and so was not efficient.

If we turn to the countries with current accounts in surplus, the assertion that their good export performance was due exclusively to workers' wage restraint and the consequent lower unit labour costs is also untrue. The determinants of competitiveness are complex and multidimensional: a company can compete on price but can also do so by offering a portfolio of products more adapted to the needs of the market, of higher added value or with more cutting-edge technology. The strengths of the supply are as important as its cost advantages, or more so. At country level, the structural conditions that raise the attractiveness of the supply have to do with the size and integration of enterprises, workforce training, the labour relations practices, the level of technology, commercial infrastructure or international relations. It is not enough just to have a cheaper workforce. In fact, elements other than cost/price advantages predominated in determining the external competitiveness of the top five eurozone economies, especially in the crisis and post-crisis years.[45] We insist on this multi-causality of competitiveness because after 2010 the excessive emphasis on wage costs led to an equally excessive emphasis on austerity.

Excess private indebtedness and sudden stop

The abundance of low-cost liquidity and the belief that there was no exchange risk allowed the European junket to keep going beyond reasonable limits. Current account deficits, to be maintained, needed other countries to be willing to finance them. As well as allowing the party to go on, these capital flows also contributed greatly to worsening productivity differentials by way of wage rises in the periphery and increased consumption. Thus, the countries of the European periphery went into a perverse spiral in which current account deficits were financed by external loans, these in turn permitted over-consumption, price and wage increases, which widened the productivity gap even further and increased the current account deficit. And so the wheel kept turning.

---

45   See Xifré (2017)

The banks of eurozone countries in surplus had been more than happy to lend vast sums of money to peripheral countries in the belief that the strength of the euro was impregnable. But when they began to doubt the creditworthiness of borrowers, their manner cooled. The willingness of third parties to finance the excess spending of others always reaches a limit. When that point arrives, adjustment should usually take place by way of a currency devaluation to rebalance external accounts. But as this route is closed off in the case of a monetary union, deficit countries continue depending completely on the inflow of capital from abroad. When capital flows abruptly reversed in 2008, the crisis erupted immediately. This sudden drying up of capital (known as "sudden stop", in the specialised literature) was the immediate trigger of the European financial crisis.[46] As the deficit countries went into recession due to this sudden reversal, consumers and businesses found that their debt levels were unpayable in due times.

Contrary to the narrative that the origin of the crisis lay in the fiscal excesses of some countries, the reality is that the phenomenon of over-indebtedness made its appearance long before any symptom of fiscal stress. It was the exorbitant and irresponsible flows of capital from the surplus countries of central Europe to the countries of the periphery that allowed them to grow beyond their means. And those who contracted the debt were not the governments of those countries, but the private sector (banks, companies and households).

Indeed, the data in Figure v-3 call into question the conventional view that the level of public debt was the main indicator of potential debt problems. The graph separates the four main components of the debt by country: government, non-financial companies, households and financial institutions. In 2008, at the beginning of the crisis, government debt as a proportion of the total debt in each country was relatively small. In Spain, government debt was 47% of GDP and represented only 14% of the total public and private debt. In the UK, public debt was 52% of GDP and also represented 14% of the total British debt. In France, government debt was 73% of GDP and 24% of the total debt. The exception was Italy, where

---

[46] There is an extensive literature that narrates and explains the phenomenon of "sudden stops" of capital in emerging economies, historically resulting in exchange rate crises, and usually accompanied by financial and sovereign crises. See Calvo et al. (2004)

government debt was more substantial and amounted to 101% of GDP and 34% of the country's total debt. Another relevant point is that the debt of financial institutions in Europe was relatively moderate in 2008. Non-financial companies and households had measurably higher debt.

FIGURE V-3
Debt Components by Country, 2008

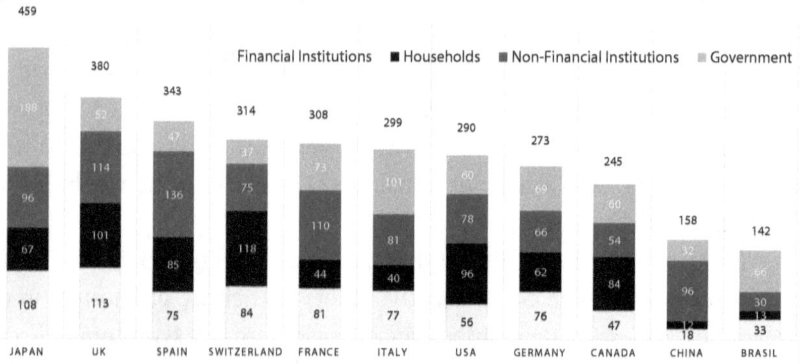

[Bar chart showing debt components (Financial Institutions, Households, Non-Financial Institutions, Government) as percentage of GDP by country:
- Japan: 459 total (Government 198, Financial Institutions 96, Households 67, Non-Financial Institutions 108)
- UK: 380 total (52, 114, 101, 113)
- Spain: 343 total (47, 136, 85, 75)
- Switzerland: 314 total (37, 75, 118, 84)
- France: 308 total (73, 110, 44, 81)
- Italy: 299 total (101, 81, 40, 77)
- USA: 290 total (60, 78, 96, 56)
- Germany: 273 total (69, 66, 62, 76)
- Canada: 245 total (60, 54, 84, 47)
- China: 158 total (32, 96, 12, 18)
- Brasil: 142 total (13, 66, 30, 33)]

Note: Debt as a Percentage of GDP. Swiss Data correspond to 2007
Source: McKinsey Global Institute (2010)

The evolution over time of the four debt components corroborates this (see Figure v-4). We take three typical countries: Spain and the United Kingdom, as examples of accelerated increase of private debt levels, and Germany, for her more temperate attitude. In the case of Spain, the public debt in the period 2000-09 diminished from 63% to 56% of GDP, but the other private debt components grew exponentially. The debt of Spanish non-financial companies went from 74% to 141%, household debt from 45% to 87% and that of financial institutions from 11% to 82% of GDP. A salient fact is that in 2007, the year before the crisis, Spain received a capital inflow of 150 billion euros. In total, Spanish global debt went from 193% of GDP in 2000 to 366% by mid-2009, due to the very significant increase in private debt. The reader may imagine the brutal impact that a sudden reversal of external financing would later have in this context of excessive private debt. That was the trigger of the crisis in Spain.

FIGURE V-4
Components of debt growth: Spain, Germany and United Kingdom (1980-2009)

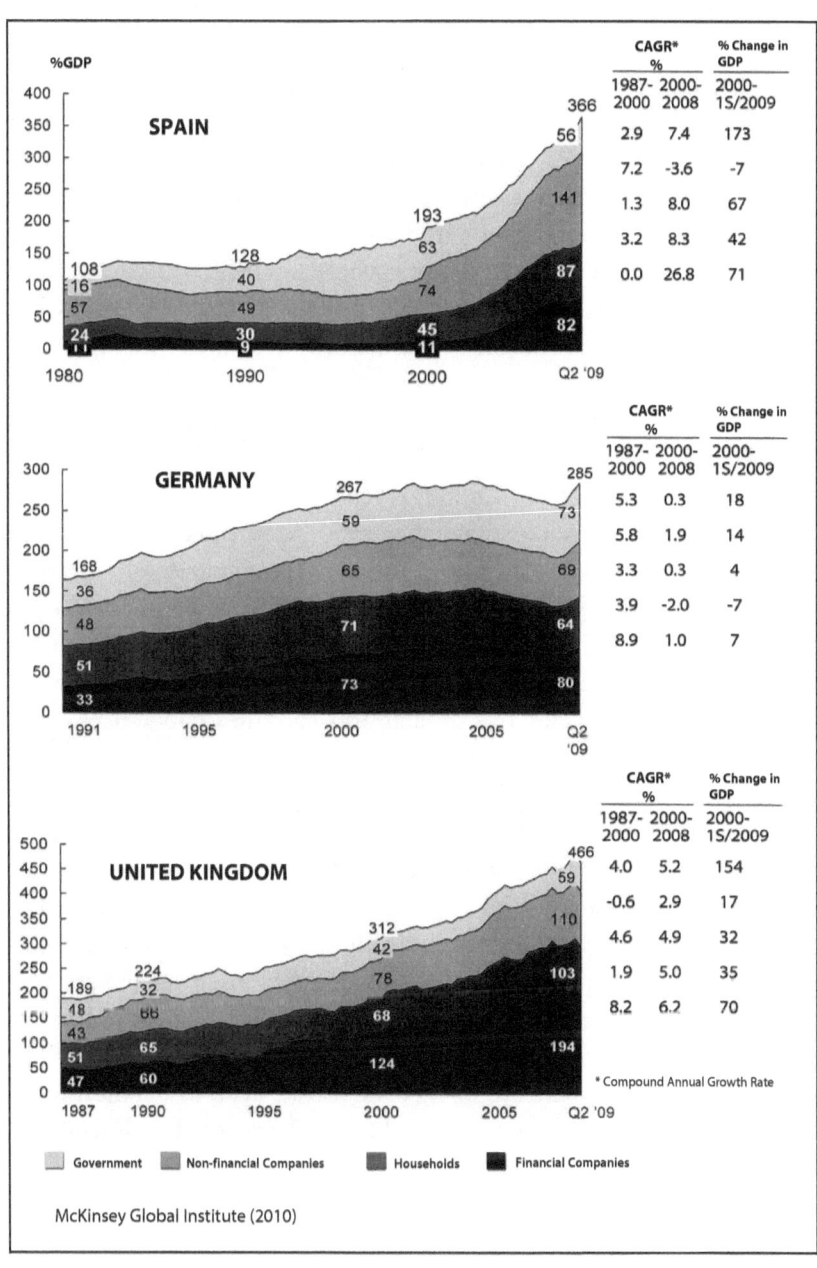

McKinsey Global Institute (2010)

Excessive growth of private debt is also observed in the case of the United Kingdom, where global debt goes from 312% to 466% of GDP in the period 2000-09. Here again, the main cause of the debt increase was not the government but the private sectors of the economy: non-financial companies increased their debt from 78% to 110% of GDP, households from 98% to 103%, and financial institutions going from 124% to 194%, the largest share. The average annual growth rates of these components between 2000 and 2008 were not as high as in Spain but were still quite high.

Contrast these figures with the case of Germany, where during the same period, the overall debt barely rose from 267% to 285% of GDP. Most of this moderate growth was in government debt, which grew from 59% to 73% of GDP, while households diminished their debt by 7 GDP points, non-financial firms increased theirs by 4% of GDP and financial institutions by 7%.

In this context of exuberant debt growth in some countries, any disturbing event would be enough to affect the confidence of foreign investors, make capital flows abruptly reverse and unleash a systemic crisis. The event finally arrived in September 2008. As was to be expected, the virulence of the markets differentially affected the countries whose structural vulnerabilities had led them beyond reasonable levels of borrowing.

The existence of the monetary union was of no help in dealing with the shock of the reverse of capital, quite the opposite. When countries have their own currencies, this sudden stop leads inexorably to a foreign exchange crisis and devaluation. Additionally, the central bank may resort to printing money to dilute the value of the debt through inflation or may even lend to the government, so it can pay its debts. However, when there is no national currency and no central bank to rescue the government, capital flight leads to a crisis of confidence in the sovereign debt as well as in the debt contracted by the financial institutions. Risk premiums are then adjusted upwards. Eventually the country becomes insolvent and must be rescued by fellow members of the union. In any case, bailout or not, in the absence of the exchange rate escape valve, the affected country is forced to enact a hard process of deleveraging of all private debt, which inexorably drags the economy into recession and unemployment. This forces it to embark on a process of deflation of domestic wages and prices, which is the only way available for gradually reversing the productivity gap. The greater the earlier productivity gaps, the more acute will be the deflation.

Good and bad disequilibria: when capital stampedes

The obligation of fulfilling the convergence criteria prior to the launch of the Union in 1999 exerted an undeniable disciplinary effect on the countries that aspired to form part of it, especially in those with past fiscal and monetary disorders (see Tables III-1 and IV-1). This would not have been possible without key advances in certain structural reforms in the public administration, in the labour market, tax systems and regulatory frameworks for competition. But after the union was constituted, it was another story. Once nominal convergence had been achieved, to get into the 1999 photo, the ease of financing allowed some countries to avoid or postpone much needed structural reforms.

How could so many people turn a blind eye to the excesses of debt and current account deficits for so long? The complacency of markets and authorities during the years of euphoria post-1999 is explained largely by the idea, prevailing up to 2007, that these disequilibria were inherent in the process of real convergence which necessarily had to occur between the least developed and more developed countries of the Union. In order for the differences in income, in infrastructure or in productivity between the core and the periphery to converge, the periphery countries needed to incur temporary imbalances in their savings and investment equation, so as to have the additional investment resources necessary to gradually close the gaps. Accordingly, current account deficits and increased external debt would be the means to the end of financing the process of raising overall productivity in the peripheral economies. It was assumed that capital inflows, and their current account deficit counterparts, were destined for investments in infrastructure, capital goods, education and efficiencies in public administration, which would improve the growth potential in the medium and long term. Consequently, what was observed in the eurozone's first years of life were "good" disequilibria.[47]

At the start of convergence processes, it is indeed not easy to differentiate *ex ante* between good and bad disequilibria. Nevertheless, with the benefit of hindsight we now know that the capital inflows in the European periphery countries did not go towards financing plant

---

[47] The pioneering analysis of good and bad disequilibria is due to Blanchard and Giavazzi (2002).

and equipment to close the productivity gap but were mainly diverted to consumption. In cases such as Ireland and Spain, investment went towards residential construction, which was the only sector that grew and created jobs. In cases such as Greece and Portugal, the capital inflows fed a rambling bureaucracy and public projects of doubtful efficiency. Most of those countries' debt went to totally disproportionate infrastructure projects or directly to finance consumption. This abundance of funding created conditions for wages and prices to increase relatively more in the European periphery, whereupon the productivity gap widened, and external competitiveness declined. From a structural point of view, the imbalances between savings and investment did not end up financing the closing of gaps. Indeed, the reverse happened: they ended up becoming "bad" disequilibria, which placed the eurozone periphery in a situation of extreme vulnerability.

Good disequilibria become bad when imbalances (between savings and investment, exports and imports, etc.) are perceived as unsustainable. Sooner or later, the merry financiers notice such unsustainability. It only needs a trigger for capital flows to suddenly revert, with the usual consequences: recession, falling tax revenues, companies and households unable to pay their debts, banks swamped by defaults, governments having to bail them out, national debt increasing and investors fleeing from the sovereign bond markets.

Incentives for fiscal indiscipline

The second core issue of the EMU concerns the fiscal dimension and is one of the most debated aspects of the design and dynamics of monetary unions. It is well known that the European Monetary Union was built on a peculiar political trade-off between the monetary and the fiscal, in which the European States were willing to relinquish their monetary independence in exchange for preserving their sovereign rights to raise taxes, borrow and spend. It was thought, especially in Germany, that the existence of a strong European Central Bank with a clear mandate to prioritize price stability, and a prohibition on financing or bailing out governments in deficit, would be sufficient to impose financial and fiscal discipline. Until the late 1990s, the disciplining effect of currency integration was the prevailing belief among economists who studied the effects of "tying one's hands" and "borrowed credibility". The countries with weak currencies wanted to shelter under the protective shield of the Bundesbank so that its proverbial monetary discipline would tie the hands of spendthrift governments and imbue them with its anti-inflationary credibility.

Contrary to this naive belief, and in line with Kenen's admonition (1969), many academics insisted that some minimum degree of fiscal centralisation or federalism was necessary for an integrated monetary area to be viable. They argued that at some point the magnitude of asymmetric shocks could be such as to require fiscal transfers to affected countries, in order to allow them to cope with the disturbance without endangering their very permanence in the Union.

Alexander Lamfalussy, a Hungarian-Belgian economist, General Manager of the Bank for International Settlements of Basel and later first President of the European Monetary Institute in 1994, warned at the end of the 80s, in a memorandum to the Delors Committee, about the dangers of a monetary union between countries with such differing propensities for fiscal deficit. Lamfalussy did not share the belief that financial markets or monetary discipline of the common currency would even out or patch over the differences in fiscal behaviour of the members of the future union. Hence, his recommendation was to make the necessary arrangements to establish a common fiscal policy, as a natural complement to the common monetary policy.

The American economist Barry Eichengreen also gave a premonitory warning in 1993:

> *"The rationale for these conditions is that admitting into the monetary union members displaying inadequate fiscal discipline will subject the ECB to pressure to purchase the debts of the lax countries, with inflationary consequences for the union as a whole. Governments which issue debt in excess of their capacity to service it might expose themselves to a 'debt run', in which investors suddenly liquidate their holdings of that government's obligations. The price of its bonds will plummet, and the ECB may feel obliged to purchase them to prevent the entire EC bond market from being demoralized. This swap of money for bonds would fuel inflation. Because the inflationary costs of the bailout are borne by*

> *all members of the monetary union, individual governments will have an incentive to run excessive deficits and issue excessive debt. Alternatively, if the ECB is prohibited from supporting the market in the bonds of an over-indebted government experiencing a run, EMU may herald a new era of pervasive financial market instability.*[48]

Eichengreen pointed to several problematic interactions that seem to be inherent in a currency union. Firstly, there are no watertight compartments where the monetary effects of countries' fiscal excesses can be isolated or neutralised. If the single central bank intervenes in the sovereign debt market to prevent its collapse, this action has an expansive monetary effect and can endanger the inflation target. And if not, it submits the union to the rigours of speculative waves that end up spreading instability to the rest of the union. Secondly, in a monetary union the problem of free riding[49] occurs sooner or later, because the costs of profligacy are diluted among all the members, while the benefits (in the short term at least) are individual, creating an incentive for fiscal indiscipline.

Perversely, free riding also works to discourage good behaviour: for example, a country that undertakes a labour market reform that lowers the natural rate of unemployment and, therefore, reduces inflationary pressure in that country, gives a marginal benefit to all members of the union because it allows the single central bank to apply a less restrictive monetary policy and, eventually, to reduce the common interest rate. The short-term costs of the reform, however, fall exclusively on the shoulders of the country undertaking it, while the other members benefit but assume no cost.[50] This unequal distribution of costs and benefits discourages the implementation of structural reforms within a monetary union.

Where free riding is most frequent and most damaging is in the field of fiscal policy. In fact, the EMU countries' behaviour was far from exemplary as regards their fiscal balances (see Figure IV-5).

---

48 Eichengreen (1993), page 1347

49 We use the term to refer to the behaviour of stowaways who travel at the expense of others, without assuming the cost, or worse, shouldering others with the cost of their actions.

50 Chari and Kehoe (2008) develop a model of temporary policy inconsistencies, which analyse the inflationary effect of labour market reforms and conclude that monetary integration weakens the incentive for reform.

Figure V-5
Fiscal Deficit (% of GDP): Germany and France vs Periphery, 1999-2017

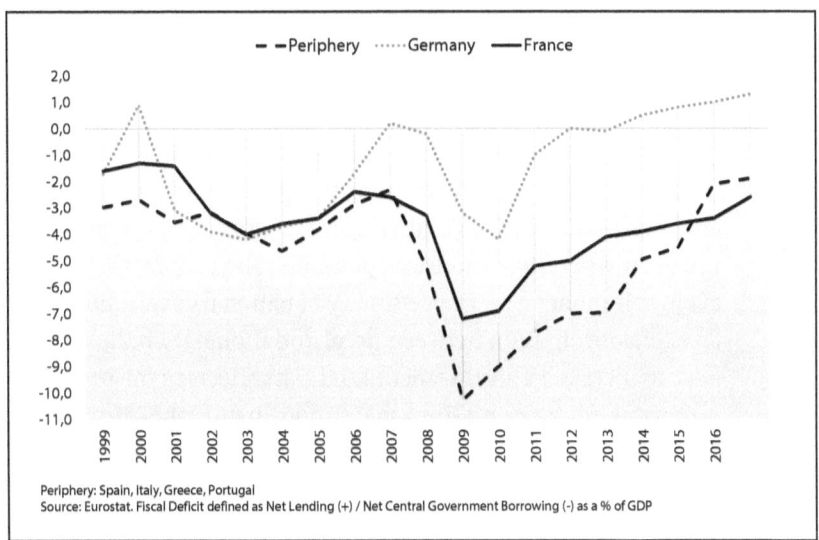

Periphery: Spain, Italy, Greece, Portugal
Source: Eurostat. Fiscal Deficit defined as Net Lending (+) / Net Central Government Borrowing (-) as a % of GDP

Between 2002 and 2005, the two leading countries of the union (Germany and France) broke their Stability and Growth Pact (SGP)[51] commitment not to incur fiscal deficits above 3 percent of GDP. The periphery countries also broke the commitment, except for Spain, which remained on positive ground every year. Between 1999 and 2007 there were 34 breaches of the SGP deficit limit. Until the emergence of the CFG in 2008, the Franco-German bloc and the Mediterranean periphery had very homogeneous fiscal behaviours. From 2009, the periphery shows a much more pronounced deterioration than the France-Germany duo. It is worth mentioning that, since 2007, France was already uncoupled from the German fiscal train and had a fiscal conduct very similar to the countries of the Mediterranean periphery. This coincides with the general loss of dynamism in the French economy.

Several factors go to explain this undisciplined fiscal slant of the European monetary union. We will mention two of them:

---

51 Prior to the start of the monetary union, aspiring countries signed an appendix to the Maastricht Treaty in 1997, called the Stability and Growth Pact (SGP). This provided follow-up and penalty mechanisms to ensure that the fiscal targets set out in the convergence criteria (i.e. not to exceed 3 per cent of fiscal deficit and staying below 60 percent in the ratio of public debt to GDP) would continue applying after the start of the Union.

1. The institutional design of the EMU gave power and independence to a single central bank whose sole responsibility was price stability. Meanwhile, governments were left with the responsibility for ensuring employment and economic growth. This was the germ of inevitable conflicts between policy objectives that can and often do collide. The conflict can lead to fiscal policies that are neither optimal nor desirable.[52] To put it another way, as monetary policy and the responsibility for controlling inflation are not national responsibilities, governments do not worry about inflation when they increase spending. The problem is that, to avoid this monetary irresponsibility of national governments, the level of coordination between fiscal and monetary policy would have to increase. This is something the architects of the monetary union did not foresee. Given that subordinating the central bank to the political say of governments is out of the question, it would have to work the other way around, i.e. the solution to the conflict would be to impose restrictions on individual governments' fiscal management in order to support the ECB's anti-inflationary goal. The facts of real life show that this rarely works out.
2. In normal circumstances a monetary union reduces the cost to a member of incurring fiscal deficits and excessive debt, thus encouraging fiscal laxity by reducing the cost of borrowing. This is because the financial and bonds markets in a union show a high level of integration. Excessive debt issues by individual national governments do raise community interest rates, but this effect is diluted in a broad and deep market, while the temporary benefit of the deficit stays in the debt-issuing country.[53] As long as normal conditions persist, countries with structural weaknesses can emit nearly unlimited amounts of debt, without suffering the disciplinary cost of rising interest rates. This was the situation that prevailed in Europe until 2008. When the sudden stop happened and the markets punished profligate countries with sudden hikes in financing costs, it was already too late.

---

52 See the model developed by Dixit and Lambertini (2003) to substantiate this conflict of interest.

53 Faini (2006) reports on extensive research on the impacts of fiscal measures on interest rates.

The disciplinary effect of the SGP in its first years of life was almost nil, in good part because of the impotence of the Council of Finance Ministers (ECOFIN) to impose the corresponding penalties. The institutional design of the Pact itself underlay its non-applicability, since the imposition of sanctions depended on a unanimous decision of the members of ECOFIN. It is naive to think that this club of the national heads of their countries' public finances would ever unanimously sanction a colleague, knowing that another day the finger could be pointing at them. In view of continued breaches, and in order to give it more flexibility to adapt to medium-term economic cycles, the SGP was reformed in 2005, but the realities of the 2008 crisis made sure it remained innocuous and toothless.

At a more fundamental level, the impossibility of the EMU fiscally disciplining its members lay in its essential weakness: its political design. The monetary union could not function as a political union as long as its members kept their fiscal sovereignty, among other things. There was, therefore, an underlying conflict of political legitimacy every time any Community body tried to impose a fiscal decision on a member of the Union. The European institutions had not been elected by the people and were not entitled to tax the citizens at national level or to define how much or on what the tax revenues were to be spent. Furthermore, the governments of EU countries could not enact non-refundable fiscal transfers to others without the legal framework of a fiscal union.

The discussion around proposals for solution was intense from 2011 onward. The proposal to create "independent fiscal agencies"[54] clashed with the same problem of political legitimacy. The only course of action that could be put into practice was on the lines of establishing EU fiscal rules, that countries would voluntarily accept by signing a tax treaty. Preferably, they should incorporate this in their Constitution or some other high-level legal framework, so as to make the fiscal indiscipline of a country politically more expensive.

The Treaty on Stability, Coordination and Governance (TSCG), known as the Fiscal Stability Treaty, was signed on March 2, 2012 by all

---

54 Debrun, Hauner and Kumar (2009) carried out a survey of the technical literature on this issue, specifically on the motives for establishing independent fiscal agencies, their possible design and the experience gained with them.

the European States except the United Kingdom and the Czech Republic. The agreement introduced the rule that the structural fiscal deficit[55] could not exceed 0.5 percent of GDP and that excess debt relative to GDP of over 60 per cent had to be dismantled within certain time limits. Sanctions for non-compliance would be imposed by the Supreme Court of Justice of the European Union. Rather than any unlikely sanctions that the Supreme Court of Justice might impose, the carrot and stick for countries to adopt these rules voluntarily were access or non-access to European liquidity or bailout funds.

The problem with this treaty, like that of the fiscal pacts that preceded it, is that they contained an intrinsic contradiction: they were inspired by the German federal model, which gives the central government the authority to impose rules on federal *Länder*. In the case of the EMU, however, countries retain full sovereignty over their fiscal matters. Obligations to EU institutions cannot override national fiscal sovereignty.

Bundesbank über alles: THE ONE-SIZE-FITS-ALL MONETARY POLICY

The third core issue defining the EMU design faults refers to the design of monetary policy. Aware as the architects of the Union were of the bias towards fiscal laxness of many European countries, they decided to incorporate into the founding Maastricht Treaty the statute of a European Central Bank with three central elements: a strict prohibition on the ECB financing fiscal deficits through operations in the primary market of sovereign debt bonds; total independence and political autonomy; and no-bailout clauses of banks and governments.[56] The backbone that should run through the entire *raison d'être* and behaviour of the ECB was the exclusive and exclusionary mandate to defend price stability.

The design of the ECB was a replica of the German Bundesbank. In keeping with its historic obsession with price stability, that condition was imposed by Germany in return for giving up its currency and joining the monetary union. The national central banks delegated monetary policy

---

55   The structural budget deficit is an estimated measure of the fiscal deficit that would exist if the economy were operating at full employment.

56   Articles 103 and 104 of the Maastricht Treaty.

to the ECB, upon which their national responsibilities were reduced to maintaining the payments system and the regulation and supervision of the local financial system.

In terms of monetary policy strategy too, the ECB was born bound to the same pillars that anchored the monetary policy of the Bundesbank. The instrument for controlling inflation was interest rates and these had to be defined on the basis of two intermediate variables: first, the evolution of monetary aggregates, mainly the M3 aggregate; and, second, the set of "all relevant indicators" to evaluate the inflationary forces at each moment.

These elements of the ECB's monetary strategy were criticized by a goodly number of economists from its inception.[57] When the ECB was created in 1999, the use of type M3 monetary aggregates as a guide for monetary policy was severely questioned, because their final relationship with the inflation indicator is too ambiguous to fulfil its purpose of guiding decisions on interest rate policy, particularly in low-inflation environments.[58] Equally disputed was the second guiding variable that groups "all the relevant indicators", because it is operationally difficult and also very opaque.

In addition, based on extensive accumulated research and experience, from the mid-1990s other central banks of large economies redesigned their monetary policy strategies around "inflation targets", which were usually established in bands around a central rate. The ECB, however, established a ceiling of 2 percent inflation rate as its goal. This approach was also questioned as it was not properly speaking a band but a cap, and furthermore was considered too low for the European situation. This ceiling forced the ECB to subject the eurozone to permanent deflationary pressure.

A monetary policy based on averages

Beyond these technical aspects related to monetary strategy, the central problem in the design of the European monetary architecture was that it applied a one-size-fit-all policy for countries which, as we have seen, had very different circumstances and structural situations. This was not just a

---

57   For details of this interesting debate, see Wyplosz (2006) and Beetsma and Giulodori (2011)

58   de Haan, Jakob, Sylvester Eijffinger and Sandra Waller (2005) validate empirically the ineffectiveness of this monetary strategy under low inflation.

design failure of the ECB as such, but a problem inherent to a monetary union comprised of countries with severe asymmetries. Divergences in terms of wage bargaining systems, trade-offs between central governments and autonomous regions, different drivers of growth (exports, internal markets, services, real estate, …), short-term cycles, assets subject to manias, etc., etc. would have required radically different monetary policies in each country, but the very essence of the monetary union precluded this flexibility.

A country like Spain, for example, that was entering the first half of the 2000s with a dangerous housing bubble fuelled by a bank credit boom and low interest rates, was crying out for the implementation of a restrictive monetary policy. Unfortunately, the Central Bank of Spain had neither the instruments nor the mandate to curb the liquidity bubble through monetary policy, while the ECB, by both design and mandate, was concerned only with European averages to set its monetary policies.[59] The inverse situation happened when the crisis exploded: what Spain and the rest of the periphery countries needed were expansive monetary policies that would counter the contractionary spiral of decreasing demand, but the medicine they got was the opposite, at least until 2012.

The specifics of individual countries were not relevant in the equations of the ECB, because interest rates could not be established on the basis of any particular situation. Thus the ECB's policy added fuel to the fire: the centralized monetary policy fed the bubbles of individual countries during the boom phase, and later potentiated the recession. The reader will recall our mention of the Walters Critique, which points to the divergence of real interest rates when countries don't have the same inflationary culture. Low real interest rates generated incentives for businesses and households to increase debt leverage, which gave a greater impetus to economic expansion, made inflation more persistent and reproduced the differential of real interest rates: a dangerous feedback loop.

The ECB was born in Maastricht, comforted in the delusion that asymmetries between countries would have vanished after the prior period

---

59 Having said that, however, the central banks of the periphery, including the Spanish, can be reproached for not using the instruments they did retain in their sphere of competence. Specifically, they could have employed banking regulation and supervision to mitigate the essential ingredient of the real estate bubble, i.e. the irresponsible expansion of bank credit. Their responsibility for allowing the crisis to accumulate is undeniable, since they had both the information and the tools to prevent banking excesses.

of convergence. When stubborn reality prevailed and the disparities of real economies persisted, self-deception gave way to the Bundesbankian dogma that these disparities were not a matter for the ECB. The national governments would have the task of evening out the real economy imbalances through structural reforms of their factor markets. The problem was that at the national level governments no longer had the means to make the process of real convergence viable, since belonging to the monetary union deprived them of the use of exchange rate and monetary policies. For example, the only way to smooth out differences in productivity in the short/medium term was through a relatively smaller rise in prices and wages compared to more productive eurozone members. The ECB's ambitious inflation target, however, conspired against this type of equalisation because it required an unsustainable process of deflation in the weakest countries. In fact, the opposite occurred and those countries incurred higher inflation that aggravated the disadvantage of higher relative costs. The other alternative would have been for the countries of the centre to agree to inflate their economies, something unthinkable to mentalities such as those of Germany and its partners in the European core.

Systemic fragility of financial markets in a monetary union: the original sin

We will now look at the financial markets. A monetary union increases the vulnerability of the financial markets, particularly the bond markets. Paul de Grauwe (2012) presents an interesting comparative analysis of the effects of the crisis post-2008 in the United Kingdom and Spain, which leads him to this conclusion. This happens because when a country joins a monetary union it relinquishes control over the currency in which it issues its debt. The monetary financing of fiscal deficits and the option of using inflation to dilute the debt are both eliminated, these being the weapons of last resort used by a State to avoid falling into insolvency. The markets can therefore force Spain into default, while the United Kingdom, not being a member of a monetary union, can issue the money needed to meet its obligations in sterling. And, as the pound sterling floats, in the end there will always be an exchange rate to calm the financial markets. In addition, during a crisis of market confidence the United Kingdom would have the advantage that her money in circulation would remain intact, while Spain could suffer a severe contraction of liquidity by euro flight from her banking system to safer havens. As is well known, liquidity problems can become solvency problems when market sentiment is adverse.

This would explain the "paradox" seen in the comparison between Spain and the United Kingdom (see Table v-1).

Table V-1
Comparative figures: Spain–United Kingdom, 2009-2014

	Spain						Average
	2009	2010	2011	2012	2013	2014	2009-2014
GDP Growth	-3,6	0,0	-1,0	-2,9	-1,7	1,4	-1,3
Unemployment Rate	17,9	19,9	21,4	24,8	26,1	24,4	22,4
Fiscal Deficit % of GDP	-9,6	-7,8	-7,6	-8,0	-4,1	-3,0	-6,7
Inflation Rate	-0,3	1,8	3,2	2,4	1,4	-0,1	1,4
10-year Bond Spread	0,6	2,5	3,2	3,9	2,2	1,1	2,2
	United Kingdom						Average
	2009	2010	2011	2012	2013	2014	2009-2014
GDP Growth	-4,3	1,9	1,5	1,3	1,9	3,1	0,9
Unemployment Rate	7,6	7,9	8,1	8,0	7,6	6,2	7,6
Fiscal Deficit % of GDP	-8,8	-7,0	-4,8	-5,4	-4,2	-3,8	-5,7
Inflation Rate	2,2	3,3	4,5	2,8	2,6	1,5	2,8
10-year Bond Spread	1,0	0,4	0,2	0,5	1,1	1,2	0,7

Source: WEO April 2017, IMF.

Despite both countries initially showing similar problems in the fundamental elements of the crisis, such as the debt levels and current account deficits, the markets punished Spain with much higher risk premiums (bond spreads) than those applied to the UK. Spain had to pay on average 210 basis points more than the United Kingdom in 2010, 300 basis points more in 2011 and 340 basis points more in 2012.

If Spain's increased financial vulnerability was one side of a double-edged sword, the other was the fact that the cost of the crisis in terms of unemployment and lost output was higher. Deflation and recession were much more severe in that country, as shown in Table v-1. The UK could allow higher inflation rates, which helped her in the dual purpose of diluting the real value of her debt and stimulating the economy through a more expansionary monetary policy, while Spain was subject to the deflationary dictates of the ECB. After the recessionary adjustment of 2009, which affected both countries equally, the UK had uninterrupted economic growth since 2010, while Spain took until 2014 to exit the recession. Most remarkable were the unemployment figures. Putting aside the structural differences of the respective labour markets, Spain saw her unemployment rate rise from 18 to 26 percent, while the UK was able to maintain her relatively low level of unemployment. The conclusion is that the adjustment process was much more costly for Spain, in large part due to the rigidity imposed by its membership in the EMU. Conscious of this fact, the markets treated Spain with greater harshness.

The rigidity and fragility inherent in the membership of a monetary union increases the probability of the affected economy being placed in a bad equilibrium, characterized by the painful succession of punitive risk premiums, chronic fiscal deficits, sovereign debt crisis, economic recession and banking crisis. Given the high level of financial market integration in a monetary union, sovereign debt problems will spread to other countries through the banking system.

The problem of countries being forced to issue debt in currencies other than their own is not new. This has been the inescapable lot of all developing (now called emerging) nations. What is new is that, owing to their membership of a monetary union, several large developed European countries are facing the same typical developing-country problem, which in the jargon of economists has been called the "original sin".[60] It's the classic problem of currency mismatch: the obligations are in a foreign currency, but money is issued in the local currency. This mismatch comes from the fact that emerging countries have insufficiently broad and deep capital markets to issue debt in their local currency.

Members of a monetary union cannot wash away their competitiveness gap by devaluing the currency. They have to undergo a process of price and wage deflation to recover the lost competitiveness. Countries trapped in these bad equilibria typically enter a destructive spiral that

---

60 The term was coined by Ricardo Hausmann in the late 90s. See Eichengreen, Hausmann and Panizza (2003), who use a large dataset to analyse the effects of original sin in the field of emerging economies.

threaten their fiscal solvency for an extended period. The original sin of borrowing in a currency over which they have no issuing authority banishes them from the earthly paradise they once thought they had entered and throws them out into a hostile and turbulent world.

A BLINKERED CENTRAL BANK: THE ABSENCE OF A LENDER OF LAST RESORT

It is disingenuous to think that a major financial crisis can leave a currency unscathed. The systemic fragility of financial markets in a monetary union points to the fourth core problem of the European monetary architecture: the omission of responsibility for the stability of the financial system from the ECB's constitutive mandate. In the design of the EMU this responsibility fell on national bodies: national central banks, national banking supervisory bodies, national securities commissions, etc. The ECB felt responsible only for price stability, and hence showed itself reluctant to engage in banking affairs. The founding Maastricht Treaty expressly forbade the ECB to have a role in rescuing banks. At bottom, the central-banker designers of the Treaty embodied in it their fear that bank bailouts might need resources that could only come from monetary emissions, since there was to be no central common budget for this purpose.

The European crisis showed that this institutional arrangement might have worked in times of steady prosperity but not in times of turbulence. The ECB had no mechanism to prevent financial systems from suffering misfortunes that would affect the very solvency of countries. The vigorous financial globalisation from 1990 meant that peaceful times in the financial sector were a thing of the past. The goal of ensuring financial stability thus became as important as that of price stability. Apart from hardliners, an incipient consensus therefore took shape between economists and policy makers that the stability of the financial system, in its dual dimension of the banking system and the sovereign bond market, should also be the European Central Bank's responsibility. If national governments were left with only fiscal policy to deal with disturbances, the supra-national monetary authority necessarily had to assume additional duties beyond merely ensuring price stability.

This position that the central banks should ensure the stability of the financial system had special relevance in Europe due to the oversized national banking systems. The reason for this hypertrophy lay in the fact that traditionally a high proportion of funding in Europe was channelled through the banks and not, as in the United States, through the capital markets. Thus, national banking systems became too large for a State to have the fiscal capacity to bail out its major banks in the event of a collapse. Between 2001 and 2007, the size of some banking systems, measured as a percentage of national GDP, went from 360 to 705 percent in Ireland, from 229 to 373 percent in France, from 177 to 280 percent in Spain and from 148 to 220 percent in Italy.

The core issue is that, on joining the EMU, the national banking systems were left without their lenders of last resort. The fragility of Europe's financial markets came in large part precisely from this absence of an ultimate lender, something that has proven to be absolutely essential throughout world financial history. If this element of fragility is compounded with that coming from the aforementioned original sin, the conditions were ripe for all kinds of setbacks.

History has shown that what makes a banking crisis truly dangerous is that, in the absence of a lender of last resort, well-known mechanisms turn liquidity problems into solvency problems. The dynamic works like this: if there is a sudden run on bank deposits, any available funds must be replaced at a much higher cost. If none are available, banks must liquidate assets (bonds, industrial investments or real estate investments) at depressed prices. In any case, the solvency of the banks is compromised by the increased funding costs or by losses from the fire-sale of assets. And if there is no funding available at any cost, the direct outcome is a large-scale run on deposits and the bankruptcy of the institution.

Although it is true that the facility of last-resort loans should not be used for tackling solvency problems, it is no less true that in a crisis the frontier between liquidity and solvency problems tends to disappear, even for healthy institutions. It can be extremely difficult to draw the line between both problems. If it turns out that the issue is merely liquidity, the lender of last resort will not need to act, since the markets would know this and be willing to provide the necessary liquidity at the corresponding price. A central bank acts when the markets are reluctant to do so, precisely because they don't know if the problem is liquidity or solvency. What matters is that the healthy part of the system does not embark on a destructive dynamic of self-fulfilling prophecy, which is where the actions of a central bank are decisive.

The vicious circle of banking and sovereign crises: the bond markets

Proposals to extend the ECB's remit also took in the capital markets, especially the sovereign bond market, an issue that sparked passionate controversy. Its statute forbade the ECB from operations in the primary sovereign debt market. The fierce opposition of Germany and its allies to any intervention in the bond market was rooted in that stance. The reality, however, was that arguments in favour of ECB intervention had solid grounds, taking into account the proven interaction between banking crises and sovereign crises. The risk of not helping the bond market was that the banks would become infected with the sovereign crisis. The same was true in reverse: not helping the banks would degenerate into sovereign crises.

This perverse feedback between banking crisis and sovereign crisis became painfully evident in the euro crisis. National banks were major holders of debt from their respective governments. The vicious circle consisted of governments rescuing their banks and then the latter rescuing the former.[61] Banking crises not only deprived governments of their main source of financing but shouldered them with the cost of bank bailouts. Conversely, the sovereign debt crisis seriously affected the balance sheet of financial institutions–through the loss of value of their investment portfolios–and thus degenerated into liquidity and solvency crises. Depending on circumstances, in some cases the original push came more from the troubled Treasury (Greece, Portugal) and in other cases more from the distressed banks (Ireland, Spain), but the pernicious feedback then occurred relentlessly in both directions.

The first and foremost transmission mechanism between sovereign crises and banking crises in the absence of a lender of last resort went via the direct fiscal impact of actions to rescue financial systems. In a second round of effects, local banks were forced for reasons of profitability or

---

61 In 2012, no less than two-thirds of the stock of Spanish sovereign debt was on the books of Spanish banks. Between October 2011 and May 2012, the peak months of the crisis, Spanish banks increased their exposure to Spanish sovereign debt from approximately 40 billion to 150 billion euros, to replace the withdrawal of funds by non-Spanish banks and investors.

political pressure to buy debt from their respective governments, and so the vicious circle ("doom-loop") of banking crises and sovereign crises kept churning. The considerable resources that governments had to inject into banks to face the violent contraction of liquidity in the months immediately after the Lehman Brothers crisis in September 2008 came from State coffers. And later on, the no less massive funds for recapitalisation and/or restructuring of banking systems also came from State coffers. The greater part of the added public debt in the crisis years came from this assistance to banks. This vicious cycle of banking crisis, sovereign debt crisis, credit retrenchment, fiscal contraction and economic recession could have been strongly mitigated–or even avoided–if the markets had known that there was a lender of last resort. In most cases, the mere knowledge of the lender's existence would have made intervention unnecessary. In other cases, the resources needed to deal with the crisis would have been much less.

In recognition of this reality, in October 2011 and February 2012 the ECB arranged two operations to inject liquidity into the banks (LTRO: Longer Term Refinancing Operations), totalling one trillion euros. Underlying this was the dual purpose of providing liquidity and at the same time allowing the banks to purchase their governments' debt, from which they benefited with a juicy interest-rate arbitrage. These operations, however, provided temporary relief, but increased the banks' exposure to their countries' sovereign risk. Indirectly, the ECB was financing governments through their banks, something which greatly scandalised the Bundesbank representatives in the ECB.

None of this, however, generated the looked-for effect of restoring confidence in the stability of the euro in the countries concerned. Only the July 2012 statement of the President of the ECB, Mario Draghi, to do whatever was necessary to save the euro, and the commitment announced shortly afterwards to an aggressive program of bonds buying, known as Outright Monetary Transactions (OMT), managed to calm the markets. This was the recognition of the need for a lender of last resort by the ECB. From the second half of 2012, the ECB showed a commendable pragmatism in its actions, especially in terms of providing liquidity to troubled banks and providing liquidity to the sovereign bond market. Unfortunately, by this time most of the damage was already done.

There were two objections to this involvement of the ECB in the bond market. The first referred to the fear that bank rescues, by their expansive monetary effect, would affect strict compliance with the inflation target. The second, and more significant, had to do with the existence of a "moral hazard", which tends to create a perverse incentive for some banks to incur excessive risks or to engage in bad practices knowing that there will be a final rescuer if things do not go well. Without downplaying any of these two very fundamental objections, the truth is that those same two problems have been faced by every central bank in the world, especially the Federal Reserve. Seen in retrospect, the risks were adequately managed by the world's leading central banks.

In the 80s and 90s a consensus formed about the importance of an independent central bank with a clear mandate for price stability. After the GFC there coalesced a consensus that the stability of the financial system should be also part of the mandate of a central bank. The ECB gradually took this on board. There is now sufficient theoretical knowledge and practical experience for a balanced handling of the conflicts that necessarily appear between an anti-inflationary objective and a mandate of financial system stability. This idea to broaden the mandate was even more relevant to the central bank of a monetary union, since the very existence of the union brought additional elements of fragility and vulnerability into national financial systems. A new paradigm emerged, according to which central banks were responsible for ensuring not only price stability, but also economic growth and financial stability. The new intellectual and operational challenge of the central banks was to define the instruments and in what degree to use them to achieve these multiple objectives. It was necessary, for example, to add to the arsenal a strong supervision of the financial system. It was also necessary, once the scope of the mandate was broadened, to establish some form of political accountability and reporting, such as that of the US Federal Reserve.

The ECB's problem was that the legal framework established in Maastricht left no room for this modern view of central banks with multiple mandates. This forced the ECB to experiment with somewhat sinuous, even at times sibylline, manoeuvres to meet the objective of ensuring the financial system's stability by acting as lender of last resort.[62] A fundamental reform of the EMU Statute would have been necessary to allow

---

62 Blot, Creel, Hubert and Labondance (2014) delve into these contradictions of the ECB's actions during the crisis.

the coordination of actions in the field of monetary policy, financial regulation, bank supervision and fiscal policy. In such a reform, a mandate to meet the aforementioned triple objective should also have been made explicit. Otherwise, the ECB would have to keep climbing into the ring with one arm tied behind its back and under the permanent, opinionated, and legal harassment of those, such as the Bundesbank and a good part of the German leadership, who did not agree with this extension of its mandate.[63]

APPENDIX V-1
WAS THERE NO ALTERNATIVE? A COMPARISON BETWEEN THE GOLD STANDARD AND THE MONETARY UNION

We said at the beginning of chapter V that the very existence of the monetary union worsened the effects of the GFC in Europe. In the absence of inter-country compensatory mechanisms, the affected economies had no option but to deal with bad equilibria through the only measure possible in the framework of exchange rate rigidity: domestic deflation. The underlying problem then would be exchange rate rigidity in the absence of alternative mechanisms for adjustment and compensation. To better understand this problem, it is useful to compare the EMU with another fixed exchange rate system, the Gold Standard, because both represent a similar approach to adapting the economy in the presence of shocks.

There has been intense discussion of the role of the Gold Standard in the lead up to the onset of the Great Depression in 1929, and then in the mishandling of this crisis. Where there is consensus is that the adjustment mechanism inherent in the Gold Standard contributed to the crisis becoming virulent and spreading international contagion.[64]

How did the Gold Standard work? Even though the system dates from 1819 with the British *"Act For The Resumption of Cash Payments"*, it was only when the

---

63 Stiglitz (2016) emphatically states that "the key macroeconomic reform [of the EMU] is changing the mandate of the ECB"

64 See the classic study by Friedman and Schwartz (1963), where the authors attribute the primary responsibility of the Great Depression to the Federal Reserve, which permitted a strong monetary expansion prior to the crisis and then orchestrated a very severe contraction during it.

United States joined the scheme in 1879 that the regime reached its zenith, which lasted until the second decade of the 20th century. In this system, certainly the most transparent and successful in international monetary history, gold fulfilled the function of unit of account. The value of all national currencies was established relative to gold, the currency-to-gold parity was irrevocably fixed and money creation was backed by gold reserves. National currencies were freely convertible into gold and total freedom was meant to exist for international trading of gold bullion. Gold exports and imports would affect the quantities of money in each economy and thus set in motion the automatic adjustment of internal prices that would restore the balance of external accounts. In cases of suspension of convertibility or modification of parity for reasons of *force majeure*–such as a war–countries committed to return to the original parity once the *force majeure* disappeared.

Consequently, two key elements defined this system. The first of these was the commitment to maintain the values of national currencies at a fixed parity to gold and, by logical transitivity, at fixed parities among themselves. The second key element was the free flow of gold between countries, without any kind of constraint. Both conditions determined how national economies settled imbalances generated by perturbations, the so-called automatic "price-specie-flow" mechanism.

How did this mechanism work? For example, if a traditional wool-producing country suffered the impact of a negative disturbance, such as when wool was replaced by synthetic textiles, it would suffer a decrease in exports, an imbalance in its external trade account and a consequent depletion of its gold reserves. Halting the depletion of the gold reserves and recovering the balance of trade was only possible by restoring competitiveness through domestic deflation. This deflation–falling internal prices and wages–would happen automatically because of the monetary contraction caused by the loss of gold reserves, since there couldn't be more money in circulation than the country's reserves of gold. This mechanism was fast and efficient but extremely painful in terms of unemployment and impoverishment of workers.

Monetary union represents a still more extreme form of exchange rigidity than gold standard, since the national currencies themselves disappear and there is no provision for a country leaving the union. As with the Gold Standard, the adjustment mechanism when faced with disturbances is exclusively internal, inasmuch as it excludes the possibility of an exchange rate adjustment among the members of the union. To restore lost balance, countries adversely affected by disturbances must undertake the same arduous and painful road of domestic deflation and economic recession. The tight straitjacket imposed by this mechanism leads to pro-cyclical policies that aggravate the crisis once it breaks out.

Both systems share the same duality: they are highly beneficial in good times, but they can also be destructive and relentless in times of crisis.[65] The Gold Standard, however, had an advantage over a monetary union: it had a mechanism for temporary suspension of the system and some leeway for parity fluctuations. The countries involved kept their own currency. When a country couldn't stay in the system through *force majeure*, it could withdraw temporarily and agree to return once the adverse circumstances were overcome, at the same exchange rate to gold as at the time of withdrawal. A second element of flexibility was the existence of certain exchange rate fluctuation bands (the so-called "gold points") that allowed exchange rate mini-adjustments. In contrast, a monetary union has no exit mechanism nor bands of tolerance.

Another disadvantage of a monetary union is that it allows imbalances to build up and persist for longer, as evidenced by what happened in Europe up to 2008. The Greek disaster would not have happened under the Gold Standard, because it would have been corrected early on by way of a loss of gold or foreign exchange reserves. This would have induced a significant drop in prices and internal salaries in Greece to recover external competitiveness. This ability to adjust on the fly (self-correction) is what made the Gold Standard the most successful and longest-running international monetary system of the past two centuries. In contrast, Greece was able to maintain a current account deficit of close to 10 percent of GDP for years, because the rest of the world believed that, with Greece being part of the EMU, there was no credit or exchange risk.[66] Instead of experiencing currency outflows and monetary contraction due to the external imbalance, money continued to flow to Greece and the bean feast could keep on going. This confirmed the dangerous feature that, in good times, the mechanisms for adjustment and overcoming imbalances simply do not work in a monetary union and the imbalances accumulate. But when the wave breaks and the financial markets discover that the credit and exchange risks are very real, the adjustment happens quickly and very destructively.

---

65 Eichengreen and Tamin (2010) highlight how exchange rate rigidity facilitates trade and integration in times of peace and prosperity but compounds the problems in times of trouble.

66 Dellas and Tavlas (2014) carried out a comparative analysis of the behaviour of adjustment processes in the gold standard and the monetary union and take the case of Greece as an element of comparison.

VI

THE POLITICAL ORPHANHOOD OF THE EURO AND THE SOLIDARITY VACUUM

We now move on to other components of the euro crisis which straddle the border between economics and politics. No known monetary union has survived in the long term without being founded on a platform of political integration or at least real solidarity among the members. The closer the bonds of economic and monetary integration, the more need there is for supra-national institutions to resolve political discrepancies, give the common currency its ultimate support and solidity, collect taxes on behalf of the Community, channel resources towards members with problems, and solve distributive conflicts.

The European edifice was not equipped with this platform of political/solidarity union. There was no synchrony between the speed of economic, social and political integration. It is fair to recognize that conditions for this degree of political integration did not exist in the preparatory years of the Maastricht Treaty. But if this was so, neither did the conditions exist for the degree of monetary integration that was finally agreed upon. The initiatives of the Single Market and the European Monetary Union were a risky leap into the void. Both compelled a European-scale globalisation, for which the citizens and socio-political structures of the Community were not prepared. The founding leaders were imbued with a lot of wishfulness and much faith in the endogenous dynamics of integration that, from crisis to crisis, would supposedly unite Europeans more and more until they entered the promised land of a United Europe. Meanwhile, on the road through the desert, there was much dogmatic belief that monetary discipline would generate fiscal discipline and financial stability, making it unnecessary to resort to mechanisms of solidarity.

A monetary union is hard to imagine without a minimum component of solidarity among its members. We don't mean solidarity in the sense of a moral category, or as a criticism of the rich not helping the poor, or as a moral appeal to share wealth with strangers. In principle, no citizen is obliged to put their hand in their pocket to help a citizen of another country. Our approach is systemic and practical: in the long run, a monetary union cannot survive between countries as diverse as those of Europe unless there is some mechanism of solidarity. Germans or Austrians can do what they want with their money, but this option is not compatible with being part of a monetary union. Similarly incompatible is a free riding attitude by a member of the union improperly incurring in fiscal deficits or excesses of debt. As the saying goes, you can't have your cake and eat it; you can't be in a union and not be supportive, in the economic sense of the term. Just as you can't be a member of a club and ignore the rules of coexistence.

Solidarity is necessary to make adjustment processes viable when fundamental equilibria are broken within a monetary union. If the entire burden of adjustment falls exclusively on countries facing difficulties, the cost in terms of economic hardship is so high that it eventually calls into question the very survival of the union. In this sense, the position of Germany and the central core of the eurozone, on not assuming their proper role in a balanced adjustment process, were responsible for the eurozone crisis taking so long to overcome and the future viability of the euro being seriously questioned.

The Euro as an Orphaned and Stateless Currency

The problem starts with the euro's stateless status. As a first point, the EMU was born in the "political asepsis" of the Committee of Governors of the European central banks. It wasn't that the governors had no clear political mandate to work on the design, but that the edifice of the monetary union was not built on the foundations of a democratically legitimate institutionality with room for fiscal solidarity or a lender of last resort. To the central bankers of that era, especially those of the Bundesbank, the possibility of monetary measures being contaminated by politics was horrifying. Largely for this reason they preferred to leave the fiscal sphere completely out of the monetary union's design so that the new currency, the euro, would be politically aseptic. Moreover, the politicians were also complicit in this design: past experience justified their concern about the inhibiting effect that exchange turbulences had had on the process of European integration, so they decided to entrust the central bank technicians with the task of isolating the currency from the fiscal vicissitudes of governments. There is nothing more pleasing to the ears of a central banker than a request to make the currency independent of political whim.

The political orphanhood of the euro has another dimension, even more fundamental than the ECB's political asepsis. We refer to the fact that the European Monetary Union was built on the basis of a divorce between the currency and the State, between monetary and fiscal affairs. This was a built-in frailty in its institutional design, possibly its main Achilles' heel. Thus the euro was born as an ethereal currency, whose issuer was not a State and whose central bank had no other responsibility than preserving the value of the currency. We say "ethereal", because the new currency broke the age-old tradition of monetary regimes in which States were the issuers of money, the creators and guarantors of the currency's value, the ultimate support of the financial system. Money, especially modern money, is a fiduciary instrument, a promise of payment which the public trust, a debt of an issuing authority. Chartalist theory postulates that money can only exist on the foundations of a legitimate centralised political entity, as a legal creation of the State, in opposition to "commodity" money, which only has intrinsic value.

The eminently political nature of national currencies does give them inherent fragility, because currencies are exposed to the political vicissitudes of the States that issue them. Fiscal storms may certainly undermine the stability of the currency, but when this happens, only the State has the ability to correct its mistakes, change course and restore the triple status of the currency as unit of measure, medium of exchange and store of value. The State, therefore, may be a source of instability, but at the same time it is the last bastion of the currency's strength, especially in times of great difficulty.

At the outset, Germany would have preferred to see the European Monetary Union built on the basis of a prior political union, but that did not appeal to France, always very jealous of not giving up its political sovereignty. The final compromise was that fiscal matters remained under the sovereign authority of States, to satisfy France, but the Treaty of Maastricht created an extremely orthodox monetary framework in defence of the stability of the euro, to satisfy Germany. This framework had to somehow replace or supplement the absence of legitimate political support for the euro. The German ordoliberal notion prevailed, according to which the euro would be embedded in a robust monetary order, integrating its member States in a supra-national community governed by regulations based on the rule of law, the free market and the inviolability of money.[67] The independence of the European Central Bank was the main constituent element of that monetary order. The member States were mandated to conform to the monetary order, to become mere executors of the regulations and to implement their national policies, especially the fiscal ones, in such a way as to not threaten the stability of the currency. That is why the central-banking architects of the system did not consider the euro to be such an orphan currency. They could not imagine that narrow national interests could someday prevail over the sacrosanct framework of the rules of the monetary order.

The stubborn reality was that the interests of governments were often not aligned with the requirements of the monetary order. The supra-national entelechy that order had supposedly created did not withstand the ravages of various economic shocks. Europe, beyond the Community rhetoric, was not a State, nor even a Federation of States. There were no fundamental institutions to carry out the functions of a State, such as a single tax authority, a defence establishment holding the monopoly on military power, or a political entity to back the currency. What existed in Brussels was not a government, but a tangle of intergovernmental agencies that tried to reconcile the interests of 28 very different countries.

The Global Financial Crisis came to reassert the importance of the idea that the State is the ultimate creator of money, the ultimate guarantor of its value, and the ultimate protector of the financial system. In a financially hyper-globalised world, there is a very high likelihood of a national banking system experiencing crisis at some point. That's when it is vital that there be a lender of last resort. The fact that it is the central

---

67 See Bonefeld (2016)

bank that acts as such a lender should not obscure the reality that the State will always be "the lender to the lender of last resort". The fiscal budget will always end up assuming the burden. The euro did not have this strength, because neither the currency nor the European Central Bank had a united European entity backing them.

Is a monetary union possible without a political union?

It has often been asserted that, in the long term, a monetary union without political union is not viable. The assertion seems to be reinforced by the fact that none of the various monetary unions in history managed to survive without the support of political union. Cohen (2003) asks this question and tries to answer it through a historical analysis of several attempts at monetary union, most of them unsuccessful, and concludes that economic ties alone are not enough to give coherence to a monetary union. A monetary union implies a supra-national delegation of important sovereign decisions. This is acceptable and sustainable only when the members share priorities and institutional and cultural ties that make them partners in a common cause. These ties are expressed in a broad web of institutional interrelationships that reflect a genuine sense of solidarity and community spirit among the countries involved. The great difficulty and length of time needed to create such a web explain why relatively few currency unions have lasted long. Europe's took several decades and remains a work in progress.

If we turn to what is so far the most successful monetary union in history, the United States of America, we find that it started with a fiscal union and then transitioned to monetary unification.[68] Simultaneously with the ratification of the Constitution in 1789, much of the powers of raising taxes, borrowing and spending of public resources moved to the federal level. It was not until 1863, with the National Currency Act, that the federal dollar was established as the single currency of the United States. The Federal Reserve system was established in 1913.

From the dream-manifesto written by Altiero Spinelli, Ernesto Rossi and Eugenio Colorni on Ventotene island in 1941, through the other

---

68 See Frankel (2015) and McNamara (2016)

founding fathers such as Schuman, Monnet, Adenauer and de Gasperi, they all visualised economic and monetary integration as milestones on a journey towards political integration, be it in the form of a Federation of States or even as a great new European State. The Frenchman Robert Schuman put it explicitly when he presented his Coal and Steel Community Plan in 1950. Jean Monnet pushed it in 1954 with the creation of the Action Committee for the United States of Europe. Four decades later, German Chancellor Helmut Kohl, in his speech to defend the proposal for monetary union in the Maastricht Treaty before the Federal Parliament on the 6th of November 1991, stated emphatically: "*It cannot be repeated often enough: Political union is the indispensable counterpart to economic and monetary union. Recent history, and not just that of Germany, teaches us that the idea of sustaining an economic and monetary union over time without political union is a fallacy*". Kohl could not have more clearly and forcefully established the link between the sphere of monetary union and that of political union. Equally striking was Chancellor Merkel twenty years later when in an interview on June 7, 2012 on the German television station ARD said: "*We need more Europe, we need not only a monetary union, but also a fiscal union, in other words, more common budgetary policy. And above all we need a political union, i.e. we need to gradually give powers to Europe, give control to Europe*".

Both the political and the technocratic forces that drove the creation of the euro were also convinced that the monetary union was not possible in the long run without political union. But given that at the moment of its creation political integration was not viable, they thought that the common currency would step up the pace towards political integration and finally end in a United Europe. This was not, nevertheless, Germany's idea as regards the sequence and precedence of the spheres of integration. In this, as in many other things, the opinions of the two main European bastions, France and Germany, diverged, although in the end they would usually reach agreement and when consensus was not possible, one of the two would yield in a civilized *quid pro quo*.

France called for the "monetarist" view (not to be confused with the concept of monetarism associated with Milton Friedman), according to which the introduction of the common currency would spark an endogenous process of greater integration in all fields, including the political. The French economist Jacques Rueff affirmed that "*Europe will be built by its currency, or it will not be built at all"* (*"L'Europe se fera par la monaie ou ne se fera pas"*). France's idea of political union, however, did not go beyond a loose confederation of nation-States (*L'Europe des Patries*), in which national sovereignties were preserved. Ultimate power would not lie with the European Commission or the European Parliament, but with intergovernmental bodies, from the European Council on down. Of course, the French expectation was always that Paris would become the *de facto* political capital of Europe.[69]

Germany, for its part, defended the "economist" view, according to which the introduction of the common currency should be the final step, the culmination of a process of increasing economic and political integration. Helmut Kohl's emphatic defence, mentioned above, in favour of a political union as a necessary condition for the survival of the euro, should be understood in this context. Four decades before, Konrad Adenauer also spoke unequivocally in favour of the primacy and precedence of political integration. Both, however, had to resign themselves, when faced with the difficulty of moving on the political front first, and accept the reality that France's priority was economic and monetary integration without concessions of political sovereignty. In the end, the French approach prevailed and the common currency was introduced before progress was made towards political integration.

However, with the benefit of hindsight, it would not be true to say that Germany was more in favour of political union than France as a precondition for the survival of the common currency. For much of the German political and bureaucratic establishment, the rhetoric about unity was, so to speak, a means of dragging their feet on a proposal they had no sympathy with, as it involved abandoning their beloved deutschmark. It was a way of saying that Europe was not yet ready for a common currency. Indirect confirmation of this interpretation is given by Germany's unwillingness to accept, both then and now, an element without which one can hardly speak of political union: fiscal solidarity. Any scheme involving the future possibility of a commitment to transfer fiscal resources to third countries without compensation was flatly rejected by Germany. Hence,

---

69 Otero-Iglesias (2014) of the Instituto Real Elcano goes into the peculiar relationship between France and Germany, in which the former dominated politically, to the point where nothing substantial moved in Europe without French acquiescence, while the latter used the French political leadership to its advantage.

fiscal integration was conspicuous by its absence in the architecture of the Maastricht Treaty.

Going in tandem with France allowed Germany to maintain an openly pro-political-union rhetoric, because it knew that its partner France would not allow excessive moves in that direction. After the euro crisis broke out, the German establishment gradually abandoned even the rhetoric, because public opinion was increasingly suspicious of pro-European solutions that implied having to open their wallets at some point. This happened particularly after Merkel felt cornered in the European Council in mid-2012, when her eurozone partners pressed her to move forward with the creation of the banking union, which necessarily included some form of common bank deposit guarantee. That sounded like a transfer union, Germany's greatest anathema.

If, as we said earlier, a monetary union needs some degree of political union, how has the euro lasted so long and overcome a crisis of the magnitude of the US sub-prime debacle, followed by the sovereign debt crisis of the European periphery? Could the link between both unions be not that essential? The answer to these questions must begin by recognising that reality is not usually black and white. When the euro was born, there already existed in Europe a non-negligible degree of supra-national institutionalism, of Community agencies that had taken on the decision-making power of governments to a significant degree. Certainly, there was no European State or Federation of European States with the symbols and rituals of a sovereign nation, but the European countries shared a fair number of institutions, functions, or attributions, which are typically essential elements of a political union. In short, the cradle where the euro was born was not a disparate group of nations, but an entity with a certain degree of political integration. We refer to institutions such as the European Parliament, the European Court of Justice or the European Commission, which represented the three powers (legislative, judicial and executive) constituting a liberal democracy within the framework of the Rule of Law. Moreover, the European Central Bank was a totally supra-national institution, perhaps the most European of them all, the most independent and farthest from the influences and vicissitudes of the governments of individual countries.

It was in this context that the euro was born, within the framework that had been building slowly since the birth of the European Economic

Community in the mid-50s. To deny these advances of European integration would be to deny the obvious. Now, these levels of integration were enough to see the emergence of the ESM, the Single Market and the EMU. They were also enough to make the monetary union prosper during almost its first decade of life, backed by the prosperity and stability of the worldwide "great moderation" before the GFC. The orphanhood of which we spoke in the previous section did not stand out in the normality of day-to-day affairs but did do so in the exceptional times that put European solidarity to the test. The test arrived with all its harshness when the Eurocrisis blew up in 2010. That is when the structure of the EMU's edifice began to creak and quiver.

Political union or solidarity union?

Unlike those who attribute the vulnerability of the euro project mainly to an insufficient degree of political union, we are convinced that the real shortcoming was not European nations' resistance to yielding their sovereignty to a United Europe, but rather the reluctance of individual countries to deal with the imbalances of wealth between them, to share the burdens of realignment when the crisis came knocking at the doors of some members, or to establish risk-sharing schemes. The key word is solidarity, understood not as generosity, charity or handouts, but as mechanisms to make it viable to restore the economic balance of the affected members, in a time and at a cost that would be politically reasonable.

We saw in earlier chapters that the crucial flaw in the design of the Monetary Union was that it did not foresee the mechanisms and institutions that could deal with the remarkably high initial degree of diversity of its members: misaligned exchange rates, dissimilar production structures, disparate unemployment rates, divergent fiscal cultures, different inflationary traditions and diverse labour markets. At the time, most of those responsible for taking the Union forward did not have a realistic view of these disparities and asymmetries. Others professed a blind faith in the subsequent capacity that the Monetary Union would have to generate procedures on the fly for overcoming disparities. In the good times, when the lake is swollen with water, a sailor doesn't worry about shoals, but when the water level drops, many shoals come to the surface. That is when tools and institutions are needed to navigate in difficult waters.

The central message of the theory of Optimum Currency Areas is clear: if there are asymmetric disparities and disturbances among members of a monetary union, there must be sufficient compensatory mechanisms to facilitate rebalancing its economies. Labour force mobility and flexibility of prices and wages are the two adjustment mechanisms that should work as a first line of defence, but in their absence there may be nothing for it but to organise fiscal transfers, sovereign debt guarantees or bank deposit guarantees. At the end of the day, some countries must be willing to provide resources to other countries to help them out of difficulties.

We insist that a monetary union requires a minimum of solidarity, one of whose main expressions is for its members to share burdens and risks, even to the point of supporting the debt of a member country in trouble. Obviously, mechanisms must have been previously put in place to avoid (or mitigate to a reasonable degree) fiscal indiscipline, free riding and moral hazard from one country to the detriment of others. Given the negative incentives to behave badly, and the effects of contagion, it is essential to formulate supra-national rules for healthy fiscal and financial behaviour, and to provide effective means to ensure compliance with them. All of these precautions, monitoring and sanctions must be present, but in the end crises always occur and there must exist some form of fiscal union with the possibility of transferring resources between members.

If the matter were as simple as lending money to one another and getting it back later, there wouldn't be much to discuss. But when the transfer of resources has no chance of being repaid, something much more solid and indisputable that an act of selfless solidarity is required. Why should the citizens of one country be forced to pay taxes to get those of another country out of a problem which they very probably generated themselves? Unilateral fiscal transfers have direct distributive implications because they move wealth from citizens of one country to citizens of another. This is where the political dimension of the problem comes fully into play. These compensatory transfers only seem possible within the framework of a superior political understanding, of an institutionalism that brings together the various nations that make up the monetary union. It need not necessarily be a new United States of

Europe or a Single European Budget, but an entity with ties sufficiently solid to sustain resource transfers with no return. Such an institutional framework must also have sufficient democratic legitimacy to administer these transfers of wealth and to impose rules for good behaviour on member States.

The hardships of the eurocrisis did not make the EU advance far enough in the direction of fiscal solidarity. On the contrary, during the development of the crisis and its aftermath, Germany was emphatic in defending the principle that no solution or scheme undertaken to address the problem could end up with any kind of unilateral transfer between countries of the union. "*The Monetary Union is not a transfer union*", was a theme constantly repeated by the German leadership. It was this principle which blocked all proposed schemes, for example to endorse or pool the sovereign debt of the countries of the union, to establish a mechanism for the resolution of banking crises, to create a European system of bank deposit guarantees or to write off part of the Greek debt. Any of these mechanisms would have been enough to stop in their tracks crisis developments which later turned out to be very costly, not only for the countries immediately affected, but also for the EMU as a whole.

Unequal sharing of the burden of adjustment

The meagre performance of peripheral European economies until several years after the GFC ended puts the spotlight on a central problem of the crisis resolution process within the EMU. It is assumed that in a community of countries that are part of a monetary union, in which there are surplus and deficit countries, countries with high unemployment and low unemployment, the burdens on the road to the recovery of equilibria should be shared. This means, in particular, that surplus countries should expand their economies to help those in deficit to overcome the imbalance more quickly. Countries with low inflation should allow it to rise to facilitate the recovery of competitiveness of countries in crisis. None of this happened in the eurozone: the lion's share of the burden of economic rebalancing fell on the deficit countries. Worse still, the restrictive policies of the buoyant countries often contributed to increase the load and make the process of recovery even slower and more painful. Germany, instead of expanding public spending, reduced it and contributed to the 32 percent fiscal retrenchment of the whole eurozone between 2010 and 2014.[70]

Mundell had already stated this in 1961, in his simple model of the adjustment process between two countries, whose smooth operation was a necessary condition for creating a monetary area (see a detailed explanation in Appendix VI-1). It is inherent to the economic life of nations that adverse situations may crop up, in the form of disturbances that can be endogenous as well as exogenous, self-inflicted as well as blameless. When these disturbances asymmetrically affect countries that are related by monetary or trade ties, they must work to adjust their economies and restore the lost balance with their partners. This will mean adjusting some key economic variables, such as the level of public spending, interest rates or the exchange rate.

The exchange rate is the key variable for restoring external imbalances. The problem of countries that are part of a monetary union is that they can no longer use the exchange rate to restore balance between them; they have lost the most valuable tool for adjustment. For this reason the fathers of the theory of Optimum Currency Areas stressed that a group of countries or regions should not give up their currencies unless they had alternative mechanisms or instruments available to compensate and replace the loss of the exchange rate instrument. As we mentioned in the previous chapter, in the absence of the exchange rate variable, these mechanisms were, among others, flexibility of prices and wages, mobility of the labour force and fiscal transfers.

One of the assumptions of the theory is that adjustments in the member countries should be coordinated. In other words, if, for example, negatively-affected countries need to reduce domestic wages and prices to restore competitiveness, surplus countries should stimulate their economies, increase salaries, accept higher inflation and thus reduce their current account surplus. And if a group of countries experiences a sudden reversal of external financing, the creditor countries should establish financial support schemes to avoid an abrupt and disorderly slide towards recession in the debtor countries. Only by the surplus/creditor members thus helping with the rebalancing of the deficit/debtor members can the monetary union be viable in the long term. Otherwise, the plight of those

---

70 See Baldwin and Giavazzi (2015)

who suffer adverse shocks not only hinders the economic performance of the union as a whole, but also erodes political support for the union itself. Even the citizens of creditor countries day by day feel more reasons to disconnect from the union.

In the eurozone crisis, most of the burden of adjustment fell on the debtor countries of the periphery. The prescription of "austerity, come what may" reflected this unbalanced view of what should be an adjustment process in a monetary union. By putting all the weight on one side, the intensity of the fiscal cutbacks, real salary cuts and debt reduction in debtor countries had to be severe. The irony is that, in the end, creditors were also affected, because the non-viability of the austerity programs made economic growth in the eurozone languish for many years. The unviability of Greek debt, for example, prevailed and creditors had to accept important write-offs. The European Central Bank had to lose its virginity and act as a lender of last resort from 2012.

For a system to work, it must act as such in all of its parts. The parts in surplus should let the automatic internal adjustment mechanisms work in them as well. If the burden of adjustment falls exclusively on the members in deficit, the magnitude of the effort and sacrifice makes the adjustment economically, socially and politically unfeasible. For some countries to be able to deflate their domestic prices and regain competitiveness, others must inflate their own. Financial surpluses must be put back in circulation.

When Germany and other core countries should have increased spending and accepted higher inflation, what happened was the opposite. The core of Europe continued with its traditional aversion to inflation, however small, and to fiscal expansion. It is very difficult for a monetary union to survive in the long term on the basis of this unbalanced distribution of adjustment effort. The reality is that, without higher inflation in the European central core, it was not viable for the periphery to implement enough internal deflation to close productivity gaps in a reasonable time and at a reasonable cost. The immediate consequence of this unbalanced process is that the gap between the centre and the periphery of Europe became wider.

Unfortunately, the European discussion took on a tone of Manichaeism that ignored the systemic nature of the crisis and its solution. The "orthodox" approach–ordoliberalism, as we'll define it later–which was imposed by Germany and seconded by its Centre-North European allies, classified members of the eurozone into two groups, the good and the bad: those who had done their job and abided by the rules (the good guys at the centre-north), and those who had squandered, cheated and broken the rules (the bad guys at the periphery). The bad had to assume the consequences of their actions under the chastening guidance of the good. This moralistic rhetoric was dressed up with arguments about the need for structural reforms. The dangerous thing about this discourse was that it exempted the good guys from their systemic responsibility of assuming their part of the adjustment.

The (difficult) political economy of the adjustment

A second element to the detriment of the debtors, on top of the imbalance in the distribution of the adjustment burden, was the slow pace of the debt restructuring process, the indecision, the setbacks, all of which contributed to aggravating an already very serious situation. There was certainly no surfeit of expertise at the technical levels of the EMU, but the main explanation for this destructive slowness must be sought in the eminently political character of the decisions to be taken. These decisions differentially affected power relationships, both among members of the Union and within countries.

Every debt crisis produces conflicts and political and social divisions both between creditor and debtor countries, and within the debtor countries, and even within the creditor countries.[71] The conflict revolves around who should bear the burden of bringing the debt down to manageable proportions: at the inter-country level the obvious question is whether the burden should fall solely on the debtors or be shared by the creditors; within the debtor countries, the debate is about how much sacrifice each group in society must make to generate the surpluses that allow the debt to be served; and within the creditor countries the conflict arises over who should absorb any eventual debt write-offs, the taxpayers or the bondholders.

By definition, in a monetary union the only form of rebalancing is via the modification of internal prices and wages. Theoretically, this internal

---

71 Ver Frieden, (2014) and Matthijs, (2013) for a more detailed development of the political economy dynamics of adjustment processes.

adjustment can be achieved by means of deflation in debtor countries, inflation in creditor countries or a combination of both. If deflation is chosen, the main burden will fall on the debtor countries and, within them, on the workers. If the route is inflation, the load will fall on the creditors and, within them, on the owners of capital and rents.

It might seem obvious that those who absorb adjustment burdens will be the debtors, but this has not always been so in episodes of debt crisis at other times in history. In the crisis of the first half of the 1930s, for example, the debtors had the whip hand and retained a strong negotiating position. In the Latin American debt crisis of the 1980s, on the contrary, the creditors could impose their conditions and the burden of adjustment fell mainly on debtors. During the exchange crisis of 1992-93 in Europe, the bargaining power was distributed fairly evenly between creditors and debtors.

In relations between creditors and debtors, each group has its negotiating weapons, some of them very powerful. The main weapon of the debtor is to withhold payment and cause serious economic damage to the creditor. The creditor's weapon is to expel the debtor from the international financial community and close future access to financial resources. The balance of costs and benefits in the case of a default is complex because there is no free lunch for anyone, neither the debtor nor the creditor. In addition to purely economic considerations, in the case of a monetary union the political costs of being expelled can be as high or higher than the financial ones. It can also be extremely costly for creditors to force a member out, because that would sow the seeds of disintegration.

Within the debtor countries, the political dispute revolves around which sectors of society and to what degree they should support the burden. Governments must make difficult decisions because each set of actions affects social groups differently. According to what decisions are taken, those principally affected can be employees, or taxpayers in general, or the beneficiaries of social programs, or financial institutions–shareholders or bondholders–or savers, or pensioners, or consumers, or a long *et cetera*. The decision to default or not in itself affects society in different ways: for example, if export sector or financial sector interests prevail, the route of default will not be taken, as happened in the case of Spain. Within the creditor countries, at some point there will also have to be some sacrifice, however small, in the form of debt relief, interest reduction or lengthening of terms. The government will have to decide if the sacrifice will be borne by the fiscal budget, i.e. by taxpayers, or be absorbed by the lending banks or the central bank.

Each decision, on either side, has serious distributional implications and, therefore, high social and political consequences. When the heads of government of creditor and debtor countries sat at the negotiating table in Brussels, Berlin or Madrid, their respective constituencies and opinion groups paid close attention to what was being decided. German Chancellor Merkel might have had some sympathy for the hardships the debtor countries were going through, but she had to keep winning elections in Germany. She could not over-irritate the dominant public opinion, which firmly believed that debtors had to atone for their sins, and that it was unacceptable for German taxpayers to have to dip into their wallets to rescue bankrupt countries. All the while the Greek Prime Minister had to give political weight to whether closing the fiscal gap was going to be handled by making the rich pay or by reducing benefits to the unemployed and pensioners.

On a different point, the collateral effect of the unbalanced manner in which adjustment policies were handled was the erosion of democratic legitimacy, both at the level of Community institutions and at that of national governments, especially in debtor countries. The low-income majorities in these countries felt that the greater part of the burden was falling on their shoulders. The debtor governments, for their part, saw their sovereignty stripped away by having to hand over to European institutions power over such important issues as fiscal budgets, banking supervision or the welfare benefits of their citizens. Europe thus became fertile soil for the emergence of political instability, anti-European sentiments, nationalism and populism.

Appendix VI-1

TWO MODELS OF ADJUSTMENT AND BURDEN SHARING

Figure VI-1 illustrates the bilateral Mundellian mechanism of price and domestic wage adjustment when the exchange rate cannot be used as the policy variable, as happens in a monetary union. If this mechanism is allowed to operate without interference, both countries, the one in deficit and the one in surplus, share the burdens of adjustment equally.

FIGURE VI-1
Automatic bilateral adjustment mechanism

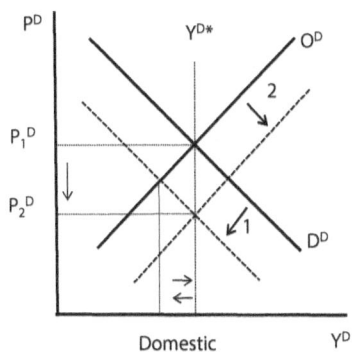
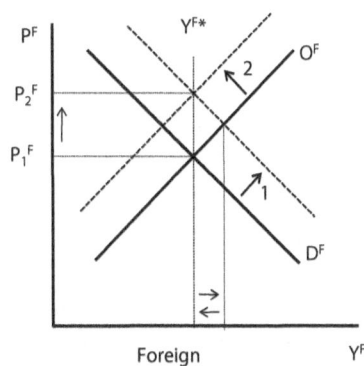

The graph on the left shows the aggregate supply and demand lines of the domestic country D and the one on the right the aggregate supply and demand lines of the foreign country F. Suppose that country D suffers a fall in external demand for its exports. As a first step, this fall displaces the domestic aggregate demand line D^D downward, and at the same time moves the line of aggregate demand in the foreign country D^F upward (step 1: displacement of the solid demand lines towards the dotted lines). In words, the fall in domestic demand implies that to maintain the same level of economic activity Y^D, domestic prices should fall from P_1^D to P_2^D; if prices do not fall, economic activity should drop. In reality, the drop in demand ends in a combination of falling economic activity and price reductions determined by the new point of intersection of the dotted demand line with the solid supply line O^D, which initially does not move. That is to say, in the domestic country the fall in demand for its exports generates a fall in the level of activity (employment), reduced prices (deflation) and current account deficit.

In the foreign country (right-hand side of the figure) there is a mirror effect: the increased demand induces an increase of activity and employment, inflationary pressures and current-account surplus. Graphically, this effect manifests as a displacement of the demand line D^F upwards and to the right, since the higher demand with a fixed initial supply translates into higher prices (step 1).

In a second step, what is the impact of these shifts in demand on the supply and on the price level? Supposing that prices and wages are flexible and that the authorities do not interfere through exchange rate manipulations or in other ways; or to put it another way, supposing that the internal automatic adjustment mechanism is allowed to function, incipient domestic unemployment will exert downward pressure on wage levels, diminishing the marginal cost of the work force and stimulating employers to increase the level of activity for the same level of prices. This readiness of business to use a larger work force and increase production is graphically represented by a displacement of the line of aggregate domestic supply O^D towards the right (step 2: displacement of the solid supply lines towards the dotted ones). This displacement (increment) of supply will continue until the point at which the economy returns to its initial equilibrium level of full employment, which is the level of economic activity Y^D at which the original supply and demand converged. That is to say, economic activity initially decreases (step 1) and then returns (step 2) to its previous level (this descent and subsequent recovery is shown by the two arrows in the figure).

Success in recovering full employment will depend on the domestic economy being allowed to reduce price levels sufficiently (deflation) so that the new dotted lines of supply and demand are at the original level of economic activity. The increase of supply induced by the fall of real wages will reduce the initial unemployment and increase production, but at the expense of causing a further fall in domestic price levels (up to P_2^D). Additional deflation will reinforce the relative improvement of domestic competitiveness and will also restore equilibrium in the balance of payments.

In the foreign country, as in a mirror, the expansion of economic activity beyond the potential level of initial equilibrium will cause an excess demand for work force and an increase in wage levels. The increase in real wage costs will discourage the use of manpower, reduce economic activity and raise the general level of prices up to P_2^F, all of which is expressed graphically with the displacement of the aggregate supply line O^F towards the new dotted line at the left (step 2). But as initially there was an increase in demand and a corresponding shift of the demand line to the right (step 1), the new equilibrium level of greater demand and less supply will be found on returning to the full employment point of economic activity, but at a higher price level (inflation). The consequent fall in competitiveness will help eliminate the surplus of the balance of payments and restore external equilibrium.

At the end of the process, and if the factor markets are operating smoothly, the domestic economy will have been able to restore employment and productive activity to its previous potential or equilibrium level, but at the cost of deflation. The foreign economy will also return to its real equilibrium level, but at the cost of inflation. An advantage of this automatic adjustment mechanism is that both countries share the adjustment burdens equally, provided none of them creates obstacles to the adjustment of prices and wages. The negative side of the process is that both countries end up with unwanted price levels and that the path to restoring balance can be very costly in terms of unemployment in the domestic country and an acceleration of inflation in the foreign country.

Suppose now that the surplus (foreign) country is opposed to stimulating its economy and accepting a certain amount of inflation. In this case, the foreign country adopts the monetary and fiscal policies needed to counteract the increased demand and keep its previous price level and economic activity. This situation is described on the right-hand side of Figure IV-2, which shows that nothing happens.

FIGURE VI-2
Unilateral adjustment mechanism

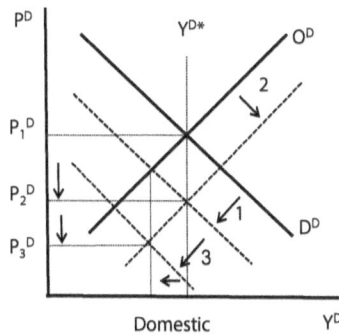
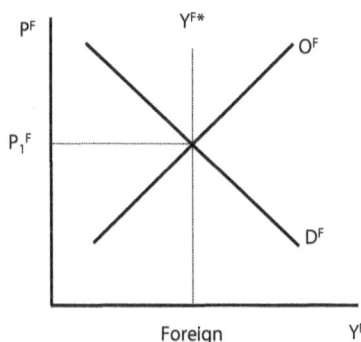

In the deficit (domestic) country, however, the refusal of the surplus country to collaborate with the adjustment forces the deficit member of the union to a further reduction of demand and greater deflation (step 3). This is so because with the foreign country keeping to the same price level, the domestic country needs to further reduce its domestic prices and salaries in order to regain its competitiveness and re-establish equilibrium. A further contraction in aggregate demand (more austerity) contributes to this process of deflation. Graphically this is reflected in a new downward shift of the demand line and a further fall of the price level to P_3^D. This unleashes a new dynamic of improving competitiveness, which is not graphically plotted in the figure. The greater domestic deflation may, via greater competitiveness, be able to stimulate greater supply and to recover something of the lost level of economic activity, but the end result will always be harder for the domestic country than the scenario shown in the Figure VI-1, in which the surplus country collaborates with the adjustment.

VII

LOST INSTITUTIONALITY, HIERARCHICAL GOVERNANCE AND DEMOCRATIC DEFICIT

After the preceding reflections in the field of political economy, from this chapter on we will be delving into the realm of politics. During the financial crisis tectonic shifts took place in how European institutions operated, which in turn reflected changes in the power relations within the EU. Henry Kissinger famously asked which phone number to call when one wanted to speak with Europe. With the events subsequent to 2008, no-one was in any doubt that to communicate with Europe the number to dial began with +4930, the Berlin area code.

More than institutional changes, we should speak rather of the de-institutionalisation of the framework of the European Union. Between Europe not being prepared, the crisis not being properly managed and its virulence forcing decisions to be taken from one emergency to the next, the EU institutions of government were first displaced by intergovernmentalism of the Heads of State in the European Council and then by German dictates. In this way, the deficit of democratic legitimacy that had been dragging on the EU and EMU since their inception was exacerbated.

The blizzard of the euro crisis swept away the principles of governance that had been so laboriously built up in previous decades. The liberal principle that the rules of the free market would take care of disciplining member countries was consecrated at the heart of the treaties constituting the union. Sovereign debt (mis)management, for example, was rewarded or punished by financial markets with risk premiums and the (un)availability of sources of funding. With the euro crisis, however, creditor governments, not markets, began to decide whether to grant or deny financial resources, set interest rates and impose adjustment programmes on the debtors. The universal and anonymous rules were replaced by the authoritarian discretion of a few leaders.

The *quid pro quo* of receiving bailouts in exchange for drastic adjustment programmes imposed by creditors clashed with the rules of coexistence that had prevailed heretofore, which had no place for this kind of imposed top-down management. And if affected citizens also perceived that the inner circles of the Community were giving special privileges to large corporate interests or to those of the hegemonic country, the stage was set for a growing disaffection with the entities known as the European Union or the European Monetary Union.

Europe became also trapped in a dysfunctional triangle between national policies, European policies and globalised markets.[72] Brussels wrote the rules, but politicians took the decisions in power bargaining, where what dominated were the respective national interests. Politicians from 28 nations took decisions under pressure from their national constituencies, which were increasingly guided by matrices of opinion opposed to the integrationist logic. And if wasn't their electorates, then the financial markets took care to instil terror when the decisions were not to their liking. This was not, by a long stretch, the best way to give governance to a political and monetary union.

Bad management, de-institutionalisation and discretion: from Brussels to Berlin

We argued in the previous chapter that it is difficult for a monetary union to survive without a supportive political umbrella. What further aggravates the difficulties is when mistakes are also made in handling the crisis, either by erroneous and ideologically-driven diagnoses or by poor management. Furthermore, dismantling the existing institutions to give way to discretionary decision-making, with the centre of power moved from Brussels to Berlin, was of no help at all. In this transition to discretionary decisions, these necessarily became less technical and more political.

---

72 See Garton Ash, (2012).

With regards to the macro-management of the eurozone crisis, Eurocrats and politicians did not have the assertiveness (or humility) to draw on the extensive experience accumulated in the world in the area of crisis resolution. This led them to make mistakes and to undertake a costly process of trial and error. The responses to the crises were late, incomplete and excessively subject to interference by politicians, who showed little understanding of the complexity of the problems and scant willingness to acknowledge mistakes.

The speed and quality of response of the EU institutions did not match the urgency and magnitude of the tasks that national governments had to undertake to resolve the fundamental weaknesses of their economies. It was up to these institutions to design general frameworks that would facilitate the successful implementation of policies at national levels. However, the European institutions were not in tune with the urgency and gravity of the problems.

The handling of the Greek debt crisis was an example of this management style: it merely kicked the can down the road rather than facing the real problem of that country's insolvency. The resolution of the banking crisis in other countries was also unduly delayed: Spain, with the connivance of the European agencies responsible, kicked that ball around for about three years. In the case of the Italian banks, the lack of definition and action lasted even longer. The European Central Bank took three years to accept the responsibility of ensuring not only price stability, but also financial stability.

In addition to managerial dilettantism, the eurozone suffered from a fundamental problem: there was a mismatch between the levels of responsibility and the levels of authority.[73] To handle a crisis, both dimensions have to work at the same level and be properly enmeshed. If the responsibility to resolve a banking crisis, for example, resides in the individual country where the banks are located, the authority and the means to initiate the rescue should also exist at that national level. Typically, the entity with the authority and means to solve a systemic banking crisis is a central bank. However, in 1999 the national central banks had delegated to the European Central Bank the only effective tool for addressing a

---

73 A contradiction highlighted by Paul de Grauwe in his contribution to the book edited by Baldwin and Giavazzi (2015)

systemic banking crisis: their capacity to act as lender of last resort on behalf of the State. The individual governments of the eurozone did not have sufficient means to rescue their troubled banks. When they initially tried to do so, levels of government debt soared, bond buyers retreated, and the crisis metamorphosed into twin banking and sovereign crises. Only the promise of Mario Draghi in July 2012 to do whatever it took to save the euro managed to stop this diabolical downward spiral in its tracks. Finally, the ECB, which did have both the authority and the means, assumed the responsibility as well.

From that moment on, the ECB took over the reins of managing the eurozone crisis. Its monetary actions helped to weather the storm and led to a gradual emergence from the pit of recession, because the EMU had neither the capacity nor the fiscal institutions to deal with the difficulties. The problem with this drift of crisis management is that it took it completely out of the reach of democratic political control. A central bank like the ECB, with the mandate of unrestricted political independence, is an essentially authoritarian (undemocratic) entity that is responsible to no-one.[74]

The eurozone crisis also to a large extent blew apart the EU institutional framework that had worked relatively well in times of normality. In its first stages, the EU institutions and bodies (the European Commission, the Commissioners, the Parliament) were fairly capable of handling the consequences of the crisis. When the Greek debt crisis blew up, however, management of the rescue had to be outsourced to a triumvirate, called the Troika, composed of the European Commission, the European Central Bank and the International Monetary Fund (an entity external to Europe). This was the first recognition that the problem had surpassed the managerial capacity of the political and technical Community bodies, which had neither the expertise nor the financial muscle to deal with the problem, while the ECB and the IMF had both in abundance.

It soon became evident, especially when after the Greek crisis the Irish and Portuguese crises hatched, that the European institutions did not have the financial resources to rescue members in trouble. In the second half of 2010, the European Financial Stability Fund and the Securities

---

[74] Schneider and Sandbeck (2018) attribute the drift of the eurozone towards what they call "authoritarian statism" to the dominant role of the ECB.

Markets Program were created and given certain funds, which turned out to be insufficient. The eurozone crisis had reached a magnitude that required the mobilisation of additional funds, which only the Member States of the EMU could make available.

Governing to prevent a crisis is not the same as paying to repair the damage once it has blown up. When it was time to reach for their wallets, to make contributions to the European Financial Stability Fund and then to its permanent successor, the European Stability Mechanism, governments were no longer willing to let the EU institutions and their officials make decisions on how much to contribute and to whom to deliver funds. Nor was it easy to make these decisions in a macrocephalic European Commission composed of officials from 28 member countries. In that moment Europe, and more particularly the eurozone, entered into a new stage of governance based on intergovernmental relations, on direct negotiations between governments.

The European Commission began to give way to the European Council, where sat Heads of State in person, rather than Community officials. Each new episode of the crisis called for a new Summit of Heads of State. That's where the fundamental decisions began to be taken, relegating the European Commission to the role of executor of the policies and guidelines emanating from the European Council. The urgency imposed by events gave pre-eminence to the intergovernmental framework, represented by the European Council, the Councils of Ministers and the Eurogroup, to the detriment of the earlier institutional architecture that revolved around the European Commission and the European Parliament.

It is true that the European Council was also a core body in the original EU architecture, but one of an eminently political nature which had not been designed or prepared to supplant and consolidate all power of decision. For a long time, the main divergence within Europe had been between the "supra-nationalists", who advocated a Community government centred on the European Commission with all its related bodies, and the "intergovernmentalists", who preferred to govern the life of the Community through direct negotiations between the Heads of State meeting in the European Council. In fact, Europe had travelled a considerable distance along the path towards supra-nationalism before 2008, that being the natural way towards more Europe and less mosaic-of-nations. Nonetheless, the progress made in overcoming excessive early intergovernmentalism and replacing it with supra-governmental bodies and mechanisms was in great measure reversed by the effects of the crisis. Even Germany, under the leadership of Merkel, moved on from its previous supra-nationalism to the intergovernmental model. When intergovernmentalism was finally imposed, a new dividing line emerged between the members of the European Community: those who assumed the intergovernmentalism of the European Commission as the channel for collective action, and the Eurosceptic nationalists who, like the United Kingdom, were not in tune with the idea of other governments deciding on their sovereign destiny.[75]

This inexorable path towards de-institutionalisation was accelerating in the same degree that the crisis was speeding up. Soon not even the European Council could avoid the gale, because it stopped working purely as a collegiate organ subject to even-handed rules of operation. France and Germany, Nicolas Sarkozy and Angela Merkel, resuscitated the Franco-German power couple that had been so ubiquitous in the early days of the European Union and later of the EMU. It became the custom for the leaders of the two major European powers to meet bilaterally prior to European Council meetings to establish joint positions. And the decisions they adopted were not small-time, for example the agreement at the Deauville meeting on October 18, 2010 on Private Sector Involvement, which spread panic in the financial markets.

But to tell the truth, this Franco-German bilateralism of 2010 was qualitatively different from that of 1990. Two decades earlier, France and Germany were talking to each other as equals in terms of power and influence. Germany might have had greater economic might, but France surpassed it in political and military power. In 2010, Germany had emerged strengthened from a decade of reforms, economic restructuring and vigorous productivity growth, which had made it the economic powerhouse of Europe. This clear economic predominance, coupled with greater assertiveness in the European political scene, had made Germany the undisputed European leader, who also had coffers full of money with which to save or condemn. France, on the other hand, showed clear signs of sclerosis due to a hyper-regulated political and economic system that did not allow the forces of productive change to develop. Aware of this

---

75 See (Bulmer, 2016)

disadvantage, the French leadership preferred to close ranks with Germany so as not to be left out of the summit of European power. But in the Sarkozy-Merkel duo, the lead singer was the German Chancellor. And when François Hollande was elected President of France in 2012, any chemistry that might have existed between Sarkozy and Merkel disappeared, France lost further ground and Germany became even more entrenched as the master of Europe.

As we shall see later, one consequence, probably unwanted by either of the two leaders, was that it placed Germany in a central position, in which the country dominated *de facto* the debate on European policies and imposed its own points of view. Now European eyes no longer turned to what the European Commission in Brussel was doing, as at the beginning of the crisis, or towards the European Council when money had to be put up, but to the Chancellor of Germany. Anything more de-institutionalising could not have been imagined. The mill of the Euro crisis had–temporarily–shredded the main institutions of the European edifice.

Concomitant with the weakening of the basic European institutions was the breakdown of a fundamental principle of the EU. The founding agreement of the European nations was that the Union was based on a body of rules, expressed in laws and regulations adopted democratically, and whose application, administration and sanctioning power was entrusted to European institutions. The virulence and speed of the crisis, however, necessitated *ad hoc* decisions for situations that were not foreseen in the European framework and for which the existing body of rules did not offer an effective solution. This is how the philosophy of rules-based governance gave way to a system of government by discretionary decisions taken at the intergovernmental level, either in the European Council, in the Franco-German bilateral agreement or directly in the German Foreign Ministry. Basic institutions such as the European Commission were relegated to the role of implementing decisions taken at intergovernmental level or directly by Germany.

Rule-based multilateralism was the philosophy of government with which the EU was founded. This multilateralism of decision processes gave way to the hierarchical imposition of discretionary decisions. The EU/EMU, which had been conceived as a system of symmetrical distribution of power, became an association of States functioning under structures of domination and subordination between creditors and debtors, between the centre and the periphery. Let us not fall into the temptation of attributing to Germany any sinister designs for European domination. What happened is simply that the EU/UME institutional edifice was not designed to handle a crisis of the magnitude experienced after 2008. What would have been required for such an event was a centralised "economic government" with effective authority and capacity to coordinate macroeconomic policies and allocate fiscal resources to stop the contagion, something that was not contemplated in the Treaty of Maastricht. In the absence of such a centralised government, the decision to save the euro at any cost forced the actions of all the players to persistently violate the principles of the Treaty of Maastricht.

Finally, as the icing on the cake, this authoritarian de-institutionalisation allowed the creditors to impose their economic model on the debtors. The debtors in crisis had based their growth on a model focused on the domestic market, in which–to greatly oversimplify–the driving forces were indebtedness and fiscal expansion. The creditors, on the other hand, had turned to export markets, for which they needed to permanently improve competitiveness through wage containment and fiscal frugality. Clearly, this second model was victorious in the euro crisis, giving Germany the moral and intellectual authority to demand that debtors adopt the competitiveness and frugality model. The adjustment policies imposed on the debtors were directed to this end. The message to the latter was very clear: permanence in the euro was conditional on their adopting the Centre-North model. The problem was that such a profound transformation would take a long time to carry out, because it clashed with deeply rooted economic cultures. Besides, this kind of imposition was certainly not part of the foundational spirit of the EU/EMU.

Deficit of democratic legitimacy

The phenomenon of de-institutionalisation and abandonment of the rule-based framework aggravated the old problem of the democratic deficit that had weighed on the life of the European Community since its inception. The more discretionary the actions of European bodies and the greater the impact of their decisions on the lives of citizens, the more naked and irritating this democratic lack became. The increasing perception of the common citizenry was that the decisions were being taken in an inner sanctum of powerful personages. Many of these decisions affected them very negatively and citizens felt that they were carrying the can for others. Many citizens also sensed that leaving the solution to the problems to Community institutions was to hand them over to the great financial and multinational interests and remove the issues from the democratic controls that guarantee a minimum of social equilibrium at national levels.

Many people were clear that there was much need for change and reform, but there had to be also a perception of a minimum of fairness and justice in the efforts to save the euro. What ultimately happened was that almost the entire burden of adjustment–and sacrifice–fell on the shoulders of the debtors, which was seen as unfair. With this perception of inequality being exacerbated by the breakdown of European institutionalism, the stage was set for questioning the legitimacy of the European construct.

Some history to explain the concept

What is the problem of democratic legitimacy? General opinion tends to associate the "democratic deficit" with the fact that Community authorities are not elected by the citizens, nor do they answer for their actions to organs of control proper to a liberal democracy at national level. Senior European officials are appointed by the member countries in a–generally not very edifying–process of lobbying and horse-trading. The Parliament, the only directly elected body, is a 751-headed Hydra that legislates a great deal concerning the lives of citizens, but that has no capacity to define the course of the EU, nor to control and demand accounts from the European institutions where the real power resides (the European Council, the European Commission or the European Central Bank).

The deficit, however, does not lie mainly in the fact that 'European bureaucrats are not democratically elected'. Every State has its army of unelected bureaucrats, which does not diminish their legitimacy to direct and settle many public issues. In the end, the bureaucrats of the European Commission and its organs have all been appointed by ministers or Heads of State who have political legitimacy in their countries of origin. Nor is it necessarily anti-democratic for certain policy areas to be delegated to Community bodies. Take the central bank as an example. It might be in the best democratic interests of a country to delegate to a common central bank the responsibility of ensuring the stability of the common currency. The questions begin when the actions of the central bank are to the detriment of certain individual countries or have internal redistributive effects in those countries. When distributive conflicts arise within a nation, there are democratic organs of political control to resolve those conflicts (parliaments, judges or, in the end, elections). But the ECB is not subject to any kind of political control. And if there is a perception that the institution is favouring the interests of the hegemonic country, the legitimacy of its actions will be questioned.

Something that really conspires against the construction of legitimacy is that at this point there is still no European *people*, a community of citizens who feel and think themselves European with the same force that they feel and think themselves French, German or Greek. When voters go to European elections, what they have in mind are primarily their own particular national problems and preferences. Almost seven decades of Europeanisation have not persuaded citizens to stop thinking first of their national interests as countries rather than of the interests of Europe. National identities remain the emotional centre of gravity. Domestic imperatives and interests still prevail over the European common good.

The first decade of the 21st century witnessed multiple efforts to adapt Community structures and their governance model to the new realities (Treaty of Amsterdam, Treaty of Nice, Treaty of Lisbon…). All these reforms and treaties, however, failed to overcome the fundamental reality that the European Union had become a burdensome and cumbersome system, both in its bureaucracy and in its only organ of direct democracy, the Parliament. Nor were they able to solve the fundamental problem of the democratic legitimacy of the European edifice.

Turning our attention to the origins of the problem of legitimacy, we saw that in the construction of the European Community, what prevailed was Monnet's concept of top-down integration managed by Community experts. Citizens did not understand the complexity of the tasks being undertaken, nor did the leadership have any particular urgency or need to explain itself. Many of the founding fathers of Europe, such as Monnet or Delors, had been or continued to be high-level public officials, technocrats trained in the elite schools of engineering or public administration. Matters related to integration, from the industrial technicalities of exploiting coal and steel to the complexities of a system of exchange rate bands, required a high level of expertise, totally beyond the understanding of common voting citizens. From the start these European bureaucracies were given the implicit mandate to deal with such technicalities, assuming that upon these small pillars of technical agreements the great edifice of European integration would be built.

The truth is that the European project was a project of the elites. The European people, or rather, the national electorates, were quite marginalised in the process, except for an occasional invitation to participate in a referendum when a fundamental change in the European Union's Constitutional Treaty was mooted. But we must also recognize that during the first four decades the European population showed a passive consensus with the project of Community elites and bureaucracies. Certainly, this role of the bureaucracies allowed a more rapid movement towards "more Europe" despite the passivity, indifference or ignorance of society. In the end, nevertheless, this elitism became a millstone for political legitimacy that ended up undermining the bases of the process.

Monnet believed faithfully in the stimulating power of crises: "*Europe will be constructed in crises and will be the sum of the solutions to these crises*". In his vision, integration would create the political consensus for more integration. Once a Community scheme was embarked on, the problems or crises that might arise would have to be solved with greater levels of integration, because retracing steps or untying knots was always much more expensive than moving forward.

In particular, European bureaucracies conceived the process as a progressive transfer of local or national functions and competencies to the supra-national Community level. By transferring certain functions up to that level, the pressure to increase areas of integration would grow, either because the Community perceived the benefits of the initial measures and insisted on advancing further (integration by positive feedback) or because the initial measures were incomplete and had to be deepened or extended to make them work or to avoid undesirable impacts (negative feedback). Some have described this negative approach as the scorched earth strategy, from which there is no return without extreme pain.[76] Just as burning ships or destroying bridges stops an army from retreating, certain Community decisions left no doors open for going back. One of

---

76 Guiso, Sapienza and Zingales (2015)

those decisions on which there was no going back was monetary unification. Helmut Schmidt, Chancellor of the Federal Republic of Germany between 1974 and 1982, said in 2007 that *"... this is the great strength of the Euro, that no one can abandon it without seriously damaging his own country and his own economy".*[77]

The process that led to the Treaty of Maastricht and then to the European Monetary Union had this same millstone of a lack of democratic legitimacy that Europe has suffered since its inception. As long as integration was accompanied by some growth and, above all, by generous subsidies, the questioning of Community elites in Brussels was modest. During the European Community's first decades of life, the democratic deficit could be compensated for by a constantly improving quality of life for European citizens, which was largely attributed to the benefits of a common market, to the structural funds that richer countries put at the disposal of the laggards, or to the generous Community subsidy policy, especially in agricultural matters. The legitimacy of the European institutions was based on the results of their actions ("output-oriented legitimacy"), rather than on the legitimacy of democratic elections or on the existence of participatory mechanisms for European citizens to take fundamental decisions ("input-oriented legitimacy"), as highlighted by the German political scientist Fritz Scharpf (2013). This second form of legitimacy was never very present in the construction of the European Community, but it was sufficiently compensated for by the first.

Popular adhesion to the common project was guaranteed until well into the 2000s, because everyone received their share, greater or lesser, of the generous policies on subsidies, structural aid, etc. This utilitarian adherence should not however hide the fact that citizens felt alienated from European institutions and felt that decisions affecting their lives were taken behind the closed doors of Community offices. When the Global Financial Crisis of 2008-09 hit Europe hard, the old democratic deficit was transformed into disinterest in, distancing from or open rejection of the European project.

The economic and social consequences of the post-2008 European financial crisis shattered the political legitimacy that had been derived

---

[77] Stated in an interview with David Marsh in 2007, in: David Marsh (2009). *"The Euro: The Politics of the New Global Currency"* Yale University Press. p. 255

from the positive performance of the Community government. All the prescriptions applied to the debtor countries had an important dose of sacrifice and deterioration in the quality of life, eroding the legitimacy based on well-being. At the decision-making level, the newly implemented governance scheme directly dissolved any vestige of legitimacy related to the expression of the will of the citizens, and even to the participation of the European Parliament and the national parliaments. The new model of crisis governance had in many respects constrained the sovereignty of democratically elected national governments. The actions of the Troika and the European Central Bank represented an intense and extensive exogenous intervention in the internal functioning of some countries of the Union.

The euro crisis placed the EMU in a dilemma: the levels of intervention required to preserve the Monetary Union had to be of such an intrusive nature that they clashed with the precepts of democratic decision-making. The Procedure for Macroeconomic Imbalances, for example, granted discretion to the European Commission and its subordinate bodies to supervise, control and sanction an indefinite range of policy areas, going beyond the division of competencies that had historically existed between national and Community levels. The new discretionary powers granted to the Community technocracy were not compatible with the golden rule of the European integration process: Community life was based on rules agreed upon by the members, which were applied within a known legal and regulatory framework.

The European Commission and the European Council ended up acting practically as foreign powers, discretionally imposing policies and reforms within the debtor countries, which only the democratic institutions of governments and elected parliaments should have been able to adopt. The constituent Treaties of the EU and the EMU never envisaged such discretionary powers for the Commission or the Council. Much less did they foresee the "ultimate power of decision" that the European Central Bank assumed in order to determine which countries received oxygen to survive and which did not. Such powers would have been understandable only within the framework of a political union. The paradox of the European democratic dilemma that the crisis brought to the surface is that an eminently technocratic body, such as the EU government, whose legitimacy was historically based on the welfare achievements it produced, was devoid of legitimacy when it most needed it.

Citizen disenchantment and integration fatigue

It is easy to explain anti-European sentiment being exacerbated during the financial crisis. The interesting thing is to note that the problem of democratic legitimacy and the alienation of citizens from Europe began long before the euro crisis, even if it was counterbalanced by handouts. Disenchantment with Europe began to take shape from the beginning of the 90s. As evidenced by the study of long-term opinion trends by Guiso, Sapienza and Zingales (2015), based on Eurobarometer surveys, the peak of identification with Europe happened in 1991, just before the signing of the Maastricht Treaty (see Figure VII-1). From then on, there was a gradual reduction in support for membership in Europe, reaching a minimum in 1996. The drop was relatively more pronounced in the southern European countries (Italy, Greece, Spain, Portugal), even though these remained the most Europhile in absolute terms. In central Europe too (Austria, Germany, France, Belgium, Luxembourg, Holland) there was a very significant decrease in positive sentiment towards membership in Europe. Since that dip, between 1996 and 2001 positive sentiment improves moderately due to the start-up of the Monetary Union. New troughs are observed in the period 2003-05. In 2009, as was to be expected, positive sentiment decreases across the entire spectrum of countries, but it does so much more sharply in the countries of the South. It is significant, and not surprising, that in the countries of the Centre and the North the drop was rapidly reversed, while in the countries of the South it continued to fall.

It is striking that after two key events, the signing of the Maastricht Treaty in 1991 and the macro expansion of membership in 2004, levels of identification with the European project fell. Paradoxically, support for Europe historically dropped at crucial moments of progress in the European integration process. This would seem to be disenchantment on the part of those who harboured illusions and hopes before decisive moments in the life of Europe, and then faced a reality that the citizens saw as disappointing.

In mid-2010s less than a fifth of Europeans favoured continuing to transfer power from national to Community levels, but most wanted to continue keeping the euro. The fact that European citizens say they neither want greater levels of integration, nor do they want to go back on what has been done, especially with the common currency, points towards a disagreement not with the idea of European integration itself, but with the way it has been implemented. Or perhaps also an intuition that breaking up the Monetary Union would be very costly for everyone. More on this in Chapter XII.

FIGURE VII-1
Evolution of positive sentiment towards European membership, 1973-2011
(EU 15)

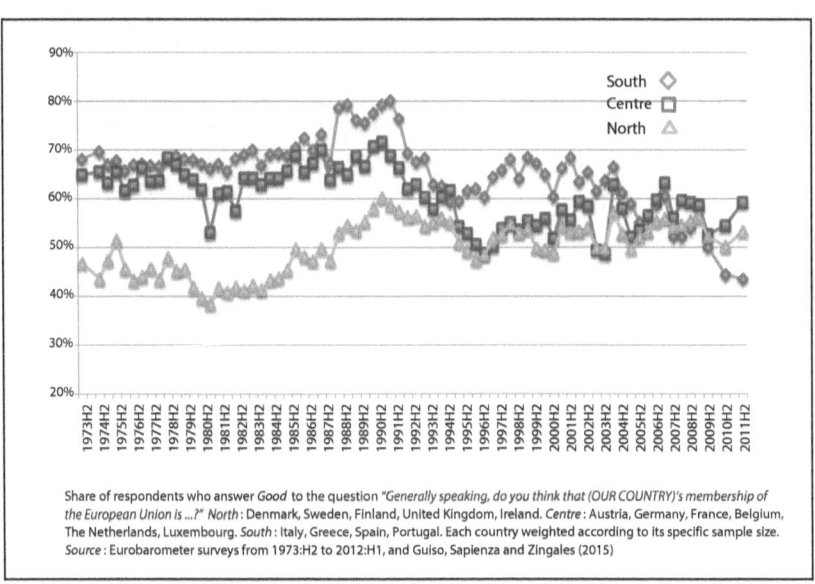

Share of respondents who answer *Good* to the question *"Generally speaking, do you think that (OUR COUNTRY)'s membership of the European Union is ...?"* **North**: Denmark, Sweden, Finland, United Kingdom, Ireland. **Centre**: Austria, Germany, France, Belgium, The Netherlands, Luxembourg. **South**: Italy, Greece, Spain, Portugal. Each country weighted according to its specific sample size.
Source: Eurobarometer surveys from 1973:H2 to 2012:H1, and Guiso, Sapienza and Zingales (2015)

The opinion studies also show that the dissatisfaction of the citizenship is transferred in equal or greater degree to their national governments, and vice versa. There is a very widespread perception that the respective governments and Community bodies do not take into account the real interests of citizens, nor allow them to participate democratically in the decisions that affect them. In addition, some significant sectors of society feel that they have been losers in the game of European hyper-globalisation and blame this on the very existence of the European Union or on the common currency. That is why European populist movements also appeal to anti-European groups. The European Union attracts a good deal of democratic frustration from citizens who feel left out by the bureaucratic elites.

The delays, half-measures and inconsistencies with which the European leadership initially addressed the structural problems of the eurozone only aggravated the fatigue of European citizens. A growing weariness of EU citizens with the cyclopean task of building the monetary and political Union conspired against the adoption of necessary correctives in the time required. This has been called integration fatigue. The euphoria of the first half of the 2000s gave way to widespread pessimism and disappointment. The Europe of the Monetary Union has performed undeniably worse than the rest of the world, indeed worse than the European countries that are not part of the Monetary Union. Growth has been slower, unemployment higher, restrictions and lack of options to deal with the crisis have been much greater than in the rest of the world. Hence, in the countries hit hardest by the crisis, integration fatigue was compounded by austerity fatigue, on having to undergo very severe fiscal adjustment processes, leading to the destructive spiral of fiscal adjustments, debt deleveraging and economic recession. The conjunction of both fatigues explains the growing detachment of large sectors of the population with the European project.

PART III

GERMANY BETWEEN HESITANCY, HEGEMONY AND COERCION

If the project of the European Economic Community and later of the European Union was an attempt to solve the German Problem by diluting Germany within a European framework, events evolved in such a way as to create a new German Problem. Certainly, the problem is different this time, because present-day Germany cannot be accused of bellicosity, but for its neighbours Germany has once again assumed the uncomfortable position of being too powerful not to upset the European balance of power, while not being large enough to exercise fully hegemonic leadership.

The intention of the victorious Allies, which the German leadership of the post-war period also subscribed to, was to transform the country into a "European Germany", and never allow Germany to turn the Continent into a "German Europe", to paraphrase the dilemma posed by Thomas Mann. In the heated debate over Germany's current role, some would describe the current situation as being closer to a German Europe. We are more in agreement with the description by the British historian Timothy Garton Ash (2012), who defines the situation as that of "*a European Germany in a German Europe*". The truth is that, according to Ash, "*Germany is key to the future of Europe, as it has been, in one way or another, for at least a century.*" A solution to the problem of the EMU is inconceivable without decisive action by Germany to fill in the pieces missing from the Union jigsaw puzzle.

Germany has been blamed for many things during the unfolding of the Euro crisis.[78] She is blamed for plunging Europe into stagnation because of her obsession with reducing fiscal deficit and debt, she is accused of not contributing to the debtors' adjustment burdens, of imposing austerity with implacable Calvinist zeal, of defending only her own interests, of taking advantage of the crisis to expand her power, etc. Many of these myths have been sufficiently rebutted or nuanced throughout the present book. In Part I we saw the central role that Germany played in the gestation of the EMU, both in promoting it and in giving it a structure and philosophy that sowed the seeds of its vulnerability. In Part II we saw the role assumed by Germany in the mishandling of the eurozone crisis. We now want to look at why Germany acted as it did, at what were the ideological drivers of her initiatives and at why she did not assume the responsibilities corresponding to a hegemonic power.

Here we will maintain a critical view of German conduct, but we steer away from the moralistic position of those who attribute to this country evil intentions or mere selfishness. Looking after its own interests was certainly a factor, but to no greater extent than for any country that does so. Germany really was convinced that what had been good for it, had also to be good for the "misguided" countries of the European periphery. It wanted to pass on to the rest of the eurozone its successful export model based on wage containment and fiscal austerity. It wanted to impress upon European economic policies the same ordoliberal stamp that had sustained the post-war German miracles, embodied in the model of the social market economy.

Our main criticism refers to the evasion of the responsibilities proper to a country that, voluntarily or involuntarily–it doesn't really matter–had attained a hegemonic position within the EMU. Holding such a position implied duties and rights, costs and benefits. When the hegemon of a monetary system refuses to assume the costs and fulfil the duties inherent to its position, the system breaks down and eventually disintegrates.

---

78   Franz Joseph Meiers (2015) gives a good account of these charges. See also Stiglitz (2016), Krugman (2014), Lagarde (2014), Kundnani (2014), Kundnani (2011), Beck and Kotz (2017)

VIII

GERMAN WAGE CONTAINMENT AND EXTERNAL IMBALANCES IN THE EUROZONE

German economic policy after the Global Financial Crisis was focussed on its own economic recovery. The situation of its eurozone partners received only marginal attention, largely because the prevailing rhetoric was that everyone should shoulder their own responsibility, especially those countries that had become irresponsibly indebted. In tune with its own economic cycle and with the own recovery evolving in a satisfactory manner, German fiscal policy was more restrictive than would have been rational in a monetary union where the bulk of the members were experiencing a severe recession. It occurred to no-one in Germany that their high current account surpluses and their banks' financing of the periphery's deficits might share responsibility in the crisis in those countries. There was also very little introspection on how German banks and investors benefited from the boom in indebtedness and consumption on the periphery.

German economic policy makers did not recognize the systemic interplay of their actions with what was happening in other corners of the eurozone. They were so convinced that their model was the right one, that they could not imagine it having negative implications for others. And if it did, their righteous certainty immunised them from any sense of responsibility (or guilt). Thus, the policies of Germany became out of sync with those of her partners in the eurozone at a time when it was most necessary to coordinate them.

At the heart of the German export economic model are wage containment and frugality. This model would be perfectly praiseworthy if

Germany were not part of the closely interconnected framework of a monetary union and did not have the overwhelming economic weight that it does have. Because of these interactions, the German model contributed to creating bad equilibria prior to the crisis in the rest of the eurozone, aggravated the effects of the crisis and placed a heavy burden on the periphery's recovery process.

Europe's deep-pocketed moral arbiter

How did Germany get to become the driver of the European bus after pleading in the post-war era to be allowed to sit in the back seat? What Germany has represented for Europe has always been immersed in paradox. The reader will recall that we began this book with a survey of Germany's key role in European history. Its central geographical position between the Great Powers of the time (France, Austro-Hungary, Russia and Britain) and the size of its territory and population made it the pivot holding the scales in the complex power relations between the Powers. Until well into the nineteenth century the fragmentation of the German Principalities did not allow the nation to become a Power in itself, but whoever managed to dominate or win over the Principalities had guaranteed control of the centre of Europe and, therefore, of the continent. After Bismarck managed to consolidate German unification under the aegis of Prussia in 1871, Germany went on to take its own place on the stage of European Powers.

The problem was that Germany was always a factor of instability in Europe, first because of its fragmentation and later because of its power. It was not, however, a Power strong enough to dominate the continent and generate the peace that an empire usually commands. For their part, the other Powers felt threatened by the economic and military might that a unified Germany was rapidly accumulating. In turn, the Germans felt permanently encircled, both geographically and politically, by the alliances that other European countries knitted together to contain the German danger. This led to a perverse feedback dynamic of mutual distrust and arms build-up, leading finally to the two world wars of the first half of the 20th century.

This digression into the past was necessary to understand how the German Problem fertilised the European Union's gestation. The European

Economic Community, including its predecessor the European Coal and Steel Community, was much more a political than an economic project, in which Germany was always the *leitmotiv*. After the Second World War, France was determined once and for all to stop Germany recovering its power. The way to neutralise it was to subsume it in European Community entities, in which France would retain political control. The United States and Britain were less emotionally and politically slanted against the Germans, but they also agreed that European unity was the best way to solve the German Problem. For its part, Germany knew that the only way to be readmitted into the international community was through its participation in European institutions. The Germans became fervent Europeanists and exemplary international citizens.

Soon, economic success put Germany in the front seat of the bus for the European trip, and in certain areas in the driver's seat. Germany was undoubtedly at the wheel in everything related to the monetary and exchange system, which since the collapse of Bretton Woods had acquired special relevance. The credentials that allowed it to assume such leadership were granted by the strength of the deutschmark and the prestige of the Bundesbank in achieving price stability. Indeed, there can be no doubt that the design of the Euro and of the European Central Bank had a markedly German stamp. Beyond its monetary leadership, Germany essayed a new economic model, the "social market economy", that allowed it to grow beyond its European peers and to become once again the premier economic power of Europe. This model was based on a scheme of co-determination and pacts between capital, labour and the State. On the productive front, Germany soon managed to recover her industrial leadership through an untiring commitment to innovation, applied research and the opening of foreign markets.

After the second German reunification in 1990, the new Federal Republic of Germany consolidated as the leading European economic power, exceeding by 1.5 times the GDP of its immediate follower, France. Its population grew to 80 million inhabitants, compared to 58 million for France. In 1995, the German economy represented 28.3 percent of the European Union's GDP. Her fiscal accounts were healthy and public debt represented between 70 and 80 percent of GDP, significantly below her peers in the eurozone. External accounts were especially strong after a decade-long national crusade to improve the country's competitiveness.

In 2010, the current account surplus of goods and services was equivalent to the entire eurozone trade surplus. The German net international position[79] in that same year showed a healthy surplus, equivalent to 25.6% of GDP. At the same time France's position was negative at 9.3% of GDP, Italy's negative at 20.2% of GDP and Spain's negative at 88.6% of GDP, to mention the four largest countries in the eurozone.

It is not surprising, therefore, that as the eurozone's financial crisis worsened, Europe's eyes should turn to Germany, the only country with pockets deep enough to deal with the bailouts that were becoming necessary. But even more than her financial capacity and the size of her economy, what gave Germany a natural leadership when the financial crisis broke out was her record as a successful country, of someone who had done her homework, someone who had managed to change from the mid-90s "sick man of Europe" to the bright star of the mid-2000s. Germany was the European country structurally best prepared to face the onslaught of the Global Financial Crisis. Fervent defenders of their own economic model, the Germans felt they had the right–and the moral duty–to tell their troubled European partners just how they had failed. Those being shaken by the turbulence of financial markets because of their high level of debt should be criticised and blamed for spending more than they should have.

Former Italian Prime Minister Mario Monti said once that *"only in Germany is economic science considered a branch of moral philosophy"*[80]. It is no coincidence that in the German language the word *Schuld* means both debt and guilt. The Swabian housewife–the prototype of good German behaviour–would never go into debt to spend more than she had. There is an implicit assumption among Germans that savings are an expression of virtue and debts of sin, rather than the expression of a complex set of economic facts and circumstances.

It was this supposed moral authority that allowed the German authorities to impose their particular interpretation of the origin and characteristics of the crisis, as well as to write the consequent recipe

---

79 *Net International Investment Position*, macroeconomically speaking, is the difference between the financial assets and the financial liabilities of the residents of a country with respect to other countries.

80 Quoted in Christopher Smart (2017)

book. As we said in Chapter IV, the Greek debt crisis provided the perfect narrative that fitted the binary moral thinking of virtuous and sinful. The fault and the obligations were all on one side, with no mention of the imbalances of the creditors who financed the boom of the debtors. As the main creditor, directly, and as a leader of the creditors union, indirectly, Germany was in a position to fix the terms and the amounts of the bailouts.

Regrettably, the recipes did not meet their goal of pulling the debtor countries out of the crisis in a reasonable time and at a reasonable cost. Moralisation obfuscated a systemic view of the crisis, a vision in which debtors and creditors should recognize their share of responsibility and contribute in a balanced way to the tasks of the adjustment process. Germany was closed to this vision, laid the responsibility completely on the shoulders of the debtors and assumed the role of the undaunted moral policeman.

It would be injurious to the truth, however, to attribute attitudes of pettiness or insensitivity to German society and its leadership. On the contrary, the German people are known for their sense of solidarity, compassion and justice. What lay behind the hard and unilateral German positions was their worldview about the way to organize as a society, their economic philosophy, their vision of labour relations and production, their own recipes for success. Germany wanted for its European partners in crisis the same model and the same paths that had led it to success. At all times, Germany was fervently convinced that what had been good for it also had to be good for the rest of Europe. That is why it never had a moment's doubt about rigorously imposing its austerity prescription on the debtor countries.

The contribution of German wage restraint to the appearance of disequilibria in the Eurozone

The imbalances that occurred in the countries of the European periphery, especially the external current account deficits, can only be understood in the context of the central European countries' surpluses, especially those of Germany. The existence of this interconnection during the initial building up of the disequilibria makes it reasonable to think that overcoming it would also require the cooperation of the surplus economies. We must be careful, however, not to oversimplify by thinking that one's loss is directly the other's gain, and vice versa. The trade deficit of the eurozone periphery is not an arithmetical mirror, a zero-sum game, of the surplus of the European Centre-North.[81] The German trade surplus was not achieved solely by selling to its European partners more goods and services than those it imported from them, since the principal destinations of German manufacturing were the Asian and North American markets.

Incomplete consensus narrative

Although there were indeed no arithmetical mirrors in the respective accounts of goods and services, there were nevertheless several indirect channels through which the surpluses and deficits of Germany and the eurozone periphery did interact. A critical and reputable voice regarding German responsibility in the periphery's disequilibrium is that of the German economist Peter Bofinger (2015), who as one of the five members of the sacrosanct *Sachverständigerrat*, the German Council of Economic Experts, can hardly be regarded as Germano-phobic. His central thesis is that the "consensus narrative"[82] on the origin of the European crisis does not take into account Germany's key contribution to creating problems in the European periphery. This consensus narrative focusses on the accelerated accumulation of private and public debt, which, when the sudden stop of capital flows to the periphery took place, degenerated into banking and sovereign crises. In more or less veiled form, this narrative points to the sole responsibility of the deficit countries themselves, which either did not want to or did not know how to stop the boom in demand that generated asset bubbles and deteriorated competitiveness by way of wage increases above productivity.

Bofinger highlights the effect that German wage containment had on the rest of Europe in the first years of the EMU. Looking back, Germany began its EMU membership in 1999 in a very compromised economic situation. The entire decade of the 90s was consumed in trying to assimilate

---

81   That would be the case in Mundell's oversimplified model of a world of only two countries, but not in the real world of multiple interconnected nations inside and outside the euro region.

82   This refers to the work compiled by Baldwin and Giavazzi (2015), a kind of manifesto signed by a very important group of economists, in which they reach a consensus on the development of the eurozone crisis and its causes.

the brutal economic impact of absorbing East Germany into the new unified nation. This was done at a very high fiscal cost in order to finance reconstruction and standardise welfare benefits for the citizens of the East with those of the West. This implied a monetary expansion by recognising the East German mark in a one-to-one exchange with the deutschmark, with consequent inflationary pressures which damaged the competitiveness of German industry. Although it is hard to believe it today, in those years there was talk of Germany as the "sick man of Europe": unemployment was high and economic growth disappointing. While the rest of the eurozone grew at an annual average of 3.2% between 1995 and 2000, Germany did so at only 1.7%.

In view of this lack of dynamism, Gerhard Schröder, once elected Chancellor of Germany in 1998, called for a "Work, Education and Competitiveness Pact" (*Bündnis für Arbeit, Ausbildung und Wettbewerbsfähigkeit*), a tripartite pact between unions, business and government. The initiative faithfully mirrored the corporatist culture of German society, which was accustomed to high level understandings between Capital and Labour under the aegis of the State. The "dialogue summits" within the framework of the Pact worked reasonably well. From them emerged the elements of consensus that Schroeder, in his second term of Social Democratic government, gathered together and presented in 2003 in the plan called "Agenda 2010." As the central core of the consensus, the unions were willing to not increase wages above inflation, under the condition that employers fulfilled their role of increasing employment. Agenda 2010 included reductions in taxes on capital, incentives for companies, measures to support productivity, drastic reductions in welfare benefits, flexibility in the labour market and wage restraint. In other words, a fully-fledged ordoliberal adjustment plan, validated by the unions.

As a consequence of Agenda 2010, from 1999 to 2008 German general unit labour costs had remained constant (see Figure V-1) and in some sectors, such as manufacturing, came even to decline by 9 percent. This wage restraint during those years when the rest of the eurozone, especially the countries of the South, went into a phase of overheating and price and wage increases, helped to further open the gap between both groups of countries. According to Bofinger, wage containment, understood as wage increases below productivity growth, contributed decisively to the formation of imbalances in the eurozone periphery countries via several channels:

- A first impact was derived from inflation differentials between Germany and the rest, which directly affected the competitiveness of exports.
- A second impact was derived from the ECB's interest rate policy, induced by low German inflation. When what the periphery really needed was a restrictive monetary policy, the ECB kept to the European inflation average and maintained low interest rates, thus adding fuel to the fire for the overheated periphery economies.
- Third, aggregate domestic demand in Germany fell appreciably due to wage restraint, which made it difficult for other European countries to market their exports in Germany.

Depressed demand in Germany and a boom in demand in the eurozone periphery created the perfect storm for the overspill of trade imbalances. Le Moigne and Ragot (2015) estimate that German wage restraint was responsible for almost half the divergence in balance of trade within the eurozone, a very significant impact.

To these channels we must add another extremely important one, not sufficiently emphasized by Bofinger in his analysis. Macroeconomically speaking (see Box VIII-1 below), current account surpluses amount to an excess of savings over national investment, with the consequent accumulation of financial surpluses in the surplus country. It was in great part these financial surpluses that, mediated by German banks, financed the Mediterranean periphery's consumption spree and caused the boom in demand, inflationary pressures, wage increases and loss of competitiveness in those countries. And it was the sudden stop in these financial flows that later triggered the chain of vicious circles that brought the eurozone into crisis.

Wage containment, hero or villain?

Depending on from which side you look at it, wage containment assumes the role of hero or villain. For the neo-Keynesians, like Bofinger and most non-German economists, it was the villain that fed the current account imbalances between the countries of the eurozone. For the Neoclassicals, among which we could also include the German ordoliberals, wage moderation and flexibility of the labour market were the cause of the second German economic miracle, which turned the German economy from the sclerotic patient of the 90s into the export champion of the first decade of the 2000s, the undisputed economic leader of Europe. This interpretation of the determinants of German growth fitted into the Neoclassical paradigm that the important thing for economic growth was to create conditions to increase the production of goods and services, that is, conditions to improve the supply side. The preferred instruments for this approach are tax cuts to capital, relaxation of regulations, especially in the labour market, and reductions in wage costs. In contrast, the Keynesian paradigm favours stimulating economic growth through the determinants that drive aggregate demand for consumption and investment.

The experience of the eurozone before the crisis, and more especially after it, seemed to validate the ordoliberal approach that emphasized the central importance of wage containment and low inflation for the achievement of competitiveness and growth. As usually happens, the victors impose their cosmology. This dispute between Neoclassicals and Keynesians would not have mattered so much, had it not been for the fact that the winning dogma prevailed when it came to explaining the causes of the crisis and designing recipes for the way out. The Germans in essence wrote the official narrative of the European techno-bureaucracy: countries that had given free rein to public spending, to excessive investments, to indebtedness and to wage increases were those that went into crisis after 2008, while those that moderated wage aspirations, controlled fiscal deficit and reduced welfare benefits were those that weathered the storm of the financial crisis without problems and achieved important surpluses in their internal and external accounts. This narrative offered the perfect justification for blaming the victims, and only the victims, for the crisis in which they found themselves. Greece fitted this story like a glove. The immediate derivation of this interpretative approach was that the recipe to get out of the crisis could not be other than wage containment, internal deflation, dismantling of labour rigidities and reduction of public spending; in other words, austerity.

With the benefit of hindsight, almost no one doubts that this recipe for austerity, without other accompaniments, deepened and extended the eurozone crisis far beyond what was reasonable and necessary. The recipe for austerity was based on a mistaken diagnosis. As so often happens, reasonable-sounding ideas, half-truths and observations are dressed up by ideology to turn them into dogma. One of those half-truths was that wage containment had been the main bulwark for the competitiveness of German products by way of lower labour costs. Bofinger himself, despite disagreeing with many points in the official German narrative, implicitly maintains that wage containment was what improved German competitiveness through labour costs and contributed to the poor balance of payments performance of its European partners.

The Dutch economist Servaas Storm (2016) questions this linear single-cause relationship between wage containment, competitiveness and trade surplus. The fact that German wage containment had occurred concomitantly with imbalances in the eurozone current accounts, does not mean that there was a causal relationship between both phenomena. Recall that competitiveness depends, among other things, on productivity factors–measured by the ratio (quotient) between the quantity produced and the costs incurred. Competitiveness, therefore, can be improved by either reducing the costs of input (the denominator of the equation) or by improving the quantity of output (the numerator of the equation). We know that German productivity, measured as output per man-hour worked, grew above that of its European partners, but empirical evidence does not support the thesis that lower unit labour costs (the denominator) were the main determinant of German international competitiveness.

Greater German productivity and competitiveness had more to do with fundamentally technological conditions than with the wage containment of German workers. The boom in German exports is mainly explained by the fortunate combination of two factors: first, a successful technological revolution in its manufacturing sector (the key *Mittelstand*) that specialized in the manufacture of sophisticated high-technology capital equipment; and secondly, a favourable situation of demand on the world market, which showed an insatiable appetite for German technological products, especially from fast-growing countries such as China, India, Russia or Saudi Arabia. The decade of the 2000s was the golden decade for the growth of emergent economies. The demand effect (the numerator), rather than the cost effect, was what drove German exports. Through commendable engineering ingenuity, German industry was able to develop sophisticated products that the world was clamouring for. This was the key to its export boom.

Nor is it true that the wage "excesses" of the countries of the eurozone periphery were the main causes of their current account imbalances.

Proof of this is that the current account deficits appeared before wages had heated up. They were initially due to the increase in imports and not to a drop in exports. This sequence was especially evident in the case of Spain. It was capital flows, mainly from German and Dutch banks, which in the first instance reheated domestic aggregate demand, increased imports and subsequently induced wage increases through the boom in demand.

As we mentioned earlier, the narrative about the causes of imbalances within the eurozone acquired great importance when designing solutions. No-one denies that wage containment contributed to improving the productivity of German workers, just as wage excess worsened the productivity of workers in southern Europe. However, the dominant single-cause interpretative dogma, according to which containment or wage excess became the main explanation for current account surpluses or deficits, led to serious policy errors. Under this approach, virtue was exclusively on the side of those who knew how to defer gratification in the best traditions of the Protestant ethic, while those who gave free rein to increasing wages and expenditure, the "profligate Latins", had a burden of guilt that they needed to expiate by way of austerity. Besides, as the fault was one-sided, the non-guilty party had no economic or moral obligation to contribute to the restitution of balance.

Economic and cultural structural dualism

In addition to the above, behind the balance of payments disequilibria in the eurozone was the structural duality between a central core of countries, basically Germany, which specialised in the production of high-technology goods with high added value, and the rest, mainly the countries of southern Europe, which were concentrated in non-tradeable productive sectors and in tradeable products of low technology and low added value.[83] Germany's manufactured exports tended to be relatively insensitive to unit labour cost, which was not the case with the products exported by southern Europe, where the comparative advantages lay to a large extent on the cost-to-price relation. Paradoxically, although Germany didn't really need to reduce wage costs to mark its strong presence

---

83   The terms "tradeable" and "non-tradeable" refer to goods and services that can be traded or not traded internationally.

in the international market of high-tech goods, it was the country that did actually reduce them. The other countries, which really did need to do it because of the type of products they produced, went in the opposite direction of increasing labour costs. The tragedy of those countries with less technological development is that the restoration of their current account balance depended to a large extent on the reduction of wage costs, which was a very counterproductive recipe to get out of the low-growth trap in which they were immersed.

The truth is that the seed of this dualism had already been planted before the introduction of the Monetary Union, but there is no doubt that since 1999 divergences of productive structures within the eurozone have been growing. The post-2008 eurozone financial crisis only aggravated this problem of structural duality, because all efforts were devoted to internal devaluation, with no oxygen left to open avenues for the growth of a higher quality export supply.

This is very bad news for a monetarily integrated area, whose fundamental postulate is that the structural divergences between its members either must not exist from the outset or should be progressively reduced by the effect of integration. Increasing structural divergences ends up inexorably undermining the foundations of a monetary union, unless there are compensating solidarity mechanisms in place. Even when such mechanisms exist, a monetary union in which the gap widens day by day is not feasible in the long term. Rather than fiscal austerity or wage deflation, what would have really helped the deficit countries of the eurozone were policies aimed at closing this structural gap, such as industrial policies to promote technological advances and increase competitiveness in higher added-value sectors and better paid employment.

It is hard to be optimistic about the prospects of overcoming this structural dualism within a reasonable time. The reason is that underlying this economic-productive dualism there also hides a socio-cultural dualism which is of equal or greater importance. Different models of society, different economic cultures and different economic models coexist within the EMU, as we have already mentioned in Chapter v.[84] At the risk of over-simplifying, we could draw the following North-South dividing line:

---

[84] Streeck, (2015) and Scharpf, (2018) have paid particular attention to this issue of conflicting social and economic models.

- A Mediterranean South, which historically has been more accommodating with inflation, which tends to spend more than it has, whose growth model has been driven by domestic demand, where fragmented unions have high bargaining power, where conceptions of equality and solidarity tend to produce outsized welfare systems and where the State intervenes significantly in economic life.
- A Central and Northern Europe, which has a strong aversion to inflation, which preaches household and fiscal frugality as a virtue, whose growth model has been boosted by the export sector, based on efficiency and entrepreneurship, where economic agents relate to each other in a corporatist and cooperative framework of moderation and where the State limits itself to preserving non-abusive competition.

There are certainly many nuances in the reality of each region and each country, some of which, like France or Austria, are difficult to pigeonhole in either of the two poles, but that does not take away the analytical merits of these idealised typologies. They tell us that there are two social models, based on different histories and cultural traditions. In the economic sphere, the Southern typology corresponds to countries with a greater tendency towards spending and indebtedness, while the Northern typology applies to countries with a greater tendency towards savings and investment. Both cultures have their own socio-economic dynamics and their own mechanisms for viability. It is relatively easy to fall into the temptation of attributing to one model or the other a moral superiority or greater power to efficiently organize society around the goal of generating well-being. Any such moral judgment will have to be based on a set of social preferences and values, which necessarily makes it subjective.

The problem is how to reconcile both cultures and models within a monetary union. The coexistence of both models brings to community life too much political abrasiveness, conflicts, endless discussions and permanent negotiations. The reality is that they are two models that cannot coexist within a fixed exchange regime, because they are doomed to diverge rather than converge. To avoid attrition, they should seek a negotiated convergence towards certain fundamental common arrangements. This is the only way for the monetary union to become viable. If not, one of the two models will sooner or later have to prevail over the other. It is not hard to guess how that will go. In economic-financial terms, there is no way that the export model, based on frugality and productivity, will not surpass the domestic market model based on distributive public spending.

The crisis of the euro made crudely self-evident the supremacy of the export efficiency model and its economic philosophy. What remains to be seen is whether the South will have the will and capacity to assimilate and internalize the culture of the Centre-North. For the entire eurozone to be on the same page in terms of economic philosophy, the Mediterranean periphery has no other choice but to adopt the Centre-North model, because it is unrealistic to think that Germany and its neighbours are going to renounce their winning formula. If this is the case, the future of the eurozone, in its current configuration of countries, looks very uncertain.

The German trade surplus: the apple of discord

At the beginning of the GFC, Germany had a current account surplus of 5.6 percent of GDP, while the average in the Mediterranean periphery was a deficit of close to 10 percent (see Figure VIII-1). After much effort, the current account of the periphery managed to leave the deficit zone in 2013, staying between 0 and 1 percent since then. The German surplus, instead of converging, rose steadily since 2008 to between 8 and 9 percent of GDP since 2015. That after 9 years of the crisis exploding the periphery is so unable to revitalize its external sector while Germany continues in such excessive surplus, is an indication of the deep imbalances that persist within the eurozone.

Figure VIII-1 reveals the profound misalignment of economic policies between Germany and the periphery. It is true that the German export sector managed to reach an enviable competitive position, but it is also true that the magnitude of the imbalance cannot be explained by simple competitive factors. Serious macroeconomic disequilibria underlie this divergence. Economic theory establishes a clear correlation between trade surplus and low levels of domestic aggregate demand, high level of savings, and fiscal surplus (see Box VIII-1 to understand the relationship between the external current account and the main macroeconomic variables). Balance of payments disequilibria are a reflection of the intertemporal preferences of societies, more specifically, a reflection of a country's preference for savings or consumption, for savings or investment. In a closed economy, by definition, saving equals investment. But in an open economy, savings can be channelled abroad rather than into domestic consumption and investment. This macroeconomic (im)balance between saving and investment is always directly manifested in an (dis)equilibrium in the balance of payments. This is because a greater propensity to frugality and savings reduces the demand for goods and services in the domestic market and, therefore, the demand for imported goods and services. If, at the same time, frugality is accompanied by deflation and low costs, as is often the case, the stage is set to improve competitiveness and increase exports. The preference of German society was definitively inclined towards savings and frugality.

FIGURE VIII-1
Current Account Balance (% of GDP) 1999-2017

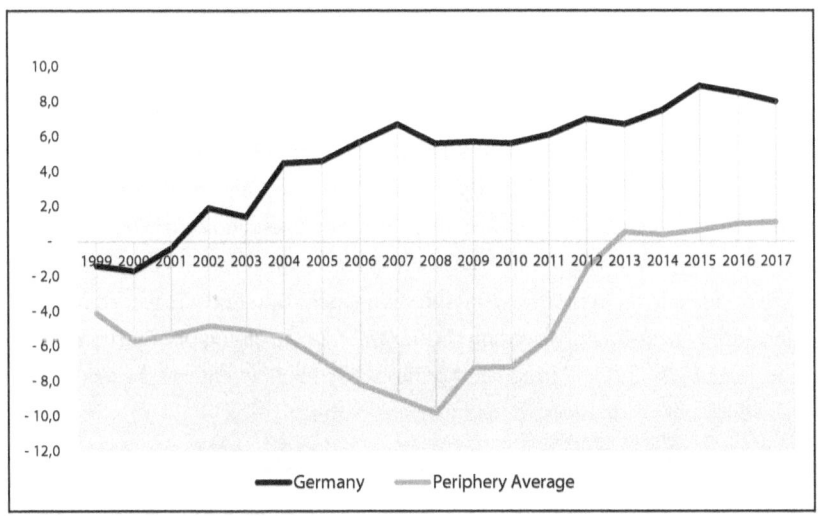

Box VIII-1
A BRIEF LESSON IN MACROECONOMICS:
THE MEANING OF THE BALANCE OF PAYMENTS CURRENT ACCOUNT

The following equation applies to National Accounts:

(1) $CA = (S - I) + (T - G)$

The equation tells us that external savings (CA = balance of the external current account) is the sum of the net private domestic savings (= savings S minus investment I) and the net savings of the government (= public revenues T minus public expenditure G).

A simple multiplication of the above equation by -1 shows the other side of the coin:

(2) $-CA = (I-S) + (G-T)$

In other words, the nation's net indebtedness (-CA) is the sum of the net indebtedness of the private sector (= investment I minus savings S) and of the net indebtedness of the public sector (= expenses G minus income T).

Another macroeconomic identity tells us that saving (S) is the part of the national product (Y) that the private sector does not consume (C) and the government does not spend (G).

(3) $S = Y - C - G$

From the equation (2) we know that to reduce the current account deficit (= nation's net indebtedness), savings must be increased, and this is achieved by reducing private consumption and/or government spending according to equation (3). This is the basic axiom of the austerity recipe. On the other side of the coin, the decrease in the current account surplus happens by reducing saving through increasing investment, increasing consumption or increasing public spending.

Interestingly, the German authorities subscribed fervently to the axiom of austerity, but not so much to the other side of the coin.

The German establishment saw nothing negative in these surpluses, rather they were considered an indication of the correctness of their economic model. External accounts were not seen as the product of policies or incentives orchestrated by the government, but as the result of a multitude of private transactions made with the expectation of obtaining a profit.[85] If a positive balance emerged from this multitude of transactions, it was because the country had a competitive economy based on structural factors. Phillip Steinberg of the German Ministry of Economic Affairs identifies no less than half of the trade surplus as being explained by those fundamental factors that have to do with an industrial structure oriented towards high-tech products and with a successful portfolio of products and customers. However, he also recognizes that persistent surpluses of such magnitude point to the existence of distortions and structural problems, such as unfavourable conditions for investment, weak domestic demand or excessive wage containment.

Other analysts, such as Hans-Werner Sinn (2016) of the IFO Institute for Economic Research, are less self-critical and offload all responsibility onto the countries that, according to Sinn, have chronic current account deficits and demand a flow of German capital surpluses to finance their deficits. The eurozone created before the crisis a false sense of absence of risk that allowed German banks to flood the deficit Mediterranean periphery with loans. Instead of complaining so much, Sinn's story continues, the deficit European partners should strive to copy the German model and become more efficient. Anything other than tightening belts would only lengthen the decline of the debtor countries.

This position is tantamount to denying that the international economy and, more particularly, the economies of a monetary union are systemically intertwined. In the boom years, Germany fed the inflationary expansion of its neighbours; in the years of the depression, it exported deflation to the debtor countries. We have insisted that the real impact of German wage containment was not so much the direct effect of costs on relative productivity, but rather the double effect of depressing domestic demand in Germany and re-heating demand in the eurozone before the crisis occurred. Agenda 2010 put German society into a mode of austerity and savings, thus hindering the export of goods from the European periphery to that country. Of great impact also was the fall in investment

---

85   Christoph Schmiedt, President of the German Council of Economic Experts (cited by Coricelli, 2017).

demand, or its counterpart, the high level of national savings, which German banks had to channel into loans to the countries of the European periphery, all of them eager for funds to undertake ambitious investment plans. It was these capital flows to the periphery that fuelled the boom in aggregate demand in those countries and the consequent wage pressures.

The percentage of GDP destined for savings in Germany is significantly higher than in the rest of the world. If we look at Figure VIII-2, we find that the German savings rate persistently exceeds that of the European Union, that of the 35 countries of the OECD (Organisation for Economic Cooperation and Development) and that of the United States. Particularly striking is the divergence with the latter, whose average savings rate since 2007 has been 17%, while that of Germany has been 27%. Significantly, Germany pulls ahead of the global pack after 2003, when the Schroeder Plan (Agenda 2010) begins to bear fruit.

FIGURE VIII-2
Comparative Savings Rates (% of GDP), 1999-2017

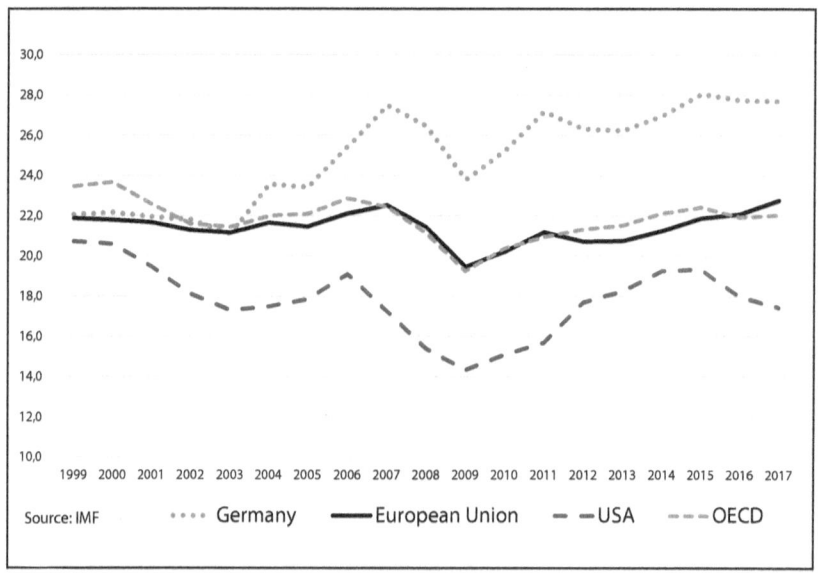

Although Germany is in the lead for savings, in terms of investment rate it is behind the rest of the world. Figure VIII-3 shows that since the beginning of the 2000s, Germany has had the lowest investment rate in the Western world, including the European Union. Only in the three years from 2009 to 2011, due to the Global Financial Crisis, was the US investment rate below that of Germany.

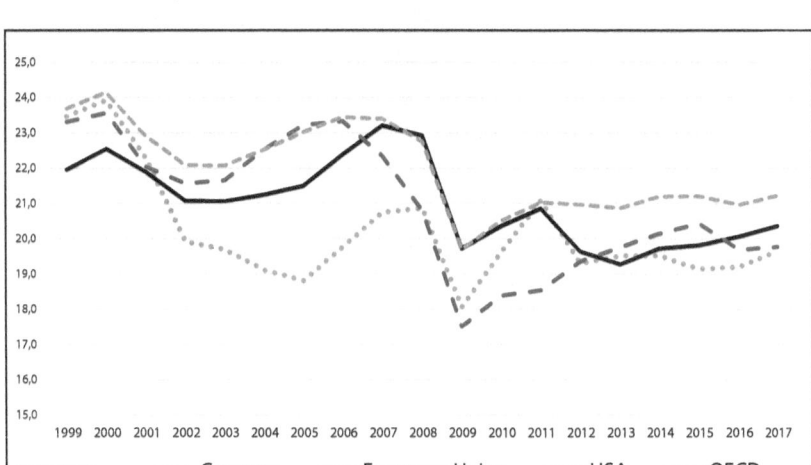

FIGURE VIII-3
Comparative Investment Rates (% of GDP), 1999-2017

The European partners complain to Germany that they should save less, consume more and invest more. The rest of the international community and the International Monetary Fund echoes the same complaint.[86] The official German vision is that the high level of savings and its mirror of trade surplus is in tune with the age-demographic changes of German society, which is aging rapidly and for whom social security must be ensured. It is estimated that by 2035 Germany will have more than 21 million people over 67 years old, half of them being older than 80.[87]

The aging population argument is valid, but the German problem for Europe is not so much that it saves too much, but that it invests too little. The general opinion is that its comfortable fiscal situation would allow Germany to increase the level of public investment without jeopardising

---

86 The Economist 2016-09-03 - More spend, less thrift

87 Fuest (2017) and Coricelli (2017)

necessary inter-generational savings. Germany has one of the lowest public investment rates in the industrialized world. Government investment has dropped four percentage points since 2000. Nor do German companies want to reinvest internally the high profits they obtain abroad. According to Marcel Fratscher of the German Institute for Economic Research, about half of the current account surplus reflects this investment gap.[88]

After so many years of moderation, the investment gaps in public infrastructure are very large, especially in educational facilities, hospital facilities, roads, military, rail networks and equipment and a long *etcetera*. Germany is also reluctant to open its service sector to competition and foreign investment. It sounds paradoxical that the service sector continues to be so internally protected in a country so focussed on exports. It is hard to understand the resistance to dismantling regulatory excesses, removing barriers to entry for investment and liberalising access to all players, including private and foreign. It is precisely in services where the investment gaps are most striking and where a policy change would be fully justified. If this happened, the effect on the reduction of the trade surplus would be significant.

These investment gaps are an additional argument for Germany to undertake a broad and sustained investment program. Collaterally, such a program would automatically create the environment for wage improvements that would stimulate workers' propensity to consume, which would increase imports from other countries on the continent. It would also be a good idea for Germany to allow its inflation to rise above the average of the eurozone periphery, so that countries in internal adjustment processes would not need to incur excessive deflation to close the productivity gap.

The German political and intellectual establishment, however, has refused to take this path of stimulating its internal economy. For one thing, monetary and fiscal activism is not at all popular, and for another, there is a united internal front, from the unions to the employers, against any measure that weakens the export position, either through wage increases or internal inflation. Stimulating its economy through domestic spending

---

88   Cited in The Economist (2017), "Vorsprung durch Angst. The good and bad in Germany's economic model are strongly linked" - Jul 8, 2017. Contrary to this opinion, Fuest (2017) argues that the German investment rate has remained stable at around 20% for the past 15 years with different levels of current account surpluses.

to the extent that it can generate pressure for wage increases or inflationary pressures is an anathema, running in the opposite direction to what has always been the economic philosophy of frugality and deep aversion to inflation.

Nor do they allow themselves to be softened by the argument that an expansion of domestic spending on consumption and investment would help alleviate the burden of austerity on their European partners. They firmly believe that the problems of unemployment and low growth in those countries are their exclusive responsibility and that they should follow the example of German containment to straighten their economies. Germany cannot apply internally those stimulus policies that have supposedly led others to the economic garbage heap. And in order that no future government can ever fall into that temptation, in 2009 Germany adopted a constitutional rule that limited the fiscal deficit. In 2010 the German government introduced a package of spending cuts with a goal of reducing the deficit to 0.35% by 2016, directly contrary to what the partners were asking for.

Another argument to justify the German refusal to jointly assume part of the burden of re-balancing Europe is that a stimulus to German domestic demand would not necessarily lead to a reduction in the trade deficit of the eurozone periphery through an increase in those countries' exports to Germany. The argument is solid, as shown by some projections based on the input-output matrix of Europe, which suggest that higher German demand would encourage exports from Eastern Europe more than those from Southern Europe.[89] As we explained above, to think that the deficits/surpluses of the eurozone countries were arithmetically mirrored before 2008, is as simplistic as believing that reversing them could be managed in a 1 to 1 ratio. Similarly, increasing German workers' salaries so that those of the periphery could recover their productivity with less of an austerity sacrifice would not have had enough impact.

The forces behind the disequilibria in balances of payments are certainly more complex, but this does not exempt Germany from the task of finding channels to facilitate the adjustment processes of the rest of the eurozone. An increase in German aggregate demand is not the be-all and end-all, but it would have other spill-over effects on the European

---

89   Input-output matrix reference in Storm (2016).

and global economy that should be considered. Another way would be the resumption of capital flows towards Europe, that allow the recycling of trade surpluses to deficit countries.

Some analysts, such as Alan Cafruny (2015), are less benevolent when they try to explain Germany's unwillingness to contribute to the re-balancing of its trading partners. They emphasize that the German growth model, the so-called export mercantilism, rests entirely on the growth of exports, especially due to the vicious cycle of there not being enough dynamism in its domestic market to sustain growth because of wage containment and fiscal frugality. According to this view, Germany benefited greatly from the EMU because it allowed it to have a currency, the euro, which was certainly undervalued compared to what would have been the strength of the deutschmark had it not belonged to the eurozone. Additionally, belonging to a monetary union protected it from possible policies of competitive devaluation on the part of its European neighbours. The imposition of austerity recipes, therefore, was not the result of a mistaken reading of the crisis, product of its ordoliberal creed, but a reflection of the conflict between the structural interests of German capital and the development needs of the eurozone as a whole.

We do not deny that Germany has substantially benefited from an undervalued euro, but we see no support for the thesis that German export success has been based on the exchange rate or even on its low labour costs. No doubt both were contributing factors, however the German competitive advantage did not rest solely on costs, but rather primarily on an economic model promoting efficiency, entrepreneurship and technological innovation. To Caesar that which is Caesar's.

The debate between Germany and the rest of the world concerning the trade surplus has reached an *impasse*. Germany does not buy the economic arguments of its critics. We believe, however, that it will probably be reasons of political economy or indeed of politics as such that should move her to do something. The first is that the breach between creditors and debtors cannot go on if they both belong to a monetary union. We have already seen the degree of disintegrating political tension that this gap created during the crisis. The extreme case of Greece showed what should never have happened between two countries of a monetary union: an irresponsible and duplicitous member, whose economic sovereignty is annulled by the creditor members. The second reason is that persistent disequilibria in current accounts end up generating tendencies towards trade protectionism in the deficit countries, which come to the fore when populism seizes political power. It is true that the normative and institutional framework of the eurozone would not allow protectionist drifts to occur, but tensions between countries would feed centrifugal forces towards the disintegration of the Union.

A third reason is that Germany is violating the limits defined by the Excessive Imbalance Procedure of the European Union, which establishes that the current account surplus should not exceed 6 percent of GDP. The reputational damage suffered by Germany was significant when, in the early years of the EMU, it repeatedly failed to comply with the fiscal deficit limit. A similar situation occurred in the decade of the 2010s with the trade surplus. This breach of fundamental rules is not in keeping with Germany's leading role in Europe. It eats away at its moral authority, something the country values highly.

Finally, the tensions that the German commercial position generate inside and outside Europe make it difficult for her to exercise what has been the maxim guiding her foreign policy since 1945: international cooperation. The vocation to resolve all conflicts through multinational cooperation, the use of bilateral or multilateral cooperation to expand her internal markets and the civic-minded nature of her engagement in the international arena have been constant in their international positioning. It is uncomfortable for a country that has always proclaimed these cooperative and consensual principles, to sit in international meetings and repeatedly hear the same complaint about its external disequilibrium.

Just how far these political considerations will weigh on motivating Germany to moderate her lonely path in future is difficult to discern. Let us hope that the fact that the euro crisis has been temporarily overcome does not diminish Germany's incentive to moderate its external account imbalance.

IX

ORDOLIBERALISM:
THE GERMAN ECONOMIC CATECHISM

The EU and the EMU suffer from both economic and ideological asymmetries, and in the long run the latter can do as much damage as the former. Very different cultures coexist within the union, different ways of understanding life and authority, different visions of work, of the balance between saving and consumption, of the role of the State in the economy and a long *etcetera*. Just as the development of the crisis brought out economic dividing lines between debtor and creditor countries, importers and exporters, technological leaders and stragglers, so did ideological splits become apparent that had a great influence on how countries managed their economies and in why they went into crisis.[90] The tolerance of a Mediterranean country towards inflation or debt is an ocean away from that of a country like Germany, for whom *Schuld* means both debt and guilt.

The victors not only write the history, they impose the ideology. Germany emerged from the eurozone crisis as the winner: its economic model had weathered the GFC storm without any major issues. Behind that successful economic model was a fairly well-defined ideology with deep roots in both the German philosophy of the State and Society and in the Protestant popular culture epitomised by the Swabian housewife. The

---

90 Some analysts explain the harsh and inefficient process of handling the crisis as a reflection of the antagonism and incompatibility between national cultures within the eurozone (Herrera, Guiso et al., 2017). In a model of choice interactions, the Greeks end up "bluffing" more than is usual for them and the Germans end up "punishing" more than is usual for them, with the consequent loss of welfare for all.

success of the model gave Germany the moral authority to tell its partners and neighbours how they should have gone about things and what was the road to straightening out their economies. And if on top of that Germany had the economic might to provide rescue resources, it was clear who was in charge. The German view of the causes of the debtors' crisis became the official diagnosis, determining what prescriptions were applied.

Ordoliberalism and the culture of stability

The interpretation and approach to the crisis meshed perfectly with what had been the dominant economic philosophy in Germany after the Second World War, known as "ordoliberalism". It was this philosophy that had inspired the foundations of the European Monetary Union and later informed the responses to the eurocrisis. Although it is true that its application during the euro crisis was full of contradictions and inconsistencies, there is no doubt that at the level of popular ideology it exerted powerful restrictions on how to deal with the situation.

The central concepts of this thought were initially developed by the Freiburg School in the years prior to World War II, one of whose main representatives was Walter Eucken (1891-1950). Wilhelm Röpke (1899-1966) also made decisive contributions to ordoliberal thinking. The school wanted to get away from both National Socialist State interventionism and *laissez-faire* liberalism. According to Eucken, the principles which constitute a free market economy are:

- Private property
- An efficient pricing system
- Primacy of the monetary order and price stability
- Openness and freedom of markets
- Legal responsibility, and
- Stability of economic policy

To understand this, it is important to emphasize that ordoliberal theory was developed by legal philosophers, not by economists (in the modern sense of the word). For them, the legal dimension gives shape to the economic sphere, and the latter would not be what it is without the legal framework.[91] As a basic principle, society must function according to rules formulated in a general way; it is the function of the State to define the formal principles and rules that govern society and the economy, enforce their compliance and penalise their non-compliance; in no case should the State assume direct functions of production or distribution of goods and services. The most important responsibility of the State is to define rules for the promotion of free competition in the markets and rein in the actions of monopolistic or oligopolistic cartels. In essence, the ordo-liberal approach advocates a strong State authority that is the guardian and defender of a free market economy, which must also operate within an ethical, social and humanistic framework. Chancellor Angela Merkel expressed it in her speech at the end of the year 2009: "... *the State must be the guardian of the economic and social order. Competition needs to have a sense of proportion and social responsibility ... These principles must be followed throughout the world.*" This last lapidary phrase of universal validity reflects the dogmatic tone customary in Germany when speaking of this ordoliberal economic order.

Ordoliberal thinking and liberalism in the style of Friedrich von Hayek and the Chicago School share the concern for the preservation of individual freedom and the conviction that competitive markets are the best environment for the development of that freedom. Where they differ radically is in the role of the State. While classical liberalism relies entirely on the power of markets to discipline and punish abuses of power by individuals or corporations, and hence its defence of *laissez-faire*, the ordoliberals propose a strong State to monitor abuses of power and punish those who deviate from the rules. The State must have the strength to create and defend the conditions that allow Adam Smith's invisible hand to operate properly; it is the "market policeman" in the words of Walter Rüstow, another of the fathers of ordoliberal thought. The role of the State in early ordoliberal thinking is so central that the economy is seen as a political fact, something that works under political rules or ceases to function if those rules are not applied. If, for example, the economy goes into crisis, it is because there has been a failure of State intervention. Either the State has not regulated enough, or has addressed the intervention inadequately, or has not been able to enforce the rules.

---

91   For a development of these concepts, see Hien and Jörges (2018)

It is the State that defines the regulatory framework within which individuals develop their actions in exercise of their freedom, and which punishes those who deviate from it. Economic agents are fully responsible for their actions. Failure to comply with the rules entails full individual responsibilities that must be sanctioned without exception. This accountability of economic agents is essential for the proper functioning of the free market system. If the allocation of responsibilities and the application of sanctions are diluted in any way, moral incentives are created for future breaches and the regulatory system breaks down. For example, rescuing a badly administered bank undermines the foundations of the system, because it exempts the owners or administrators of that bank from assuming their responsibilities and the consequences of the bankruptcy. The same applies to rescuing profligate governments.

Before Konrad Adenauer and his Minister of Economy, Ludwig Erhard, entered government, ordoliberal thought had hardly left the academic ivory tower of abstract ideas. It was in the 50s and 60s when ordoliberalism found expression and concrete application in the economic model driven by Adenauer and Erhard. The model that produced the German miracle of the post-war period was called the social market economy (*Soziale Marktwirtschaft*), a very German combination of a free market under rules of high social and ethical content. The principal rule was the prohibition of positions of abuse of economic power that could dampen free competition. In addition to ensuring free competition, the State was responsible for guaranteeing that the economic system did not abandon those in need of social protection and that there was an equilibrium between the interests of capital and labour. As Karl Schiller, an SPD Finance Minister, liked to say: *"As much Market as possible, as much State as necessary"* (*"So viel Markt wie möglich, so viel Staat wie nötig"*). This social responsibility of the State is the second great difference between ordoliberalism and other branches of neoclassical liberalism. Certainly, the model then underwent changes over the following decades and absorbed many elements of American neoclassical liberalism, but it always preserved the essential features of ordoliberalism of the Freiburg School, regarding the central role of the State and its social responsibility.

As regards the implications of this philosophy as a guide for decisions on economic management, the model was dressed up with several elements that later became pillars of the EMU edifice:

- Price stability as the supreme objective; independence of the Central Bank
- Principle of fiscal probity (equilibrium): spending based on income; not living beyond one's means; an aversion to contracting debt
- Principle of non-rescue (no bailouts): countries, banks and, in general, economic subjects must assume the consequences of their policies and actions
- Faith in the disciplining effect of financial markets

These four elements are part of the "stability culture" (*Stabilitätskultur*) that is so characteristic of German economic thought. The deep aversion to inflation found its realisation in the sacrosanct respect for the political independence of the central bank, entrusted with the single objective of preserving price stability. The mentality of saving for lean times and the aversion to borrowing in order to spend more than one has is the guarantee that monetary stability will not be undermined by the fiscal conduct.

These pillars of the stability culture were embodied in the agreement establishing the EMU. We commented in Chapter III that France was the country that most proactively pushed the idea of the monetary union and that for Germans giving up the deutschmark meant a difficult sacrifice. The only way to overcome the resistance of the Bundesbank and the German leadership was to ensure that the Maastricht Treaty incorporated these elements of the German stability culture. The independence of the European Central Bank was the embodiment of a monetary order in which monetary policy was elevated to a legal Olympus and led by a supra-national power free of political whim. In this way, the currency was "de-nationalised" so that no government could manipulate it. The States kept responsibility for fiscal management, but always (supposedly) under the restriction of the supreme good of currency stability. Under the agreement establishing Maastricht, fiscal policy had to support and be subordinated to monetary policy through a regulated framework. The construct of the monetary union contemplated no sort of fiscal transfers or risk sharing schemes or shared responsibilities, since this would have violated the principle of individual responsibility of the States and would have undermined the discipline of the members of the union.

Very much in line with the German mindset, the design of the Maastricht Treaty was based on the presumption that the rules of no monetary financing of fiscal deficits and no rescue would be enough to guarantee stability. The naiveté came, first, from believing that everyone was going to respect the rules and, second, from trying to apply the same set of fixed and general regulations to countries as structurally different as those that were going to coexist within the EMU.[92]

Once monetary policy had attained absolute supremacy and national fiscal policy was subordinated to the stability of the currency, the union's equilibrating mechanism *par excellence* became the adjustment of the job market to achieve competitive labour costs. Ordoliberalism, like neoliberalism, is based on the conviction that flexible prices and (falling) wages are the solution to the problem of unemployment. In the economic literature this is called the automatic adjustment mechanism of prices and internal wages, which characterizes all fixed exchange rates. In this scheme, therefore, wage containment is in the first rank among economic policies.

Ideological differences between Germany and Latin Europe

A useful approach to understanding this German economic philosophy is to contrast it with other ways of thinking, and what better contrast than that offered by the thinking of France, the second pole of the duo that has governed Europe? Brunnermeier, James and Landau (2016) have taken on the task of contrasting the views of Germany and France on the economy in general and on the principles that should govern their conduct in economic matters (see Table IX-1 for an outline of the different views). Here we will refer only to the principles and ideas most pertinent to the handling of the crisis. As Europe's Mediterranean South is closer to French thought and the North and Centre closer to German thought, we could draw an ideological dividing line between the Anglo-Saxon and Protestant Centre-North, and the Latin and Catholic Mediterranean South. The Centre-North gives precedence to rules, rigour and consistency, while the Mediterranean South places an emphasis on flexibility, adaptability

---

[92] Scharpf (2018) also attributes this naive belief to ordoliberal thinking's faith in rule-based systems.

and innovation. Expressed as a cliché, it's Kant *vs.* Machiavelli, rules *vs.* discretionary action.

TABLE IX-1
Divergent views between Germany and France

Ideological-political differences		
ISSUE	GERMANY	FRANCE
State	Federal	Centralised and unitary
Constitutional order	Social State ruled by law, based on rules, checks and balances	Rule of law, based on rules subject to political control
Democracy	Parliamentary	Presidencial
Values	Solidity, rigour, frugality, stability of rules	Solidarity, flexibility, adaptability, innovation
Predominant ideology	Ordoliberalism	Keynesian activism
Responsibility of economic agents	Unmitigated	Subject to political control
Differences in economic systems		
Industrial (union) relations	Consensual, centralised and corporate	Conflicting and fragmented
Markets	Commercial freedom and open financial markets	Promotion of "national champions"
Macroeconomic policy	Regulated monetary framework that prioritises price stability	Active management of the economy for the achievement of growth
Central Bank	Independence, single mandate of price stability	Objectives of stability and growth with political control
Banking	Federally decentralised, dispersed	National and concentrated
Exchange rate regime	Flexible according to fundamentals	"Strong", fixed franc
Fiscal Union	Opposed to fiscal transfers, except in full political union	Reluctant to yield sovereignty, but open to solidarity transfers

Based on Brunnermeier et al. (2016)

As we said earlier, the central backbone of German thought is that society and the economy must operate under a set of stable rules, whose application and power to exact penalties is guaranteed through bodies of vigilance and control imbued in the Social State ruled by law. This need to live under stable rules made sense after the traumatic experience of National Socialism. In fact, ordoliberalism of the Freiburg School was born as a reaction against the arbitrary totalitarianism that had seized hold of Germany in the decade previous to the Second World War.

According to the principle of responsibility (*Haftungsprinzip*), citizens, whether individuals or corporations, are solely responsible for their actions and must be held accountable for compliance with the rules. If an individual bank or a National Treasury becomes insolvent, they must fully assume the consequences of their actions, no matter how harsh these consequences may be. The markets constitute the first line of enforcement, the second line being bankruptcy and the final one the law. Rescues or debt forgiveness would go against the principle of responsibility and would set precedents that would wipe out the *raison d'être* of having a world of rules, which is precisely to discipline economic agents in order to encourage good practice. The moral hazard of knowing that bad behaviour might one day be rewarded with a rescue or pardon would undermine the foundations of the system and create incentives for free riding. The State is not an insurer against private risks.

It is this principle of liability, and the moral hazard of not respecting it, which explains the aversion of Germany to using the Central Bank as a lender of last resort. When a debtor, whether sovereign or private, receives debt relief, it loses the incentive to correct its mistakes in the future. Additionally, the monetary expansion that would result from rescuing banks would endanger what for Germans is the only goal of a central bank: to maintain price stability. A system of firm rules, both monetary and fiscal, is what will prevent overspill from bad fiscal management and consequently spares the Central Bank from the political pressures that could undermine its independence.

In the intellectual and political tradition of Graeco-Latin Europe, on the contrary, the rules certainly exist, but they are not the absolutist entities that they are in Central and Northern Europe. Just as the establishment of rules is the product of democratic confrontation and negotiation, their application must also be subject to political negotiation, especially when to apply them implacably might have serious social consequences. Particularly in times of crisis and turbulence, regulated frameworks must be able to adapt flexibly to new circumstances. It would not be in the democratic spirit for the government to be absolutely bound hand and foot by regulatory schemes that might well have made sense under normal circumstances, but do not in times of crisis.

For Latin countries, the principle of individual responsibility should not exclude the parts of a system (the members of a community) from assuming their own share of responsibility, even if indirectly and in due proportion. For example, for Southern European banks to become over-indebted in the way they did, banks in creditor countries had to lend them sums of money that exceeded reasonable risk limits. Certainly, the responsibility of the lender is not the same as that of the borrower who fails to pay up, but there are strong economic and political reasons to justify the burden of regaining equilibrium being undertaken as symmetrically as possible.

Applying these contrasting philosophies to the fiscal sphere, German thinking refused any mutualisation of sovereign debt without prior fiscal union being attained; in the meantime, each country had to be liable for its own debt and rescues were totally prohibited. This position left debt default as the only escape valve of a monetary system as rigid as a monetary union. France, on the other hand, considered fiscal bailouts an indispensable stability mechanism against adverse asymmetric economic shocks, just as the theory of Optimum Currency Areas had initially postulated. Interestingly, Germany was usually more willing to transfer certain fiscal powers to Brussels, something that for France was politically unacceptable. On the other hand, France was more willing to consider transfers of fiscal resources to countries in crisis, whereas Germany closed its ranks against any type of fiscal transfer. Behind this friction we observe once again the contrast: the principle of individual responsibility in a rules-based world *vs.* flexibility seasoned with solidarity.

True to this principle of responsibility, Germany would not allow any rescue package not conditional on the recipient's future good behaviour. The rules of this good behaviour were included in the Treaty on Stability, Coordination and Governance (TSCG) of March 2012, which established:

- A structural deficit ceiling and a balanced fiscal budget
- A public debt burden cap (60 percent of GDP)
- An automatic correction mechanism in case of deviation from any of these rules

- Obligation to give the maximum legal status to the TSCG within each country

As for the basic recipe for restoring lost fiscal balances, the German position was consistent with its philosophy of individual responsibility and its attachment to frugality: countries that had incurred excess spending had to submit to the rigours of austerity, reduce expenses and increase taxes. Only purification through austerity, accompanied by structural reforms on the supply side to improve growth potential, could put those economies back on the path of healthy economic growth. The Latin partners, for their part, did not believe in the healing properties of austerity and saw in it risks of self-destruction or aggravation of the crisis. Betting on a deficit reduction by contracting demand was to flog the dead horse of a demand already depressed by the debt crisis. What was necessary was rather to stimulate aggregate demand to give social and economic viability to structural reform programs.

In the area of banking, Germany tended to interpret bank problems as an expression of underlying structural failures, so they were to be handled as if they were solvency problems. Irrigating the troubled banks with liquidity was not going to solve the problems at the root, but rather avoid or delay a necessary restructuring. France and the countries of the South tended to consider banking problems in terms of illiquidity, which had to be addressed through a proactive and aggressive policy of injecting liquidity into financial systems. In the original design of the EMU, the responsibility for financial assistance fell to the national central banks, which was tantamount to saying that it fell on the shoulders of the taxpayers of the respective States. When in 2011-2012 the banking crisis became systemic in several of the countries of the periphery, it became evident that no national State had the financial muscle to support its banking system on its own. It was at this time that most of the members of the eurozone entrusted the European Central Bank with the mission of stabilising the European financial system, which it did very effectively.

This intervention of the ECB as lender of last resort generated discomfort in the German government and open rejection by the Bundesbank. Its approach was that this lifeline was going to generate the wrong incentives by saving the rescued financial systems and their national treasuries from the need to undertake the reforms that would place them on the path of financial discipline. According to Germany, the ECB's aid was preventing the curative powers of market rigour from having their effect; rather, they helped to prolong the same dependence on external financing to cover internal deficits that had been evident since the dawn of the Monetary Union. Opposition to the ECB's action came to the point of questioning its legality before the German Constitutional Court on the grounds that the Maastricht Treaty expressly prohibited the bailout of governments or financial systems. A second argument was that the monetary expansion derived from aid would undermine the sole mandate of the ECB to preserve inflationary stability. France and the Mediterranean periphery did not share this restrictive view of the ECB's mandate. For them, a central bank is not a separate solar system, but part of the same entity, the State, which also has a social responsibility to preserve the stability of the financial system.

PRINCIPLES, PRAGMATISM OR SELF-INTEREST?

The clash of ideas between Germany and France has allowed us to bring the contrasting ideologies between two approaches to the euro crisis down to earth. Let us now take another step towards the real world and ask ourselves how coherent Germany has been in applying these principles. Rhetoric is one thing and implementation another. When the crunch came for the eurozone, Germany had to set aside several ordoliberal principles, sometimes because the virulence of the markets gave no room for manoeuvre, and at other times because its own interests were threatened. Critics point out that Germany always liked to impose strict rules on its partners but was more flexible when it had to apply them to itself.[93] They mention as background the breach of the fiscal deficit limit in the first decade of the 2000s, when for three consecutive years Germany exceeded the limit and was not penalised for it. Then, as the GFC exploded, the German authorities were eager and generous in rescuing several German banks, ignoring the moral hazard they talked so much about. They also

---

93 In the book edited by Thorsten Beck and Hans-Helmut Kotz (2017), several of the contributing authors highlight the constant deviations of Germany from the regulated ordoliberal framework during the years of the euro crisis (see especially the contributions of Feld, Köhler and Nientied, Michael Burda and Charles Wyplosz).

consented to deviations from principle in the initial rescues of Greece or when France and Spain incurred fiscal deficits above the limits. The German government preferred to turn a blind eye to the ECB's liquidity injection operations in 2011 and 2012, because that lowered the pressure of having to become the lender of last resort for some of its banks with large exposures to the South. Neither before, nor much less after the GFC, was Germany faithfully compliant with ordoliberal principles.

The underlying problems with rule-based systems are twofold. Firstly, their champions do not envisage a serious crisis arising as long as everyone abides by the rules. And secondly, when the crisis erupts, the rules become such straitjackets that governments have to resort to discretionary measures, the management and administration of which the system is not prepared for. In the case of the eurozone, this discretionality not only generated inefficiencies and delays, but put Germany in the spotlight and made it the final decision maker–something the Germans had always tried to avoid. This dragged it into a political diatribe from those who complained that the decisions of the European Council and other Community bodies responded to the particular interest of Germany.

Take the case of banking as an illustration. Contrary to what one might think, German banks faced very serious problems when the crisis broke out in 2008. The leading private and public banks, in their eagerness to become first-rank international players, had allowed themselves to be dragged into the speculative frenzy of the American sub-prime bubble and other bubbles in Europe. As a result of bad investments, several banks had to be rescued or nationalised in 2008-2009.

At the end of 2008, the Merkel government provided SoFFin, (*Sonderfonds für Finanzmarktstabilisierung, Special Financial Market Stabilisation Funds*), the entity in charge of bank rescues, with the significant sum of 672 billion dollars (equivalent to 20% of GDP) in guarantees and liquid money to address the serious situation of German banks. To get an idea of the magnitude, this amount was similar to the 700 billion authorised for the US Troubled Asset Relief Program for the same purpose, which only represented 4.75% of the North American GDP; that was, in relative terms a quarter of the resources needed by Germany. A frenzy of bank rescues took place between the last quarter of 2008 and the first half of 2009: Hypo Real Estate, a subsidiary of the Hypo Vereinsbank, was rescued and then nationalised; the second-largest private commercial bank, Commerzbank, was rescued in exchange for transferring to the State 25% of its capital; the regional State banks Bayerische Landesbank, West Landesbank and HSH Nordbank also received important injections of capital.[94]

Additional to the effects of the sub-prime crisis, the leading German and French banks also had a high exposure to Greek debt. In order to protect their banks, Germany and France initially refused to apply write-offs (cuts) to the Greek debt and opted for the rescue route, supplying Greece with new loans to pay the old ones. Not only did this solution contradict the prohibition on bailouts enshrined in the Treaty of Maastricht, but it went against the rationale that no more debt should be loaded upon a debtor who is already insolvent. In this way, the problem of the banks was transferred to the European governments, and ultimately to the taxpayers. Once the banks were outside the danger zone, France and Germany proposed the policy of Private Sector Involvement for the second Greek rescue package of 2012. Besides that, the essence of the creditors' strategy did not change: delivery of new resources to pay off old debt and cover new deficits. According to a study of the European School of Management and Technology in Berlin (ESMT), almost half of the 216 billion euros of the two initial Greek rescue packages was for paying interest due, recapitalising banks and repaying loans, all of them measures to alleviate the problems of the creditor banks.

These things are what have called into question the double standards of the German approach to the financial crisis: orthodoxy for the debtors and pragmatism and self-interest for the creditors. Not every step was successful, however. Private Sector Involvement, for example, at that time of turbulence in the markets and with no additional measures to stem the haemorrhage, was a very bad move by Merkel, which aggravated and accelerated the crisis. This aggravation forced Germany to do or permit things it had always tried to avoid, such as bailouts, monetary expansion (quantitative easing) by the ECB or the supervision of its banks by external bodies. This contradiction is what Matthias Matthijs (2016) has called the "Berlin puzzle".

---

94 Deutsche Bank, flagship of German banking, did not receive resources directly, but by then had already sown the seeds of its later decline as a global player.

A possible explanation of this puzzle is the hypothesis advanced by David Art (2015), who contends that what appeared to be Germany's mistaken policy decisions actually were pieces of a well-designed strategy after the Greek debt crisis of 2010. This strategy required a high degree of turbulence in financial markets to break down the resistance of German public opinion as well as the constitutional objections that were preventing rescue efforts. The dilemma had to be presented in terms of preserving the stability of the euro and not in terms of solidarity with the debtors or lifebelts for the creditor banks. Preserving the euro was something that the Bundesbank and constitutional judges considered a high priority but helping out irresponsible debtors was not an argument acceptable to anyone, especially to the German public. Seen from this perspective, the 2011 Private Sector Involvement decision would not be the "serious error", for which Merkel was so criticised, but part of a congruent strategy of pushing the financial markets to the brink of collapse to weaken internal resistance and force deep reforms on the debtors.

We do not share this hypothesis of a cold Machiavellian strategy on the part of the German authorities. What happened was simply that the financial crisis was aggravated by inefficient and belated management by the Community institutions, with Germany at the head. Not only was the Community's structure not prepared for a crisis of this magnitude, but a lack of understanding of the problem and ignorance about the instruments for handling it was evident at every level. That Germany would later take advantage of this deterioration to boost its own policies is another matter.

We agree with the position of Feld, Köhler and Nientiedt (2017), authors close to the Freiburg School, that Germany's key actions during the eurozone crisis were not really moulded by ordoliberalism, but that what predominated rather was pragmatism, the defence of the *status quo* and the national interest. They point to the fact that most German economists do not differ so radically from their colleagues in other places, especially those of the Anglo-Saxon neoliberal world. Their approaches could not get too far away from reality, unless they lived in academic ivory towers. Where Germany remained more aligned with ordoliberal ideology was in interpreting the causes of the crisis and applying to the debtors the recipe book of austerity and structural reforms, tailored to a German standard. In other words, rigidity without and flexibility within.

This incongruence between internal and external conduct explains how much of the behaviour and policy decisions of the German authorities during the euro crisis deviated from ordoliberal precepts. To tell the truth, these precepts were formulated at such an abstract and general level that they gave room to different solutions.[95] For example, there was intense debate within the ordoliberal camp about which stability should be preserved, that of the European Union's institutionalism–the *Ordnungsgefüge*–or that of the euro. Saving the euro meant bypassing some established rules of the ordoliberal order. In the end, the pragmatism of saving the euro prevailed.

Hien and Jörges (2018) also believe that the direct influence of ordoliberalism on German economic policy has been overestimated. Most German economists and policymakers are closer to Anglo-Saxon neoliberalism than to the ordoliberalism of the Freiburg School. The influence was, rather, indirect through the cultural values underlying ordoliberalism, with its strong roots in the Protestant ethic. More than among economists, this culture is still very present in the German population and influences political discourse in a way that strongly restricts the choice of policy options. As an example, let's take the concept of solidarity, so crucial for the survival of a monetary union. From the purely ordoliberal perspective, social aid must be limited to what is strictly necessary for each citizen to have the incentives leading to virtuous behaviour: hard work, frugality, responsibility. Everyone should live on the fruits of their labour and not spend more than they have. The danger of welfare aid is that it tends to generate counterproductive incentives and end up being a "total catastrophe for the State and society", in the words of ordoliberals. General unemployment insurance, for example, has no place in this concept of solidarity, much less saving a bank or a bankrupt country.

The original contribution of the Protestant ethic to ordoliberal thought is undeniable, but with the passage of time political reality forced compromises with more socially-minded political or confessional tendencies. When Germany was shaping its economic model in the 50s

---

95   Jacoby (2014) justifies these contradictions in the fact that ordoliberalism is not a completely developed theory of economic life and that therefore can shelter very different recipes under one umbrella.

and 60s, the strict Calvinist-Lutheran ethic had to make concessions to the Catholic vision of society, which was much more paternalistic and inclined to social justice and redistribution of wealth. The Catholic Chancellor Konrad Adenauer and the Protestant Minister of the Economy Ludwig Erhardt, with the help of the economist Alfred Müller-Armack, arrived at the symbiosis of the *"soziale Marktwirtschaft"* model (Social Market Economy). This model combined the original principles of the ordoliberal heritage, more rooted in Protestantism, with elements of social justice and income redistribution, more rooted in Catholicism. The social dimension owed as much to the State's vigilance against abuses of market power, as to the welfare system.

Ordoliberal ideas had and still have a powerful draw in German public opinion, because they appeal to the common sense of the Swabian housewife and are rooted in the atavistic depths of northern Europe's Protestant morals (Schmidt, 2016). German public opinion–fed by newspapers in the style of Bild Zeitung, a popular tabloid, or the Frankfurter Allgemeine Zeitung, organ of the educated Centre Right–remained attached primarily to a simplified version of ordoliberalism that quickly labelled the eurozone crisis as a consequence of and a deserved punishment for wasteful southerners and siesta takers. This gave them the moral high ground to defend the particular interests of Germany, and especially to avoid having to pay other people's bills.

It is this grassroots support for ordoliberal ideas that explains their persistence in German political discourse. Merkel had to keep winning elections and for that she needed to connect with the popular version of ordoliberalism predominant in the electorate. It is also true that, on top of electoral expediency, a large part of the German establishment agreed with the ordoliberal ideology. A conspicuous and convinced representative of this thought was Wolfgang Schäuble, Minister of Finance from 2009 to 2017, who proudly and repeatedly cited his ordoliberal origins (he was born and studied in Freiburg, the cradle of ordoliberalism). For Schäuble, the cause of the euro crisis was that some countries were living beyond their means before the crisis erupted, and so could not demand unconditional support or solidarity. Any help should be conditional on changes in behaviour in the direction of more work, more productivity, frugality, responsibility, self-sufficiency.

X

AN INCOMPLETE AND DISFUNCTIONAL HEGEMONY

The history of international monetary systems implies that their sustainability over time will depend mainly on political conditions, more specifically on the ability and willingness of the hegemonic member of the system to continue providing the elements that confer stability and cohesion on the system. Applied to Europe, the survival of the Monetary Union in its current form will depend on the willingness of Germany to exercise its (benevolent) hegemonic responsibility and therefore to assume its share of the stability burdens in the future. Has Germany met that responsibility? Has it really felt that it has it? It is no exaggeration to say that the success or failure of Germany in its task of stabilising and uniting the eurozone system means the success or failure of the EMU project. And if the eurozone of 19 were to implode, the European Union of 27 would have a very uncertain future. Everything points to the fact that, just as the main driver of the decision to form the EMU was political, making it viable in the future will be a political decision as well.

It is therefore worth trying to understand how the web of power relations within Europe was shaped and what role Germany assumed within that web. The country emerged from the crisis as the centre of economic and political power in Europe: the lines of negotiation and decision passed inexorably through Berlin, which became in many aspects the *de facto* capital of Europe. The force of numbers and events put it in a dominant position, but also placed it at the focus of criticism. The irony of history was that, due to the crisis, the European Union, which supposedly was born to tame Germany, became the stage for Germany to emerge as the new dominant power. During the euro crisis, a benevolent leadership was expected of Germany, which she could not or would not accept. This made her a target of accusations, much to the frustration of the Germans, who felt misunderstood after having devoted so much effort to the process of European integration.

If the European integration project was born largely as a way of solving the German Problem, the evolution of events put Germany in a position where the problem reared up yet again, albeit in new ways, and some of the stereotypes and prejudices that had pursued Germany for two centuries resurfaced. To what extent did Germany contribute to becoming the target of so much criticism and go from being seen as the good citizen, to being vilified by many as an implacable, insensitive and selfish power?

Much of the problem was in the German aversion, after the Second World War, to assuming positions of leadership or strength that could resuscitate the ghosts of the past. This ambiguity between *de facto* domination and the discomfort of exercising a hegemonic role explained a good deal of the contradictions and inefficiencies of how the crisis was handled. What coalesced in Europe in the decade of the 2010s was a dysfunctional hegemonic system, in which the leader that was in fact dominant did not assume its collective responsibilities, entailing significant costs. Nor was it able to win over the other members to its ideological creed.

This was the concern of Radoslaw Sikorski, Polish Foreign Minister, when in a speech in Berlin in November 2011 he warned: "*I will probably be the first Polish foreign minister in history to say this, but here it is. I fear German power less than I am beginning to fear its inactivity. You have become Europe's indispensable nation. You may not fail to lead.*" Matthijs and Blith (2011) were even more emphatic in stating that "*The complex of causes of the eurocrisis does however have a common root: Germany's failure to act as a responsible hegemon in Europe*".

Theory of hegemonic stability

We must take a moment to understand the concept of hegemony, which will help us to answer the question of whether Germany behaved as a hegemonic power in the European Monetary Union. As we proceed to define the terms hegemon and hegemony, the reader is invited to imagine how Germany might fit into these concepts. The term *hegemony* comes from the Greek and means "*leadership, preponderant influence, dominant position*". In ancient Greece, the title of hegemon was used to describe both the chief commander of the army, as well as the city-State that led the coalition against other City-States, such as Athens or Sparta as the case may be. In more political terms, hegemony implies a certain relationship of dominance and subordination between two or more States. Typical examples of hegemons were Rome in the Roman Empire, Spain in the Spanish Empire, Great Britain in the British Empire, Prussia in the German Confederation, Russia in the Soviet Union or the United States in the Western Alliance.

It was the German political scientist and constitutionalist Heinrich Triepel who developed the theory in depth in his 1938 work on hegemony.[96] Hegemony is defined on a spectrum between simple influence and pure domination. When the relationship between two or more States is based exclusively on the strength of one of them to impose its decisions, we cannot speak of hegemony, because this must be based on a recognition of hegemonic leadership by the States being led. The hegemon derives its legitimacy and stability from this recognition. In the absence of voluntary recognition and subordination, this is not hegemony but simple imperial domination. Neither is a hegemony a relationship based on simple influence of ideas, ways of life or social models. In its origins, then, hegemony is born of a reciprocal understanding, of a communion of interests, of a sense of belonging, whether this understanding has been embodied in a legal agreement or through a special degree of influence of one country over others.

In general, the hegemon is a *primus inter pares* that has grounds for having earned its status as a leader and continues to work permanently to preserve the group's cohesion and nourish the reasons why the other members adhered at the time. The power and influence that the hegemon can exercise over its followers depends mainly on its ability and capacity for influencing the will of other States. This power and influence must be based on four necessary conditions:

---

96   Despite the suggestive title ("*Ein Buch von Führenden Staaten*") and the period in which he wrote it (1937-1938), Triepel managed to avoid any reference to or apologia for the National Socialism of the time.

- A sufficient base of economic and military power
- Ability and capacity to impose and implement its ideological, social, political and economic model
- Willingness to assume the hegemonic role and the duties that this entails
- Acceptance of the hegemon by the other member States of the community

In the end, what is at issue is that the hegemonic leader manages to implant its own political, cultural and socio-economic model in the other members. This can happen through one of the following three ways, or a combination of them.[97]

- External induction: rationally motivated acceptance of norms in exchange for incentives and/or perks provided by the hegemon
- Normative persuasion: acceptance of norms due to the subordinates' own conviction
- Appropriate conduct: a middle way by which members behaviour is "politically correct" and they interpret their role and follow the norms expected of them in the hope of being rewarded with some collective benefits

Subsequently, the theory of Hegemonic Stability was developed. This initially applied more to the world of international economic relations but is perfectly extendable to the world of geo-economic relations between countries. In his book on the causes of the Great Depression of 1929, Charles Kindleberger (1973) attributed the severity and destructive force of the crisis to the absence of a hegemonic leader which could have taken the actions necessary to tackle the ravenous contagion that sank the world economy into 10 years of depression.[98] Great Britain had emerged decidedly weakened from World War I and at the time did not have the financial muscle necessary to provide the global financial system with the necessary liquidity. The United States had suffered little during the war and

---

97 See Ikenberry and Kupchan (1990)

98 Kindleberger (1973)

continued its unstoppable economic rise, but it had not yet internalised its new importance and showed no interest whatever in taking over the Western world's leadership.

The central message of this approach is that without a hegemonic leader playing its part to the full, international economic and financial systems tend to be unstable. According to the theory of Structural Neorealism (Waltz, 1979), international relations tend to be naturally anarchic and fragmented. Economic agents, including States, tend to compete and contend uncooperatively in a zero-sum game, which sooner or later unleashes destabilising destructive forces. Aware of this reality, Kindleberger linked the success of a monetary order to the existence of a hegemon able to assume collective responsibilities in solidarity.[99] According to Kindleberger: *"A stable monetary order requires a hegemon powerful enough to resolve collective action problems and extend concessions to subordinate allies"*. The hegemon must take on a good dose of solidarity: *"... the international economic and monetary system needs leadership, a country which is prepared, consciously or unconsciously [...] to take on an undue share of the burdens of the system, and in particular take on its support in adversity by accepting redundant commodities, maintaining a flow of investment capital and discounting its paper."*

Two functions of the benevolent hegemon are central to the Kindleberger postulate:

- ability to solve problems of collective interest, and
- willingness to take on a disproportionate share of the system's burdens, grant concessions to allies and apply penalties to dissidents.

The resolution of problems of collective interest is equivalent to what in the social sciences is called the provision of "public goods", such as the security and defence of the nation or the protection of the underprivileged, tasks usually undertaken by the State or delegated to third parties under public economic tutelage. Extended to the international sphere,

---

99 Curiously, the German Minister of Finance, Wolfgang Schäuble, who played a leading role during the Eurocrisis, gave a nod to Kindleberger by subscribing to his vision that only a lead nation, a benign or stabilising hegemon, could create a stable global economy. In Europe, according to Schäuble, that role corresponds to Germany and France jointly (cited in Kundnani, 2014).

someone has to provide certain goods to the nations, such as the institutions to keep order in world trade, international law or the preservation of the global environment. In the sphere of international economic and financial relations, essential public goods are the provision of international liquidity, a legal framework for trade, the protection of private property and, above all, the economic and financial stability of the system. Referring specifically to the crisis of the Great Depression, but applicable also to other crisis events, Kindleberger identifies five public goods that the benevolent hegemon must provide:

- Serve as a market for goods that cannot find a buyer (distressed goods)
- Provide short-term liquidity and long-term countercyclical loans
- Coordinate macroeconomic policies
- Stabilise exchange rates
- Act as a lender of last resort during financial crises

As these are public goods, no-one can be excluded from their benefits, but neither is anyone willing spontaneously to assume their cost on their own for others to benefit. At national level, therefore, it is the State that assumes the production of public goods, directly or indirectly. At the level of a community of nations, it is a *primus inter pares* or dominant State that must assume that function, since otherwise the system will drift towards anarchy and instability.

The second element or function of the benevolent hegemony is a willingness to grant concessions to allies. To be considered as such, the hegemonic country must assume the lion's share of the costs of producing public goods. Since cooperation between nations and economic-financial integration are public goods of the first order, especially in a community united by a common currency, the hegemon must absorb an outsize burden of the costs of preserving such cooperation and integration. There are two reasons to justify the disproportionate costs assumed by the hegemon. The first is that, if it did not do so, there would be no justification in holding the title of hegemon, nor would the other members of the community have any reason to recognise it as such. The system of hegemonic relations has to provide sufficient incentives to countries that want to belong to a relationship of "consensual domination", the main one being the hegemon's willingness to provide public goods at its own expense. The second reason is that the hegemonic power receives important benefits derived precisely from its hegemonic condition. Think of the exorbitant privilege[100] that the dollar becoming the world reserve currency since World War II has meant for the United States. Or think of the benefits for Germany of the undervaluation of the euro with respect to a hypothetical deutschmark, which allowed it to have competitive prices for export. Or Germany's prerogative in setting the terms of the financial bailouts of the debtor countries while saving its own banks. The disproportionality of the common costs corresponds to the disproportionality of the benefits. It is an equitable relationship.

In addition to being able to increase through incentives the benefits of belonging to the system, the hegemon must be able to impose and enforce sanctions on members who do not behave according to the rules. Now, fulfilling the rules cannot depend only on the hegemonic member's power of coercion or sanction. There is a need for it to create incentives to motivate the adherence of the other members. It is also necessary to have a broad network of links, co-dependencies and mutual commitments, as well as a sense of community and belonging; all duly reflected in a framework of common institutions.

Strictly speaking, nothing forces the hegemon to pay a club maintenance charge higher than what would correspond mathematically to its "shares" in the club (measured, for example, by its relative economic weight or the size of its population). That is why the country willing to assume these disproportionate costs is usually called in the theory a "benevolent" hegemon. In contrast, a hegemon that only agrees to pay a fee strictly proportional to its size is called a malevolent hegemon, where this malevolence can range from not accepting disproportionate charges to abusing its power and extracting additional benefits from the partners. This malevolent way of exercising hegemony is not viable in the long term, because it would lack the essential element of recognition from the other members of the group and would end up becoming pure domination. Consequently, only a benevolent hegemon can really exercise a stabilising role as we have defined it here.

---

100   A term coined by former French President Giscard d'Estaing and treated in extenso in the book by Barry Eichengreen, *"Exorbitant Privilege"* (2011) to refer to the position of the US dollar in the world economy.

The term benevolence can easily lend itself to confusion, because it tends to be associated with kindness, generosity, or altruism. The hegemon does not need to have any of these attributes: when it assumes a greater part of the community burdens, it is doing so in its own interest and fully aware that the benefits derived from its hegemonic condition more than compensate for the possibly higher costs. It is essential, however, that the partners recognise this supposed benevolence and not feel threatened or intimidated by the senior member. The hegemon must know how to control its power and never abuse it, but rather emphasise that its actions are for the collective benefit, that the cooperative arrangement is good for everyone, both leader and followers.

Why do stable hegemonic systems eventually tend to destabilise? Gilpin (1987) states that the hegemon acts in its own interest at all times, even when being benevolent. There comes a time, however, when the hegemon wearies of its role and loses the motivation to continue assuming the duties associated with it. This fatigue is usually associated with one of two factors, or with a combination of them:

- The maintenance costs of the hegemonic system increase substantially, either as a result of a systemic crisis or due to endogenous dynamics that require an ever-greater level of integration.
- The emergence of more dynamic economies, whose strengthening is interpreted by the leader as free riding on its generous contributions. The leader begins to perceive the emerging countries as rivals and threats to its leadership, as a result of which it demands greater contributions and begins to renege on its previous commitments to security, defence, protection of the environment, etc.

By way of illustration, the first fatigue factor seems to be more applicable to the case of Germany in the European Monetary Union today, while the second would apply to the foreign policy swing of the United States during the Trump presidency. When Trump demands that Europe pay a larger share of the cost of NATO, or renegotiates NAFTA, or raises American trade barriers to Chinese products, he is renouncing the role of the US as a benevolent hegemon.

Hegemons in monetary systems compared

The importance of the hegemon for the stability of a system is most apparent when, through its own decision or by *force majeure*, it fails to fulfil its duties. In the sphere of international monetary arrangements we find several notable examples showing the connection between the success or failure of the monetary systems and the disposition of the hegemonic country to assume its burdens and responsibilities.

A brief review of the monetary systems of the last two centuries, and especially of the causes of their failures, points to certain common elements:

- No matter how symmetrically and politically balanced the system aims to be at its outset, sooner or later it evolves towards hegemon-and-subordinates, centre-and-periphery patterns.
- The conduct of the hegemon in favour of the collective interest creates in the rest of the members a sense of community and solidarity.
- The willingness and/or capacity of the hegemonic member to continue providing the goods of collective interest necessary for the operation of the system is essential for its survival.
- When the hegemonic member puts its national interests before those of the group, especially in a crisis context, the system comes to an end.

Just as the presence of a dominant individual country is necessary for the existence of an integrated monetary system, this same presence can become–in fact tends to become–the main impediment to its functioning and continuity. There follows a brief historical review of four monetary systems.

In the case of the Latin Monetary Union (LMU) created in 1865 by France, Belgium, Italy, Switzerland and Greece, France assumed the role of the hegemonic axis of the system.[101] The monetary standard was based on bimetallism, of which France was an ardent defender. Gold and silver coins circulated simultaneously with an official conversion parity

---

101 Fendel and Maurer (2015)

from gold to silver and vice versa. As with any bimetallic system, the distortions caused by arbitrage between both types of coinage each time the market value of the metals moved away from the value implicit in the official parity, created permanent conflicts between the members of the union. When Switzerland tried to leave the LMU in the mid-1870s and adopt the Gold Standard, France imposed an exit barrier in the form of an obligation to redeem all Swiss silver coins against payment of gold at the overvalued official parity. The Bank of France had a long tradition of doing good business with arbitrage, as well as a sizeable reserve position in its own silver coins and in those of other countries of the union. With members forcibly retained within the union because of the high cost of redeeming their silver coinage, the LMU languished until the 1920s, and its members opted to join *de facto* the Gold Standard, in which most of the world economy already coexisted. In the end, the stubborn and self-interested French defence of bimetallism ended the Latin monetary union, which she had created, and with it her chances of having a dominant presence in the international monetary system of the 20th century.

In the case of the Gold Standard, the leader of the British Empire, Great Britain, exercised its hegemonic responsibility up to 1914, and the system worked smoothly until then. From 1914 to 1918 the arrangement had to be put on hold because of the First World War. With the restoration of the Gold Standard after the war, Britain was no longer in an economic position to assume the burdens of hegemony, since it emerged from the conflict economically very weakened. But the new rising hegemonic power, the United States of America, was not yet aware of its new place on the world stage and of the demands inherent in it. Thus, the monetary system of the Gold Standard disintegrated and the world economy entered a black phase of isolationism, protectionism and confrontation between the Wars.

It was not until after the Second World War that the American attitude changed, when it pushed for the implementation of the Bretton Woods system, an exchange rate and monetary arrangement in which the dollar fully assumed its status as the world's reserve currency and the American Federal Reserve played the part of *de facto* world monetary authority. Originally, the Bretton Woods system was also conceived as a symmetrical monetary scheme, with a standard denomination different from the currency of any member country. In real life, however, the United States emerged from the war with such economic power compared to its European allies, that the dollar soon came to occupy the position of the system's "numerary", reserve currency and currency of account, to which other currencies were referred. The Federal Reserve became the central bank of the system, whose monetary policy determined the world rates of interest and inflation. The moment came, however, when the United States negligently disregarded its obligations as the hegemonic pivot of the empire of the dollar. Another war, that of Vietnam, placed the hegemonic power in a conflict between its own national interest and the collective interest of the world, a conflict that the Johnson and Nixon governments resolved in favour of its national interest, leading to the collapse of the system in 1971.

The European Monetary System, established in 1979, also wanted to be a symmetric system with the ECU as numerary, but it soon became *de facto* an asymmetric system in which the deutschmark evolved to be the reserve and intervention currency, at the same time that the Bundesbank assumed the leading role in European monetary policy. The two main reasons for Germany assuming this role were the considerable size of its economy and financial market, as well as its reputation for inflationary containment, the credibility of which was borrowed by the other European countries in exchange for submitting to its monetary designs. Additionally, the foreign exchange intervention mechanisms of the EMS were designed in such a way as to favour the country with the reserve currency and place the burden of adjustments on the shoulders of countries with weaker currencies.

Once again, the problems and national interests of the hegemonic country ended up superimposed on the responsibility of leading a collective. The surprise fall of the Berlin Wall at the end of 1989 and the subsequent unification subjected Germany to a severe monetary and fiscal shock, which spread to the rest of Europe through the Bundesbank's monetary policy and ended up generating the crisis of September 1992. This crisis practically defeated the EMS, because there was an asynchrony between the monetary policy requirements of Germany and those of the rest of Europe, a conflict that was resolved in favour of the hegemonic member and that triggered violent speculative attacks against the weaker currencies of the other European countries.

These historical experiences show that the sustainability of monetary integration schemes depends in the end more on political than economic conditions. They also confirm the theory's postulate of the crucial importance of a hegemonic State with the will to make the arrangement work effectively on terms acceptable to the other members.

Did Germany measure up to its hegemonic responsibility?

Turning our attention to the issue that concerns us in this chapter, the question is whether Germany assumed the role it theoretically should have assumed as the hegemonic centre of the EMU. Throughout this book we have made multiple references to Germany's actions before, during and after the crisis. In the light of these actions and with the help of the interpretive framework of the theory of Hegemonic Stability we have to conclude that the balance is tilted towards the negative side, in that the eurozone did not have a benevolent hegemon to help it adjust and stabilise the system when a group of its members suffered a severe shock after the Global Financial Crisis.

As with the other monetary systems mentioned above, the euro was born with the best intentions as part of a symmetrical monetary order, in which the currency was an *ex nihilo* and stateless creation. Once again, however, the old dilemma of asymmetry reappeared. Firstly, there was the extrapolation of a Bundesbank that indirectly took control of the new European Central Bank via its Statute. Secondly, Germany's economic and financial weight, far from declining in relative terms, continued to grow once Schröder's Agenda 2010 began to bear fruit in the mid-2000s. Finally, thanks to the 2008 financial crisis, a monetary union system that theoretically was to root out the predominance of one currency or its central bank, evolved *de facto* towards a centre-periphery scheme, in which Germany exercised a dominant influence in the EMU's decision-making. The rescue schemes for the periphery countries and the imposition of ordoliberal austerity consolidated the fundamental asymmetry of the EMU system, in which Germany emerged as the undisputed centre of power.

That at least is how the narrative of both friends and foes would have it. But can post-2009 Germany really be classified as a <u>benevolent</u> hegemon in the sense of Kindleberger? If we stick to the economic sphere, Germany failed to live up to its responsibilities as the hegemonic leader of the system. A series of benefits are often associated with the hegemonic position, such as:

- Monetary policy adapted to its specific needs and cycles
- Influx of capital and financing at lower cost
- Undervalued currency
- Privileged protection of its banking system when it comes to rescuing debtor countries.

The hegemon must know how to recompense these benefits with gestures of solidarity and, above all, by assuming the responsibilities of the office. To have lived up to these responsibilities, Germany would have had to invest more effort and resources in:

- Qualitatively improving–or in many cases transforming–the eurozone institutions for the sake of financial stability
- Achieving a better balance between the burdens of intra-community adjustment processes, in the sense of contributing to the economic revival of its fellow EMU-members with their own economic expansion
- Facilitating the creation of fiscal stabilisers to mitigate the serious social impact of the adjustment processes in the debtor countries
- Putting in place credible backstops to wind down destructive situations of financial panic

Germany's attitude towards the eurozone during the pre-crisis phase resembled in many respects the attitude of benign neglect that the United States had had towards the accumulation of tensions in the Bretton Woods system in the years prior to its collapse. Germany did not ignore the financial bubble that had been growing in Southern Europe or Ireland before 2008, but its own banks were inflating the bubble with excessive loans to the banks in the periphery. This allowed it to recycle the excess funds associated with its current account surplus, which in turn reflected the internal imbalance between too much saving and too little consumption. Also, its own companies were benefiting from the boom in demand for consumer and investment goods in the countries of Southern Europe. Germany, together with France, undermined the foundations of the Stability and Growth Pact, when in 2003-2005 it did not comply with the permitted fiscal deficit limits and blocked the imposition of the fines contemplated in the Pact. That was not behaviour compatible with the moral authority of a leader. With that dam broken, the fiscal discipline of the rest of the members of the monetary union ceased to be an inviolable principle.

Once the crisis erupted, Germany adopted a strategy of muddling through, especially during the first years, reflecting considerable ambiguity in the face of the crisis: doing enough to avoid blowing the European project apart, but resisting the application of policies that would affect her particular interests, displease her internal constituents or imply costs for her own pocket, even though those policies could have nipped the problem in the bud. The pressure of German monetary orthodoxy hindered the ECB's ability to face the immense financial crisis that was brewing in 2010-2011. This orthodoxy commended an act of remarkable wrong-headedness, when the interest rates were raised twice in 2011 simply because European average inflation exceeded the established goal by 0.6 percent. The rescues of Greece, Portugal and Ireland came late and in insufficient quantities, largely due to German reluctance to any kind of bailout of "wasteful" governments.

Obfuscated by the ideological veil of ordoliberal thought, the German leadership mistakenly interpreted the crisis of the periphery of the eurozone as a consequence of the fiscal indiscipline of those countries, the roots of which could be found in the Mediterranean culture of working little, saving less and living beyond one's means. The fact that before the outbreak of the financial crisis, the fiscal accounts of the debtor countries were balanced, at least as balanced as the accounts of the central core of Europe, was overlooked. Also overlooked later was the fact that fiscal deficits were not the primary source of the debtors' crisis but were a consequence of the particular manner in which the financial crisis was dealt with.

Given this biased interpretation, the recipe to get out of the crisis could only be austerity: spend less, collect more taxes, privatise and thus reduce the fiscal deficit. This austerity would also have the positive side effect of depressing domestic prices and wages (a so-called internal devaluation) and thus recovering external competitiveness to reduce the trade balance deficit. There was no talk in the diagnosis of the factors that had led to the boom in demand on the eurozone periphery: a monetary policy of low interest rates, coupled by large capital flows from German and other European big banks. It was not mentioned that, with the exception of

Greece, the crisis was triggered by the abrupt withdrawal of this capital, which forced a brutal deleveraging of banks, businesses and households on the periphery, provoked the bursting of real estate bubbles, bank failures, plummeting aggregate demand, recession, falling tax income, sovereign debt to rescue the banks and fiscal deficit.

We do not say that the troubled countries had not committed excesses of indebtedness but there was much moralistic finger-pointing on the part of Germany: other people, the debtors, were the only ones responsible for their excesses; they had to learn to live within their means; the debts had to be repaid with no concessions, because if they were condoned, it would create incentives to continue misbehaving in the future; the debtors had to undertake structural reforms similar to those of Schröder's Agenda 2010. There was a total rejection of any fiscal support scheme "for free" for the countries in trouble, with the argument that the Community treaties prohibited bailouts and that approval of the German parliament would be required to authorise this type of transfer with no return.

There is nothing wrong with a country pursuing its own interests and avoiding placing other people's burdens on the shoulders of its own citizens; this attitude, however, was compatible neither with the responsibility of leadership that voluntarily or involuntarily fell upon Germany, nor with equitable sharing of the tangible benefits derived from its hegemonic position within the eurozone. As when we spoke of the concept of solidarity in chapter VI, we are not using these terms here in the sense of morality or altruism. We are simply pointing to the axiom that a system such as a monetary union needs certain structures and rules to function, one of which is the figure of a benevolent hegemonic centre:

- to ensure the provision of certain public or collective goods necessary for the stability and survival of the system,
- that is willing to assume a substantial share of the cost of that provision, and
- that by its conduct generates in the other members of the group incentives first to associate, and then to remain in the club.

But this was not the way in which Germany saw its obligations. It did not want to take responsibility as a benevolent hegemon, because it did not see itself as such.

Some analysts, such as Matthijs (2014), clearly define Germany as a coercive hegemon, especially if its performance is analysed in comparison with that of the United States during the CFG. Both countries saw and defined their leadership in very different, even opposing ways. While Germany acted within the dichotomous ordoliberal interpretation of the causes of the crisis, the United States recognised its systemic nature, provided the necessary liquidity, encouraged the lender of last resort to act, and harmonised the monetary and fiscal stimuli. In short, the American authorities assumed the responsibility and cost of providing stability to the financial system. Meanwhile, Germany's coercive approach tried to offload most of the burden of adjustment onto the shoulders of the debtors and felt no responsibility to provide stability to the system.

The European Monetary Union survived the euro crisis because the European Central Bank filled the gap left by Germany as a dominant member. While this country reneged on its duties as a benevolent hegemon, the ECB had to take on the task of stabilising the system by acting as lender of last resort.

The mark of history and German foreign policy

Germany never wanted to see itself as a hegemon, because it went radically contrary to the image it had cultivated after the Second World War as a good citizen of the world, humble, cooperative, civilized and peaceful. Assuming positions of dominion or preponderance was not in its spirit; the word hegemony was not to be spoken. A past of almost two centuries in which Germany was seen as a problem, as a threat to peace because of its spirit of domination, had to be left behind. The past decisively coloured its foreign policy and how it understood its space within Europe.

In Chapter 1 we recalled that before the nineteenth century, when Germany did not yet exist as a nation but rather as a loose confederation of principalities and City-States united by a common language and culture, its central geographical position among the three European powers, France to the East, Russia to the West and Austria to the South, turned German territory into a battlefield for European supremacy. Whoever dominated the German centre, dominated Europe. After the defeat of the Napoleonic armies in the early nineteenth century and the subsequent agreements of the Congress of Vienna in 1814, the largest German principality, Prussia, emerged as a new military and political player on the European scene. What was really important in the new situation was that an increasing number of German principalities gradually amalgamated around the Prussian centre of power, forming a Confederation that became the embryo of the subsequent German Nation-State. The final impulse was given by the 1871 Pact of Versailles, after another victory of Prussia over France, when the North German Confederation proclaimed itself the German Empire, after which all the German States and principalities agreed to form part of the Confederation under the leadership of Prussia.

From that moment on, Europe's German Problem was that Germany had a size and economic might that made it a major power factor on the European stage, which could not be ignored. That might, however, was not enough to exercise a hegemony that would be recognised and accepted by the rest of Europe, nor was it enough to explicitly assume the cost of that hegemony. This ambiguity made Germany an uncomfortable neighbour, too big not to fear, but too small to have its hegemony accepted. Or to put it the other way around: too big to be loved and too small to be feared. Large enough to be blamed for everything bad, but too small to fix it. These are all variants of the same ambiguous reality.

To this ambiguity was added a deep distrust of the other European Powers towards the supposed expansionist pretensions of the German Empire, whose counterpart was a German fear of being encircled and annihilated by those Powers. Hence, from the second half of the 19th century, a dynamic of action and reaction, arms races and self-fulfilling prophecies arose, which led to the two World Wars of the 20th century. Unlike the post First World War scenario, when the weak leadership and lack of understanding of the victorious Powers allowed Germany an accelerated recovery, after the Second World War the Allied Powers took care to divide Germany up geographically, subjecting it to territorial occupation and stunting its economic potential. France and Russia were especially against allowing the loser to raise its head.

The German strategy to confront this enclosure was twofold. On the one hand, the Foreign Ministry developed an active policy of opening up towards Eastern Europe and Russia, the so-called *Ostpolitik*. On the other hand, it entered into a strategic alliance with France to promote the European Union. The Franco-German axis was present in all the crucial decisions taken to advance European integration. Germany had no problem putting France into the political driver's seat of the European project, in exchange for recognition as a full nation.

After 1945, Germany, although defeated and subjugated, continued to be the focus of attention and concern of European and even world politics, at least while the Cold War lasted. What to do about Germany remained the European problem *par excellence*. The initiatives of cooperation in military defence, NATO, the Coal and Steel Community and even the European Economic Community were born in the omnipresent shadow of the German Problem. The Allied Powers, especially those of the old continent, saw these initiatives as a way to set Germany on the path of civility, a way to subsume its power within international structures. The Germans, for their part, saw their incorporation into these supra-national institutions as the gateway to readmission into the international community.

After the war, German society made the decision to do everything necessary to be no longer seen as a problem. To this end, Germany did its part:

- De-Nazification efforts were profound, as was the reconversion of minds towards the promotion of peace and democracy.
- The contribution to the progressive construction of European political and economic bodies was fervent and generous.
- Foreign policy was marked by containment, avoiding the spotlight and framed around the principles of civic-mindedness and international cooperation.

However, the depth of the open wounds and the legacy of distrust meant that during the post-war period there was no important decision on the European playing field over which the ghost of Germany did not hover.

In its determined purpose of regaining its status as a good citizen, post-war German foreign policy had a profound aversion to the limelight and an even deeper aversion to what might sound like hegemonic pretensions. This is one of the keys to interpreting why Germany was against acting alone in the foreign policy field after 1945. Rather than going it alone, it chose not to act or simply treated the issue in question with benign indifference. That is why all the European initiatives in which it was involved went in tandem with France. After unification in 1990, Germany received many nudges from the United States to take the step of becoming its privileged Western leadership partner. Ignoring these siren songs, Germany preferred to continue facing inward towards Europe and promoting the monetary union project at the behest of France. The problem was that this special relationship cooled during the crisis, first because both governments had divergent theoretical and political approaches and secondly because France was economically left behind. Add to this a lack of chemistry between the new leaders (Hollande and Merkel), and we have an additional reason for Germany to avoid taking on the leadership of Europe on its own.

This explains why, when by the logic of events Germany acquired such an economic preponderance, especially after 2008, it was still reluctant to assume a leadership that it never wanted nor sought. Hence the epithet of "reluctant hegemon" that explains to a large extent the ambiguity with which Germany acted before, during and after the eurozone's financial crisis. It was *de facto* the leader of Europe but pretended not to be.

Europeanism was one of the backbones of German foreign policy. Germany knew that the only way to cast off the yoke imposed by the victors was through integration into European organisations in which other countries, especially France, maintained political control. Diluted within Europe, its old rivals, especially France, were reassured because they felt that the German recovery would not lead to its own strengthening but to that of Europe. This explains the enthusiastic German support for all Community initiatives, including those in which its own balance of costs and benefits was negative, such as the Coal and Steel Community or the Common Agricultural Policy. The Monetary Union was of no particular interest to Germany, but it accepted it for the sake of the European project of ever-closer political and economic integration.

The other backbone of German foreign policy, and probably the one with the most desired outcome, was the project to reunify the two Germanys. It was a very long-drawn-out project, which required much perseverance and consistency, much skill and capacity for balance, because the divided Berlin, and the divided Germanys had become the ultimate symbol and battlefield of the Cold War. The Federal Republic of Germany, with its political, social and economic system, unquestionably belonged to the Western Alliance, but it also needed to keep open permanent channels of communication and relations with the Soviet Union, without whose cooperation reunification would not be possible. Once the first generation of leaders (Adenauer, Erhard, etc.), whose inclinations were more Atlanticist and Anglo-Saxon, passed into retirement, the Social Democrats, under the leadership of Willy Brandt, developed the so-called *Ostpolitik*, a policy of rapprochement and cooperation with the Soviet Union and the other countries of Eastern Europe, which from time to time caused some discomfort on the part of the Western Allies.

The abandonment of militarism was a third element characterising foreign policy. After the War, the prohibition on military rearmament was blunt, limited armed contingents being only gradually allowed, but always under the umbrella of European defence schemes or within the framework of NATO. For its part, the German nation gladly accepted this limitation, first from its own clear conviction and secondly because the United States, France and Britain offered sufficient protection in the framework of the Cold War.

Non-militarism allowed Germany to emerge as a markedly civil society, a connotation which came in useful when with the passage of time it became undeniably a power. Being called a civil power[102] represented a danger to no-one. This civism became the fourth defining element of German foreign policy. The concept was also applied to Japan, another defeated and demilitarised regional power, which also developed a growth model focussed on exports. In the sphere of international relations, a civil power recognizes the need for cooperation with other players for the achievement of international objectives, particularly economic objectives, as a means of achieving foreign policy goals.[103] In the interests of these objectives, the civil power is willing to transfer fragments of sovereignty to supra-national institutions. For the sake of civilised international relations, the existence of a rules-based international legality and the proper functioning of multilateral organisations for cooperation are of

---

102   Term coined by Francois Duchene at the beginning of the 70s and then applied by Hanns Maull (2001) to Germany and Japan.

103   Hans Kundnani (2011, 2014) has investigated German foreign policy from the perspective of its export-oriented economic model. His is also the concept of "geo-economic power" applied to present-day Germany.

capital importance. That was the central goal of German foreign policy: to "civilise" international relations and provide the right environment for international trade. Commercial expansion, not territorial expansion, and the power of trade, not of arms, marked the new positioning of Germany in the international sphere. We could describe the German State, meaning no negative connotations, as a Mercantile State in which State and business, hand in hand, devoted immense efforts towards promoting the companies' presence in foreign markets.

The Watershed of the Second Unification

1871, the year of the first reunification, marked a before and after for 19th century German foreign policy. 1990, the year of the second reunification, represented another turning point in German foreign policy, although quieter and, fortunately, less problematic. Just as a new nation arose from the 1871 process, rather than a mere aggregate of mini-kingdoms or principalities, after 1990 another nation was born (or resurged), rather than a simple aggregate of the West and the East. From that moment there was a gradual change of identity, characterised by a greater confidence and assertiveness of Germany as a nation. The great goal of reunification had come about. Forty years of struggle had managed to overcome the resistance of the Allies and position the country as a civil and civilized power. The Germans felt that they were once again a normal nation, that the country had ceased to be an occupied territory, that the family had been reunited, that the guilt had been basically expiated and the ghosts of the past had been exorcised.

Unified Germany became a nation of 80 million people, well above the 58 million in France or the 57 million in the United Kingdom. The early years were difficult because of the enormous economic sacrifice the West made to absorb the problems of the East and bring its population up to the level of social welfare and standard of living of their compatriots in the West. Doing so without allowing inflation and fiscal deficit to spill over represented a juggling act for the government. The zealous struggle against inflation was handled by the Bundesbank, with the result that growth languished for almost a decade. When Gerhard Schröder was elected Chancellor in 1998, his main initiative was to convene a tripartite pact between government, unions and business to revive the languishing economy.

Be that as it may, German foreign and domestic policy had taken on an air of normality, with important repercussions. The first was that the country began to speak more freely of its own national interest and to be more aware of its position of power in Europe. In the international sphere, to the extent that the German economy depended more and more on exports, a greater pragmatism imbued its relations with other countries. Slowly there was a transition from being a civil power absolutely committed to multilateralism towards an economic power that realistically pursued its own objectives. This transition would not seem so relevant but for the context of the long previous period, in which to speak of Germany's own interests was a kind of taboo.

After overcoming the rough patch of the 90s (as the "sick man of Europe"), the 2000s saw Germany pull ahead of its European partners. In addition to Schröder's Agenda 2010 paying off, the launch of the European Monetary Union in 1999 also triggered dynamics that widened the gaps between Germany and its eurozone partners, a subject with which we have dealt extensively throughout this book. When the 2008 financial crisis broke out, the position of German economic dominance in the eurozone was definitively established, making the German government the arbitrator and guide of European policy. As never before in the first six decades of the post-war period, Germany assertively defined its own interests and had no qualms about imposing its preferences and recipes on European countries subjected to the ravages of over-indebtedness.

In the German mindset it was not, however, an exercise of pure and simple imposition. For all the evolution towards normality, Germany remained reluctant to exercise positions of domination or leadership. Its actions, therefore, were wrapped in the ideological guise of ordoliberal thought, which dressed up the real fact of domination, making it look like the inevitable application of the truths of that catechism. That guise provided it not only with a biased interpretation of the crisis, but also with the justification for the recipe for austerity imposed on those countries. The German economic success, a kind of second miracle, had supposedly proved that this special German way of doing things, of understanding the State, society and economy, was right and that what had been good for Germany also had to be good for others. Angela Merkel expressly stated this in 2014: "*What is good for Germany is also good for Europe*".[104] In the light of such self-assertiveness, there was no shortage of commentators recalling moments of Germany's historical past, specifically the Bismarck era, when the nation felt it was endowed with exceptionalism (*Sonderweg*) to fulfil a special destiny.

In addition to its deep ideological convictions, German conduct in the eurozone crisis was constrained by the export model, the backbone of its economic success. The German economy could not assume its share of the adjustment burden because that would have required it to inflate its economy and allow an internal revaluation, that is, a relative increase in prices and internal wages, which would have meant a loss of export competitiveness. Aside from going against the German anti-inflationary culture, this type of policy would have directly undermined its growth model, in German view.

This is how the events of the eurozone crisis signalled another rupture in Germany's attitude towards Europe. Berlin had emerged from the crisis as the only intact economic power. Europe's second and third economies faced serious difficulties. Italy was crushed by the weight of its huge public debt, the weakness of its banks and the scant export dynamism of its industrial sector. France languished under the weight of an interventionist and protective State, a suffocating public administration and confrontational labour relations. The old Franco-German alliance did not survive the lack of empathy between Hollande and Merkel. In other circumstances, the natural tendency of Germany would have been to stand to one side, let everyone sort themselves out, not impose, not lead. The problem was that the crisis revealed a real existential risk for the euro. Either act or the Monetary Union would be dismembered. So, in seeking to save the Monetary Union, Germany acted with greater assertiveness and firmness to promote solutions concordant with its ideological mindset.

Outside of Europe, Germany continued to behave in much the same way as before, prioritising the use of soft power through the promotion of reciprocal trade relations and a reluctance to use its economic leverage. Towards Europe, however, the exercise of power was forceful. When its interests were threatened, as with the real risk of implosion of the euro after the outbreak of the Greek crisis, its intervention was energetic and

---

104   Quoted in Meiers (2015)

determined, protected by its economic supremacy. In the multipolar international framework, though, where its economic power ranked in fourth or fifth place, its foreign policy continued to lean towards multilateral diplomacy and the defence of regulated frameworks that favoured trade. In this broader framework, Germany still shunned being seen as a great power, using military force or imposing its leadership.[105]

International relations expert Hans Kundnani (2011) has developed the thesis that Germany was and behaved as a "geo-economic power" within Europe and that this is the new way in which the German Problem has resurfaced.. The Eurocrisis gave Germany a definitive leadership position, more thrust upon it than sought. Unlike in the past, such leadership became a peaceful and civilized way of promoting an economic model. There had been a shift from geopolitics to geo-economics and Germany had decidedly become a geo-economic power.

The term "geo-economic power" refers to a condition of international power in which commercial mechanisms replace military methods for exercising power or pressure: it is the use of capital rather than firepower, civil innovation rather than military technological advances and market penetration rather than military bases.[106] Internally, this international positioning on the basis of trade involved a close interaction between the State and business corporations in a relationship of mutual interdependence and mutual (and consensual) manipulation, characterising what we referred to above as the Mercantile State. Japan would also qualify under this definition, as would China, the difference being that Japan and Germany do not possess or use military power to leverage their economic power.

It is beyond dispute that in the 2000s Germany reached the status of a geo-economic power, at least in its European sphere of influence. The discussion is centred rather in just how powerful that power has been, and what cultural, ideological and institutional factors have restricted its hegemonic exercise. Certainly, the relative size of the German economy compared to its European partners is less impressive than that of the United States or China with their main partners. If we take the three

---

[105] A military parade *a la* Champs-Élysées (Paris) would be unthinkable on Unter den Linden (Berlin).

[106] The concept was developed by Edward Luttwak (1990)

largest countries after the United States, the American economy in 2015 was 1.6 times greater than the Chinese, 4.1 times greater than the Japanese and 5.4 times greater than the German. But if we take the three largest European countries after Germany, the German economy in 2015 was barely 1.4 times greater than the French, 1.8 times greater than the Italian and 2.8 times greater than the Spanish. According to these proportions, Germany seems to have been more of a *primus inter pares* than a classical dominant power. To take just one example, Germany would not have had the ability to rescue Spain, much less Italy, when in 2011-12 they both suffered the severity of their sovereign debt crises. Given these proportions, Germany's historical situation was reaffirmed, in the sense that it was and still is too large not to be determinant but is not large enough to exercise true hegemony.

As we have stressed, cultural and ideological factors as well as the weight of history have limited the exercise of supremacy within Europe. In Germany there is neither the social consensus nor the internal disposition to assume an open hegemony, let alone the willingness to assume the cost that this would eventually entail. Any solution that involves the risk of resource transfers to other countries without return–the unmentionable transfer union–is categorically rejected.

Last but not least, Germany did not succeed in selling its social and economic model to the rest of Europe. For its Latin partners, the ordoliberal culture and the strictness of the export model were difficult to digest. In contrast to how Rome in its time fortified its hegemony through its imperial subjects' acceptance of the *lex romana*, or the United States was able to sell its capitalist model and the "American way of life", Germany failed to establish the supremacy of its model by consensual means. This failure meant that German domination had to be based more on economic than on cultural power.[107]

For these reasons of insufficient cultural power, insufficient size and, above all, lack of disposition, we agree with Kundnani's description of the German model of domination within Europe as a geo-economic "semi-hegemony", because it indicates the predominant economic power

---

107 Cox (1983) emphasises that for a country to become a proper hegemon it needs to transplant its way of social and economic organisation to the group of countries under its sphere of influence.

base and the *sui generis* detachment from its duties.[108] Germany did not want to assume the obligations that a full hegemony entailed, especially that of assuming most of the costs of endowing public goods.

The solutions Germany put on the table were mostly zero-sum[109] results, in which profits for some were losses for the others. The blame for entering into a crisis belonged entirely to the debtors and Germany had no obligation to assume any portion of the costs of adjustment. The Germany of the Eurocrisis cannot be classified as a benevolent hegemon, in the sense of the concept developed by Kindleberger. Neither can it be classed as a malevolent hegemon, because it had no conscious intention of exploiting its partners. Nor can it be classified as pure and simple domination, because as we have already seen, this position was very far from Germany's possibilities and mindset. Nonetheless, it matters not at all how reluctant and dysfunctional the hegemony was. The fact remains that Germany acted as a hegemon and failed in the task of stabilising the eurozone.

Reasons for the reluctance: some more benevolent interpretations

We must be careful when drawing historical parallels between the situation in Germany now and in the past, especially when those times were rife with conflict and bellicosity. Where the reference to history is certainly pertinent is with respect to the problem of the size and geographic location of Germany. The element in common with the past is its being in the middle of Europe, having a size and economic power superior to that of the rest of the neighbours, but not being big enough to fully exercise the role of hegemon–and be recognized as such.

German intellectuals and analysts refuse to look beyond this problem of size and location. The majority of the German political establishment

---

108 Kundnani (2014) draws a parallel between this current semi-hegemonic position and that between 1871 and 1945, when ambivalence concerning the size of Germany (the German Problem) was a source of instability in Europe. We feel, however, that drawing parallels between such radically different historical moments leads to more confusion than insight.

109 This concept comes from game theory and describes a situation in which the gains or losses of each participant are counterbalanced mathematically with the losses or gains of the other participants.

sincerely rejects the idea that their country is playing or has an interest in playing a hegemonic game.[110] They think that the conduct of Germany during the euro crisis was no different from what could have been expected from a creditor who undertakes the necessary and usual actions to get their money back, using the typical tools of creditors in episodes of sovereign debt problems. The panoply of instruments included collection warnings, restructuring agreements with longer term concessions, interest rate reductions and new loans to honour the maturities of the old ones, conditional on certain reform programs in the debtor economies. Such methods, these analysts say, were no different from those traditionally used by the IMF when it has been asked to deal with countries in trouble.

Germans are uncomfortable when someone draws parallels to the past. They think that this is overstating things, that the explanation is simpler: the approach to the euro crisis was no more than an expression of the ordoliberal ideology that has traditionally imbued the political, business and academic establishment. This thinking was not only deeply rooted in the cultural and ideological tradition of German society, but its universal validity was vindicated by the success story of its economy. Seen from this angle, Germany only wanted to apply to its troubled eurozone partners the same recipes that it had applied to itself for decades. What had been so productive for her, would surely also work for her neighbours.

A central ordoliberal principle is each person's individual responsibility for their own actions and its consequences. When that responsibility is not insisted on effectively, the system of rules and incentives falls apart. Consequently, so the German line went, Germany could not permit the debtor countries of the eurozone periphery to evade the consequences of "excesses" during the boom years. It was up to them, not to Germany, to tighten their belts, reduce their fiscal deficit and regain their external competitiveness. For this reason, a symmetrical adjustment, as advocated by many, went against this principle of responsibility. Calls to prop up Germany's own domestic demand or to orchestrate stimulus packages for debtors in recession were categorically rejected. The rejection was motivated by ideology, not hardness of heart.

There is another aspect of ordoliberal ideology that hindered the exercise of a supra-national hegemony. Ordoliberalism advocates an order

---

110   See Mertes (2015)

governed by a body of rules of conduct, which the State is responsible for applying and enforcing. These rules apply to persons or legal entities who are the subjects of a State that acts with full political legitimacy. But when that philosophy extends to the sphere of a community of sovereign nations, the problem of legitimacy rears its ugly head. When the rules have not been established by a democratically elected State, but by opaque Community entities through a process of intergovernmental negotiations, their imposition provokes rejection. There is no way the application of the principle of responsibility can be linearly transferred from the level of the citizens of a country to the level of the sovereign nations of a community. If it is also perceived that the rules have been dictated by the dominant member of the community and that the distribution of costs is unfair, the conditions are set for a crisis of hegemonic legitimacy or, at the very least, a rejection of the policies issuing from the hegemonic centre.

Let us take a moment briefly to look at this issue of ideology in the context of the discussion on Germany's obstacles to exercising hegemony. An essential element of all hegemony is the ability to influence the thinking, way of life and model for political and economic organisation of the societies under the influence of the hegemon. Did Germany succeed in having its European partners accept and assimilate the ordoliberal ideology? It seems not. The German prescriptions for handling the crisis were seen as being imposed by the country that had the whip hand and that, by the way, was also mistaken in its diagnosis. Furthermore, there was too much misalignment between the Nordic, Anglo-Saxon, Calvinist, strict, austere culture, and the flexible, negotiating, supportive Latin culture, little given to deferring gratification. If we take the United States as a reference hegemon, that country has been much more successful in orchestrating role models, cultural patterns and ideological consensus. Recall, for example, the "Washington consensus", formed in the 80s and 90s as a set of precepts to deal with debt crises in developing and emerging countries. In retrospect, many criticisms can be made of these precepts, but it cannot be denied that the Washington consensus was embraced at the time by both creditors and debtors. Such a consensus did not exist in Crisis Europe.

Defenders of Germany's reluctance to assume a more active leadership role also point to its constitutional structure. The German political system does not favour the exercise of leadership either, still less of a sufficiently executive and assertive hegemony. To ensure that the past could not be repeated, the Allies fragmented the country into a federal system that is politically, fiscally, and financially decentralised. The regional States, the *Länder*, enjoy a lot of autonomy. The head of government, the Chancellery, is not endowed with executive powers like those with French-style presidential regimes. The electoral system is designed in such a way that it forces the majority party to govern through coalitions. In addition, the Constitution of the Federal Republic of Germany contains a large number of institutional checks and balances that limit the decision-making capacity of the executive branch. Among these, for example, is an active German Constitutional Court that has set limits to several European initiatives, including some issued by the European Central Bank.

On another front, the new generation of German political leaders–we say "new" in comparison with that which led the country until the end of the 90s–showed no willingness, talent or inclination to assume leadership positions in Europe. This is a generation born in the post-war period, career civil servants and party officials who respond more to local interests than to great Europeanist visions. The issues that dominate political discussion nowadays are deliberately narrow, cautious and unexciting. We find ourselves with the paradox that while German power has grown, its political class has become parochial.[111]

It is not easy to resolve the dilemma in which Germany finds itself enmeshed. If it insists on the condition that recipients of any type of aid behave "as they should", it is accused of coercively imposing its economic model. But if it generously agrees to help without imposing conditions, its own electorate–and probably its Constitutional Court as well–would strongly oppose. In either case, Germany is in the dock.

To attempt a–simplistic–summing up, we would say that the good moral conscience of the Germans, or the question of the Greeks or Italians feeling dominated by Germany, does not much matter. Our interest here has been to provide evidence and arguments that go beyond perceptions and shed light on how conducive German actions have been for preserving the stability of the monetary union and optimising the welfare level

---

111   Garton Ash (2013) elaborates the changes in the German political landscape of the last couple of decades.

of all of its members. Such actions cannot be evaluated as those of just one more member of the Union, but of a member who holds a position of privileged power and on whom, therefore, the survival of the Union greatly depends. From this perspective Germany, as a hegemonic leader, has not lived up to its responsibilities and its conduct has generated more harshness than necessary, and more impoverishment than welfare. Seen from this angle, its hegemony has failed.

PART IV

DESIRABLE, POSSIBLE, AND PROBABLE FUTURES

Where does Europe find itself today, in the second half of 2018, and where can it go from here? It is futile to try to predict, as if this were an exact science, the future evolution of the European Union and particularly of the European Monetary Union. What we can do is to understand what the options are for the European project, what proposals are on the table, what degree of consensus they have and how viable they are. Two things are certain: first, that the edifice of the European Monetary Union is far from safe against a new major crisis; and second, that a future crisis will represent a new existential risk for the Monetary Union, but this time without the political will to save the euro.

We will begin with a discussion of the economic options. The debate is split between two large groups: those who think that the Monetary Union edifice is incomplete and that it mainly needs solidarity (risk sharing) schemes so as to properly confront a new crisis; and those who think that the Union is complete and that the only thing needed is market discipline and for everyone to abide by the rules. The second group refuses outright to share risks, meaning the game is deadlocked.

Important efforts are being made to reconcile both positions, but in the end both the problem and the solution are political in nature. Today, European integration is facing into a political headwind. The euro crisis and the refugee crisis tore up the European nations' consensus on Europe and its integration project. In fact, the risks of disintegration are very real. Brexit is just one chapter in a long history of misunderstandings.

The emergence of nationalist and anti-European populism throughout Europe has drastically reduced the establishment's political room for manoeuvre in undertaking any kind of meaningful reform. This being the case, it would seem that the sensible strategy would be to realistically evaluate what is possible, unwind what must be unwound, mainly the Monetary Union in its current form, and envisage a much more flexible, plural and democratic Europe.

XI

THE DESIRABLE: PREPARE FOR THE NEW CRISIS

Until 2015, the performance assessment of the European Union and particularly of the European Monetary Union was mostly negative, both among academic analysts and in the perception of the ordinary citizen. It was felt that the Monetary Union had not brought the expected growth and prosperity. The sacrifices that a good number of its member countries had to make to face and overcome the onslaught of the Global Financial Crisis and its delayed European version were really substantial. And when the turbulence of the crisis calmed down after 2013, subsequent growth was poor and unemployment levels remained at abnormally high levels. The legacy of high public debt left by the crisis limited the use of fiscal policy to stimulate growth.

The unequal distribution of the burdens of economic adjustment between the members of the Monetary Union generated disputes and resentments. The Monetary Union, designed to unite, became a source of disunity. The cracks in solidarity, coupled with the hardships of the recession, created a breeding ground for the emergence of dangerous nationalist-populist tendencies, mostly ultraconservative, that began to hoist anti-Europeanism as one of its main political banners. Previously taboo topics, such as exiting the euro or the European Union, began to be openly debated. There was a revival of calls to rebuild barriers to people which it had taken decades to tear down. Anti-European forces in the United Kingdom, which had always been lying in wait, seized the moment to tilt the June 2016 referendum towards exit from the European Union.

As of 2016, however, all the European economies began to grow moderately, largely as a result of the reforms implemented to get out of the crisis, but also supported by a strong global boom. As a result of the improvement, the criticisms of integration began to soften, zeal for reform in the eurozone lost momentum and deep divergences concerning the way forward flourished in the absence of the unifying urgency of the crisis. The dividing line between the European Centre-North, led by Germany, and the South, led by France, resurfaced again and again in whatever proposal was put on the table to redesign the architecture of the monetary union. The crude reality is that Europe, particularly the EMU, is not prepared for the new crisis that will one day inevitably occur. Much progress was made between 2011 and 2014, but it will definitely not be enough if the various reform packages are not completed.

What future awaits the EMU and, in consequence the European Union? What are the main challenges that lie ahead? What proposals for reform of its institutional architecture are on the table? What are the medium-term scenarios? Two things are clear. The future of the EU is closely linked to that of the EMU: the EU can hardly survive in its current form if there is a traumatic disintegration of the Monetary Union–and we do not see how such a disintegration can happen without a good deal of conflict between countries. The second aspect is that the crisis of 2010-12 is not going to be the last existential crisis to threaten the euro. Until mechanisms are in place to allow the most affected members to make the necessary adjustments at a reasonable cost and in a reasonable time, the political will to preserve the union–on either side–is likely to disappear.

THE CALM BEFORE AND AFTER THE STORM: THE STATE OF THE UNION

Since 2015, all eurozone countries have been growing moderately with the exception of Greece, which only began to do so in 2017. Unemployment rates fell consistently. Despite the slowdown in world growth in 2018, the outlook for growth towards 2020 is still positive, mainly fuelled by the fiscal stimulus of the United States. As for the eurozone, growth estimates for 2019 and 2020 are more modest but are still in positive territory. If nothing bad happens before 2020, we would be looking at five years of growth without major upsets.

Several positive elements have been visible in this recovery of Europe, unlike the bonanza that existed before 2008:

- Economic growth has not been based on credit expansion and accumulation of debt, but on recovery of demand.
- The traditional debtor countries have managed to put their current account balance of payments in the black. This means that they have not financed growth with foreign capital, so some have been able to amortise external debt while others have not needed to increase it.

It is fair to acknowledge that the countries of the European periphery, except for Italy, have done their job by getting their economies in order and undertaking some structural reforms. Today they are standing on more solid foundations, which will allow them to face the next recession with more fortitude. Their better external position will lower the friction between creditor and debtor countries, so the new conflict will rather revolve more around different economic philosophies, different economic models and different visions of what to do with the eurozone and with Europe.

Legacies of the crisis: sovereign debt and bank delinquency

Despite the good economic news, there are important threats on the horizon: Brexit, Italy, trade wars, populism... Europe cannot rest on its laurels. As the historian and expert in financial crises Carmen Reinhart (2018) recalls, a recovery is not the same as a resolution of the crisis. Suffice it to recall the long periods of economic lethargy that followed the Great Depression, the lost decade of Latin America, or the procrastinated Japanese banking crisis of 1992. Political risks and past debt burdens lurk. The very low interest rates may rise at some point, depriving governments of oxygen and slowing economic growth. And if the rates do not rise, the monetary authorities will not have the tools to face a new slowdown of economic activity. Taking a longer view, the population is aging and productivity is not growing fast enough.

Sailors usually relax and doze after a long and difficult storm. But if they do not pump the water from the ship's hold while the calm lasts, another storm will catch them out with a reduced capacity to face the turbulence. And if it also turns out that the last storm showed that the rigging and navigation system were faulty, all the more reason to take advantage of the good weather to undertake the necessary repairs. It is also very likely that the captain's style of command during the last storm was not up to the job, in which case it is time to review it.

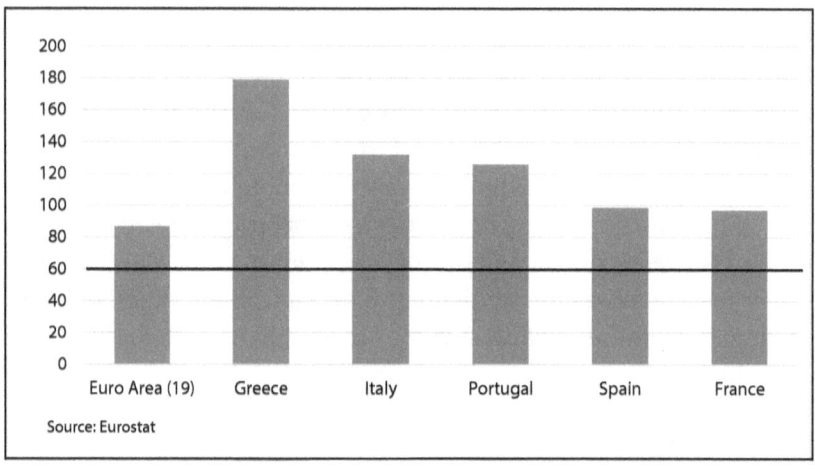

Figure XI-1
Total Public Debt (% of GDP), 2017

Source: Eurostat

The financial legacies left by the eurozone crisis–in our simile, the water in the hold–are twofold: high public debt and a significant portion of the banking loan portfolio of doubtful recoverability. As regards the burden of government debt, its increase since the eve of the GFC has been significant. All the countries of the Mediterranean periphery are appreciably above the threshold of 60 percent of GDP established in European regulations (see Figure XI-1). At the end of 2017, government debt in Greece was close to 180 percent of GDP, in Italy 132 percent, in Portugal 126 percent, and in France and Spain close to 100 percent. These debt burdens impose a straitjacket on fiscal management, which in a monetary union is where the main responsibility lies for facing disturbances. A minimum room for manoeuvre is also needed for making structural reforms viable. In the second half of the 2010s, the debt burden has been bearable, due to almost negative interest rates, and it has not been necessary to borrow more in a context of moderate growth. But two things are true: someday interest rates will rise and/or someday growth will stop. With higher interest rates, debt service will become more onerous, and with less growth, tax revenues will fall. The moment the financial markets begin to question the fiscal sustainability of some country, speculative attacks will skyrocket and the wave of contagion will begin again.

Neither has the legacy of the banking crisis been solved. At the end of 2016, the gross amount of delinquent loans in the European banking system amounted to 5.1% of the total loan portfolio, well above the 1.5% of the US and Japan.[112] This percentage was equivalent to one trillion euros, with Italy accounting for 300 billion euros (equivalent to 17 percent of its gross loan portfolio), followed by France (150 billion, equivalent to 4 percent of its gross loan portfolio), Spain (139 billion, equivalent to 5.6 percent of its gross loan portfolio) and Greece (120 billion, equivalent to 45 percent of its gross loan portfolio). Of those amounts of loans in trouble, no more than half were covered by provisions, when it would be orthodox for provisions to cover 100 percent of such delinquent accounts. This legacy of past-due loans would not be so menacing if it were not for the fact that deposit protection and bankruptcy resolution mechanisms are not yet ready to prevent a new destructive spiral of sovereign debt crisis and banking crisis.

Another manifestation of the persistence of banking problems is the accumulation of imbalances between the central banks of the eurozone, the so-called Target 2 Balances (T2B). The ECB functions as the platform for the eurozone payment (clearing) system, in which some countries are in financial deficit while others are in surplus. In practice, those in surplus extend credit lines to those in deficit that are automatic, unlimited and with no expiry term. Until 2008 the inter-country accounts were balanced, but with the explosion of the crisis the positive and negative balances began to grow to threatening levels. At the end of 2017, the German central bank had a positive balance of close to 900 billion euros, while Spain and Italy had negative balances of 374 and 440 billion euros respectively. These considerable amounts are expressions of snowballing economic imbalances within the eurozone. No-one knows how these obligations can be wound down or how they could be honoured in the event of a disintegration of the eurozone.

---

112   See the Report of the European Systemic Risk Board (2017)

Italy is the best demonstration of the risks that still lie in the eurozone (see Box XI-1). Many think that the country will be the weak link where the stability of the eurozone will break next. It has a debt burden that exceeds 130% of GDP, a banking system that is not yet healthy and an economy that lacks the stimulus to grow. The window of respite of moderate growth and a calming of the markets that opened after 2015 will close again one day, either for political reasons or due to a new recessive cycle. The markets know that none of the Community institutions, not even the European Central Bank, currently have the capacity to handle something as big as the eventual Italian black hole. If Greece triggered so severe a crisis in 2010, imagine the impact of a destabilisation of the Italian bond market.

Box XI-1
ITALY: THE UNMANAGEABLE THREAT

Italy is today the biggest threat to the EMU. It is the third largest economy of the eurozone and one of the six signatory countries of the Treaty of Rome. Its economy has been virtually stagnant for several decades: its real GDP per capita is today lower than when the European Monetary Union started in 1999. For decades its burden of public debt has been, along with that of Greece, the highest in Europe: 110 percent of GDP in 1999, 132 percent today, well above the 60 percent agreed threshold for being part of the EMU. The levels of public and private investment have been consistently below the European average, as has productivity, despite having some export clusters of high added value.

The main problem in Italy is that it has kept postponing and avoiding the reforms that would have been necessary to eradicate the inefficiencies of its political, social and economic system. The country has historically suffered from high levels of corruption, much of which goes unpunished because of a dysfunctional judicial system.[113] The levels of tax evasion/avoidance are also high, as is the bureaucracy in a bloated public administration. In the economic sphere, the rigidity of the labour market hinders entrepreneurship, innovation and new investments. The banking system has the highest delinquency rate in Europe

---

113   See Roubini and Rosa (2018)

(after Greece), a sign that a clean-up of the financial system is still pending. Fiscal management is chronically in deficit, just as chronic as the virtual stagnation of the economy.

After the coming to power of the populist coalition formed by the right-wing Northern League and the leftist Five-Star Movement, a serious political risk was overlaid on top of the economic problem. The platform on which those parties were elected preached an end to fiscal austerity and to submission to the "dictates of Brussels". The complicated political dynamics of the governing coalition makes a clash with Brussels inevitable at some point. If the plans proposed in the respective electoral platforms are enacted, such as the introduction of a universal basic income (M5S) or a flat tax rate (Liga), the fiscal deficit would shoot up, in contravention of European directives. If Brussels sanctions Italy, it would fuel the fire of anti-European nationalism within Italy. If not, the credibility of the rules and sanctions in the EMU would suffer a fatal blow. Damned if they do, damned if they don't. In a first round of tinkering with the 2019 budget, Italy has given way to the EU's firm position, but the conflict has barely begun.

Sooner rather than later, there will come a time when the financial markets will become reluctant to continue with the eternal debt roll-over. In that case, a restructuring of the immense Italian public debt will be necessary, which would trigger a tsunami of unpredictable consequences. Europe has neither the mechanisms nor the financial resources to face this eventuality today. Nor does it seem that it will have the political will to do so. In the Italian case, the only way to face the crisis would be to avoid it.

More Europe or less?

What lines have been laid down in the current debate within the eurozone? A recurrent dialectic is the question of whether to move towards more Europe or less Europe. More Europe means extending the scope of the supra-national Community bodies, ceding more sovereignty over decisions to these bodies and progressively incorporating more elements of a political and fiscal union. Less Europe means giving back to the members of the Community their fiscal sovereignty and their autonomy in social and migratory policies, among other things. This devolution would relocate political legitimacy back to national levels, where it had always been. Proponents of this line think that the Monetary Union was a step too far in the process of European integration, a step that should not have been taken, something for which Europe was not prepared, something that was not even necessary in order to safeguard the benefits of commercial and economic integration.

The Heads and officials of the Community bodies in Brussels, understandably, would want more Europe. In their opinion, a monetary union is not viable in the long term without significant progress towards a greater political union that would give democratic support to the surrender of sovereignty to supra-national entities. In the fiscal area, these entities would be in charge of transferring Community resources to countries affected by disturbances, to prevent them entering destructive spirals of fiscal crunches and economic recessions. Financially, these entities would exercise effective regulation and supervision of the financial system and securities markets. And when a banking crisis erupts, Community funds for deposit guarantees and resolution of bank failures should have enough European fiscal support to nip spirals of contagion in the financial markets in the bud.

Today, most of the eurozone countries have not been won over to such a surrender of sovereignty. France protects zealously its fiscal autonomy. The countries of the European Centre-North especially, headed by Germany and the Netherlands, emphatically reject any scheme that leads to automatic fiscal transfers from one country to another. That is why the European Commission has been looking for intermediate roads that could be negotiable, but they all include a certain degree of solidarity that could lead at some point to fiscal transfers between member countries of the Monetary Union.

The institutional architecture of the eurozone saw some important advances during the peak years of the crisis, but it has stalled halfway and seems unable to prevent or handle future crises. This is especially true in relation to the two Achilles' heels of the eurozone monetary construct: the lack of fiscal integration and the absence of a banking union. Activity on both fronts was almost feverish during the crisis; however, all the reforms began to stumble when they came up against the real heart of the problem: the acceptance that a monetary union may at some time need some kind of fiscal solidarity. Today economists like to use the concept of risk-sharing, but the euphemism does not change the essence that in a monetary union in the end someone has to save someone else's bacon. Certainly, this issue is not easy to solve because it involves the serious risks of moral hazard, free riding and disincentives for reforms. Neither are the citizens of the buoyant countries willing to open their wallets to help "spendthrifts". Meanwhile, in the absence of real solutions in both areas, Eurocrats have continued to do what they have always done very well: set rules about rules, procedures about procedures, and further entangle the regulatory web.

At the political level, it would take one of two things to escape from the labyrinth in which the EMU finds itself: the leadership of a benevolent hegemon willing to assume the cost of securing that common good known as financial stability; or the formation of real consensus among the principal members of the Union to achieve that same goal of stability. The first route meets reluctance from the only country with the capacity to assume the hegemonic role, Germany. And the second route would involve the revival of the Franco-German axis, the same one that energised the great advances of the first five decades of the EU and later of the EMU. Conspiring against such a revival is not only the growing gap in economic power between the two countries, but more importantly the deep ideological differences between them. And the differences are not only between these two; intra-European rifts are another legacy left by the eurozone crisis: North against South, creditors against debtors, ordoliberals against Keynesians, elites against ordinary citizens, liberals against populist nationalists.

The atmosphere today in Europe does not favour major changes. Now then, if the eurozone wants to avoid lurching from one crisis to another, something must be done to make the euro viable. Most analysts agree that the next crisis may again bring with it an existential risk to the EMU and, by extension, to the EU. What would be needed to preserve the macro-financial stability of the Union? Can members of the eurozone live with the Solomonic option of having "less Europe" politically, but with greater fiscal and banking integration? What should be the minimum scope of such integration and how viable is it?

While it is true that the EMU today is better prepared than before 2010, no-one knows how well the edifice can withstand a category 4 or 5 hurricane. While other alternatives take shape, Europe must shore up the current edifice of the EMU if it does not want its collapse to drag down the larger edifice of the European Union. The EMU edifice has design flaws, certainly, but it is of little help to keep pointing the finger at the architect without proposing realistic solutions that take into account the political reality of Europe. Doing nothing is not an option. The EMU exists and, while it lasts, Europe must make the best of it.

Risk sharing or submitting to discipline?

The main European economic debate today focuses on the dichotomy between those who advocate solutions involving some degree of risk sharing and fiscal transfer, and those who reject this in order to submit all members of the Monetary Union to the rigours of market discipline and orthodoxy in the handling of fiscal and banking affairs. A dynamic process of conflicts and alliances has centred on this dichotomy.[114] If we draw a line with shared risk at one end and market discipline at the other, and then place the eurozone countries along that line, we can identify three major coalitions:

- Countries of the South (France, Greece, Spain, Italy, Portugal and Belgium), led by France, located closer to fiscal solidarity and risk sharing
- Countries of the North, Centre and East (Germany, Finland, Slovakia, Holland, Austria), led by Germany, located towards the defenders of fiscal and market discipline
- Small countries, located in intermediate positions and forming circumstantial alliances on one side or the other (Luxembourg, Ireland, Cyprus, Slovenia, Estonia, Latvia, Lithuania, Malta)

So far it has been impossible to carve out a minimum of consensus to move towards real solutions. The coalitions have had to make mutual concessions in a dynamic of permanent negotiation. On this spectrum, Community institutions such as the European Commission and even the European Central Bank under the leadership of Draghi tend to view with

---

114   Wasserfallen and Lerner, (2018) have drawn up a map of competing groups between the extremes of the dichotomy between solidarity and individual responsibility.

sympathy proposals with some content of solidarity and risk sharing. The route that these Community bodies have navigated to present proposals is to find a common ground that reflects the minimum that one side would demand and the maximum that the other side would be willing to accept. In general, this lowest common denominator tends to fall far short of what would really be needed to give strength to the Monetary Union edifice. And in any case, very little has materialised from all the proposals and counterproposals. The Single Resolution Mechanism created in mid-2014 as part of the banking union project agreed in 2012, was the last substantive reform approved by Europe in financial and economic matters. It would be worrisome if a new crisis were needed for the path of necessary reform to be resumed.

The Southern bloc–and secretly the EU institutions also–advocate the establishment of mechanisms to stabilise economies *ex ante*, for example by making funds available to soften the impact of negative shocks. And if, in spite of everything, an economy should become destabilised, there must be *ex post* mechanisms to staunch the bleeding and mitigate the impacts of crises. All these mechanisms include a fair degree of risk sharing–and possible unilateral transfers–among the members of the union. The Centre-North-East bloc, led by Germany and the Netherlands, rejects risk sharing outright, because this would generate incentives for bad behaviour and avoid undertaking structural reforms to attack the causes that led to the crisis in the first place. What is needed to get out of the crisis and not fall back into it is a reinforcement of fiscal rules and more market discipline.

The great challenge to moving towards some degree of consensus is to ensure that stabilisation mechanisms and collective insurance programs do not degenerate into the need for permanent unilateral transfers from some countries to others or weaken the sense of urgency of structural reforms. Both are valid concerns for those who advocate market discipline programs. If they are not addressed, it will be difficult to move forward. To make the euro viable in the long term, some compromise must be found between both positions, but not by having them Solomonically meet halfway, which would be the same as not getting anywhere. The schemes that are adopted must genuinely attack the root of the problem of the euro's inherent instability.

Some economists and research centres have been making significant efforts to reconcile positions, such as the proposals made in the document presented at the beginning of 2018 by a group of 7 French and 7 German economists (called the 7+7 Group)[115], entitled *"Reconciling risk sharing with market discipline"*. The position of ECB President Mario Draghi (2018), expressed during a conference at the Institute of the European University of Florence, in which he elaborated on the advantages of risk-sharing schemes to prevent financial crises, also points in that direction. The essence of both approaches is that sharing risks and market discipline do not have to be mutually exclusive but should rather be complementary.

The message of the 7+7 Group is that risk-sharing schemes in the banking system not only reduce the overall risk of a country's banking system, but also that of its individual banks, which is the ultimate goal of market discipline. These economists also agree that it is possible to reconcile the necessary fiscal discipline with growth policies that hinder the appearance of the destructive spirals of the past, when a banking crisis led to a sovereign crisis and this in turn led to fiscal deficit, austerity, recession and more fiscal deficit. The group's policy recommendations seek three objectives:

- Eliminate the vicious cycle between banking crises and sovereign crises, forcing banks to reduce their holdings of their governments' debt securities
- Increase the resilience of economies in the face of adverse shocks through risk sharing fiscal schemes
- If all else fails and governments or banks become insolvent, allow orderly debt restructuring

A banking union to reduce vulnerability

What does the concept of risk sharing mean for the financial and banking sector? Let us first identify the problem. Chronologically, the post-2008 eurozone crisis was a banking crisis rather than a fiscal one. The bitter lesson was, firstly, that without a credibly solid banking sector there is no macro-financial stability and, secondly, that once a banking crisis is unleashed there is no national capacity within the framework of a

---

115 See Bénassy-Quéré et al., (2018)

monetary union to stop the haemorrhage and contagion. In the absence of a lender of last resort, the national treasuries do not have the muscle to stop the free-fall of their banks and, when they try to do so in the early stages, it is at the cost of turning the bank debt into sovereign debt and unleashing the doom-loop between banking crisis and sovereign crisis. Due to the pre-eminence of bank financing, European banks have become too large to be rescued by their respective national States.

Against the background of this diagnosis, the proposals to confront the inherent financial instability of the eurozone seek to create a banking union, since European banking is still highly cantonised. This union has three basic components: a common structure for supervision, a common mechanism for resolution of bank failures and a collective deposit guarantee. In the first component, progress since 2012 has been significant. In the second and third, we know what needs to be done, the mechanisms are designed, and the institutions have been created, but there remains the not so minor detail of who pays if the existing dams–that is, the funds available at national and/or Community level–are breached. If the crisis once again became systemic today, the available funds would not be enough to handle it. In light of this, the markets would exert extreme pressure to cover the potential losses and force the EMU to make existential decisions, in the style of Mario Draghi's *"whatever it takes to save the euro"*.

It is not wise, however, to make the survival of the eurozone depend on one-off heroic decisions which do not arise from an institutional, legal and regulatory framework that has been previously reformed to address systemic financial crises. The rescue policy adopted by the ECB in July 2012 teetered dangerously on the edge of illegality, in which the Maastricht Treaty and the ECB's statutes had to be reinterpreted too loosely. The objective is that in future both the Banking Resolution Fund, for the management of insolvent banks, and the Deposit Guarantee Fund have ultimate Community fiscal support, making them credible. In addition, history has repeatedly shown that the simple (credible) promise of an ultimate backstop often makes the use of these funds unnecessary. This was demonstrated during the 2008-10 financial crisis in the United States, where the FDIC did not need to use its credit line with the US Treasury. Nor did the ECB incur losses due to its July 2012 commitment. If the commitment of the authorities is credible, the deposit insurance funds provided by private banks would be sufficient to handle the specific situations of bank failures.

Paradoxically, the "no rescue" clause, written in letters of fire in the Maastricht Treaty and repeatedly violated in the eurozone crisis, can only be realistically fulfilled if there is a Banking Resolution Fund and a Deposit Guarantee Fund that are credible, as well as an orderly bankruptcy mechanism for banks. When the economic agents (depositors, investors, other financial institutions) are aware of this, the speculative attacks will cease the moment each one has covered their risk, a moment that will come much earlier than it would without these mechanisms of protection and resolution.

It turns out, then, that the commitment of the authorities to providing public funds–the ultimate backing–to stop financial panic in an orderly way is what would make private schemes of risk sharing, such as deposit protection, work. It would also most probably obviate the use of public resources. Even if the systemic crisis were of such a magnitude that the ECB or the EU Funds had to disburse some resources, the amount of these would be appreciably lower than those that would have been needed without the existence of the common backstop. This is how the communal willingness to share risk reduces the overall risk of the banking system and, therefore, the risk of individual banks. Hence, public support schemes decisively reduce the vulnerability of the financial system.

Obviously, any risk-sharing scheme must be accompanied by the satisfactory functioning of the mechanisms for common banking supervision. Macro-prudential regulations should also be adopted to eradicate several of the cancers that led to banking crises in the past, especially the doom-loop between banking crises and sovereign debt crises. For example, balance-sheet limits on exposure to government debt should be established, as well as limits and/or prohibitions on government guarantees to banks.[116]

Were the three pillars of the banking reform to be implemented, the conditions for a true banking union would exist. The benefits would range from reducing the likelihood of systemic crises to stabilising credit flows. Just as an example, consider the case of a bank with presence in several European countries, which could offset losses in one country affected by the recession with reasonable profits in other countries that are

---

[116] There are countries, such as Italy, which still vigorously resist regulations limiting the holding of government debt by the banks. Tabellini (2018) argues that such a restriction would hit highly indebted governments, since it would deprive them of their quasi lender of last resort–their local banks–with the consequent risk of destabilisation.

not affected. It would not be forced, as happened in the eurozone crisis, to completely shut off the credit tap. These supra-national banks could assume a good deal of the counter-cyclical stabilising role that usually corresponds to fiscal management. Hence, a banking union works as a totally private risk-sharing insurer.

Shared fiscal stabilisation

While a banking union does not meet with much resistance, a fiscal union of similar depth encounters widespread rejection. No government, not even those embracing the philosophy of risk sharing, would be won over to the idea of surrendering the last stronghold of national economic sovereignty, which is the power to collect taxes and decide on what they are going to be spent. The underlying–and difficult–problem is that this power is now the exclusive right of national governments according to the Constitutions of all the European countries, as recognised by the Maastricht Treaty. It would require a profound reform of the constitutional framework of the Union to enable this cession of fiscal sovereignty, something unthinkable at the moment. Nor do airy proposals for a European "super-minister" of Finance arouse enthusiasm.

The good news is that these conventional forms of fiscal integration, which attract so much resistance and require so many legal reforms, are not the only way to achieve the goal of stabilisation. Other second-best programs could serve the same purpose, which is to prevent economies from destabilising in adverse circumstances. This does not require huge masses of resources.

In the theory of Optimum Currency Areas, starting especially with the contribution of Kenen (1969), some degree of fiscal transfer has always been considered necessary as part of the stabilisation mechanisms in the absence of exchange rate flexibility. We saw in earlier chapters that what perpetuated the euro crisis and made it more destructive was the recessionary spiral that generated the perverse dynamics of austerity, recession and speculative attacks. Behind this spiral was the inability of the debtor countries to mobilise fiscal resources to stabilise the economy in the early stages of the crisis. As the financial markets were aware of this fundamental fiscal weakness, their speculative attacks on the bond markets of the affected countries did not cease until they entered into that vicious cycle.

Looking to the future of the eurozone, the reasons for endowing it with some common capacity for stabilisation are very strong. When a country loses its fiscal room for manoeuvre for facing a negative shock, market forces–what others call speculative agents–will push it to the verge of bankruptcy, at which time the community must decide whether to rescue it or open the exit door from the Monetary Union. During the euro crisis the decision was to rescue, but at a very high cost, whether in the form of resources used or wealth previously destroyed. If the markets had known from the outset that there was enough fiscal capacity at the Community level to allow the country to stabilise its economy and resume the path of growth, speculative attacks would have ceased early on–in fact they would not even have occurred–and the bailout cost for the Community would have been much lower or even non-existent.

Those who advocate market discipline resist these mutual fiscal support schemes, because they consider them a reward for past bad behaviour and a disincentive to undertake the necessary reforms going forward. This is not a trite argument, but two considerations are necessary. The first, related to the past, is that economies are not always destabilised because of bad economic policies; under certain circumstances, irrational markets can punish a country perceived as potentially vulnerable to a disproportionate degree and beyond what would have been necessary to correct the faults that might objectively have been present. This market overshooting may end up taking a country into a state of fiscal unsustainability that would have been perfectly avoidable with moderate initial Community support. Secondly, going forward, the eurozone crisis has shown that countries end up being brought to such a weakened position that their room for fiscal and political manoeuvring to undertake timely reforms at a reasonable social cost is very limited.

True, the bailouts of debtor countries during the euro crisis constituted a terrible precedent. It has been shown that they generate the most perverse incentives, undermine the European Constitution and do not prevent a high cost in lost welfare. The Greek tragedy should not be repeated. That is why the new architecture of the European Monetary Union should foresee mechanisms for an orderly restructuring of sovereign debt, when at the end debt restructuring is the only solution. The earlier in the crisis process the restructuring occurs the better, so there must be incentives that reduce its cost and the potential for contagion.

One thing is certain: these ordered restructurings can be necessary to avoid the accumulation of unmanageable debts that make all the effort and sacrifice of structural reforms useless. Market discipline does not work when the debt legacy makes the long-term viability of reforms not credible. Heavily indebted countries must receive support to place themselves on a sustainable path of debt management, that is, a path that will gradually reduce the debt burden. Market discipline, in the form of austerity, is certainly not the solution, as the euro crisis showed. This is a lesson that the European Centre-North orthodoxy should not forget.

Between 2011 and 2013, European bureaucracies were frantically generating directives and rules to "tighten the belts" of their members. All of these reforms were necessary and useful, but they did not eradicate the scepticism about the capacity of the EU institutions to enforce the rules and impose sanctions when breaches occurred. Based on this scepticism, among other things, some economists proposed to accept reality and give control and responsibility over their fiscal management back to national governments.[117] This proposal for devolution, however, has to be accompanied by penalties for the misbehaviour of governments. If a country messes up and falls out of favour with investors, it will not be bailed out and will have to assume the full cost of restructuring its debt.

Taking fiscal responsibility back to national level is not incompatible with the desirability of having risk sharing schemes to help stabilise a country hit by shocks. Clearly, the right to receive support is contingent on the country committing to Community rules of good fiscal practice. If, on the contrary, the country has behaved irresponsibly, it can have no access to stability guarantee funds and its destiny will be one of default and debt restructuring. Carrying out this complex process in an ordered way means that procedures need to be established beforehand and that there exists a credible and solvent institution to supervise them. This task would fall to the European Monetary Fund, tailored to the IMF model and immune from the whims of governments that so often affect other Community institutions. The Fund should be provided with sufficient resources to help restructured countries to get back on the path of sustainable growth and debt service.

---

117 See, for example, Eichengreen (2017)

Being willing to enforce the constitutional ban on rescues is music to the ears of those who advocate market discipline. However, willingness is a far cry from effective execution. Experience dictates that the more a situation deteriorates, the more expensive it is not to rescue, but at the same time the authorities tend to delay acting until they are forced to renege on their initial commitment not to rescue. That is why clear rules of early action should be defined so that the restructuring of debts is less costly than a subsequent bailout.

The risk with this policy–and with the disciplinary approach in general–is that it can generate panic in financial markets and push all agents to divest themselves of assets they consider at risk in a possible future restructuring.[118] These reactions of panic and contagion can lead a country or a bank to insolvency, even if its economic and financial fundamentals are basically healthy. This is where solidarity advocates say that the discipline of no-rescue needs to be accompanied by risk-sharing schemes so that speculative attack situations are limited to cases in which distrust is justified by the proven insolvency of a debtor and not by irrational panic.

The ease with which panic can be unleashed is often directly correlated with burdens inherited from the past. A banking system that has an unresolved problem of old delinquent accounts or a government that carries a heavy debt on its shoulders is more prone to be attacked by speculative forces. This greater vulnerability is one of the costs of legacies of the past. Another cost is that, if the legacy is high, the probability that market discipline fails or that structural reforms do not achieve their goal is also high. The measures adopted will lack credibility: no-one believes that Greece can grow and generate employment under the burden of a public debt over 170% of GDP; and if it does not grow, it will not reduce debt, nor have lasting political stability.

Germany and its market discipline allies are thus right not to agree to creating risk-sharing mechanisms, as long as the risks inherited from the past (old delinquency or old debt) are not isolated from the new risks arising from the day-to-day operation of the economies or the banks. Legacy costs must have a parallel and separate solution to present and

---

118 Micossi (2018) and Tabellini (2018) express this concern, probably very influenced by their proximity to the Italian situation. They argue that attempts to apply market discipline can generate instability and panic.

future risk-sharing schemes. In the case of banks, solutions along these lines may be to sell delinquent portfolios to specialised entities, amortising bad loans at a loss or creating a "bad bank" to absorb unhealthy assets. Significant progress has been made in this direction, but much more needs to be done and more public support would be required, in the style of the US government's Troubled Asset Relief Program during the 2008-09 crisis. In the case of sovereign countries, reduction programs are more complex, but this should not serve as an excuse to kick the can of solidarity eternally down the road, because what will be at stake in the next crisis will be the survival of the eurozone.

We close this section with a summary of proposals that have been made to mobilise common fiscal resources in favour of stability:

Table XI-1

Proposals for fiscal stability mechanisms

PROPOSALS	COMMENT
EUROPEAN STABILISATION MECHANISM (ESM) Created in September 2012 to deal with bailouts during the euro crisis	The problem with the ESM, in the first place, is that it did not have and does not have sufficient funds to face a crisis of the magnitude suffered by the eurozone. In the second place, the strict conditionality attached to the granting of resources has a clear pro-cyclical bias, which would aggravate the crisis instead of alleviating it. Under pressure from Germany, the ESM was created as an intergovernmental body, which is not controlled by the European Commission, nor subject to EU laws.
EUROPEAN MONETARY FUND (EMF) The European Commission has been proposing to convert the ESM into a true Monetary Fund along the lines of and with the capabilities of the IMF	The concern of the Centre-North-East alliance, especially Germany and the Netherlands, is that the creditor countries would not have control—in other words a right of veto—over who is being supported and under what conditions. Meanwhile, the concern of the Mediterranean periphery is exactly the opposite: that the creditors will use the Fund to discretionally impose their policies, as has been happening with the ESM. For the moment, the EMF is still in the freezer.
EUROPEAN INVESTMENT FUND The Fund would be financed with fiscal contributions from all the members. The purpose is to prevent the fall in investment in times of fiscal crisis, since investment projects are the first to be cut in the face of falling revenues.	Even though the Fund in itself has consensus, the amount of resources to be assigned to it does not.

TABLE XI-1 (cont.)
Proposals for fiscal stability mechanisms

PROPOSALS	COMMENT
UNEMPLOYMENT COMPENSATION FUND Funded with contributions from members as a percentage of GDP. The goal is that in recessive phases unemployment benefits should act as a counter-cyclical fiscal stabiliser.	The resistance to this type of compensation fund is high, because unemployment rates within the eurozone differ widely and countries with lower rates fear that transfers of resources will flow only to countries with high unemployment rates. A compromise solution could be for transfers of resources to be conditional on structural reforms to increase the flexibility of the labour market.
RAINY DAY FUND Proposal made by the IMF as a mechanism to accumulate resources during times of prosperity (0.35% of GDP per year has been proposed) that can later be used in times of recession.	This fund does not enjoy the support of Germany and the alliance of Nordic countries, which prefer that each country use its surplus resources to reduce debt levels during booms.
ISSUANCE OF SECURE BONDS The palette of proposals in this area is broad (European Senior Bonds, securities backed by sovereign bonds, etc.), but all have the purpose of increasing the security of sovereign bonds issued by countries.	The issuance of a purely European risk bond encounters open resistance from the Centre-North countries.
COMMUNITY GUARANTEE FOR THE FIRST TRANCHE OF SOVEREIGN DEBT Only debt issued below the threshold of 60% of GDP would enjoy Community support. Above this threshold, only the issuing country would be responsible, with the consequence that the risk premiums of this second tranche would be significantly higher.	This proposal could evolve into a possible common ground, but it has not yet been seriously considered at EU-official levels.

The proposals the European Commission has been putting on the table since the end of 2017 are more aggressive and point to Europe having a common Treasury capable of issuing Eurobonds and managing its own budget by the mid-2020s. That budget would perform functions of macroeconomic stabilisation in times of crisis. For the moment, Germany and its allies want to have nothing to do with a sizeable eurozone budget, nor common unemployment insurance, nor to mutualise the issuance of debt.

As regards the European Monetary Fund proposal, Germany would be willing to support the transformation of the ESM into an EMF, as long as this new body is subject to intergovernmental control, that is, outside the decision-making power of the Community organs. Additionally, countries that receive resources from the Fund must submit to strict conditionality. *Nihil novi sub sole.* Germany insists on focussing on rules of fiscal health, simple and strict, whose compliance is reinforced. A new element of the German position is the focus on setting and sanction limits on debt levels as a percentage of GDP (a torpedo aimed at Italy …), in the style of the limits traditionally set for fiscal deficits. It also supports the creation of a debt restructuring mechanism, which would manage the "bankruptcy" of undisciplined countries.

The moral hazard of solidarity

The German argument against any solidarity mechanism that involves sharing risks is that these schemes will ultimately mean sharing burdens, in which resources will always flow in one direction, from donors to beneficiaries. It is not difficult to guess who the donors would be, and who the beneficiaries. The moral hazard of such a situation is that profligate countries or irresponsible bankers would end up being rewarded for their bad behaviour. When economic agents know that others will eventually bear the costs of their misbehaviour, the incentives are there to keep misbehaving. A typical example is that of the banker who knows that he will be helped by the State, tacitly encouraging him to happily grant credit or make unduly risky investments.

The best antidote against moral hazard, according to orthodoxy, is the discipline of the market and an insistence on individual responsibility. At least, that's how it's supposed to work. The problem is that discipline is not always effective in achieving its purpose. When, as a consequence of poor behaviour, a whole financial system or a whole country threatens to go down the drain and take others with it, the cost to society of letting them go can be unjustifiable. That's when programs of fiscal solidarity and risk sharing, when applied timely, acquire a social and economic justification. The Maastricht Treaty prohibited the ECB from acting as lender of last resort and did not contemplate fiscal rescue mechanisms at EMU level. Market discipline at its purest. In the end, however, the ECB had no choice but to exceed its mandate in the absence of a fiscal solution to the eurozone crisis.

The classic risk sharing scheme is the Central Bank's role as lender of last resort. Of course, knowledge of this final possible rescue could relax the discipline of bankers, but there are ways to mitigate the harmful influence of moral hazard. The very existence of shared protection schemes (fiscal stabilisation funds, bank deposit guarantees, etc.) in intermediate phases of the process of deterioration significantly reduces the probability of defaults. And if there is also an orderly procedure for bankruptcy or debt restructuring, the costs of default decrease to the point that the markets consider it a real possibility and act accordingly, punishing bad behaviour through high risk premiums. Paradoxically, in the absence of any credible risk-sharing scheme or an ordered default procedure, the opposite effect could occur: a default would be so catastrophic that it would not be credible, in which case the markets would not act accordingly, that is, they would not reward the good players and punish the bad ones.

The no-bailout clause was never really credible in the eurozone, neither before nor after the crisis. The supposed discipline of the market did not work before 2010, because no-one imagined the possibility that the Monetary Union could abandon one of its members. Neither did it work afterwards, because the fundamental unsustainability of the debt levels made the no-bailout promises just as unbelievable. Only during the brief window between the end of 2010 and mid-2012, when, in a context of chaos and lack of Community coordination, investors started to contemplate the possibility of a Greek bankruptcy and corresponding Grexit, market discipline did work, but in so destructive a way that a rescue became inevitable.

The central point of the 7+7 Group approach is that the absence of intermediate risk-sharing schemes with a credible no-bailout rule prevented the effective performance of market discipline. In other words, shared-risk schemes and market discipline are not irreconcilable opposites but can complement and reinforce each other. This is good news, because it would open the doors to understandings between philosophies that today are at odds in Europe. Is this a delusional hope?

Anything can happen, again

What to do with the Monetary Union? The economic, technical and rational response is that the necessary changes have to be made in its financial architecture in order to provide it with tools to allow it to face financial crises without each of them representing a new existential risk. Each of the conflicting ideological sides has its own recipes, on which they cannot agree. In particular, Germany and its peers in Centre-North Europe will avoid any steps towards a possible transfer union. It is not, as some moral judges suggest, that rich countries are simply selfish and do not want to support the poor. The fact is that these countries are firmly convinced that solidarity schemes are unnecessary if all members of the eurozone comply with the established norms in a disciplined manner. On the contrary, solidarity would serve rather as a disincentive to do things properly and undertake the necessary reforms.

Eurozone reform is deadlocked. This does not mean that there have been no incremental changes to improve the euro area's resilience in the face of negative shocks, but we do not expect them to be substantial enough to face a major financial crisis with confidence. There have been and will be times of greater or lesser progress in the reforms: from 2010 to 2013 many good things were done in the eurozone, but from 2014 to 2016, virtually nothing was accomplished. In 2017 the "Macron effect" appeared, which once again re-enthused European sentiment with its visionary rhetoric. When in 2018 this effect began to fade, the change of government in Italy and renewed immigration fights were an alarm bell to Germany that it had to concede something if it did not want to be isolated in Europe. However, in the purest Community tradition, the EMU and particularly Germany will not take decisive steps until the euro is once again subject to a new existential threat. In 2012, it was the ECB (Mario Draghi) who saved the euro *in extremis mortis*, with the passive and reluctant assent of Germany. Over the following four years, EU governments practically outsourced dealing with the stability of the eurozone to the ECB. For how long will this go on?

In 202?, when a new crisis appears and the new European Monetary Fund does not yet have sufficient Community fiscal support to confront it, what card up the sleeve will be needed to save the euro again? The ECB cannot continue propping up the euro indefinitely, because no central bank can or should be continually solving political or constitutional deficiencies.[119] The logical and sensible thing would be to take advantage

---

119   This is also the firm conviction of Pisani-Ferry (2016)

of the years of tranquillity to build mechanisms and institutions to fulfil the stabilising role that the ECB has played up to now. It should surprise no-one that this is not happening, in line with how sluggishly reform processes have traditionally operated in the European Community. In the midst of a new crisis Germany will have to decide if it is worth saving the euro or not. If it considers it worthwhile and the cost is manageable, the options will remain the same as in 2012: either the ECB starts issuing money to buy troubled debt, or the European national treasuries undertake to foot the bill.

XII

BETWEEN DISINTEGRATION AND ORDERLY RECONFIGURATION

With the benefit of hindsight, many now say that taking the step of creating the Monetary Union was a mistake, although none of the critics of the time hit on what would become the triggers of the euro crisis.[120] Ashoka Mody (2018) even describes the EMU as a "tragedy". Martin Feldstein (2016) accuses the European leadership of exceeding the mandate originally granted by the people to create a common space for the free movement of goods, services, capital and people. In his opinion, it was this extra step that ended up moving the United Kingdom away from Europe, until finally it decided to leave. Others long for the old European Monetary System, which, although certainly not immune from turbulence, countries could leave with relatively little trauma. The problem is that once a country enters the putative earthly paradise of a monetary union, leaving it individually has an incalculable immediate cost. As the experienced Financial Times commentator Martin Wolf said: *"Creating the eurozone is the second-worst monetary idea its members are ever likely to have. Breaking it up is the worst."*[121]

Rather than Bill Clinton's 1991 campaign slogan "It's the economy, stupid", in the case of the European Union, it should be: "It's politics, stupid".

---

120 We share the opinion that it was a mistake, but it is also true that in the 80s, when the EMU project came to fruition, little was known about the great revolution that was coming with the liberation of financial flows and globalisation.

121 https://www.ft.com/content/44c56806-a556-11e4-ad35-00144feab7de

The economic risks that threaten the EMU are multiple and serious, and oceans of ink are still being spilt to propose solutions. However, the problem of the Union is eminently political: the reasons that created it were political, the causes that keep it paralysed are political, and the forces that can save it or keep it wearily alive will be political until some big event decides its fate. The fundamental problem of the EMU has been and still is the disconnect between the economic logic that should underpin the edifice of the Monetary Union and the political will to do what must be done. To put it in simpler terms: there is no political disposition to cede the terrain of fiscal sovereignty that would allow the implementation of solidarity or risk sharing schemes among the members of the Union. Moreover, there is no political will for solidarity to go beyond strictly stabilising the currency, and still less for including elements of equitableness to help close the social and wealth gaps between the members of the eurozone. Without this solidarity, a monetary union composed of countries so different from each other has no prospect of surviving in the long term.

Hypothetically, this asymmetry between the need to share fiscal resources and the willingness to do so could have been corrected by the presence of a strong member of the Union to take on the responsibility of providing stability to the system. But the aversion to fiscal transfers has prevented Germany from fulfilling the role of a benevolent hegemon. Germany, under pressure from its citizens, had a condition for agreeing to the wishes of France in establishing the EMU: the Monetary Union must never become a transfer union (or a debt union). National sovereignty on taxes and spending was irrevocable. Risk-sharing proposals presented by the European Commission or the southern Mediterranean countries have smashed against this rampart time and again.

It is no exaggeration to say that the EMU stands or falls because of Germany. Other analysts dilute the responsibility more and place it on the shoulders of the Franco-German axis. That may have been the case in the past, but today the potentials of the two countries are tilted in favour of Germany. And in any case, France is also a staunch defender of its own fiscal sovereignty. Both countries are somewhat schizophrenic in their European rhetoric: both sing the praises of a united Europe, but neither is willing to give up an iota of their fiscal sovereignty. The difference is that the French are more willing to open their wallets to contribute to a common European budget.

If, as we fear, Germany and its Centre-North allies continue to kick the can of fundamental EMU reforms down the road, the time will come to do two things: first, and for the time being, continue to build second-best defence mechanisms against financial instability and, second, make orderly plans for reconfiguring the eurozone. The most viable alternative is for the strongest countries to take the exit door and unite around a newly revalued "euro *bis*", more in line with their high-productivity export model. In this way, the Mediterranean periphery would remain inside the current euro, devalued against the "euro *bis*" and not subject to the tensions that arise from very competitive exporting economies coexisting with economies more focussed on their internal markets.

The delayed and mishandled management of the eurozone crisis aggravated political tensions within the EMU. The recipe of confronting the insolvency of countries via new loans tied to harsh fiscal conditions, but without reducing the debt burden, led to impoverishment and unemployment. The coercive methods applied to the debtors damaged what had been the consensual and respectful code of conduct with which Europe had been built. Much-needed cohesion fractured along several ideological and geographical lines: pro-European democrats vs. Eurosceptic populists, ordoliberals vs humanists, Southern Mediterraneans vs Centre-North Anglo-Saxons, etc. When economic tensions began to ease, the refugee crisis of 2015 became Europe's new divisive problem. Merkel's handling of the crisis was severely questioned both inside and outside of Germany. The stress put on Italy and some Eastern European countries as the first barrier to entry for illegal migrants to the European continent, fuelled the growth of populist tendencies of left and right in those countries.

We are not ignorant of the magnitude of the economic cracks that present an existential risk for the European Monetary Union, but repairing them would be relatively easy were it not for the political threats that menace Europe. We will comment on four of them. The first is the breakdown of the Franco-German alliance upon which the edifice of the European Union historically rested. The second is the growing disaffection of citizens towards European institutions, to which they do not ascribe democratic legitimacy. The third refers to the refugee crisis and, more generally, to problems of migration. And the fourth is the spectre of populism that today haunts Europe from end to end. It is these political realities that make the prospects bleak for economic reforms that offer real solutions to the design failures of the Monetary Union. How close are we to the disintegration of the current European construct? Does Brexit represent the first link in this disintegration process?

The political situation at world and European level is more unstable today than in recent decades. Who would have thought before 2016 that the United States was going to become the great destabilising factor for the world order built after World War II? Or that the United Kingdom was going to get into such a level of internal disarray due to the dispute surrounding its relationship with Europe? Political events are more unpredictable today. Against the backdrop of this instability, the question of the risk of Europe's disintegration has come to the fore.

If things are handled properly, the probable dissolution of the European Monetary Union, as we know it today, need not degenerate into a total collapse of the integration that Europe, with so much determination and effort, brought about after WWII. Other forms of peaceful coexistence and constructive cooperation were and still are feasible. Two conditions, however, must be respected: first, the edifice must have a solid foundation of democratic legitimacy and, second, any new integration must respect the immense variety of cultures, social preferences, economic structures and even political models that still coexist today in the mosaic of European peoples. Probably the resulting "united" Europe will look nothing like the current rigid, uniform, invasive, crisis-driven EU. The integration needs to be multi-level, multi-sphere and multi-speed.

Can the Franco-German axis save the euro? The sacred and uneasy alliance

France wanted the euro and Germany backed it up. Each of the two countries had its own political agenda. The decision to create the Monetary Union paid no heed to questioning from the ranks of academic economists, particularly economists from the United States. Instead of giving economic ties enough time to gradually weave the web of social and political amalgamation, the decision was to jump into the void of the Monetary Union with the hope that this would subsequently force the political project to mature. Instead of synchronising the social models and policies of the countries in parallel with economic integration, the focus was exclusively on the economic. Time has proved the academics right. The introduction of the euro not only did not bring the promised prosperity and integration among peoples but has become an existential threat to the European Union itself. Something that was destined to unite, has become a source of disunity and discord.

The fates of the EMU and the EU are closely intertwined. Even the scarcely visionary German Chancellor, Angela Merkel, was clear when in May 2010, in the midst of the Greek crisis, she said that "... *if the euro fails, not only will the currency fail but also Europe, and with it the idea of the European Union*".[122] The tone is understandably somewhat grandiloquent and agitated in a context as hectic as the moment in which the Greek crisis was infecting the rest of the periphery. However, in the background of those words was a particular vision of the European project, the same as that promoted by her predecessors Willy Brandt, Helmut Schmidt and Helmut Kohl, the vision of an ever closer Union, in which the common currency was a central cog. Other visions, however, would have been and are possible.

One of the problems that Europe has faced in recent decades is that, for better or for worse, there has been an absence of inspiring leadership. We say for better or for worse, because inspiration in the wrong direction can do a lot of damage, but a lack of inspiration to galvanise people can make them miss the train of history. We have not seen again the like of politicians such as Monnet, Pompidou, de Gaulle, Moro, Adenauer, Brandt, Kohl and others who lived through the war. In their place have come party functionaries and career civil servants more concerned with parochial than universal issues, experts in the intricacies of bureaucracies and sniffers of the winds of public opinion. Their actions are governed by opinion polls, rather than by they themselves, as leaders, giving form and direction to the collective thinking, as their predecessors did.

The Franco-German alliance has also been a victim of this mediocrity. After the presidencies of François Mitterrand and Jacques Chirac, Germany was left without a real interlocutor and fellow traveller, not only due to the lack of empathy of the subsequent presidents Sarkozy and Hollande

---

122 Merkel, Angela (2010), "*Scheitert der Euro, dann scheitert Europe*", Rede vor dem Deutschen Bundestag am 19. Mai 2010. https://www.bundestag.de/dokumente/textarchiv/2010/29826227_kw20_de_stabilisierungsmechanismus/201760

with Chancellor Merkel, but to the stagnation of the French economy. The economic gap between the two countries has widened strikingly since the beginning of this century.

That is why, in the greyish context of the current European leadership, the election of Emmanuel Macron in 2017 as president of France meant a flash of hope. He won the presidency comfortably on a liberal and pro-European platform, without concessions to the populism of the right-wing Marine Le Pen. He warned of the existential risk that threatened Europe and devised a vision to revitalise it.[123] In his analysis, Europe is weak internally and externally, has no capacity for action or reaction against major contemporary challenges. His main argument was that Europe needed to re-democratise, re-enthuse its citizens and reincorporate them into the project of its reconstruction.

Aware of the minefield that surrounds the purely economic issues, the focus of the new French president concentrated on initiatives around the security and defence of Europe. The Trump administration's questioning of its commitment to defend Europe put the continent on high alert. Macron proposed the creation of a European military intervention force, a defence budget and a common military doctrine. The securing of external borders and a common policy of refugee asylums were also two components of this integration in security and defence.

Germany's attitude and commitment to joining this security and defence initiative will be revelatory. At the level of rhetoric, Germany will support the idea of a European army, but it remains to be seen how much supra-national autonomy it is willing to grant and how much it is willing to contribute to the budget. NATO was born and endured because the hegemon of the Western Hemisphere was willing to bear a disproportionate share of its costs. Now that the Trump administration has declared itself unwilling to continue assuming that role of benevolent hegemon, NATO will begin to wither and will end up being replaced by other alternative arrangements.

The Germans have been severely criticised for their low level of military spending and for their alarming deficiency in military readiness.

---

123 See the main ideas in Macron's Speech at the University of La Sorbonne in September 26, 2017. https://www.theguardian.com/world/2017/sep/26/profound-transformation-macron-lays-out-vision-for-post-brexit-eu

A good fraction of its arms and means of transport are outdated. Most military expenditure goes to salaries and pensions. Data from NATO reveal that in 2017 German spending on military equipment, research and development reached only 0.17% of GDP, while in France it represented 0.42% and in the United Kingdom 0.47% of GDP.[124] An approximate calculation reveals that since 1990 France has cumulatively used 30% more of its GDP than Germany for military expenditure. The comparison starts in 1990 because up till then Germany contributed in proportions similar to its main European partners.

Curiously, the change in the trend of Germany's military spending occurs after the reunification of the two Germanys. There are many interpretations and hypotheses, but what is relevant here is that this neglect of military spending was not very supportive of its Western partners and allies. Such neglect in no way corresponded to Germany becoming the leading European economic power, let alone to any glimpse of a comprehensive hegemonic role. Germany has been a free rider in terms of security and defence. Its security has been guaranteed first and foremost by the United States, both directly and indirectly through NATO. The second pivot on which it has historically leaned has been France, which became more relevant after Germany distanced itself militarily from the United States and Britain with its decision not to support the invasion of Iraq in 2003. In the peculiar figure of "shared leadership", France traditionally provided security to Germany and projected European military power on the world stage, while Germany provided France with financial and economic power.[125] In this question of the military, however, France took on a disproportionate share of the burden.

Tooze and Vallée (2018) hit a nerve when they draw a parallel between the financial "legacy costs" (debt burdens from the crisis) and the legacy cost of Germany's military investment deficit of recent decades. One of the main reasons for Germany not to accept risk-sharing schemes in the fiscal and banking field has been precisely that legacy issues must be resolved first. Would Germany accept the obligation to resolve its own past military legacy and retroactively level up with its main partner, France, so as

---

124   Figures from Tooze and Vallée (2018)

125   See Harold, (2017)

to become an equal partner in the great European project of assuming the reins of its own destiny in terms of security and defence? A certain coherence of positions would be expected.

In fiscal matters, Macron proposed the creation of a European Finance Minister and a common eurozone budget but did not specify amounts or ways to fund them, aware of German reluctance on this issue. That is why he made it clear that the common budget is not for mutualising debts or solving the financial problems of a particular country. Nor was he specific when he brought up the possibility of a two-speed Europe, which would allow countries that want to deepen integration to advance at greater speed, while the rest would remain in the *status quo*. Would these two speeds also apply to the eurozone? Would the eurozone end up as two currency zones with two different euros? This is probably not what Macron had in mind, because a common currency zone, by definition, cannot have two speeds in the fiscal or financial sphere.

The reaction of Germany to the French proposals was slow and lukewarm, to the disappointment of those who thought that Merkel and Macron were going to revive the Franco-German axis. In a typical Merkel gesture, and leaving nothing to chance, the German chancellor took nine months to react to Macron's proposals. She did so in an interview with the German conservative newspaper Frankfurter Allgemeine Zeitung[126], instead of presenting it in a formal speech before an important audience, as Macron usually does. Beyond some minor concessions, in essence the German position regarding risk-sharing schemes has not changed:

- The German acceptance of converting the European Stability Mechanism (ESM) into a European Monetary Fund (EMF) is conditional on two elements: first, that the Fund be outside the control of the European Commission and, second, that the restructuring and rescue decisions of a country in trouble be taken consensually by the intergovernmental method and under the ultimate control of the respective parliaments. In practice, this amounts to a right of veto for Germany on fundamental decisions of the Fund. Worse yet, the proposed decision mechanism makes decision-making

---

[126] See "*Europa muss handlungsfähig sein*", June 3, 2018. https://www.bundeskanzlerin.de/bkin-de/aktuelles/europa-muss-handlungsfaehig-sein-1141498

virtually impossible with the urgency and depth that such situations often require.
- Germany wants nothing to do with a European finance ministry, nor a significant common budget; at most, it accepts a moderate investment fund for technological innovation and for facilitating structural reforms in countries subject to EU rescue programs. The fund would be modest, in the order of 0.2% of the eurozone's GDP (Macron suggested a common budget ten times higher).
- Germany agrees to move towards a banking union, but does not give a date for implementing the deposit guarantee fund and warns that the legacy of old non-recoverable assets should be resolved first. The new European Monetary Fund could support the Bankruptcy Resolution Fund only from 2024.

Merkel says she agrees with a joint force of military intervention but warns that there will be times when Germany will not participate and that the German parliament will always have the last word. In any case, there are good reasons to doubt that Germany will commit to a joint defence scheme with France that can measure up to the challenge of the withdrawal of the US commitment to the defence of Europe. France and Germany have very different histories. The former has traditionally fulfilled its role unapologetically as a world military power. The latter will have difficulty in putting behind it the fervent non-military pacifism it had to embrace after 1945.

At the fiscal level, Merkel warns again that solidarity among European partners should never become a "debt union". It is the well-known German "yes, but no". The Franco-German summit held in June 2018 in Meseberg ratified this position of minimum agreements.[127] There were some small steps in the right direction, but crucial issues such as measures to break the perverse link between banks and their governments, create secure European debt securities, institute a sovereign debt restructuring fund or expand the mandate of the ECB were not agreed upon.

After this bucket of cold water, the "Macron moment" that oxygenated the European scene in 2017 began to fade. Within his own country, the Macron brand also lost its shine less than two years after his being

---

127 See Meseberg Declaration of June 19, 2018.

elected. This is not at all a minor issue, because it is difficult for Europe to move in any direction without an understanding between France and Germany. This was the case throughout the second half of the last century and it continues to be so in this new century. On its own France does not have the economic strength or leadership to set the European train, and particularly the train of the EMU, on the track of real solutions. Germany may have economic power, but it has always refused to act and lead alone on the European scene.

Will France and Germany be able to agree on a vision of Europe, a shared project that transcends their own particular interests to re-lead the continent? We are sceptical. Certainly, we will see in the future good collaboration between the two countries in other areas such as the military, refugee policy, tax harmonisation, social policies, etc. The importance of this willingness to collaborate in other areas should not be underestimated, because one of the problems that the process of European integration has had in the past has been to force integration in the commercial and monetary spheres, without doing the same in others. At the end of the road, however, the EMU is a primarily monetary-fiscal-financial project and there must be a basic agreement between the two main members on how to make the Union viable. The chances of the two countries' positions on Europe converging significantly in a joint platform looks very remote.

As if these disagreements were not enough cause for concern, differences between the various European sub-blocs have also been emerging with increasing force. Traditionally, France and Germany would meet before European summits, agree on the agenda and were then able to agglutinate the positions of the rest of the countries around them: Germany managed to channel the concerns of the countries of Central, Northern and Eastern Europe, and France did the same with the countries of the Mediterranean. In the wake of the bitter discrepancies that arose around the euro crisis and, worse still, the refugee crisis, Italy, for one, is reluctant to align itself with France on many issues,[128] just as the Netherlands is with Germany. For example, the (minimal) Meseberg agreements were questioned by an important group of countries comprising the Netherlands, Denmark, Estonia, Finland, Ireland, Latvia,

---

128   Beyond the basic differences, an irrational and incomprehensible antagonism has developed between the new governments of Italy and France.

Lithuania, and Sweden, all of which are radically against sharing risks with other countries.

Questioning the "sacred alliance" used to be taboo in France and Germany. But in view of the difficulty of forming a joint platform for action, some German experts in international relations and even government figures have recommended that Germany open up to new flexible alliances with other European countries. Ursula von der Leyen, German Minister of Defence, put forward the proposal in 2015 in her speech to the Munich Security Conference, stating that Germany was willing to "*lead from the centre*" in terms of security and defence.[129] In the elliptical language of diplomacy, she did not refer directly to the geographic centre of Europe, but to creating new alliances and associations in which–as the speech says–Germany was the centre that would supply its best resources and capabilities. Naturally, experts in international relations soon began to put names to this centre and associate it with Central and Northern Europe. Beyond the old, somewhat stagnant alliances, the suggestion is that Germany seek flexible coalitions and build a political centre with countries like Sweden, Denmark, Finland, Austria and the Benelux countries.[130] All of them are nations with which Germany historically maintains close relations, based on geography, standard of living and cultural affinity, but which had traditionally been treated as junior partners in the task of shaping the direction of the European Union and the EMU.

This openness to a new political centre is not a minor matter. Traditionally European countries, especially those in the Centre-North, have been cautious and have avoided turning their greater affinity into formal and visible alliances. If the Centre-North alliance were consolidated as a potential alternative to the Franco-German engine, Europe would be moving towards a deepening North-South division. It would not be that the Centre-North would advance faster than the South towards more Europe, but that it would move towards a Europe different from that advocated by

---

129 Ursula von der Leyen, Leadership from the Center , February 6, 2015. https://www.securityconference.de/fileadmin/MSC_/2015/Freitag/150206-2015_Rede_vdL_MSC_Englisch-1_Kopie_.pdf

130 See for example Janning and Möller (2016), from the Office of the European Council on Foreign Relations in Berlin.

its Latin partners. It would not be long before the idea arose of two monetary blocs, two euros, two central banks. These are processes that, once they start rolling, are not easy to control as regards their final destination.

The refugee crisis and nationalist populism: a new existential threat

Two macro events have shaken the foundations of the European edifice in the decade of the 2010s: the euro crisis of 2010 and the refugee crisis of 2015. In both events Germany played a leading role. Both events changed the face of Europe and the place of Germany within it. In both, also, Germany's hegemonic leadership was seriously questioned, although for opposite reasons and by different countries. In the euro crisis, Germany's performance was perceived as coercive, interventionist and selfish, all attributes that the German leadership had always tried to avoid as part of its pacifist repositioning campaign after the war. In the refugee crisis, Germany suffered retaliation for its coercive past.

When the turbulence of the eurozone crisis was already calming, a new crisis, the massive refugee influx of 2015, took over the European scene. Since the spring of that year, an unprecedented flow of refugees, mainly from Muslim countries in a state of civil war (Syria, Libya, Afghanistan), flooded the coasts of the European Mediterranean. 2013 and 2014 had already been critical, with 431 thousand and 627 thousand first-time asylum seekers respectively, but in 2015 the number of asylum applications more than doubled to reach 1.3 million people, with a similar number in 2016 (See Figure XII-1).

It was at that moment that Chancellor Angela Merkel, in an unexpected gesture and out of character with her prudent nature, decided to unilaterally open the borders of Germany to the rivers of refugees who had overflowed Europe's external borders by land from the Balkans. In Merkel's decision there was a mixture of moral imperative to address the humanitarian crisis, and of pragmatism in handling a situation that was already out of control. At first, a large part of the German population, generous and supportive by nature, showed moving gestures of a "culture of welcome". That year, 2015, Germany channelled almost 40 percent of the total asylum applications of the European Union, being accompanied in this disproportionate effort only by Sweden and Hungary. In 2016, Hungary stepped back and Germany handled 60 percent of Europe's total asylum applications, adding more than 1.2 million refugees in two years. More than a wave of immigrants, it was a tsunami and this time Germany did assume, as benevolent hegemon, an outsize share of the problem.

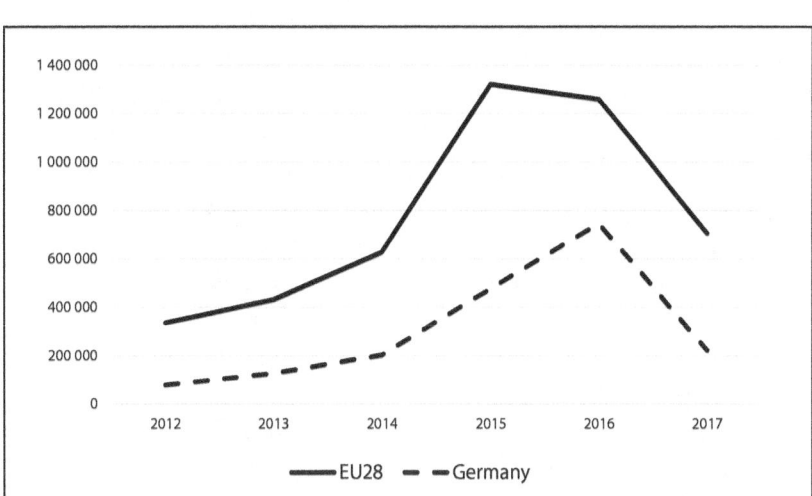

FIGURE XII-1
Number of first-time Asylum Applicants, 2012-2017

Merkel's subsequent efforts for all European countries to assume their share of the refugee burden fell on deaf ears. The system of welcoming immigrants that Europe had been applying, agreed in the Dublin II Regulation, was swamped and pulverised by the avalanche from the Mediterranean. The truth is that this system was not equitable, because it was based on the principle that asylum applications had to be processed in the country of first entry into the European Union, that is, in the Mediterranean countries of Southern Europe. This regulation placed most of the political and social burden on these countries; Greece and Italy thus felt left on their own by Europe.

The open rejection of many countries in Southern and Eastern Europe to the refugee quota system was a major blow to the leadership of Germany as the proponent country. The rejection made evident the limits to an exercise of soft hegemony that offered nothing in return, nor wanted to use coercive means to force the European partners to accept their proportional share. Some saw in this refusal sweet revenge against Germany for the coercive style with which it had handled the Eurocrisis.[131] Public opinion and the governments of the European partners were uncomfortable in observing the latent contradiction between its approach to the refugee crisis, in which Germany demanded solidarity and the assumption of equitable shares of sacrifice, and its approach to the sovereign debt crisis, in which each debtor had to assume its own individual responsibility.

Internally, German public opinion also turned in a few months against Merkel's policy of welcome. Radical populist forces found a growing echo in the population, to the point that the government faced a serious internal rebellion within the coalition, especially on the part of its Bavarian counterpart, the CSU, which demanded a reduction in the number of immigrants to 200 thousand per year and the return of refugees to the country that had originally granted them asylum. The right-wing conservative nationalist AfD rode on this wave of citizen anxiety caused by the "Muslim invasion" and improved its electoral share in the general election of 2017, going from 4.7 to 12.6 percent, which made it the third force in parliament with 94 deputies.

On the other hand, the incipient steps of some European countries towards erecting internal borders within the Union threatened to blow up the Schengen and Dublin Agreements. All this forced the German government in March 2016 to negotiate an agreement with Turkey–the key country through which the largest number of refugees from the Middle East flowed–to take back contingents of migrants stuck in Greece. These negotiations and other measures of internal hardening of asylum procedures made it possible to reduce the number of asylum applications in Europe in 2017 to little more than half. However, Germany continued to confront the problem that refugees admitted by other periphery countries sought sooner or later to continue their journey on to Germany. Imposing barriers at the German border would violate Community agreements on free internal transit but doing nothing would end up undermining the political base of the Merkel government. A diabolical dilemma.

The ultimate cause of this convoluted situation is that Europe did not really have a common refugee management policy, a common

---

131   Vision shared by Janning and Möller (2016) and Seung-Jae Oh (2016)

asylum-granting agency and intra-European quota agreements. The fact that the 2015-16 emergency has been overcome does not remotely contradict the claim that the refugee problem, and the problem of immigrants generally, represent the second existential threat to the European Union. Merkel said in an interview in June 2018: "*I now consider that the issues of securing borders, a common asylum policy and attacking the causes of emigration are truly existential issues for Europe*".[132] The refugee crisis–compounded by the continued economically motivated migration from Africa–has shocked and divided Europe. Due to the migrant pressure and the rise of populist movements, the members of the Union have looked out for their particular interests, Community discipline has been broken and fundamental pillars of the Union, such as the Schengen Agreement, have faltered. It has been a sober awakening after a decades-long dream of integration. The problem is still there and will continue for a long time.

Although the neighbours did not see it that way, the positive side of the "welcome culture" is that Germany showed its most pluralistic and inclusive side and that the liberal forces of openness remained vigorous.[133] Another positive aspect is that, unlike its conduct in the eurozone crisis, Germany acted in this case as a benevolent hegemon by accepting a disproportionate number of refugees. It did so to help countries on the periphery of the EU, aware that they could not handle by themselves an avalanche of refugees that might have the potential to destabilise their internal politics.

But it also demonstrated the deep divide between its population and the political class, between an increasingly nationalist right and a liberal centre-left, or between the modernising urban masses and the conservative suburban and rural masses. The importance of this internal divide must not be underestimated in a country in which one of the keys to success had always been the ability to understand one another and create consensus. Since 1945, the vast majority of German society consistently and enthusiastically supported the European integration project. Today this can no longer be said to be the case. The refugee crisis and the problem of immigration in general

---

132   Angela Merkel FAZ-Interview , "Nun sehe ich die Themen Grenzsicherung, gemeinsame Asylpolitik und Bekämpfung der Fluchtursachen als wirkliche Existenzfragen für Europa". https://www.faz.net/social-media/instagram/kanzlerin-angela-merkel-f-a-s-interview-europa-muss-handlungsfaehig-sein-15619721.html?premium

133   See the extensive report on Germany in The Economist of April 14, 2018.

has been responsible for sowing the seeds of political instability within the principal country of the European Union, to the point that it cannot be ruled out that a European crisis might one day flourish in Germany and the country might become the problem rather than the solution.

The euro crisis and the refugee crisis had two elements in common. In the first place, both caused serious–irreversible?–damage to the cohesion of the European community of nations: the euro crisis due to disputes between debtors and creditors, the refugee crisis due to the lack of intra-Community solidarity. In the second place, both created the breeding ground for the emergence of new nationalist populist movements or the strengthening of existing ones. It is these populist forces that represent one of the greatest threats to the future of the EU, since they are all militantly anti-European. We are not talking about the (unlikely) risk that eventual populist governments decide to withdraw from the eurozone or the EU, so much as the paralysis of the urgent reforms that Europe should undertake to survive in the long term. Unfortunately, the reality is that every Head of Government who sits in European Council meetings makes their decisions based on how each issue affects their electoral prospects in the face of populist opponents.

The aftermath of the eurozone crisis ended up convincing large sectors of the most severely hit countries, the debtors, that economic development was leaving them behind, that the political establishment no longer represented them, and that European institutions were insensitive to citizens' problems. The lower income sectors perceived that they had to pay a disproportionate part of the cost of solving a banking crisis generated by the rich. They perceived that the EU, far from closing the gaps, had enlarged imbalances between countries. They found that internal social inequality had increased after the crisis. Above all, they perceived that the sluggish post-crisis economic growth was never going to give them the pre-crisis employment opportunities they had once had. In the creditor countries, despite having been less affected, the lower income sectors also felt abandoned by an economic system unable to improve their standard of living, a system in which employment conditions were increasingly precarious and where the gap between technologically skilled and unskilled workers widened day by day.

Globalisation has become the focus of populist rage. The commercial, economic and monetary union of Europe has been the product of a hyper-globalisation process six decades long. As many comparable precedents show, globalisation always has winners and losers. The least competitive countries tend to lose, and within them the less technologically developed sectors and the less skilled workers. The problem with globalisation, and Europe is no exception, is that the new global structures do not have the mandate to redistribute their gains and compensate the losers to correct the inequalities created. This task is left to national governments, which have the democratic mandate of social justice, but lack the material capacity to implement it in a globalized frame. As Meyer (2018) points out, the EU's Community structures were only mandated to promote negative integration, that is, integration by removing barriers and regulating markets. They did not, however, have the mandate to integrate "positively" through redistributive actions to preserve social cohesion among the member countries. The other focus of populist anger has been liberal ideology. There is nothing more liberal than the removal of barriers between markets, an activity that has been at the heart of the European project. This means that the EU integration project is inevitably branded as liberal, and is rejected by those who are discontented with the current state of affairs.

The breeding ground has been prepared for the emergence of populist nationalist movements throughout the continent. All of them contain chauvinistic elements of rejection of the foreign and exaltation of the native, both culturally and economically, usually packaged in simplistic and authoritarian quick-fix approaches. Large social groups feel insecure, threatened by the opening of borders and international economic liberalism. The reaction has been a *volte-face* towards protectionism and commercial retaliation.[134]

To the feeling of economic insecurity from globalisation is added the perceived immigrant threat: threatened jobs, endangered cultural identity, formation of urban ghettos, the threat of terrorists infiltrating among asylum seekers... This popular perception of the magnitude of the immigrant problem is often very distorted, as evidenced by an opinion study conducted by Harvard University.[135] People, especially those with a lower level of education and job training, tend to associate

---

134 Conti et al. (2018a) offer a detailed analysis of the return to nationalist "sovereignty" throughout Europe. Glencross (2013) warns of the very real threat of a regression to a purely national vision of democratic legitimacy and the consequent de-legitimisation of anything supra-national.

135 Stantcheva (2018)

immigrants with threatening races or religions, and to believe that they are unemployed, have no training, and live off government handouts. It is no coincidence, therefore, that populist currents were strengthened relatively more in countries where the problems of immigration were more acute or had more resonance among the majorities disadvantaged by globalisation. In Greece, Italy, Hungary, Poland and Austria, populist parties or coalitions came to power. In the Netherlands, France and Germany, the populist offensive has still been contained, but the menace is latent and nearby. Populist parties, even without being in power, have the capacity of disrupting daily political life.

In this way, an additional existential threat has been added to the financial vulnerability of the European edifice: the political vulnerability represented by the gradual rise to power of political groups that are markedly nationalist and anti-European. This new vulnerability does not distinguish between creditors-debtors, rich-poor, North-South. In fact, the threat has already appeared in the principal member of the Union, Germany, where it can no longer be taken for granted that the majority continues to support the project of a liberal European union, which has been the quintessence of Germany's foreign policy position since the Second World War. Even if the populists do not come to power, the German government will have little room for manoeuvre to advance a forthright European agenda. And if they do come to power, nothing in Europe will be as it was before. Either way, if it is true, as we firmly believe, that Europe's destiny will depend on what Germany does or, more to the point, does not do, the auguries for the future of the Union are not good.

Brexit: the first step on the path to European disintegration?

Given the deep political division that criss-crosses Europe and how different are the visions of what should be done, one cannot ignore the question of how close we are to a process of disintegration.[136] What would

---

136 (Dis)integration should not be conceived in all-or-nothing terms. As pointed out by Webber (2018), the concept has several dimensions. These include a sectoral one, which refers to the reduction or expansion of the scope of competencies that are the subject of (dis)integration; a vertical one, which refers to how many competencies are handled at the supra-national or intergovernmental levels, and a numerical one, regarding the increase or decrease in the number of members.

it take to confront the existential threats? What unifying forces created and preserved European integration in the past? Are they still present? It does not seem so. The European leaders of the first and second generation of the post-war period showed a strong willingness to promote European integration. The common people were never an active part of the process, but they supported it pragmatically because of the material benefits that the European Community increasingly provided. Today, however, the third generation of leaders has a parochial mentality and governs through the rear-view mirror of what the opinion polls dictate. They are not guided by any vision. And the population has seen its standard of living deteriorate as a result of the crisis and is therefore suspicious of everything that comes out of Brussels.

The long-standing detachment of the United Kingdom from Europe placed it in a third ring of the constellation of European countries that made up the EU. The second ring was made up of the countries that were not members of the EMU (Bulgaria, Croatia, Czech Republic, Denmark, Hungary, Poland, Romania and Sweden), but that honestly wanted to play under EU rules. And the first ring, the hard core, were the remaining 19 countries that were also part of the EMU. The problems and the spirit of integration of each group were different. However, even though the case of the United Kingdom was too specific to draw general conclusions, it was not the only country that felt uncomfortable with the direction that Europe had taken. The central problems of Europe affected the three rings, although to different degrees, as were the margins of manoeuvre that each ring had to handle their differences from European uniformity.

Why is the United Kingdom leaving?

After almost seven decades of uninterrupted expansion, the second largest member of Europe,[137] the United Kingdom, decided in June 2016 to get off the European train. 51.9 percent of voters opted to leave the European Union. The result of the referendum took many by surprise. It is true that current events tipped the balance towards leaving, but the undeniable fact is that half the voting population was against European membership.

---

137 France and the UK compete for second place: in GDP the UK is larger, in population France slightly exceeds it if we include the French overseas territories.

Does Brexit represent the first step in the process of the European Union's disintegration? We start with a potted history of the UK's relationship with Europe to help understand the true dimensions of the event. We explained in Chapter II the very *sui generis* relationship of the United Kingdom with Europe. The British, with characteristic ambivalence, never wanted to be part of the hard core of European integration. They wanted Europe to come together, they actively worked for it, but they were always watching the game from the side-lines and keeping open the option of going on and off the pitch whenever they wanted. They wanted a seat at the European table, but always asked for a special menu to pick from. To use a very British expression, they wanted to have their cake and eat it.

From the beginning there was a fundamental divergence with respect to the purpose of Europe. France and Germany promoted the grand vision of a Europe increasingly integrated economically and politically, ordered and governed by rules defined, interpreted and enforced by Community bodies. The British, on the other hand, drew close to Europe for exclusively mercantile interests. Recall their economic hardships of the 60s and 70s. They needed access to the European common market to counter the deep economic decline derived from the loss of the Empire and from the mistaken economic policies of Labour governments. But they were not interested at all in being part of the process of deepening the European Union in areas other than the commercial. On the contrary, the British conception was opposed to everything that meant the transfer of regulatory authority to supra-national bodies. In the political realm, the United Kingdom always resisted any initiative that would mean supra-national power structures or federalist schemes. Everything had to be resolved in the intergovernmental sphere (negotiations between countries), always preserving the power of veto or, in its absence, the UK's right not to participate (opt out).

It would not be true, however, to generalise and say that all of the British rejected the idea of Europe. Scepticism about the idea of a united Europe divided the British establishment and public opinion from the beginning, both transversally and vertically. So much so that it is very likely that a hypothetical referendum on Europe at any time in the 1990s or 2000s would have yielded the same divided result that we saw in June 2016 and that the balance could have tipped in any direction depending on the current events of the moment.[138] In view of this deep split, David Cameron had to promise, in his 2015 electoral manifesto, that he would call a referendum on the United Kingdom remaining in Europe if his party won the election. It was a dangerous move–irresponsible, according to many–because any referendum result was possible, with immense and long-lasting consequences for the country. Whatever the outcome, the problem of the division of British society with respect to Europe was not going to disappear. These are situations in which one questions the reasonableness of methods of direct democracy for resolving such complex issues with such an impact on the life of a country.

Cameron led a rational campaign to convince the electorate of the economic benefits of being members of the EU, while negotiating with the rest of the European partners a series of "concessions" that would make remaining more palatable. Cameron was concerned that Europe was increasingly becoming the Europe of the euro and that the problem of monetary union was taking over the agenda of the European institutions, especially the European Council, European Commission and Parliament. The EU countries which were not also part of the EMU felt themselves to be "second-class members", not so much because they were not involved in the project of an increasingly united Europe (ever closer union), which did not interested them, but because they were losing their voice in European affairs. The United Kingdom wanted to guarantee the option of not participating in supra-national initiatives (opt-out), but to continue to maintain its privileged seat at the table of European decisions. The attitude of the European partners in the negotiations was open and constructive, especially so that of Germany, because no-one wanted Brexit. In the end, the negotiations were quite successful for the British side, except in the attempt to put additional restrictions on the access of EU citizens to the United Kingdom. That would have amounted to a breach of a core value of the EU.

Cameron, and the members of his government who favoured remaining, put forward all kinds of arguments and facts during the referendum campaign to demonstrate technically that the balance of costs and benefits was tilted in favour of staying in Europe. On the side of Brexit supporters, however, irrational, sentimental and atavistic

---

138 A speculation that we share with de Burca in his contribution to the book by Martill and Staiger, editors (2018)

arguments predominated.[139] As pro-Brexit Minister Michael Gove said during the referendum campaign, *"people in this country are tired of experts ... of organisations with acronyms that say they know what is best but are consistently wrong"*. There were insistent references to the danger of a loss of national identity, to the threat to jobs because of immigrants, to the insolence of Brussels bureaucrats in trying to impose regulations and trample Britain's thousand years of sovereignty. These arguments, added to the dream of recovering Britannia's greatness in the world, resonated more with the electorate than the rational reasons for remaining, especially among less educated and older segments of the population.

The double existential crisis experienced by the European Union in the 2010s (the euro crisis and refugee crisis) was rich fuel for the Eurosceptics' fire. Despite not forming part of the EMU, the management of the euro crisis showed the ugly face of an incompetent European institutionalism, which had to be supplanted by the hegemonic imposition of one of its members. The dictates of Berlin, plus the repressive attitude of Brussels, revived British aversion to all forms of foreign interventionism. On the other hand, the situation of migrants from the countries of Eastern Europe newly incorporated into the European Union–a million of whom had settled in the UK after 2004–was the banner waved by Leave supporters during the campaign. The straw that broke the camel's back (or rather, the storm surge in the river) was the wave of refugees across the Balkans in spring-summer of 2015. Germany's initial open-arms policy and its aim to distribute the refugees through a quota system was probably the factor that finally tipped the balance and turned the anticipated 48-52 into 52-48 in favour of Brexit.

Two years after the decision to leave the EU, the balance of events tilts more towards those who predicted negative economic consequences. Favourable winds from the global economic boom since 2016, however, have cushioned the short-term economic effects of Brexit, but the long term looks negative. Even a prudent central banker like Mark Carney, Governor of the Bank of England, speaking to the Cabinet in September 2018, could not avoid painting a highly negative outlook in the case of an abrupt departure with no agreement. According to Carney, the pound sterling would continue to depreciate, inflation would increase, as would

---

[139] Slogans like "We send the EU £350 million a week. Let's fund our NHS instead" were appealing to vast groups of voters.

interest rates, real estate prices would fall drastically and the unemployment rate would rise to double digits.[140] An exit with agreement would be less traumatic but would still be negative in the long term. The City of London would cease to be the financial centre of Europe, because the financial institutions domiciled there would lose their passport rights, that is, their ability to use their banking licence in any of the EU countries. The service sector which accounts for three quarters of the British economy, would be left out of any agreement, hard or soft.

At the beginning of 2017 the May government drew some "red lines" for the negotiation of exit: access (without membership) to the Common Market of goods, agreement (without membership) to remain in the Customs Union, non-jurisdiction of the European Court of Justice, immigration control of European citizens, and keeping the border between Northern Ireland and Ireland open and free. "*No deal is better than a bad deal*", was her slogan. The European Union, for its part, adopted a firm negotiating position and was not willing to renounce its constituent principles and values. Any member wishing to suspend their membership of the Union in future, had to know the consequences that awaited them.

The Irish border proved to be an almost insurmountable obstacle. In December 2017 the UK and Europe agreed on a "backstop" provision, which essentially was a binding assurance that there will not be a hard (physical) border between Northern Ireland and the Republic of Ireland. This is because the existing international treaty between the UK, the Republic of Ireland and the EU known as the Good Friday Agreement precludes a physical border. For Europe the only way to keep this border open would be if the United Kingdom agreed to maintain the rules governing commerce in the European Union. Otherwise, the United Kingdom could only aspire to an agreement similar, for example, to that between Europe and Canada, or Europe and Norway, with real customs borders. Brexiteers, however, are deeply concerned that the proposed backstop would leave the U.K. tied indefinitely to many EU laws. At the time of writing, there appears to be no way to square the circle in this Irish border matter.

---

140   Statements by Mark Carney, Governor of the Bank of England. https://www.theguardian.com/politics/2018/sep/13/no-deal-brexit-could-be-as-bad-as-2008-financial-crash-carney-says

In view of the strong response of the European negotiators, May's government was forced in mid-2018 to work out a new negotiating position that crossed several of the red lines laid out previously, leading to a serious split within the ranks of the Conservative Party. At the level of British public opinion there remained a large radicalised anti-European sector, but a significant segment that had voted for leaving in the 2016 referendum realised the costs of exit and the fallacy of most of the promises of greatness made in the campaign. So much so that to the question of whether the United Kingdom had done well or badly in voting for Brexit, 48 percent of respondents in mid-2018 felt it was bad, versus 42 percent good. A year and a half earlier, in February 2017, the figures were reversed (48 percent thought it was good and 41 percent said it was bad). It is not surprising, therefore, that qualified voices were raised calling for a new referendum on the UK's membership in Europe. Whether or not there will be a new referendum, the United Kingdom has no choice but to reach some kind of agreement with the EU, because a no-deal exit would be highly damaging, indeed almost catastrophic. Nevertheless, nothing can be ruled out in this contest of irrationality, even a no-deal Brexit. The foreseeable outcome, however, will probably be an initiative by UK Parliament to take control over the process to break the deadlock and choose between one of the alternative approaches, i.e. a Norwegian-style agreement or a custom union for goods. The EU could extend the deadline of March 2019, if it sees a real prospect of reaching an agreement.

Let us now return to the initial question about whether Brexit could represent the beginning of a process of disintegration in Europe. The immediate answer seems to be no, that the United Kingdom has been a unique case in the history of the European Union, a member who never fully wanted to be there, who always kept one foot in and one out. On the other hand, the firmness of the EU's negotiating position and the realisation of the enormous cost of leaving will act as a deterrent to similar initiatives. A more careful look at the subject, however, brings us to more nuanced conclusions. The disagreements of the United Kingdom with Europe were not exclusive to that country but were increasingly shared by other Community partners.[141] Brexit was a country-specific

---

141   This is a repeated theme in several of the contributions to the book edited by Martill and Staiger (2018) on the causes and consequences of Brexit.

manifestation of several crises and questionings that criss-crossed Europe and that have been mentioned throughout this book:

- Questioning of the democratic legitimacy of Community decision-making processes
- Tension between national sovereignties and supra-national Community powers
- Popular anxiety about the handling of immigrants and refugees
- Tension between members and non-members of the EMU
- Discomfort about German domination

The fact that the other EU partners were united in their negotiating position *vis-à-vis* the United Kingdom did not mean that some of them did not share several of the concerns that pushed that country into Brexit. Tacitly, the British government had become the spokesperson for other countries that were also unsatisfied with incursions into their national terrains or with the top-down imposition of economic and political models. Several countries in Eastern Europe, for example, resented the pressure to adopt the one-size-fits-all liberal politics prevalent in the EU. In the stance on immigration and refugees, many EU members were in sympathy with the British position. Brexit will not be the trigger for a chain of exits, but it was certainly the manifestation of centrifugal forces of disintegration within the European Union.

How will Brexit affect the France-Germany duo? The United Kingdom was the third *primus inter pares*, with whom the Franco-German axis was in frequent conflict, but with which on occasion one of the two countries forged circumstantial alliances, Germany more than France. With the forthcoming departure of the United Kingdom from the European Union, the France-Germany alliance becomes even more relevant, but also more difficult, because a dynamic of two is very different from a dynamic of three. The country most affected by the withdrawal of the UK from Europe will be Germany, since Germany loses an ally to which it has been the closest ideologically thanks to their shared liberal philosophy. Germany is united with France through more tangible interests, but it is not easy to maintain a common agenda when there are such distinct ideological visions. Neither does Germany benefit from the perception, which could be generated with the departure of the UK, that its position of domination in Europe has increased. So much so that Germany has no choice but to keep insisting, now more than ever, on the historic alliance with France.

What will be the new position of the United Kingdom on the stage of European and world power? For Germany and the rest of Europe, Brexit has lessened in importance. The departure of the second largest European economy, with a volume of 15% of the EU's GDP, is certainly no small thing, but its negative economic effect will be felt disproportionally in the UK itself. The country exported 43% of its goods and services to Europe in 2017, while exports from the rest of Europe to the UK accounted for just over 15%. Brexit supporters' belief that, once released from trade commitments with the EU, the country can enter into beneficial trade agreements with other countries, looks somewhat illusory. The Trump administration, for example, has already warned that its priority is to sign an agreement with the European Union first. As for its political weight on the world stage, the outlook is even less favourable. British ex-minister Malloch-Brown (2018) describes the claim that Britain will once again lead the vast Anglo-Saxon world as "comic delirium". Rather, leaving Europe seems to have made it lose its way, as shown by its flirtation with the anti-liberal Trump administration. The growing hostility towards immigrants and refugees also risks it losing its way in terms of the democratic liberal values that for hundreds of years were the beacon that illuminated the European continent.

The second (dis)integration ring: Europeans outside the euro

Eight countries (other than the United Kingdom) are members of the EU but not of the EMU. Of these eight members of the second ring, six are countries of Eastern Europe and the remaining two are Denmark and Sweden. We asked earlier whether Brexit has been a preamble to a wider process of disintegration in Europe. Of the group of countries in this second ring, only Denmark and Sweden would have a comparable level of political and economic development to the United Kingdom, but in the past their liberal tradition has made them relatively immune to populist anti-immigration demagoguery, which was one of the main motivations for the British referendum. The Swedish general elections in September 2018, however, sounded warning bells. The slide towards populism did not occur to the degree that analysts had predicted, but the traditional parties continued to lose votes in favour of the populist Swedish Democrats as immigration and crime were central themes of the electoral campaign. In Denmark, the Danish People's Party, which flies the banner of nationalist and Eurosceptic populism, became the party with the second highest number of votes in the 2015 elections. However, unlike in Britain, Danish and Swedish societies do not share the insular aversion that half of the British have traditionally felt towards the tutelage of the European Union. Nor are these societies characterised by tendencies of isolationist nativism.

As to the Eastern countries, resentment over Germany's unilateral and overbearing handling of the refugee problem opened a deep rift in its traditional alliance with the Eastern countries. The refugee crisis also brought out fundamental divergences in their socio-political models and underlying ideologies. In contrast to Western liberalism, traces of authoritarianism and populism arose in many Eastern countries, like ghosts of the communist past.

The disruptive power of populist nationalism is impeding a unified European perspective on dealing with the refugee problem and immigration in general. The problem is not so much that the number of refugees is unmanageable, but rather the "anti-community" way in which the problem is being addressed. To begin with, Europe has become a neighbourhood where the predominant attitude is to see how I can offload problems onto someone else, in a kind of beggar-thy-neighbour rivalry. By the Dublin Agreement, border countries have to deal with the flood of immigrants and process asylum applications. Partly because of their inability to do so, but also as retaliation, peripheral countries have opened corridors for immigrants to keep moving towards the central countries. These, in turn, have taken steps towards erecting internal borders to keep the problem at the periphery. There has been a blatant lack of Community discipline as everyone looks after their own national interests. Each new populist government feels it has the right to redefine the terms of previous agreements and erect internal borders. Never before have the founding principles of the European Union been so openly undermined.

The dispute concerning the refugees was the main reason for their distancing themselves, particularly with respect to Germany. Merkel's unilateral decision in the summer of 2015 to open the borders to refugees caused deep discomfort in the Eastern countries and was considered an invitation for new waves to invade Europe. The Eastern countries, particularly those on the Balkan route, were the main victims, as this was the entry corridor for refugees from the Middle East. The new flows were simply unmanageable for those countries individually. Initially, Hungary cooperated with the German initiatives, but soon Viktor Orban turned his policy around 180 degrees and embraced the position of totally rejecting taking in refugees under the quota system that Germany intended to impose. The Group of Visegrád, conformed by Hungary, Poland, the Czech Republic and Slovakia, was diametrically opposed to Germany in the whole handling of the matter. In the aftermath of the refugee crisis, the four governments turned in varying degrees towards less liberal and more populist positions, thus drawing a new dividing line on the European map: the East-West line–yet another line for a fragmented Europe.

Some Eastern European countries, such as Hungary, Poland and the Czech Republic, especially the first two, could be candidates for leaving the EU in view of the authoritarian and anti-immigrant drift of their governments. Authoritarian governments have been installed that have set themselves the task of subverting the democratic order from within, that is, abusing their electoral majority to curtail the independence of the judiciary and the legislative branch. For the first time in the history of the EU, the European Parliament has opened the doors to suspending Poland's and Hungary's voting rights in EU institutions and submitting them to the scrutiny of the European Court of Justice. This level of confrontation may well trigger concrete actions in those countries to disengage progressively from the European Union.

It should also be born in mind that the "Europeanness" of these Eastern countries does not have the historical and cultural roots of the other countries of Western Europe. The foundations of the Europe of the 6 in 1957, then the 9 in 1973 or the Europe of the 15 in 1995, is very different from the Europe of the 28 after the expansion to Eastern Europe. A fair number of countries that joined since 2004 do not share the liberal values of mature Western democracies. Their eager application for EU membership was due more than anything to the need to overcome their communist past and escape from the Russian sphere of influence. Once inside, however, utilitarian links of commerce and Community subsidies have mattered more than a true identification with European cultural identity. Those same utilitarian links will probably draw out the process of breaking up with Europe, but there is no doubt that a tectonic fault between Eastern and Western Europe now exists.

Eurozone disintegration scenarios

The acid test of European integration, its real existential threat, will be the capacity of the European Monetary Union, its first ring of integration, to remain cohesive. The future of the EU is tied to that of the EMU, now for worse rather than for better. When evaluating possible disintegration scenarios, it is necessary to be clear on a fundamental difference with respect to the second and third rings in Europe: in the face of an exit from the EU, the room for manoeuvre of an EMU member is not equal to that of a member that only belongs to the EU. If the United Kingdom had been part of the eurozone, the mere announcement of the referendum would have unleashed such instability in the British financial markets and such capital flight that it would have had to be immediately dismissed. The eurozone countries could not disengage from Europe through a civilized and democratic referendum.

Any other member of the EU that were also a member of the EMU would have to think very hard before leaving unilaterally. Greece peered briefly into the abyss of exit and had to retreat in terror. The EMU has no established legal, operational or economic mechanisms for the withdrawal of one of its members. Nor are there any legal or operational mechanisms for expelling a member who refuses to comply with Community rules.[142] In the founding treaties, affiliation to the common currency was always considered irrevocable. If a member of the EMU were to fall within the framework of Article 50, which has opened the door for the UK's exit from the EU, this would automatically imply an exit from the EMU, for which there is no legal framework. A complicated situation.

Apart from the enormous practical difficulties, the cost-benefit balance of a unilateral exit for countries in financial straits is immensely unfavourable. To begin with, it would have to settle the debt derived from its Target 2 Balance in the European Central Bank, whose magnitude would undoubtedly be unmanageable. Resolve is shaken when the costs of an exit from the Monetary Union are calculated. The mere suspicion of contemplating this measure would trigger a massive bank run, the erection of a financial *corralito* and the disappearance of credit in the economy.

---

[142] See Füst (2018), which discusses in detail the legal ways to exit the EU and the convenience of an exit clause from the EMU, similar to Art. 50 of the Treaty on European Union.

Once the exit was accomplished, all debts and obligations would have to be denominated in the new local currency, accompanied by a generalised tearing up of contracts among all the economic agents. Many companies with liabilities in euros or that need access to external financial markets would become unviable, which would aggravate the general wave of bankruptcies. All these problems, however, would not save the country from the cost of having to recover competitiveness through structural reforms and a decrease in real income for the population.

In view of these exit costs, the fact that the euro remains vulnerable adds urgency to the problem. Sluggish growth throughout the eurozone, together with persistent unemployment in its periphery, prefigure a scenario of vulnerability, both on the socio-political front and on the fiscal. The heavy legacy of debt cannot be eased without economic growth. Disruptions of a political or economic nature will inevitably arise, giving rise to speculative attacks in the bond markets. With decisive action towards banking and fiscal union the prospects of surviving these attacks would be greater. However, the reality is that there is no consensus on advancing towards these levels of union that entail some degree of risk sharing.

Aside from fiscal solidarity, among the members of a monetary union there must also be agreement regarding the monetary policy objectives as well as the balance of power in terms of monetary decisions. When national interests diverge and especially when some country has greater power than others to impose the direction of monetary policy based on its economic structure and its own national interests, the seeds of discord are sown. The perception of inequality and unequal distribution of burdens is the most corrosive element in an integrated monetary area.[143]

All that has been here said about the faults and cracks in the EMU edifice allow us to say that the risks of disintegration in the eurozone are very real. There remains the question of what form it would take. We visualize several possible routes of disintegration:

- Pedalling to stay upright
- Anomie

---

[143] Berthold et al. (2014) studied the reasons that prevailed in the disintegration of four historical monetary unions and reached the conclusion that the two main causes were unequal degrees of influence on monetary policy and divergences on policy objectives.

- Orderly breakup of the euro
- Chaotic breakup of the euro

These routes do not have to be mutually exclusive. Multiple forces working simultaneously to undermine the foundations of the EMU might produce parallel scenarios. For example, judicious schemes might be put in place to arrange an ordered dissolution of the euro, only for some event to spin the process into chaos. Anyone thinking that the outcome is predictable is kidding themselves.

Pedalling to stay upright

The laws of bicycle dynamics dictate that you have to keep pedalling to stay upright. The eurozone has been doing this for several years: there is no agreement on which direction to go in, except that we must keep pedalling so that the edifice of the monetary union does not collapse. This is a negative consensus, in which all members of the eurozone want to avoid collapse but disagree on what kind of future should be built. The pedalling is not for going forward, but simply for not falling.

We could also characterise this scenario as business as usual. The European Commission, the European Parliament and all the dense network of EU institutions stay intensely active, but this does not mean that the Union is moving towards any definite destination. Community institutions can churn out long shelves of resolutions and guidelines and nevertheless not attend to the core problems of the Union. It is the well-known European custom of muddling through.

At first glance, pedalling just to avoid falling down does not seem to be a scenario of disintegration, but rather one of conservation. The problem is that not doing anything substantial to repair the EMU edifice is a sure recipe for one day falling off the bicycle. It is highly likely that disruptive events will occur to put stability to the test and make the rider fall.

Anomie / anarchy

The greater threats of European (dis)integration do not arise only from members leaving. The EU has taken care to raise the cost of Brexit enough that other countries, members of the EU but not members of the EMU, think twice about it. And the members of the eurozone have the Greek example as a reminder of the financial setback that would accompany just the suspicion of a unilateral abandonment of the common currency.

Disintegration is more likely to take place surreptitiously by simply ignoring Community rules and questioning the established order. There have already been precedents with France's and Germany's flouting of the fiscal deficit rules for several years in the first half of the 2000s, or the blind eye that the Community authorities had to turn ten years later to the breach of the deficit reduction programs by Spain, Portugal, France and Italy. Both episodes showed that at the moment of truth the institutional decision-making mechanisms of the European Community lacked the teeth to enforce the rules and punish offenders. However, there is an important difference with the type of indiscipline that Europe has been experiencing recently. Previously, breaches were sporadic, the product of unfavourable circumstances, and the offenders showed repentance. Now they are intentional and lasting breaches, tantamount to "not caring a fig". They are not an expression of temporary indiscipline, but of a questioning of the system of rules itself and of the legitimacy of supra-national bodies' actions on national issues.

Take the case of Eastern Europe. The anarchy, selfishness and de-legitimisation that flourished in the handling of the 2015-16 refugee crisis, as well as the non-acceptance of Community directives in this and other matters, prefigure a much more serious kind of breach, because it not only reveals a non-compliance but a non-acceptance of the rules. In addition, the rebellion of the Eastern European countries against the refugee regulations and the outright rejection of resolutions on refugee distribution quotas introduced a fracture–perhaps an irreparable one–in the historic alliance between Germany and this group of countries. The aggravating circumstance was that not only was a special relationship breaking down, but that yet another important group of countries was rejecting Germany's leadership in Europe.

If we turn to Southern Europe, we know that the Italian government elected in 2017 would have preferred not to have the straitjacket of belonging to the Monetary Union. Italy has serious problems of lack of growth drivers, which do not allow it to absorb unemployment and reduce the debt burden. The temptation to use fiscal expansion to revitalise growth is very great. Imagine the highly likely situation of the Italian government adopting a fiscal policy contrary to Community guidelines. If the Community bodies decided to relax the rules or turn a blind eye, they would have no moral authority to enforce those rules for the other countries of the Union. And if to avoid this collapse of discipline, the EU authorities insisted that Italy comply with the rules, they would enter into open conflict with a government that is itself an enemy of integration, thus fanning the flames of anti-Europeanism within Italy. Either scenario would have bad consequences. The harsh reality is that, in the longer term, Italy will find it very difficult to revive its economy in the context of a Monetary Union dominated by the deflationary policy dictated by Germany. There will come a day when this problem will lead to open rebellion, probably when the next existential crisis presents itself. And note that other Southern economies in the eurozone share similar problems.

If anything has been wired into the process of building the European edifice, it has been a respect for rules and regulations. Rules-based order has been an essential part of the DNA that ordoliberal Germany injected into the EMU. With the spread of populism, however, this axiom of regulated order is being severely questioned. Populist leadership is distinguished by two features. In the first place, it proclaims itself as the only interpreter and representative of the people, which is why it devalues representative democracy and seeks to create a direct relationship between the leader and the people, which is an essential feature of authoritarian democracies. In the second place, populists harbour a contempt for the established order, which they consider an instrument of domination by the globalising elite. The logical consequence of both features is that the rules do not have to be respected when they come between the leader and his people.[144] This de-legitimisation of the rules adds to the many fronts in the populist attack on the European project.

Whether through confrontation with the Community authorities, lack of respect for established norms or rejection *per se* of the established order, the European Project is being challenged in a fundamental way. The conflict in the eurozone will no longer be just between those who can or cannot meet Monetary Union standards, but between those who want to belong to it and those who do not.

---

144   See Meyer (2018)

Orderly breakup

It is noteworthy how speaking publicly about a possible exit from the eurozone is no longer a taboo subject. Even the Germans themselves are not embarrassed to talk about it. Minister Schäuble laid it on the table to threaten Greece, when that country was reluctant to sign the rescue agreement in July 2015.[145] The implicit message of the German minister was "if you don't like it, there's the door." 154 German economics professors raised the issue in a public letter dated May 2018, when they asked that an "orderly exit mechanism" be drawn up.[146] Paolo Savona, the (vetoed) candidate for the Finance portfolio of the new Italian government, proposed it unambiguously. Reaching the point of saying this openly is a sign that the credibility of the commitment to the irrevocability of the euro, the quintessence of a fixed exchange rate regime, has begun to crumble. Once this point is reached, the future is not what it used to be. These fissures in the credibility of the commitment will radically change the dynamics of the next financial crisis for the worse. All the more reason to take the needed reforms seriously or prepare for the worst.

No-one, however, wants to crash out of the EMU and still less to do so unilaterally. Because of the serious implications of a non-consensual collapse, the voices that advocate an ordered dissolution of the Monetary Union are becoming more frequent and uninhibited.[147] Anglo-Saxon economists have traditionally shown a certain abandon in questioning the experiment of the European Monetary Union. An example is the working paper by Barry Eichengreen, published in the summer of 2007 by the National Bureau of Economic Research, with the title "*The rupture of the eurozone*", in which he affirmed that the possibility could not be discounted that some eurozone members could re-introduce their own currencies. Note that in mid-2007 the eurozone was still living its moment of glory. He even pointed to the strong

---

145 Wolfgang Schäuble, "Anmerkungen zu den jüngsten griechischen Vorschlägen" , Handelsblatt, 12 July 2015.

146 These 154 professors say that the eurozone needs "ein geordnetes Insolvenzverfahren für Staaten und ein geordnetes Austrittsverfahren." ("An ordered insolvency procedure for States and an orderly exit procedure"). See Frankfurter Allgemeine Zeitung 2018-05-22 - "Ökonomen-Aufruf: Euro darf nicht in Haftungsunion führen".

147 See Melitz (2014), Stiglitz (2016), Rodrik (2017), Scharpf (2018), among many others.

possibility that the deserter would be Germany, which would happen if the decisions of the ECB became politicised and inflation grew as a result.[148]

After the eurozone crisis, Stiglitz (2016) has been particularly emphatic that a friendly divorce is preferable to the continuation of an unsustainable state of affairs such as the current one, in which fundamental reforms are not being undertaken to give proper sustenance to the Monetary Union. The divorce could take the form of the creation of two or more monetary blocs within Europe, which would consist of groups of countries with greater affinity.

Unlike the Anglo-Saxons, European scholars and particularly Germans have been more cautious in their calls for an agreed breakup of the eurozone. That is why opinions such as that of the respected German academic Fritz Scharpf (2018), director emeritus of the Max Plank Institute for Social Studies, who proposes the dissolution of the eurozone in its current form, are especially relevant. His proposal is a transition to a European Monetary Community, initially composed of two strata: a hard core of a few countries that would remain in the EMU and the rest that would reintroduce their own currencies, which would fluctuate within bands with respect to the euro. The framework of this flexibility would be regulated by the European Exchange Mechanism II,[149] the same system that was established in 1999 to manage the exchange relation with the euro of European countries that were not part of the euro or that were candidates to enter the eurozone later on.

What stands out is the brazen "Germano-centric" tone of Scharpf's proposal. Although he acknowledges that it would make more economic sense and would be technically more viable for Germany and its peers to leave the euro and form another monetary bloc, Scharpf believes that this solution is utopian, because it would go against the *"fundamental ideological commitment of the principal German political groupings on European integration"*. Additionally, the decisive political power of the export industry and the unions would never allow Germany's membership in the eurozone to be questioned. The practical consequence of this

---

148 However, Eichengreen (2007) concludes by saying that the longer the Monetary Union survives, the less likely it is that one of its members would leave.

149 In 1999 the European Exchange Mechanism II replaced the European Exchange Mechanism of the EMS, which had governed European exchange relations since 1979. Mechanism II was designed for regulating the relationship with the euro of the countries that were candidates to join the EMU. At present, only Denmark is a member of this mechanism.

approach is that it should be the countries of the Mediterranean periphery that should apply to leave the euro, given their inability to compete and grow economically within the EMU straitjacket. It's as clear as a bell: those who do not fit the dictates of the ECB's "strong euro" will have to start packing their bags and looking for alternative monetary arrangements. This would amount to a *de facto* expulsion, as a result of which these countries would have to face a storm of speculative forces.

We suspect that Scharpf has said openly what is today a widespread, albeit unvoiced, thought in Germany. We have not been accustomed to such German assertiveness, but we need to recognise that it is the logical consequence of ordoliberal thought. It is also a reflection of the German establishment's growing conviction that there is such a deep structural divergence among the EMU economies that it makes long-term coexistence under the same roof of a common currency impossible. Faced with the impossibility of living together, the best thing is a friendly separation (if Scharpf's proposal can be described as friendly).

We totally disagree with Scharpf's exit proposal, mainly for practical reasons. When the time comes, it is Germany and its peers who should set out its separate stall around a new currency (the euro *bis*). It is much easier for a strong country to leave the Monetary Union than for a weak one, because the latter would suffer huge capital flight in the expectation of a devaluation of its currency. If, on the contrary, the expectation were for revaluation, the outgoing strong country would not suffer speculative attacks, even though capital controls and mechanisms for recycling funds would have to be established to avoid affecting the banks of the countries that stay with the weaker currency. Once the divorce is complete, the exchange rate of the different euro blocs would fluctuate to reflect competitiveness differentials, preferably within certain limits or bands, in the style of the Exchange Rate Mechanism of the EMS that was in force in Europe before the introduction of the euro in 1999.

The practical difficulties of divorce would be enormous in any case. For starters, in all the eurozone legislation there is not a single reference to a membership exit procedure. This exit regime would have to be created *ex nihilo* and should contain at least the following elements:

- Procedures and deadlines for a consensual exit and a transitional regime.

- Procedures for the management of public and private external debt, which contemplate the eventual need for debt restructuring.
- Reformulation of the European Exchange Mechanism.
- Schemes for technical and financial support during the transition.

Chaotic breakaway

Undoubtedly, a friendly divorce and the creation of two or more eurozones is a less explosive scenario than the chaotic departure of some individual members. This last scenario–the abrupt voluntary departure of an individual member–is unlikely. More to be expected would be scenarios of consensual and orderly attempts at forming blocs. But it cannot be ruled out that things might go wrong under any of the options, in which case order could turn into chaos. Thus, it could happen that:

- exit negotiations reach an impasse,
- the markets do not believe in an orderly breakup and bait themselves into attacking the outgoing countries,
- the legacy of old debt is not manageable, neither in a friendly nor an unfriendly way, or
- a sudden catastrophic event occurs (a "black swan").

The timing and outcome of a chaotic breakup, by definition, are unpredictable, just as the probability of their occurrence is also unpredictable. Today, this scenario is not on the horizon and no-one wants it, but everything will depend on whether any of the other three scenarios manages to endure over time. The options of pedalling to stay upright or of anomie are the least stable, since disturbances can push the eurozone to the threshold of breakup without the time to handle it in an orderly and consensual manner.

DISSENT, CONSENSUS AND NEW VISION: THE NEED TO REWIND AND RESHAPE

The forces of disintegration are powerful, public opinion is divided and governments have serious disagreements about what should be done to prop up the European edifice. Can a new vision of Europe be put together in this context? As a first step, all the players need to put their feet on the ground and evaluate what is possible and viable. The leaders of the European institutions and some Heads of Government continue to insist irrationally on an ideal European project that today would have no chance of materialising. They look like captains who have decided to go down with the ship they have built and skippered themselves. Part of coming down to earth is knowing when to regroup, rewind and establish a stronger position to start rebuilding the European project.

What do Europeans think and want?

In this convoluted panorama, what do European citizens want? How solidly and homogenously does public opinion support the European project? The first thing to note when analysing opinion polls is that the relationship of citizens with the European Union and the euro is highly utilitarian: in times of economic crisis and increased unemployment, identification with the Community project goes down.[150] The second aspect is that, despite the multiple problems that afflict the Union, even in its worst moments more than half of Europeans continue to support the existence of the EU. At the end of 2007, in the wake of the Global Financial Crisis, 58 percent of Europeans considered the European Union "a good thing".[151] That favourable opinion fell to 47 percent in 2011, then gradually recovered as the euro crisis was overcome, to reach 60 percent again in 2018. Looking ahead, the same percentage believes that their country would fare better in the future within the EU than outside it. When citizens are asked if their country should withdraw from the EU, a resounding 77 percent would be against leaving; even in countries like Greece and Italy, 58 and 56 percent respectively want to stay in the European Union.

In eurozone countries perception of the benefits of the euro has also improved from its lowest point in the euro crisis in mid-2011. Interestingly, in the midst of the crisis, 56 percent of citizens in the eurozone

---

150 Roth et al. (2018) provide empirical evidence that economic performance factors are the main determinants of public support for the euro.

151 All the survey data presented here have been taken from Eurobarometer surveys in the respective years.

still considered the euro a good thing for their country. That support was higher than that enjoyed at the time by the EU as a whole. The favourable perception towards the eurozone also improved along with the economic recovery, to reach a solid 64 percent at the end of 2017. These numbers are very significant and surprising at first sight. With all the severity of the euro crisis, a higher proportion of citizens have had and still have a more positive perception of the euro than have of the European Union.

If majority popular support towards the EU and toward the EMU continues to be solid, the reader will ask why it is so hard to implement the reforms that would shield the Union from future crises. The reason lies in the fact that beneath this vague general support lie many contradictions and broad ranges of opinion. A fundamental contradiction is that while citizens support the idea of the European Union, a large majority is demanding that the authority and powers of Brussels be given back to the national sphere. 74 percent of European citizens, for example, want their own governments to take decisions about immigration and refugees. Even in such fundamental remits as internal migration and trade, 66 percent of citizens believe that each national government should be able to decide which citizens of other EU member States are admitted. 51 percent prefer their own governments to decide on trade agreements with third countries.

The broad spectrum of opinions, on the other hand, reveals deep discrepancies that persist between countries of the Union and even within each country. As usual, statistical averages hide profound differences. A first level of differences is found in the different degrees of support shown individually by member countries. The range goes from 82 percent in Luxembourg who consider that the euro has been good for their country, going through 76 percent in Germany, to lukewarm supporters like Greece with 57 percent, Cyprus with 48 percent and Italy with 45 percent. These differences seem to reflect, first, how well each country did during the crisis and, second, that there are countries that are dissatisfied with the euro, particularly Italy.[152]

More critical and differentiated still are positions on how Brussels has handled the economic crisis. While 61 percent of Germans and 54 percent of the Dutch have a favourable view, only 12 percent of Greeks, 23 percent

---

152   Italy is a good example how the EU or the EMU serve as scapegoats for a long history of domestic mismanagement.

of Italians and 35 percent of the French think that Brussels has handled economic problems properly. Even more negative is the perception of the handling of the refugee problem, especially in the border countries of the EU.

A second level of divide runs through the socio-educational structure within countries: while 70 percent of white-collar employees have a favourable opinion of the euro, only 47 percent of manual workers think that the euro has been good for their country. 72 percent of those who stayed in the education system until the age of 20 or more have a favourable opinion of the euro, but only 42 percent of those who did not stay in the education system past 15 thinks that the euro has been something good. There is also a difference in positions according to age: while only 58 percent of people over 50 have a favourable opinion about the EU, a solid 73 percent of young people between 18 and 29 support the EU.

A third level of division occurs within the political spectrum of each country. It is to be expected that those of populist-nationalist leanings, left or right, have a bad opinion of the euro and the EU. The Pew Research Centre survey of spring 2017 reveals that the populists usually have mostly unfavourable opinions towards the European Union. The populist parties group together those who are disillusioned with globalisation with those who disagree with the liberal principles that are the DNA of European integration. They blame the EU and liberalism for the negative impacts of globalisation.

It is the confluence of these three lines of division that complicates the task of generating consensus on how to advance the process of European integration. While Germany, for example, is happy with the *status quo* of the EMU, Italy thinks it needs fundamental reforms. While the population with a high level of education appreciates the benefits of the Monetary Union, the blue-collar less well-educated have a mostly unfavourable opinion about the euro. And while those who are politically in the liberal-democratic wing favour European integration, the populists advocate national retrenchment.

Additionally, opinion studies reveal another fact that seriously slows down the advance of integration. We refer to the feelings of distrust towards Community institutions. At the beginning of 2007, 57 percent of European citizens tended to trust the institutions of the European Union. This confidence falls to 31 percent at the beginning of 2012, where it remains practically until the beginning of 2016, to recover later up to

42 percent at the end of 2017. This means that between half and a third of those who think that the EU and the euro have been good for their country distrust the European institutions. Mistrust is especially high in the countries most affected by the euro crisis: only 22 percent of Greeks, 33 percent of Cypriots and 36 percent of Italians trust EU institutions. In addition to distrust, half of citizens (49 percent) think that things in Europe are going in the wrong direction.

With this high level of distrust and disapproval in many countries, it is difficult for European institutions to work out consensus positions that also have democratic legitimacy. It is also an uphill struggle to get the population re-enthused and re-identified with the European vision held by the Eurocrats. In the decades of constructing the EU and the EMU, the population accompanied their national leadership in their European vision. There was a "permissive consensus" in which ordinary citizens and the national elites charged with actively negotiating the European project passively concurred. With the passage of time and especially with the euro crisis, this consensus has progressively melted away. A relationship of conflict between national elites has emerged, along with an alienation between the population and their respective leaders within each country.

The battlefield of the proposals

Regrettably, and in parallel with the divisions in public opinion, the proposals for action are also at loggerheads. Simplifying greatly, we can identify four battle lines, where the opposite sides are not always composed of the same countries or social groups. As regards the scope of reforms, one side, led by the European Commission and France, starts from the diagnosis that the EMU edifice is incomplete and has some flaws in its original design. As a result, what is needed is more Europe, the links within the Union must be deepened, institutions must be created or transformed. This group is usually imbued with a lot of enthusiasm and is proactively in favour of the European idea. The other side, led by Germany and the Netherlands, thinks that the economic and monetary union is basically complete and that what is needed is simply mechanisms to enforce compliance with Community regulations. This line of conflict coincides with the economic dichotomy that we mentioned in the previous chapter, between defenders of risk-sharing schemes and advocates of market discipline.

A second battle line is transversal to this first one and refers to where the centre of power in the European Community is to be located. Obviously, the European Commission and the European Parliament want the power of decision to reside in the Community bodies and institutions. They advocate the "Community method" to carry out the reforms, which consists of:

- Legislative initiatives under the exclusive responsibility of the European Commission in collaboration with the Council of Ministers. The European Parliament legislates and controls. These three bodies make up the "institutional triangle" of the EU.
- Decisions by qualified majority (except for some matters, like taxation, that require unanimity).

The other side, which includes Germany and France, advocate the "intergovernmental method", in which ultimate power of decision lies in the European Council, made up of the national Heads of Government, and decisions are usually made unanimously. The European Parliament has a basically consultative function in this view.

A third battle line divides the Left and the Right. There is a substantive discussion that has not been resolved or that, to be more exact, is being resolved in a direction that will not give political stability to the eurozone system. One of the main reasons for the disenchantment with the European project of a Monetary Union is that it has not fulfilled the original promise that it would correct the productive and income differences between the member nations. That was the basis for the enthusiasm with which many countries decided to the join the EMU. Practically all the reform proposals being discussed in Brussels today are aimed solely at giving stability to the current system, i.e. at stability for the euro, not at how to make the promise of social equity and general prosperity a reality. How social stability and the stability of the euro can be reconciled remains an open question.

A forth battle line refers to the desired future of Europe. Macron, Merkel and Juncker may have many differences between them, but they agree that they want to deepen the European Union and the Monetary Union. Others, including the author of this book, think that we have to start unwinding Europe; they advocate less Europe and greater role for national democratic institutions. Their main argument is that the creators of the European project went too far in implementing integrationist advances beyond what was prudent and when conditions were not ripe. They put Monnet's strategy into practice, according to which, once some new scheme of integration was in place, the problems and crises arising from it would have to be solved with more integration. An example of the recklessness of this scorched-earth philosophy was the introduction of the euro contrary to most technical opinion. With the aim of advancing integration in the economic, financial, and monetary spheres, many other aspects were left behind, for example European-level harmonisation of social policies, labour regimes, tax policies or the levelling-up of living standards. Two of these mismatches were especially relevant: the first in the political sphere, reflected in the inability to give democratic legitimacy to Community bodies; and the second in cultural identity, by not getting citizens to identify with a European citizenship. Instead of continuing to deepen economic, financial, and monetary integration, say the unwinders, the EU should pause and synchronise the different levels of integration that have been left behind. In some cases, such as fiscal management, autonomy of decision should even be given back to national authorities, accompanied, of course, by a credible no-bailout policy in cases of mismanagement.

As the reader will appreciate, the debate on the future of Europe is intense and complex. In our opinion, the approach should not be based on a wishful thinking but on a realistic appreciation of what is possible. The reality is that the political conditions do not favour more Europe, more transfers of power to Community bodies, more areas of integration, except in less contentious areas such as defence and security. There are profound divergences both between countries and within countries about the way forward. Populist nationalism is tearing apart societies from the inside. The man in the street does not trust the national technocratic and financial elites and trusts even less the supra-national ones. In this context of disagreements and divisions, any substantial progress towards integration will be questioned and will aggravate the problem of the democratic legitimacy of the European project.[153]

One of the most difficult problems when facing the future of Europe is that of coexistence between the eurozone and the rest of the EU. Eight

---

153   Glencross (2013) sees the risk of a return to a purely national definition of democratic legitimacy as a consequence of the questioning of Community government actions.

countries (other than the United Kingdom) are members of the EU but are not part of the EMU. The type and depth of political union that each group requires is radically different, but the one that takes the lead and sets the pace of integration is the eurozone subgroup. The European Commission is the supreme organ of the 27 nations, but its focus is on how to solve the problems of vulnerability that a common currency generates. The euro and its problems have dominated the European agenda to a too great extent. In the European Parliament there are already proposals to create a "sub-parliament" of the eurozone. How this fragmentation of Community structures can work is a complicated and uncertain issue, but it is necessary to gradually "de-euro-ise" the European Union. So far, non-euro countries have been treated as second-class Europeans or, at best, as Europeans transitioning towards the EMU, rather than their option for monetary independence being respected as fully valid. This silent discrimination was not the main reason for the UK's leaving Europe, but there is no doubt that neither did it encourage it to remain.

A flexible, plural and democratic Europe

We believe that this thorny issue of coexistence between euro and non-euro countries is an excellent opportunity to test the concept of what is called a multi-speed Europe. Despite its widespread use, we think "speed" is an unfortunate term here, because it semantically implies the vision that all members are hurtling towards the same goal of full monetary and political union, albeit at different speeds. We prefer to talk about a Europe of several "spheres of integration". The new concept of European Union needs to leave behind the idea of one-size-fits-all and constitutionally incorporate the idea of multiple spheres of integration and the free decision of countries to join one sphere or another.[154] In fact, the launch of the euro with only 11 members in 1999 was the most authentic implementation of the idea of multiple spheres of integration. Another case is the Schengen Agreement, where only 22 of the EU's 28 are members of the free internal mobility pact. What is missing is a change of mentality

---

154 You can be a member of a sports club without necessarily joining all its areas of activity. One can subscribe to a basic membership with entitlement to use of the pool, gym and restaurant, or expand the membership to the tennis courts or golf links. Each level of membership will have its cost and specific regulations.

so that the different spheres are not considered simply as stages towards the same collective goal of absolute union, which everyone must reach even if at different speeds. We are certainly not advocating a capricious cherry-picking: there should be certain precedences and mandatory combinations of spheres of integration, but freely chosen. Belonging to the Monetary Union, for example, would mean belonging to the banking union. But being a member of the Monetary Union should not be a prerequisite to being part of the customs union or the common market.

In order to advance, Europe urgently needs new leadership with a new vision that citizens perceive as fair, balanced and inclusive to the benefit of all of society and not only of powerful interest groups. It needs radical reform proposals to create a more open and dynamic society, with greater social permeability, greater tolerance and diversity.[155] The *sine que non* is that all this be perceived by citizens as something democratically legitimate. The permissive consensus of the initial decades certainly facilitated the construction of the European edifice, but its political base had feet of clay because a supra-national level of institutions with democratic legitimacy was never created. Like it or not, democracy continued and continues to be tied to national authorities, despite the enormous efforts that have been made to raise the profile of the European Parliament. When successive crises eroded the consensus between and within countries, this weakness in the base legitimacy of the European construct emerged with all its harshness. Unlike the national democracies, the European Community has no way of resolving social or distributive conflicts in a way that citizens perceive as legitimate, so its decisions are usually severely questioned when they affect national interests or interest groups within nations.

To illustrate the point, take the case of the European Central Bank, the central pillar of the EMU. The independence of the ECB from any political interference was the central tenet of the new monetary order, the *sine qua non* for Germany to accept the euro, as well as a way for other countries to borrow the credibility of the deutschmark. The reality is that its policy of one-size-fits-all and its exclusively anti-inflationary mandate negatively affected national economies, either to reheat them or to deepen the recession, making the ECB *de facto* the conductor of their economic policies, without having received such a mandate. The

---

155   Legrain (2017) insists also on constructing "positive political alternatives".

statutes of the modern central banks certainly protect them from political vagaries, which is good, but this does not mean that they do not have to report to some superior democratic body. Not so in the case of the ECB, which does not report to anyone, even though it continually takes decisions that have distributive implications in member countries and that, therefore, should be subject to political control.

The lesson that Europe has to learn is that what has already been built or what is going to be built must have a solid political foundation. A common currency is not a simple technocratic construct; it is a political decision that must be embedded in a network of democratic institutions that confer legitimacy on the functioning of the Monetary Union.[156] Beyond economic and financial reforms, the sustainability of the euro will depend on whether the EMU can orchestrate a degree of democratic support similar to that enjoyed by economic institutions within a nation.

Now then, it is pertinent to ask oneself if it is realistic to expect that a new leadership will emerge that inspires new enthusiasms around new visions. How can these visions be created and shared in a context of so much division and divergence of positions? It sounds beautiful and inspiring to ask that Europe be rebuilt on new democratic foundations, but how is that to be achieved in practice and at the present time? Some European leaders, such as Macron and the heads of European institutions, prefer to keep to the wishful pro-European rhetoric of constant calls to continue advancing towards more Europe. They feel that it is not up to them to propose other options that could be interpreted as a retreat in the process of union.

Europe and the eurozone, however, need to be rethought with a cool head. There is a need for realistic ways to shore up existing advances, but also to retrace some steps that should not have been taken. The easiest thing to retrace is to return to national levels everything that is not strictly necessary to keep at Community level, according to the principle of subsidiarity that should always have guided the construction of the EU. This was one of the constituent principles of the European Treaties, which excluded the intervention of the Union when a matter could be effectively served by the Member States. To the extent that more decision-making

---

[156] In the compilation of works by Matthijs and Blith (2016) on the future of Europe, Kathleen McNamara elaborates on this *"forgotten democratic embeddedness"* of the European institutions and describes it as the main cause of its uncertain future.

power is maintained at national levels, more areas of the Union will be subject to democratic control. Over the decades, however, the natural tendency of Community bureaucracies has been to absorb and control more and more areas of action and decision. Fiscal management, for example, should be preserved within the scope of national parliamentary control, which does not contradict the need for countries to eventually contribute resources to, for example, common mechanisms for economic stabilisation or bank deposit insurance. The *sine qua non*, of course, would be the enforcement of the non-bailout rule as well as orderly default procedures. Security and defence, the fight against terrorism or asylum policies, on the other hand, are typically matters that require a high level of coordination and supra-national cooperation.

One of the things that has most disturbed the balance between national and supra-national levels, between democracy and technocracy has been the euro. The introduction of the euro forced the pace of integration beyond what Europe could assimilate politically and culturally. It cultivated integration under hothouse conditions when it would have needed much more time, much more harmony between different areas, much more popular identification with Europe. The parents of the euro knew that the region was not yet ready for such a step, but they pushed it forward anyway in the traditional manner, expecting that things would straighten themselves out as time went on and that crises would take care of moving the Community towards higher levels of integration. Certainly, crises oblige us to do many things, but then the legitimacy or acceptance of new policies or structures is not guaranteed.

The retreat of a hegemon and the new Europe

How won over is Germany to the task of regrouping the Europeans and taking the lead in giving another boost to integration? What room for manoeuvre does its leadership have to shore up the European project? What idea of Europe does it have in mind?

Germany had many reasons to promote European integration in the past, especially political ones. As we said, two major objectives guided German foreign policy after the Second World War. The first was to convince the international community of its pacifist and civic-minded intentions through a style of international politics marked by cooperation among nations and active participation in multilateral institutions. The second was the reunification of the two Germanys, achieved in 1990. For both objectives, it was absolutely essential to actively promote European integration. Europe became the playing field of the new Germany: everything within the Union, nothing outside of it. Once both objectives were achieved, German foreign policy underwent a subtle but important shift: it did not stop being pacifist, civic-minded and multilateralist, but it became more conscious of its own interests and was not ashamed to defend them.

In the constellation of power inside Germany, both the unions and the idealist left, represented by the SPD, as the export industry, represented by the conservative parties CDU/CSU, made the European project the top priority of the second half of the past century. For German industry, the European common market meant expanded business opportunities. The euro made it possible to put an end to revaluation pressures on the deutschmark, which were threatening industry's external competitiveness. Over time, however, things changed: the second German Miracle driven by Schroeder's Agenda 2010 opened new emerging markets to the export industry and gave it new intrinsic competitive advantages that did not depend on the relative value of the currency. Europe thus ceased to be so important for German industry.

For the political establishment, the euro crisis and later the refugee crisis made it more difficult to reconcile their pro-European idealism with the growing discomfort of German public opinion with the generous reception of refugees or the possibility that taxes paid by German citizens could be used to rescue "profligate" countries. The decisions that had to be taken in both crises were controversial and alerted the German citizenry to how expensive it could be to meet the responsibilities of a benevolent hegemon. The strengthening of populist-nationalist movements had a lot to do with this discomfort of the traditional electoral base, which was moving towards other options that directly questioned the European ideal. In order to stop this movement, both the Social Democratic SPD and, above all, the Christian Social CDU/CSU had to moderate their own pro-European stance. Euroscepticism also ended up taking over ample sectors of the German population and its political establishment. Chancellor Merkel began to go to European summits with her hands tied by the fear of upsetting her voters and the radical sectors within her government coalition if she dared to support decisions that implied concessions or an excess of pro-European solidarity.

When in Chapter X we spoke of the type of hegemony that Germany should have exerted during the euro crisis, we mentioned the circumstances that can make a benevolent hegemon abandon its responsibilities. The most common circumstance is that the hegemon perceives that the costs of preserving the economic and political order, particularly during and after a crisis, are becoming excessive and/or that the other members of the system are taking advantage of the leader's generosity. Usually, the costs of maintaining the hegemonic system increase substantially over time, either as a result of a systemic crisis or due to endogenous dynamics that require an ever-greater level of integration. By costs we mean not only the material costs in terms of money but also the internal political cost of continuing to embrace the idea of Europe and support its continuity.

It is becoming increasingly evident that Germany is not willing to assume the responsibilities and obligations of a benevolent hegemon, at least as conceived by its European partners. Neither does it want to be a coercive hegemon, which is not in its makeup nor fits the new identity that it laboriously constructed after the war. The paradox of Germany today is that the country is perceived by the rest of Europe as a dominant and imposing leader, without it perceiving itself as such.

Beyond the perception that each party may have of itself or of the other, the reality is that today Germany has a dominant position in the eurozone and benefits from such a position. The countries of the Mediterranean periphery and the East resent this German domination and the impositional style it adopts, not so much for the leadership in itself, but for the fact that there is no correspondence between the benefits associated with this domination and the contributions necessary to bring together the Union and preserve its stability. We believe that this contradiction between the *de facto* coercion exercised by Germany and the non-assumption of its responsibility is acting as one of the main disintegrating factors in Europe.

The logic of the internal and external political constellation will make Germany less and less benevolent towards Europe. In its fourth term, the Merkel government faces a dual pressure: externally, its traditional Centre-North allies, led by the Netherlands, have hardened their position against a Europe of solidarity; internally, the populist Alternative for Germany party (AfD) has *de facto* become the third strongest political force, attracting the votes of the dissenting right. Clearly the partners in government (SPD and CSU) are suffering the wear and tear of governing and being punished by their electorate. Both pressures have minimized the room for manoeuvre of the pro-Europeans within the Merkel government. And to complete the negative picture, the figure of Merkel herself has undergone an unremitting decline from the very beginning of her fourth term, which even throws doubt on her ability to finish her mandate. Whether she does so or not, the political capital she would need to put forward significant reforms in Europe has already vanished.

What we are going to see in the future is a much more assertive German leadership in terms of the vision of Europe it advocates. Practically non-existent is the possibility that Germany will consent to risk-sharing schemes where its taxpayers' money could be used obligatorily and without previous parliamentary authorisation for rescuing depositors, banks or the treasuries of other nations. The German vision of Europe can only be coherent with the elements of the ordoliberal philosophy that are rooted in German collective thought, mainly with the principle that each must take responsibility for their actions. And if this implies that a "profligate and imprudent" nation has to be declared bankrupt and that its debt must be restructured at the expense of investors, then so be it. And if this implies that that nation must leave the Monetary Union, then so be it. And if countries in similar circumstances want to form a new currency zone, then so be it.

The idea of making the Monetary Union "more flexible" seems to be gradually permeating the thinking of the German leadership. There is enough evidence that the one-size-fits-all policy is not compatible with the deep divergences between countries, which far from diminishing over the years, as expected by the founding ideologues of the EMU, have actually worsened.[157] However, let us call a spade a spade: making the EMU flexible is a euphemism for being ready to let the Union fragment, to let some countries leave it. A monetary union, by definition, cannot be flexible, because it is the maximum form of exchange rate rigidity, in which there is no space for persistent differences of inflation, fiscal imbalances or equally persistent external imbalances. The only way for

---

157 Botta *et al.* (2018), Wortman (2018)

these differences to coexist with the Monetary Union is when there are also persistent mechanisms of transfer of resources from one country to another. As this latter element of compensation is not going to exist in the EMU in the foreseeable future, the alternative will be inexorable: either the countries in trouble adjust and are ready to accept severe recession and hardship, or the markets will take care of forcing them out of the eurozone. Even in the case of recessionary adjustment, the political dynamic will sooner or later put into power the political forces that do not want to remain in the eurozone.

Germany is not going to rescue Italy if the markets force it into default, not only because of the enormous size of the Italian debt, but because there will be a lack of political will in Germany to do so. During the euro crisis of 2010-12, Germany still thought that if the euro failed, the European Union would fail. It is still true that one failure would lead to the other, at least to the failure of Europe as we currently know it, but this is already being accepted as unavoidable.

We could go further and affirm that the death of the European Union, as we know it today, will not be as mourned as it would have been a few years back in Germany and elsewhere. Rather it could give rise to a new historical moment in which the limits of integration are recognized realistically. From the ashes of the euro's failure could arise a new, less absolutist, European Union, with room for more flexible configurations, where a common currency is maintained only by the countries that really meet the conditions for it, where there may be two or three "euros". The common currency will no longer represent an existential risk for all other areas and spheres of the EU. The new Europe will have a less demanding and comprehensive least common denominator than at present and will allow choice from a variety of spheres of integration according to national preferences and interests. National democracies will regain control of how much Europe they want and at what speed. They will have a palette of options within which to decide whether to advance in common security and defence, in flexible schemes for monetary and financial policy coordination, or in a fully-fledged monetary union. The new Community language should contain words such as "alternatives", "flexibility" or "free choice" instead of impositions or uniformity for the sake of an ideal of Europe. This absolutist idea of Europe–the reader will forgive the heresy– may have made sense in the aftermath of the two world wars but is no longer in tune with the diversity of the 21st century. A Europe in which, for example, countries that have decided not to be part of the Monetary Union are not considered second-class Europeans. In short, a Europe that democratically respects its great cultural, social and political diversity.

The spokesmen for the old European ideal will not share these ideas. They will argue that, today more than ever, Europe needs to have a single voice, to form a solid unity in the face of serious global threats.[158] The Trump administration keeps subverting the international liberal order that was painstakingly created in the post-war decades, both in terms of security and defence, and in terms of trade relations. The Russian government of Putin is behaving like an international bandit, as shown in the annexation of Crimea or in the cyberattacks on multiple organisations and governments. China, the emerging hegemon, is not a reliable ally that could offer an alternative to the Atlanticism that has characterised the international posture of Europe. Security and defence are certainly natural areas of integration for Europe, especially in the context of current threats from the West, the East and the Far East. These threats cannot, nevertheless, be the reason to press for more Europe in every field.

An advantage of this more flexible and diverse Europe is that it would not require as much from a benevolent hegemon as it does today. On recouping a good degree of the symmetry of power lost during the project of an ever more united Europe, hegemonic roles would be less appropriate and would be less necessary for the survival of the mosaic of integrations. Germany would thus be relieved of a responsibility she never wanted to have. This does not mean, however, that Germany would not have a very central responsibility in leading the process of rewinding and reshaping Europe, especially of the EMU. And once this process is concluded, the might of Germany will continue to give it a leadership responsibility in Europe, even if it is qualitatively different from what was needed in a monetary mega-union of 19 countries.

---

158   Good examples of this position are two respected European politicians, the ex Swedish Prime Minister Carl Bildt (2017), or the ex German Foreign Minister Joschka Fischer (2018)

EPILOGUE

The European soul is conflicted and restless. Its feelings towards what the European Union represents–in all its forms–are full of contradictions and confusions. Citizens mostly say that they want to remain in the Union but are dissatisfied with the Community institutions and where they are taking integration. They do not trust them and feel they are dominated by bureaucratic elites that are distant from ordinary citizens. They blame the European Union for almost all the ills that affect them. Interestingly, countries in which citizens have less trust in the Community government are those in which distrust of their own national governments is also greater. One wonders, then, if the disenchantment in those countries is really with Europe or is rather a feeling of being fed up with any kind of government or political leadership, be it national or European.

European citizens have a positive vision of the EU but want to devolve some attributions that are at the heart of the Union, such as trade agreements, back to national level. More critically, they want national governments to control the freedom of movement and residence of European citizens in their countries, challenging one of the four sacred freedoms of the European treaty. Instead of an ever more united Europe, there seems to be a turn towards national sovereignty.

We observe a similar dichotomy regarding the euro. Citizens mostly want to preserve the euro, but they are not happy with the Monetary Union, its institutions and its policies. The more affected was the economy of a country during the euro crisis, the greater the discontent. They feel that the distribution of responsibilities and burdens under the austerity policies was not equitable. Here again there is doubt about whom the discontent is directed at. The fact that citizens of the countries of the

Centre-North of Europe manifest a majority support towards the institutions and policies of the Monetary Union and that these countries have been the ones that had the best economic performance during the crisis, forces us to wonder again if the level of discontent or support has to do with the euro as such or with the economic situation of each country.

Electors can give a majority vote to parties that openly oppose the country's membership in the Monetary Union, as in Italy, and at the same time affirm that they do not want the national currency to be restored. They are the first to demand that their government give in and negotiate, when the country looks into the abyss of a possible exit from the eurozone. Their intuition tells them that their future pension in local currency would be worth a fraction of its value compared to what it would be if they stayed within the eurozone. However, those same citizens are not willing to accept the policies and reforms necessary for staying within the common currency. The rejection is generated mainly because of the perception of inequity of the economic model that has been associated with the euro, both internally in the respective country and at the Community level. One factor that increases discomfort is the feeling that the Monetary Union is dominated by one particular country.

To keep piling on contradictions, citizens living in euro-using countries find it very difficult to separate the European Union from the European Monetary Union. They usually blur the differences in outline and scope of each of the two spheres of integration; they perceive them as the same thing with the same destiny. Their likes and dislikes regarding each of these two spheres of integration go in unison. This confusion, which affects many political leaders as well, has hindered the construction of the European Union edifice for two reasons. First, because by blurring the contours of the EU and the EMU, the Eurocrats have created a *de facto* division between first-class European citizens (those in the EMU) and second-class citizens (those who decided not board the Monetary Union train or have not yet been able to). Not being part of the EMU sounds like not really being part of the EU either. Second, because it has brought upon the EU a charge of totalitarianism that it should never have had. A monetary union, by definition, does not admit fundamental divergences within it, whereas an economic and political union does allow diversity of economic and political structures, as well as diversity of levels of integration.

Almost two decades after its launch, the final verdict is that the Monetary Union has not been able to provide citizens with the added well-being and prosperity promised to them. The eurozone grew by less than the developed world during the pre-2018 boom years and took longer and suffered a greater cost than the rest of the industrialised West in overcoming the Global Financial Crisis. What was then the point of embarking on so uncertain an adventure as a monetary union?

Despite all the criticism and unwillingness to do what is necessary to preserve the euro, European citizens do not want to abandon their common currency. Beyond the instinct of people wanting to preserve the value of their future pensions, there is another explanation for this persistence of the "*animus communionis*": the fire that fuels the love for the euro has much to do with the power of utopias. The search for the El Dorado of a common currency and the consequent exchange rate stability has been a constant in the economic history of humanity. Monetary integration and exchange stability are associated in the historical memory with periods of peace, international cooperation and prosperity. Time and again, countries dream of the utopia of a common currency; sometimes they succeed in making it real, but they almost always fail to maintain it in the long term. However, regardless of the failures, the attraction of utopias always remains alive. Utopias are precisely that: powerful ideas that are never extinguished and are constantly reborn in different ways.[159]

But the reality is that there are too many contradictions and inconsistencies of positions on the common currency to give solid political support to the EMU, the very centrepiece in the edifice of European integration. If to this problem of perception we add the long litany of omissions in its original design, the misguided policies, the dissent about and postponement of fundamental reforms, the future of the euro looks, to put it mildly, very uncertain. The euro was able to survive its first existential crisis thanks to the fact that the ECB decided to ignore the Maastricht rules–Germany being forced to turn a blind eye–and act as a lender of last resort. A new existential crisis, which will undoubtedly arise someday, will find that the support mechanisms have still not been created and, above all, that either there is no political will to rescue union members

---

[159] In "The Utopia of the Common Currency" (*La Utopía de la Moneda Común*, Purroy, 2014) I explain why it is so hard to build a monetary union and why harmony is fated not to last.

in trouble or that the resources needed to rescue them are too large and are therefore unmanageable.

We have been critical of the role played by Germany during and after the euro crisis. Its responsibility came from action, but even more so from omission: it did not want to assume the obligations associated with its position as *de facto* hegemon in the eurozone. The reasons for Germany reneging on that responsibility, far from disappearing, are gaining strength over time, so we cannot expect the euro to be propped up by the most powerful member of the Monetary Union. The Germans did not feel that they had such a responsibility at the time and feel it even less so now; they never accepted the position of hegemony and still less the duties associated with it. The point here is not whether they would have liked to act as benevolent hegemon or not, but that their *de facto* position was hegemonic and with it came a series of privileges and benefits. The benevolent hegemon recognises this fact and compensates the rest of the members for these privileges by absorbing a disproportional part of the cost of maintaining the stability of the system. Only then can a monetary union survive in the long term.

During the euro crisis Germany acted as if it subscribed to the thesis that the EMU was basically unsalvageable because of the deep economic and cultural divergences between its members and that, consequently, it did not make sense to devote so much effort and resources to save the members in trouble. The truth is that this was neither its belief nor its conscious motivation at the time. Over the years, however, this belief has quietly taken shape in the German establishment and underlies the views that currently make up the country's position. By standing firm on the principle of market discipline and refusing to arrange schemes of solidarity support in the event of the destabilisation of some weak member of the eurozone, Germany is sending the clear message that the euro club is only for those that can abide by its strict rules of fiscal discipline and external competitiveness. Otherwise, members who do not comply with the rules must withdraw from the club, period.

This being the case, the chances of the eurozone surviving in its current form in the event of a new existential crisis are very low. Hence our recommendation to work on creating a formal framework that allows for a friendly separation of some members or groups of members of the Monetary Union. Obviously, the natural candidates to take the first step out of the euro should be Germany and its peers from the Centre-North. For countries with weaker currencies, the mere hint of a possible exit would subject them to a speculative spiral of unpredictable consequences. Again, Germany is not making things easy for the weaker members of the Monetary Union, with its refusal to consider taking the step of forming a new currency zone in its area of influence. Whoever takes the initial exit step, creating this framework is an arduous, long and complex task, which is why it should commence while the waters are calm. Otherwise, when a new crisis occurs, the breakdown will be chaotic and extremely costly for all.

There is another powerful reason to take seriously this task of creating a framework for friendly separation. The monetary union of the 19, representing more than four fifths of the EU, has placed the European Union in a situation of permanent stress and even danger. The euro, which was born to further unite, has become an element of discord. And what is worse, it brings to the European Union a great burden of rigidity and totalitarianism, forces it to invade sovereign spaces that it should not invade and adds fuel to the fire of the lack of democratic legitimacy. The current symbiosis between the EMU and the EU is contrary to the idea of a flexible, plural, multi-sphere and democratic European Union. For the sake of Europe, the euro, in its current form, should disappear and give way to less rigid exchange rate systems, in line, too, with more flexible models of political integration.

BIBLIOGRAPHY

Aizenman, Joshua (2014), "The Eurocrisis: Muddling Through, or on the way to a more perfect Euro Union?", *NBER WP 20242*, June.

Alesina, Alberto., and Robert. J. Barro (2000), "Currency Unions", *NBER WP 7927*, Sept.

Alesina, Alberto., R. J. Barro and Silvana Tenreyro (2002), "Optimal Currency Areas", In: *NBER Macroeconomics Annual 2002*, April.

Almunia, Joaquín et al. (2018), "Quit kicking the can down the road: a Spanish view of EMU reforms", *Elcano Royal Institute*, May.

Arahuetes, Alfredo y Gonzalo Gomez-Bengoeche (2018), "Debt mutualisation, inflation and populism in the eurozone", *Royal Elcano Institut, Technical Report*, April.

Art, David (2015), "The German Rescue of the eurozone", *Political Science Quarterly*, Vol. 130, Nr. 2.

Ash, Timothy Garton (1994), "Germany's Choice", *Foreign Affairs Magazine*, August.

Ash. Timothy Garton (2012), "The crisis of Europe. How the union came together and why is falling apart", *Foreign Affairs*, October.

Ash, Timothy Garton (2013), "The new German question", *The New York Review of Books*, August.

Baimbridge, Mark. and Phillip Whyman (2015), *Crisis in the eurozone. Causes, Dilemmas and Solutions*, Palgrave Macmillan.

Baldwin, R., (2006), "The Euro's Trade Effects", *Working Papers Series*, No. 594, March.

Baldwin, Richard and Francesco Giavazzi, editors (2015), *The eurozone Crisis. A consensus view of the Causes and a few possible solutions*, CEPR Press.

Beetsma, R. and M. Giulodori (2010), "The Macroeconomic Costs and Benefits of the EMU and Other Monetary Unions: An Overview of Recent Research", *Journal of Economic Literature* 48, 603-641, Sept.

Beck, Thorsten and Hans-Helmut Kotz, editors (2017), *Ordoliberalism: a German oddity?*, CEPR Press.

Bénassy-Quéré, Agnes et al. (2018), "Reconciling risk sharing with market discipline: A constructive approach to euro area reform", *CEPR Policy Insight* No. 91, January.

Berger, Helge, Giovanni dell'Ariccia, Maurice Obstfeld (2018), "Revisiting the Economic Case for Fiscal Union in the Euro Area", *IMF Research Department*.

Bernanke, Ben (2015), *The courage to act. A memoir of a crisis and its aftermath*, W.W. Norton and Co, New York

Berthold, N., S. Braun and M. Coban (2014), "Das Scheitern historischer Währungsräume", *Beiträge, Universität Würzburg*.

Bini Smaghi, Lorenzo and Michala Marcussen (2018), "Delivering a safe asset for the euro area", *VOX, CEPR Policy Portal*, July.

Bildt, Carl (2017), "Can Europe sustain the Macron moment", *Project Syndicate*, December.

Blot, Christophe, Jerome Creel, Paul Hubert, Fabien Labondance (2014), "Dealing with the ECB's triple mandate?", *Revue de l'OFCE - Debates and Policies, HAL Archives Ouvertes*, October.

Blanchard, Oliver y Francesco Giavazzi, (2002), "Current Account Deficits in the Euro Area: The End of the Feldstein-Horioka Puzzle," *Brookings Papers on Economic Activity* 2.

Blyth, Mark (2013), *Austerity. The history of a dangerous idea*, Oxford University Press

Blyth, Mark and Matthias Matthijs, editors (2015), *The future of the euro*, Oxford and New York: Oxford University Press.

Bofinger, Peter (2015), "German Wage Moderation and The eurozone Crisis", *Sachverständigerrat, Social Europe*, December.

Bonefeld, Werner (2017), "Stateless Money and State Power: Europe as ordoliberal Ordnungsgefüge", *Department of Politics, University of York*, York.

Bordo, Michael and Harold James (2013), "The European crisis in the context of the history of previous Financial Crises", *NBER WP 19112*, June.

Botta, Alberto et al. (2018), "Divergence between the core and the periphery and secular stagnation in the eurozone", *GPERC 63, University of Greenwich*.

Brunnermeier, Markus, Harold James and Jean-Pierre Landau (2016), *The euro and the battle of ideas*, Princeton University Press.

Bulmer, Simon (2014), "Germany and the eurozone Crisis: Between Hegemony and Domestic Politics", *West European Politics*, 37:6, August.

Bulmer, Simon and William E. Paterson (2013), "Germany as the EU's reluctant hegemon? Of economic strength and political constraints", *Journal of European Public Policy*, August.

Cafruny, Allan (2015), "Europe's Twin Crises: The logic and tragic of contemporary German power", *Valdai Papers 10*, February.

Calvo, Guillermo, A. Izquierdo y L.F. Mejía (2004), "On the Empirics of sudden Stops: The Relevance of Balance-Sheet Effects", *Inter-American Development Bank*, Research Department, July.

Chari, V. and P. J. Kehoe, (2008), "Time Inconsistency and Free-Riding in a Monetary Union." *Journal of Money, Credit, and Banking*, 40(7).

Churchill, W. (1946), Speech, University of Zürich, 19/IX/1946. http://www.churchill-society-london.org.uk/astonish.html

Cohen, Benjamin (1993), "Beyond EMU: The Problem of Sustainability", *Economics & Politics*, Vol. 5, Issue 2, July.

Cohen, Benjamin (2003), "Are monetary unions inevitable?", *International Studies Perspective*, Vol 4, July.

Conti, N., Di Mauro, D. and Memoli, V. (2018a), "The European Union under Threat of a Trend toward National Sovereignty", *Journal of Contemporary European Research*, Vol 14 #2.

Conti, Nicoló, Borbala Göncz and José Real-Dato, editors (2018b), *National Political Elites, European Integration and the eurozone Crisis*, Routledge, London.

Coricelli, Fabrizio (2017), "Surmounting the German Surplus", *Project Syndicate*, September

Cox, Robert (1983), "Gramsci, Hegemony and International Relations: An Essay in Method", *Millennium: Journal of International Studies*, Vol. 12, No.2

Debrun, X.; D. Hauner and M. Kumar, (2009), "Independent Fiscal Agencies", *IMF, Journal of Economic Surveys*, Vol. 23, No. 1

de Grauwe, Paul, (2005), "Are Latin America and East Asia optimal currency areas?", *Paper prepared for the 10th Annual Meeting of the Latin American and Caribbean Economic Association*, Paris, October.

de Grauwe, Paul (2012), "A fragile eurozone in search of a better governance", *The Economic and Social Review, Vol. 43, No. 1.*, University of Leuven.

de Grauwe, Paul and Yuemei Ji (2015), "Has the eurozone become less fragile? Some empirical tests", *CESifo Working Paper 5163*, January.

de Grauwe, Paul y F. Mongelli (2005), "Endogeneities of optimum currency areas. What brings countries sharing a single currency closer together?", *Working Paper* No. 468, European Central Bank, April.

de Grauwe, Paul and Yuemei Ji (2012), "Self-Fulfilling Crises in the eurozone: An empirical test", *CEPS Working Document No. 366*, June.

de Haan, J., S. Eijffinger and S. Waller, (2005), *The European Central Bank: Credibility, Transparency and Centralisation*. The MIT Press, Cambridge, MA.

Dellas, Harris and George S. Tavlas (2014), "The Gold Standard, the Euro, and the Origins of the Greek Sovereign Debt Crisis", *CATO Journal* Vol 33 No. 3.

Dixit, A. y L. Lambertini, (2003), "Symbiosis of Monetary and Fiscal Policies in a Monetary Union." *Journal of International Economics*, 60(2).

Draghi, Mario (2018), "Risk-reducing and risk-sharing in our Monetary Union", *Speech at the University of Florence*, 2018-05-11

Eichengreen, Barry (1991), "Is Europe an Optimum Currency Area?", *NBER Working Paper 3579*, January.

Eichengreen, Barry (1993). "European monetary unification", *Journal of Economic Literature*, Sept.

Eichengreen, Barry (2007), "The Breakup of the Euro Area", *NBER Working Paper 13393*, September.

Eichengreen, Barry (2000), *Vom Goldstandard zum Euro*, Berlin: Verlag Klaus Wagenbach. 2000
Eichengreen, Barry (2011), *Exorbitant Privilege: The Rise and Fall of the Dollar*, Oxford University Press, Oxford.
Eichengreen, Barry (2017), "The Euro's Narrow Path", *Project Syndicate*, September.
Eichengreen, Barry and P. Temin, (2010), "Fetters of Gold and Paper", *NBER Working Paper Series, Working Paper 16202*, NBER, Cambridge, July.
Eichengreen, Barry and Charles Wyplosz (2016), "Minimal conditions for the survival of the euro", *Intereconomics*, January-February.
Eichengreen,, Barry et al. (2013), "The eurozone crisis, Phoenix or lost decade?", *BEHL Working Paper Series* WP2013-08, University of California, Berkeley, May.
Eichengreen, Barry, R. Hausmann y U. Panizza (2003), "The Pain of Original Sin", August.
European Commission (2017), "White paper on the future of Europe", March.
European Systemic Risk Board (2017), "Resolving Non-performing loans in Europe", *ESFS*, July.
Faini, R., (2006), "Fiscal Policy and Interest Rates in Europe." *Economic Policy*, 47.
Feld, Lars (2018), "Whither a fiscal capacity in EMU?", *VOX, CEPR Policy Portal*, July.
Feld, Lars P., Köhler, Ekkehard and Nientiedt, Daniel (2017), "The dark ages of German macroeconomics", *Freiburger Diskussionspapiere zur Ordnungsökonomik*, No. 17/03.
Feldstein, Martin (1992): "The case against EMU", *The Economist*, June 13.
Feldstein, Martin (1997), "The Political Economy of the European Economic and Monetary Union: Political Sources of an Economic Liability", *The Journal of Economic Perspectives*, Vol. 11, No. 4, Autumn
Feldstein, Martin (2012), "The Failure of the Euro: the Little Currency That Couldn't", *Foreign Affairs*, January-February 2012.
Feldstein, Martin (2015), "Ending the euro crisis", *NBER Working Paper 20862*, January.
Feldstein, Martin (2016), "How EU Overreach Pushed Britain Out", *Project Syndicate*, June.
Fendel, Ralph and Maurer, David (2015), "Does European History Repeat Itself?", *Journal of Economic Integration*, Vol 30 No. 1, March.
Fischer, Joschka (2018), "Reclaiming European Sovereignty", *Project Syndicate*, July.
Frankel, Jeffrey (2015), "Causes of eurozone crises", *VOX CEPR's Policy Portal*, September.
Frankel, Jeffrey (2015), "The euro crisis: where to from here?", *Journal of Policy Modeling 37*, March.
Frankel, J. and A. Rose, (2002), "An Estimate of the Effect of Common Currencies on Trade and Income", *The Quarterly Journal of Economics*, Vol. 117, No. 2.

Frankfurter Allgemeine Zeitung, 2018-05-22–"Ökonomen-Aufruf: Euro darf nicht in Haftungsunion führen".
Franks, Jeffrey et al. (2018), "Economic Convergence in the Euro Area: Coming together or drifting apart", *IMF WP 18-10*.
Frieden, Jeffry (2014), "The Political Economy of Adjustment and Rebalancing", *Department of Government, Harvard University*, June.
Friedman, Milton (1997), "The euro: Monetary unity to political disunity?", *Project Syndicate*, August
Friedman, M. and A. Schwartz (1963), *A Monetary History of the United States*, National Bureau of Economic Research, Washington.
Füst, Clemens (2017), "The Politics of Germany's External Surplus", *Project Syndicate*, 2017-07-17.
Füst, Clemens (2018), "[Art. 50] Ways to leave the Euro–Does the eurozone need and exit clause?", *ESMT Berlin Forum*, September.
Gilpin, Robert (1987), *The political economy of international relations*, Princeton University.
Germond, Carine and Türk, Henning, editors (2008), *A History of Franco-German Relations in Europe*, Palgrave MacMillan.
Glencross, Andrew (2013), "The EU response to the eurozone Crisis: Democratic contestation and the new fault Lines in European integration", *Europa-Kolleg Discussion Paper* No. 3/13, Hamburg, July.
Gross, Stephen and Chase Gummer (2013), "Ghosts of the Habsburg Empire: Collapsing Currency Unions and Lessons for the eurozone", *East European Politics and Societies and Cultures*, August.
Guiso, L., P. Sapienza and L. Zingales (2011), "Monnet's Error?", *NBER Working Paper 21121*, April.
Herrera, Helios, Luigi Guiso and Massimo Morelli (2016), "Cultural Differences and Institutional Integration", *Journal of International Economics*, Vol. 99 Suplem. 1, March
Hien, Joseph and Christian Joerges (2018), "Dead Man walking, Current European Interest in the Ordoliberal Tradition", *European University Institute, EUI Working Papers, LAW 2018/03*.
Hill, Christopher (2018), "Turning back the clock. The illusion of a global political role for Britain", in: Martill Benjamin and Uta Staiger (eds) (2018).
Ikenberry, G.J.; and C.A. Kupchan (1990), "Socialisation and Hegemonic Power", *International Organisation Vol 44, 3*.
Jacoby, Wade (2014), "The Politics of the eurozone Crisis, Two Puzzles behind the German Consensus", *German Politics and Society*, Issue 111 Vol. 32, No. 2
James, Harold (2012), *Making the European Monetary Union*, Bank for International Settlements.
Janning, Josef and Almut Moeller (2016), "Leading from the Centre: Germany's new Role in Europe", *ECFR* July.
Jenkins, Roy (2001), *Churchil*, Macmillan.

Judt, Tony (2005), *Postwar: a History of Europe since 1945*, Penguin.
Kawalec, Stefan and Ernest Pytlarczyk (2013), "Controlled dismantlement of the eurozone: A proposal for a New European Monetary System and a new role for the European Central Bank", *National Bank Of Poland, Working Paper,No. 155*, Warsaw
Kennen, P. (1969), "The theory of optimum currency areas: An eclectic view", in: Mundell, R. y A. Swoboda, " eds., *Monetary problems of the…*
Kindleberger, Charles (1973), *The World in Depression 1929-1939*.
Kindleberger, Charles and R. Aliber (2011), *Manias, Panics and Crashes. A History of Financial Crises*, 6th Edition, Palgrave MacMillan, UK
Kösters, W. et al. (1998), "Der Euro kommt zu früh", *Frankfurter Allgemeine Zeitung*. http://www.berndsenf.de/pdf/155%20Profs%20Der%20Euro%20kommt%20zu%20fr%FCh_980209_KoBog.pdf
Krugman, Paul (2012), "Revenge of the Optimum Currency Area", in *NBER Macroeconomics Annual 2012*, p. 439-448.
Krugman, Paul (2014), "The timidity trap", *New York Times, March 21*
Kundnani, Hans (2011), "Germany as a Geo-Economic Power", *The Washington Quarterly, 34, 3*.
Kundnani, Hans (2015), *The Paradox of German Power*, Oxford University Press.
Lagarde, Christine (2014), "A new multilateralism for the 21st century", *The Richard Dimbleby Lecture*, February.
Lane, Phillip, (2006), "The Real Effects of European Monetary Union", *The Journal of Economic Perspectives*, Vol. 20, No. 4
Lentner, H. (2005), "Hegemony and Autonomy", in: *Political Studies, 53, 4*
Le Moigne, M. and X. Ragot (2015), "France et Allemagne: Une histoire du désajustement européen", *OFCE, Working Paper*, June.
Luttwak, Edward (1990), "From geopolitics to geo-economics", *The National Interest, Summer*
Marsh, David (2009). *"The Euro: The Politics of the New Global Currency"* Yale University Press.
Martill, Benjamin and Uta Staiger, editors (2018), *Brexit and Beyond, Rethinking the Futures of Europe, Brexit, Yet another crisis for the EU*, UCL Press.
Marzinotto, Benedicta (2017), "A Turning Point for Europe", *Project Syndicate*, April.
Matthijs, Matthias (2013), "The Euro Crisis and the Erosion of Democratic Legitimacy: Lessons from the Gold Standard", *John Hopkins University SAIS*, July.
Matthijs, Matthias (2014), "Reading Kindleberger in Washington and Berlin. Ideas and Leadership in a Time of Crisis", *John Hopkins Univ. SAIS*, November.
Matthijs, Matthias (2016), "Powerful rules governing the euro: the perverse logic of German ideas", *Journal of European Policy*, Vol 23, No. 3, April.
Matthijs, Matthias and Mark Blith (2016), "The Future of the Euro, Possible Futures, Risks and Uncertainties", in: Mark Blyth and Matthias Matthijs, editors (2015), *The future of the euro …*

Matthijs, Matthias and Mark Blith (2011), "Why Only Germany Can Fix the Euro, Reading Kindleberger in Berlin", *Foreign Affairs Snapshot*, November.

Maull, Hanns (2001), "Germany's foreign policy post-Kosovo: Still a 'Civilian Power'?" in: Sebastian Harnisch and Hanns W. Maull, editors (2001), *Germany as a civilian power? The foreign policy of the Berlin Republic*, Manchester.

Maull, Hanns W. (2018), "Germany's leadership in Europe, Finding its new role", in Ebert and Flemes eds, *Regional Leadership and Multipolarity in the 21st Century*, Vol. 3, Issue 1, February.

McKinnon, R., (1963), "Optimum currency are as", *American Economic Review*, 52, Sept.

McKinsey & Company, (2010), "Debt and deleveraging: The global credit bubble and its economic consequences", *McKinsey Global Institute*, January.

Meiers, Franz-Josef (2015), *Germany's Role in the Euro Crisis. Berlin's Quest for a More Perfect Monetary Union*, Springer International Publishing.

Melitz, Jacques (2014), "Why Europe needs two euros, not one", *VOX, CEPR's Policy Portal*.

Merkel, Angela (2010), "Scheitert der Euro, dann scheitert Europa", Speech before the German Bundestag, May 19, 2010.

Mertes, Michael (2015), "Too Big for Europe, Too Small for the World, The German Question Reconsidered", *Israel Journal of Foreign Affairs*, Vol 9, No 3.

Meyer, Niclas (2018), "EU break-up? Mapping plausible pathways into alternative futures", *LEQS Paper* No. 136/2018, August.

Micossi, Stefano (2013), "The eurozone crisis and EU institutional change: A new CEPR Policy Insight", *CEPR*, April

Micossi, Stefano (2018), "The crux of disagreement on euro area reform", *VOX, CEPR Policy*, April

Mody, Ashoka (2018), *Euro Tragedy. A Drama in nine acts*, Oxford.

Mongelli, Francesco (2008), "European economic and monetary integration and the optimum currency area theory", *European Commission, Economic Papers 302*, February.

Mundell, R.A., (1961), "A Theory of Optimum Currency Areas", *The American Economic Review*, Vol. 51, No. 4, Sept.

Mundell, R. and A. Swoboda, editors (1969), *Monetary problems of the international economy*, University of Chicago Press, Chicago.

Obstfeld, Maurice (2013), "Finance at Center Stage: Some Lessons of the Euro Crisis", *European Commission, Economic Papers 493*, April.

Obstfeld, Maurice (2014), "Trilemmas and Tradeoffs, Living with Financial Globalisation", *University of California, Berkeley*.

Ohr, R., Schäfe, W. et al. (1992), "Die währungspolitischen Beschlüsse von Maastricht: Eine Gefahr für Europa", http://wirtschaftlichefreiheit.de/wordpress/?p=20212

Otero-Iglesias, Miguel (2014), "Germany and political union in Europe: Nothing moves without France", *Royal Elcano Institute WP 8-2014*, August.
Pisani-Ferry, Jean (2016), "Preventing the Next eurozone Crisis Starts Now", *Project Syndicate*, December.
Pissani-Ferry, Jean, Zettelmeyer, Jerome (2018), "Could the 7+7 report's proposals destabilise the euro, A response to Guido Tabellini", *VOX CEPR Policy Portal*, August.
Purroy, Miguel I. (2014), *La utopía de la moneda común. El debate sobre integración monetaria y régimen cambiario*, Amazon/Kindle Edition.
Purroy, Miguel I. (2015), *Régimen cambiario y estabilidad inflacionaria. Visión desde la economía política*, Amazon/Kindle Edition.
Reinhart, Carmen and Kenneth Rogoff (2011), "From Financial Crash to Debt Crisis", *American Economic Review*, Vol. 101 No. 5 August
Rodrik, Dani (2017), How Much Europe Can Europe Tolerate, *Project Syndicate*, March.
Rose, A.K., (2000), "One money, one market: the effect of currency unions on trade," *Economic Policy* 30.
Roth, Felix Edgar Baake, Lars Jonung and Felicitas Nowak-Lehmann (2018), "Revisiting Public Support for the Euro 1999-2017", *University of Hamburg*.
Roubini, Nouriel and Brunello Rosa (2019), "Italy's Slow-Motion Euro Train Wreck", *Project Syndicate*, June
Ryan, John y John Loughlin (2018), "Lessons from historical monetary unions - is the European monetary union making the same mistakes?", *International Economic Policy*, Springer, April.
Scharpf, Fritz. (2013), "Political Legitimacy in a Non-optimal Currency Area", *MPIfG Discussion Paper*, No. 13/15,
Scharpf, Fritz (2018), "There Is an Alternative: A Two-Tier European Currency Community", *MPIfG Discussion Paper* 18/7, July.
Schmidt, Vivien (2016), "The resilience of 'bad ideas' in eurozone crisis discourse", *Boston University*, April
Schneider, E. y S. Sandbeck (2018), "Monetary integration in the eurozone and the rise of transnational authoritarian statism", *Competition & Change*.
Schweiger, Christian (2018), "Germany's role in the EU-27. Leadership constellation after Brexit", *German Politics and Society*, Vol. 36, Issue 127 Chemnitz University of Technology.
Simms, Brendan (2013), *Europe: The struggle for Supremacy. 1453 to the present*, Penguin, London.
Simms, Brendan (2017), *Britain's Europe. A Thousand Years of Conflict and Cooperation*, Penguin, London.
Sinn, Hans-Werner (2016), "Europe's Emerging Bubbles", *Project Syndicate*, March.
Stantcheva, Stefanie (2018), "The Fog of Immigration", *Project Syndicate*, August.

Steinberg, Federico and Mattias Vermeiren (2016), "Germany's Institutional Power and the EMU Regime after the Crisis: Towards a Germanized Euro Area?", *Journal of Common Market Studies*.
Stiglitz, Joseph (2016), *How a common Currency threatens the future of Europe*, W.W. Norton&Company.
Storm, Servaas (2016), "German wage moderation and the eurozone's crisis: a critical analysis", *Delft University of Technology*.
Storm, Servaas (2016), "Response to Peter Bofinger's 'Friendly Fire'", January (https://www.ineteconomics.org/perspectives/blog/response-to-peter-bofinger)
Streeck, Wolfgang (2015), "German Hegemony Unintended and Unwanted", *Le Monde Diplomatique*, May.
Szász, André (1999), *The Road to European Monetary Union. A Political and Economic History*, Palgrave Macmillan, London.
Tabelini, Guido (2015), "The main lessons to be drawn from the European financial crisis", *VOX CEPR's Policy Portal*, September
Tabellini, Guido (July 2018), "Risk sharing and market discipline. Finding the right mix", *VOX CEPR's Policy Portal*, July.
Terzi, Alessio (2018), "Macroeconomic Adjustment in the Euro Area", *CID Harvard, WP 88*, February.
The Economist (2016), "More spend, less thrift: German Surplusses", Sept 03.
The Economist (2017), "Vorsprung durch Angst. The good and bad in Germany's economic model are strongly linked", Jul 8.
Thorsten Beck and Hans-Helmut Kotz, editors (2017), *Ordoliberalism: a German oddity?*, CEPR Press.
Tooze, Adam and Shahin Vallée (2018), "Germany's Great European Heist", *Project Syndicate*, May.
Tortola Domenico and Lorenza Vai (2015), "What Government for the European Union? Five Themes for Reflection and Action", *Istituto Affari Internazionali*, Documenti IAI 15, September.
Triepel, Heinrich (1938), *Die Hegemonie. Ein Buch von Führenden Staaten*, W. Kohlhammer Verlag, Stuttgart und Berlin.
Walters, Alan (1990), *Sterling in Danger: Economic Consequences of Fixed Exchange Rates*, London: Fontana.
Wasserfallen, Fabio and Thomas Lerner (2018), "Political Conflict in the Reform of the eurozone", *University of Salzburg*, March.
Webber, Douglas (2014), "How Likely Is It That the EU Will Disintegrate? A Critical Analysis of Competing Theoretical Perspectives", *European Journal of International Relations* Vol. 20, 2, June.
Webber, Douglas (2019), *European Disintegration? The politics of crisis in the European Union*, Red Globe Press, London
Wortman, Marcus (2018), Convergence and Divergence in the EMU, *Dissertation Georg-August-Universität Göttingen*.

Wyplosz, Charles, (1997), "EMU: Why and How It Might Happen", *The Journal of Economic Perspectives*, Vol. 11, No. 4, Autumn.

Wyplosz, Charles, (2006), "European Monetary Union: the dark sides of a major success", *Economic Policy*, April.

Xifre, Ramon (2017), "Non-price competitiveness factors and export performance: The case of Spain in the context of the Euro area", *FUNCAS, SEFO* Vol. 6 No. 3, May.

Thirion, Gilles (2017), "European Fiscal Union, Economic Rationale and Design Challenges", *CEPS Working Document,* No 2017-01, January

LIST OF TABLES, FIGURES AND BOXES

1. **TABLES**

TABLE III-1: EMU - Representative Convergence Variables, 1998 . 99
TABLE IV-1: Inflation in the eurozone and selected countries, 1990-2007... 104
TABLE IV-2: Interest rates in the eurozone and selected countries, 1990-2007... 106
TABLE IV-3: Evolution of sovereign debt burden (% of GDP), 2007 vs 2016.. 132
TABLE V-1: Comparative figures: Spain–United Kingdom, 2009-2014.. 170
TABLE IX-1: Divergent views between Germany and France...... 249
TABLE XI-1: Proposals for fiscal stability mechanisms 309

2. **FIGURES**

FIGURE IV-1: Evolution of risk premiums, 1999-2007 107
FIGURE IV-2: Convergence of per capita GDP and growth differences, 1998-2016 108
FIGURE IV-3: Evolution of risk premiums, 2008-2015 119
FIGURE IV-4: EMU Public Debt 2011: size (billions) and weight (% of GDP)... 120
FIGURE IV-5: Average Growth: Eurozone (EMU-19), USA and OECD 128
FIGURE IV-6: Growth: Centre vs Periphery, 2010-2017 129
FIGURE IV-7: Periphery Growth, 2010-2017.................... 130
FIGURE IV-8: Periphery: Unemployment Rates, 2010-2017 131
FIGURE IV-9: Centre: Growth Rates, 2010-2017 132
FIGURE V-1: Unit Labour Cost, 1999-2016..................... 151

FIGURE V-2: Current Account Balance (% of GDP) 1999-2017.... 153
FIGURE V-3: Debt Components by Country, 2008................ 156
FIGURE V-4: Components of debt growth: Spain, Germany and
    United Kingdom (1980-2009)............................ 157
FIGURE V-5: Fiscal Deficit (% of GDP): Germany and France vs
    Periphery, 1999-2017 163
FIGURE VI-1: Automatic bilateral adjustment mechanism 197
FIGURE VI-2: Unilateral adjustment mechanism 199
FIGURE VII-1: Evolution of positive sentiment towards European
    membership, 1973-2011 (EU 15) 215
FIGURE VIII-1: Current Account Balance (% of GDP) 1999-2017.. 233
FIGURE VIII-2: Comparative Savings Rates (% of GDP), 1999-2017 236
FIGURE VIII-3: Comparative Investment Rates (% of GDP), 1999-
    2017 237
FIGURE XI-1: Total Public Debt (% of GDP), 2017 294
FIGURE XII-1: Number of first-time Asylum Applicants, 2012-2017 327

3. BOXES

BOX IV-1: The sub-prime bubble 110
BOX IV-2: Manias and bubbles: the dynamics of financial crises... 112
BOX IV-3: The perverse dynamics of deleveraging.............. 133
BOX VIII-1: A brief lesson in macroeconomics: the meaning of the
    balance of payments current account.................... 234
BOX XI-1: Italy: the unmanageable threat 296

INDEX

7+7 Group 302

Adenauer, Konrad 50, 59, 64, 66, 186, 187, 246, 258, 278, 319
AfD 328, 364
Agenda 2010 151, 152, 225, 235, 236, 270, 273, 280, 362
Ash, Timothy Garton 13, 73, 202, 217, 287, 373
Assembly of the European Council 56
austerity fatigue 216
austerity prescription 223
austerity program 193
 fallacy of composition 137

bad equilibria 171, 177, 220
Bank for International Settlements 97, 161, 377
Banking Resolution Fund 303, 304
banking union
 and bank deposits guarantee 188
 and Bank Resolution Mechanism 301
 and financial stability 303, 359
 German proposals on 323
 requisite for a monetary union 147, 298
 the three pillars of banking reform 304
Berlin puzzle 255
Bernanke, Ben 125, 126, 374
Bismarck, Otto von 34, 37, 38, 41, 220, 281

Bofinger, Peter 224, 225, 226, 228, 374, 381
Brandt, Willy 66, 278, 319
Bretton Woods 71, 81, 82, 83, 84, 85, 86, 87, 113, 150, 221, 268, 271
 and Europe 82
 collapse of 65, 93
 monetary system of 83, 268
Brexit 22, 58, 61, 76, 289, 293, 334, 336, 338, 339, 340, 345, 378, 380
 2016 Referendum 335
 and EU disintegration 318, 332
 comparison to Sweden and Denmark 340
 effect on the Franco-German axis 339
 impact on the UK 340
 Irish border backstop 337
 previous EU negotiations 335
 reasons for discontent towards Europe 338
 Theresa May's red lines 337
Bundesbank 16, 73, 87, 90, 96, 97, 98, 127, 161, 166, 167, 175, 177, 182, 221, 252, 256, 269, 270, 279
 and creating the EMU 97, 166
 and EMS design 66, 86, 90, 269
 and opposition to the EMU 96, 247

Chartalist theory of money 65, 183
Churchill, Winston 52, 53, 54, 55, 56, 57, 375

385

Churchill, Winston (*continued*)
   British ambivalence towards Europe 15, 52, 56
   Speech University of Zurich 55
   theory of the three circles 57
civil power, Germany as 278
Cold War 47, 48, 50, 51, 278
   Germany at the centre of 46, 276, 277
Common Agricultural Policy 60, 277
community method 356
competitive advantage of Germany 240
Congress of Vienna 30, 31, 32, 35, 39, 275
CSU 328, 362, 364
culture of stability 20, 96, 244, 247

Deauville Agreement 118, 139, 206
debt restructuring 194, 302, 306, 307, 311, 312, 323, 351
de Gaulle, General Charles 15, 49, 55, 61, 62, 63, 64, 65, 66, 71, 319
Delors, Jacques 69, 71, 74, 88, 89, 161, 210
democratic legitimacy 19, 23, 79, 210, 317, 318, 355, 357, 359, 371
   based on participation or on results 212
   Brexit and questioning of 339
   challenged by populism 357
   concept of 209
   deficit of 208
   erosion by adjustment policies 196
   erosion by the de-institutionalisation of EU governance 201
   evolution of public perception about 214
   fiscal transfers and 191
   national vision of 331, 357
Deposit Guarantee Fund 303, 304
d'Estaing, Giscard 66, 71, 79, 265
deutschmark 16, 28, 65, 66, 72, 73, 74, 85, 86, 87, 89, 90, 92, 96, 187, 225, 240, 247, 265, 269, 359, 362

and export model 150
and weakness of the franc 65, 71
credibility of 359
German reluctance to renounce to 73
hegemony in the EMS 82
revaluationist pressures 362
stability of 221
Draghi, Mario 70, 122, 129, 134, 139, 175, 204, 301, 302, 303, 313, 375
Dublin Agreement 341
   Regulation II 327

ECOFIN 92, 165
economist view 187
Eden 57
Eden, Anthony 56
Eichengreen, Barry 71, 85, 145, 146, 161, 162, 171, 179, 265, 307, 348, 349, 375, 376
EMS crisis 1992-93 90
EMU's design faults 143, 300, 318, 355
Erhard, Ludwig 246, 278
Eucken, Walter 244
European Central Bank 17, 28, 69, 70, 73, 88, 89, 97, 100, 104, 106, 116, 117, 118, 121, 122, 166, 172, 185, 188, 193, 203, 209, 213, 247, 274, 287, 296, 300, 375, 378
   2009 interest rate increase 127
   and financial system stabilisation 252
   and ordoliberal monetary order 184
   and Target-2 balances 343
   and the Troika 204
   Committee of Governors 70, 97
   European last instance of decision 213
   extrapolation of the Bundesbank 221, 270
   lender of last resort 134
   political control of 359

price stability mandate 160
slow response during euro crisis 203
statement of July 2012 122
European Coal and Steel Community 50, 56, 221
European Commission 19, 22, 69, 70, 74, 88, 92, 116, 117, 121, 123, 124, 140, 187, 188, 204, 205, 206, 207, 209, 213, 298, 309, 316, 322, 335, 345, 356, 358, 376, 379
and Excessive Macroeconomic Imbalance Procedure 213
EU reform proposals 300, 310, 355
Greek bail-out 139
European Council 19, 56, 69, 70, 74, 79, 85, 86, 87, 88, 89, 123, 187, 188, 201, 205, 206, 207, 209, 213, 254, 325, 330, 335, 356
European Defence Community 51, 52, 56
European Economic Community 15, 22, 50, 56, 58, 60, 61, 66, 69, 81, 82, 84, 150, 188, 217, 221, 276
European Financial Stability Facility 139, 204, 205
European Financial Stability Mechanism 139
European Monetary Fund 307, 310, 313, 322, 323
European Monetary Institute 89, 100, 161
European Monetary System 16, 66, 378
asymmetry of 269
French support to 66
revival of 315, 350
European Stability Mechanism 139, 205, 322
euroscepticism 362
eurozone disintegration scenarios 343
exorbitant privilege 71, 96, 265

expansionary fiscal contraction 135
export mercantilism 240
export model, German 218, 281
export model vs. internal market model 17, 232
exposure to government debt, limits on 304

Federal Reserve 84, 111, 113, 125, 126, 127, 176, 177, 185, 268, 269
Feldstein, Martin 146, 315, 374, 376
fiscal austerity 17, 19, 124, 135, 230
and export model 218
fallacy of 134
Italian government policy platform 297
fiscal indiscipline 18, 165
euro crisis diagnosis 127, 272
factors conducive to in EMU 163
incentive for in a monetary union 144, 160, 162
mitigation mechanisms 190
fiscal solidarity 16, 18, 21, 22, 191, 298, 311, 344
and EMU design 182
countries in favour of 300
German rejection of 187
in EMU design 182
fiscal union 190, 305
in the USA 185
legal framework for fiscal transfers 165
Merkel's statement 186
prerequisite of debt mutualisation 251
Franco-German axis 22, 55, 275, 299, 316, 318, 322, 339
Franco-German Friendship Treaty 64
free riding 162, 182, 190, 250, 266, 299, 387
Freiburg School 244, 246, 250, 256, 257

geo-economic power 37, 278, 282
geo-economic semi-hegemony 283
German Confederation 32, 34, 35, 261, 275
German Constitutional Court 253, 287
German Empire 35, 36, 37, 39, 275
German foreign policy 37, 42, 52, 77, 274, 276, 277, 278, 279, 362
  and civism 278
  and the reunification project 277, 279
  construction of a liberal EU 332
  main objectives after WW II 361
German non-militarism 278
German Problem 14, 15, 20, 25, 27, 29, 36, 40, 43, 46, 47, 48, 50, 52, 55, 217, 220, 284
  European integration as a solution to the 217, 221, 260, 276
  fall of the Berlin Wall and the 72
  in the interwar period 43
  the new hegemony 275, 282
Global Financial Crisis 17, 18, 19, 103, 104, 109, 134, 184, 212, 219, 222, 237, 270, 291, 352, 369
  US vs Europe 125
globalisation 18, 105, 113, 141, 147, 315, 331, 332, 354
  and populist rage 330
  effect on currency unions 146
  effect on financial stability 172
  hyper-globalisation in Europe 181, 215
Gold Standard 41, 177, 178, 179, 268, 375, 378
great moderation, the 105, 141, 189
Greek rescue package 116, 119, 255

Haftungsprinzip 20, 250
hegemon 14, 20, 21, 93, 143, 218, 260, 261, 262, 263, 264, 265, 266, 267, 271, 273, 274, 283, 284, 286, 320, 361, 362, 363, 366, 370, 374

benevolent 264, 265, 299
benevolent and Germany 270, 316
benevolent and Germany in the refugee crisis 327, 329
benevolent and public goods 264
coercive 274
etymological origin 261
reluctant 277
hegemonic stability, theory of 262
hegemony 14, 15, 16, 33, 36, 40, 48, 50, 66, 71, 72, 82, 83, 93, 100, 260, 261, 264, 265, 274, 275, 283, 284, 285, 286, 287, 289, 327, 363, 370
  classic theory of 261
  concept of 260
  dilemma of hegemonic asymmetry 270
  Great Britain in the Gold Standard 268
  ideological influence and 286
Hollande, Francois 207, 277, 281, 320

integration fatigue 23, 214, 216
intergovernmentalism 67, 201, 206
intergovernmental method 322, 356
investment rate in Germany 236

James, Harold 97, 374, 377
Jenkins, Roy 54, 377

Kenen, Peter 145, 161, 305
Kindleberger, Charles 111, 112, 262, 263, 264, 270, 284, 378, 379
Kohl, Helmut 66, 68, 72, 73, 186, 187, 319
  and *Ostpolitik* 77
  on fiscal and political union 73, 186
Kundnani, Hans 218, 263, 278, 282, 283, 284, 378

Lamfalussy, Alexander 161
legacy costs 321

Lehman Brothers 109, 111, 126, 175
lender of last resort 17, 18, 101, 113, 124, 134, 137, 139, 143, 173, 174, 175, 182, 184, 185, 193, 204, 252, 254, 274, 303, 304
   2008-2009 Federal Reserve conduct 126
   and benevolent hegemon functions 264
   and Maastricht Treaty 176, 311, 369
   and the doom loop of banking and sovereign crisis 144, 172, 173
   classic form of risk sharing 312
   German reluctance to 250
Less Europe vision 297

Macmillan, Harold 61, 373, 378, 381
Macroeconomic Imbalance Procedure 123, 213
macro-prudential regulations 304
market discipline 21, 289, 300, 301, 302, 306, 308, 312, 356, 370, 373, 381
   and debt legacy 307
   and no-bailout rule 312
   and risk of instability 308
Martin Wolf 315
McKinnon, Ronald 145, 147, 379
Mercantile State 279, 282
Merkel and Macron
   response to Macron's proposals 322
Merkel, Angela 319, 379
   and ordoliberalism 245, 258
   and the Deauville Agreement 139, 255
   and the Franco-German alliance 207, 277, 281
   and the refugee crisis 317, 326, 327, 328
   in her fourth term 363
   on consequences of the euro failure 319
   on refugee policy 329
   we need more Europe 186
military budget 320
Mitterrand, François 66, 68, 319
   policy of the franc fort 71
Mody, Ashoka 315, 379
monetary order 16, 83, 184, 247, 263
   and the role of ECB 359
   need of a stabilising hegemon 263
   ordoliberal concept of 184
   ordoliberal primacy of 244
   symmetrical and asymmetrical 270
   without a State 184
Monnet, Jean 49, 59, 65, 101, 186, 210, 211, 319, 357, 377
moral hazard 22, 140, 176, 190, 250, 253, 299, 311, 312
More Europe vision 297, 355
Mundell, Robert 145, 147, 192, 224, 378, 379

nationalist populisms 290, 331
   and the refugee crisis 326
   as sequels of the euro and refugee crisis 330
   disruptive power in European politics 341
NATO 29, 49, 50, 51, 52, 64, 65, 78, 266, 276, 278, 320, 321
net international position of Germany 222

one-size-fits-all monetary policy 18, 166
Optimum Currency Area 305, 375, 378
Ordnungsgefüge 257, 374
ordoliberalism 20, 193, 256, 257, 258
   and automatic adjustment mechanism 248
   and National Socialism 250
   and the first German economic miracle 246

ordoliberalism (*continued*)
  as order governed by rules and sanctions 285
  dominant economic philosophy 244
  essential features of 246
  in German public opinion 258
  social responsibility of the State in 246
original sin 169, 171, 172, 173
Ostpolitik 77, 275, 278
Outright Monetary Transactions 122, 175

permissive consensus 355, 359
Pleven, René 51, 56, 66
political union 18, 59, 96, 165, 185, 186, 187, 188, 213, 249, 358, 368, 380
  and fiscal solidarity 182
  and Franco-German rhetoric 188
  Angela Merkel on 186
  Churchill on 56
  French vision of 187
  German ambiguity on 187
  in the More Europe vision 297
  or solidarity union as alternative 102, 189
  requirement for monetary union 18, 183, 185, 186, 187, 298
Pompidou, Georges 65, 66, 319
populism 138, 241, 290, 320, 326, 341, 373
  challenge to democracy and order of rules 347
  emergence after the euro crisis 196
  in Sweden and Denmark 340
  threat for Europe 293, 317
principle of responsibility 20, 250, 251, 285, 286
Private Sector Involvement 118, 206, 255, 256
Prussia 15, 27, 32, 33, 34, 35, 220, 261, 275

public goods 14, 40, 263, 264, 265, 284
public investment gap 238

refugee crisis 22, 23, 289, 317, 324, 326, 328, 329, 330, 341, 342, 362
  and benevolent hegemon 14
  and British referendum 336
  European anomie in the 346
  quota system 327
  Visegrad group 341
risk premiums 106, 107, 119, 120, 122, 170, 171, 201, 310, 312
risk-sharing schemes 144, 189, 321, 355, 364
  7+7 Group proposals on 302
  and no bailout discipline 308
  German position 322
  legacy costs and 309
  lender of last resort and 312
  Mario Draghi's Florence Conferenc 302
  solidarity and 22
Röpke, Wilhelm 244
rules vs. discretion 249
Rüstow, Walter 245

Sarkozy, Nicolás 118, 139, 206, 207, 320
savings rate in Germany 236
Scharpf, Fritz 150, 212, 230, 248, 348, 349, 350, 380
Schäuble, Wolfgang 20, 258, 263, 348
  and euro break-up 348
  and ordoliberal thinking 258
  and stabilising role of the hegemon 263
Schengen Agreement 69, 329, 358
Schmidt, Helmut 66, 212, 258, 319, 380
Schröder, Gerhard 151, 225, 270, 273, 279, 280
Schuld, meaning of 222, 243

Schuman, Robert 49, 50, 56, 59, 186
second reunification of Germany 221, 279
Securities Markets Program 116, 205
Sikorski, Rodoslaw 260
Simms, Brendan 30, 36, 37, 47, 52, 74, 380
Single European Act 66, 67, 68, 75, 87, 93
Single Resolution Mechanism 301
Snake system 86
social market economy 20, 218, 221, 246
socio-cultural dualism 230
SoFFin, Special Fund Financial Market Stabilization 254
solidarity 12, 14, 16, 18, 21, 22, 24, 35, 63, 102, 181, 182, 185, 187, 189, 190, 191, 223, 230, 231, 249, 251, 256, 257, 258, 263, 289, 291, 298, 300, 301, 308, 309, 311, 313, 316, 323, 344, 363, 364, 370
  concept of 189, 257, 273
  duties of the hegemon 263, 267, 271
  in the refugee crisis 328, 330
  political 147
Stability and Growth Pact 123, 163, 272
  German and French breach of the 163
Stiglitz, Joseph 177, 218, 348, 349, 381
Storm, Servaas 228, 239, 381
structural duality 229, 230
Structural Neorealism 263
sub-prime 17, 110, 111, 112, 114, 115, 125, 188, 254, 255
sudden stop of capital flows 224

trade surplus of Germany 224
transfer union 188, 191, 283, 313, 316
Treaty of Amsterdam 78, 210
Treaty of Lisbon 79, 210

Treaty of Maastricht 66, 68, 69, 139, 184, 208, 255
  and democratic legitimacy 212
  and fiscal integration 188
  and fiscal sovereignty 305
  and German Constitutional Court 253
  and no-bailout clause 139
  and prohibition of monetary financing 248
  Articles 103 and 104 166
  culture of stability in the 247
  phases towards EMU 88
  role of the ECB 134
Treaty of Nice 78, 210
Treaty of Rome 56, 58, 60, 61, 68, 69, 81, 296
Treaty of Versailles of 1919 39
Treaty on Stability, Coordination and Governance 165, 251
Trichet, Jean Claude 117, 122
Triepel, Heinrich 261, 381
Troika 116, 117, 121, 130, 204, 213

Unemployment Compensation Fund 310
unilateral adjustment mechanism 199
unit labour costs 151, 154, 225, 228
Ursula von der Leyen 325

Versailles, 1871 Pact of 15, 35, 36, 39, 41, 46, 275

wage containment 25, 219, 226, 227, 228, 229, 235
  and competitivity 208, 227
  and economic model 150
  and export model 218
  and ordoliberalism 248
  and subvaluation 240
  and unit labour cost 154
  condition for external balance 153

wage containment (*continued*)
    impact on the rest of Europe 224, 225
Walters, Alan 148, 168, 381
Werner, Peter 81, 84, 85, 87, 88, 235, 374, 380

Western European Union 51, 66
Work, Education and Competitiveness Pact (Schroeder) 225

ABOUT THE AUTHOR

Miguel I. Purroy, PhD in Economics (UCAB, Caracas) and degrees in Economics, Political Science and Philosophy from the Universities of Hamburg and Munich, has taught Macroeconomy and International Monetary Economics at the Universidad Central de Venezuela and the Universidad Católica Andrés Bello. Author of several books in the field, he has been a Member of the Board of the Central Bank of Venezuela in the 1990s and was the Andrés Bello Fellow at St. Antony's College, the University of Oxford, during 1995-1996. He has also held leading positions in financial institutions.

For more information on the author see: www.miguelpurroy.com.

www.ingramcontent.com/pod-product-compliance
Lightning Source LLC
Chambersburg PA
CBHW030606220526
45463CB00004B/1180